YHWH EXISTS

Books in the YHWH Exists Series:

YHWH Exists
Volume 1

YHWH Exists
Volume 2 Series:

Does Jesus Exist?
The Quest for Biblical Truth &
the Suffering Servant in our Modern World
Volume 2, Book 1

The Suffering Servant, Part 1
Volume 2, Book 2
(forthcoming in 2025)

The Suffering Servant, Part 2
Volume 2, Book 3
(forthcoming)

The Day of YHWH/
The Day of the Lord
Volume 2, Book 4
(forthcoming)

Does Jesus Exist?

The Quest for Biblical Truth & the Suffering Servant in our Modern World

YHWH Exists:
Volume 2
Book 1

Jodell Onstott

Yah Tzidqenu

EMMANUEL
ACADEMIC

Greenville, South Carolina

©2024 By Jodell Onstott

All rights reserved, including the right of reproduction
in whole or in part in any form.

www.emmanuelacademic.com
www.yhwhexists.com

All Scripture references are derived from The American King James Version (Stone Engelbrite) unless otherwise specified.

All dictionary references are from Merriam Webster's Ninth New Collegiate Dictionary unless otherwise specified.

All websites and web links accessed October 2024 unless otherwise specified.

Library of Congress Cataloging-in-Publication Data
Library of Congress Control Number: 2024917654

Dedication

To my amazing and patient family, who allowed me to seek, research, and write this book.

Thank you for allowing me the time. I know it comes at a personal cost to each of you when you would rather be doing fun activities or spending more time together.

I pray this book is a blessing to you and your future.

Table of Contents

Abbreviations... xv

Scripture Abbreviations... xix

Acknowledgments... xxi

Note on Sources.. xxiii

Preface: A Sleeping Giant?...................................... xxv
    I. The Modern Suffering Servant xxv
    II. Is America Lost?....................................... xxvi
    III. A Godless Nation?..................................... xxix
    IV. Bridging the Chasm xxxi
    V. Awakening to Strength and Unity xxxii

Introduction: The Crux of the Issue............................ xxxiii

1. Prove All Things.. 1
    I. The Church's Legacy..................................... 1
    II. Freedom from Religion 2
    III. The Journey to Know God............................... 3

2. Wrestling with God 5
    I. Reasoning Together: *The First Step*.................... 5
    II. Fighting the Good Fight 5
    III. Struggling with God................................... 6
    IV. Hope Renewed 7
    V. Accepting Paul's Challenge 7
    VI. Prevailing with God 8
    VII. About this Book 8
    VIII. An Unexpected Journey 9

3. When God Knows Your Name 11
    I. Knowing You by Name 11
    II. God's Personal Name 12
    A. I Am: *The Second Step* 12
    B. Polytheism... 14
    C. Baal 14
    D. The Lord... 16

4. Knowing God by Name 19
    I. Confronting Inherited Lies: *The Third Step* 19
    II. Warning: Do Not Add or Take Away 20
    III. Forgetting YHWH's Name 21
    IV. John Jacob Jingleheimer Schmidt 22
    V. Power in the Name of YHWH 22
    VI. Finding Strength in the Name of YHWH 23
    VII. When the World Knows YHWH by Name 23
    VIII. The Lie Continues 24
    IX. A New Dawn 25
    X. The Divine Name & The Son of Man 25

5. Breaking Relativism's Spell 29
    I. Relativism's Spell 29
    II. Religion's Complicity 30
    III. Discovering the Plan 30
    IV. Dare to Join the Quest 31
    V. Precepts Light the Way 31
    VI. Precepts of Justice 33
    VII. Why Did David Love the Law's Precepts? 34
    VIII. Precepts Define Truth 35
    IX. When Did Truth Begin to Exist? 36

6. Divine Bondage? 39
    I. Remembering the Law of Moses 39
    II. A Singular Road 40
    III. The Road of Prosperity 41
    IV. The Law of Liberty 42
    V. Should We Remember the Law? 43
    VI. It Is Too Difficult! We Can't Do It! 43
    VII. These are the Words 44
    VIII. The Way of Righteousness 45

7. Does the New Testament Uphold Divine Law? 49
    I. Upholding Righteous Identity 49
    II. Law is Valid as Long as Heaven & Earth Exist 50
    III. Jesus Upholds the 10 Commandments 50
    IV. Defraud Not & the Law of Moses 51
        A. Jesus Upholds the Law before His Death 51
        B. The Apostles Uphold Divine Law after Jesus' Death 52
    V. Hebrews on Perfection 53

    VI. Jesus Upholds the Law as Truth..54
    VII. How Do We Awaken from Sleep?..55
    VIII. Testing the Path 56

8. It's All Relative 59
    I. Individual Discretion 59
    II. Gaslit Much?..60
    III. Finding Identity in God 62
    IV. How Can We Recognize Truth?...62

9. Precepts of Truth 63
    I. What is Truth?...63
        Definition of Truth 65
    II. Constancy: 1st Precept..66
        Definition of Constancy...67
    III. Fidelity: The 2nd Precept 67
        Definition of Fidelity..68
    IV. Faithfulness: The 3rd Precept 68
        Definition of Faithfulness...69
    V. Righteousness: The 4th Precept...69
        Definition of Righteousness...70
    VI. Righteousness Is Not Arbitrary: the 5th Precept 70
        Definition of Arbitrary...71
    VII. Verifiable..71

10. "It's Hard to be a Diamond in a Rhinestone World" 75
    I. A Righteous Difference...75
    II. Monotheism..76
    III. Customs 77
    IV. Shocking Claim 78
    V. YHWH vs. Manmade gods 79
    VI. Why Doesn't Divine Law Work?...81

11. YHWH Sues Israel...83
    I. YHWH'S Controversy 83
    II. The Covenant Lawsuit...83
    III. The Indictment 85
    IV. Law for the Future?...86
    V. When Men Cancel YHWH's Law 86
    VI. Out with the Old Rhinestones, in with the New..................88
        A. Continuing the Dialog, Repeat Step 1 88
        B. Modern Controversy?..88

12. Historicity of the New Testament: Archaeology ... 91
  I. Equal Weights and Measures ... 91
  II. Archaeology ... 92
    A. The James Ossuary ... 92
    B. The Talpiot Tombs ... 93
      1. The Garden Tomb ... 93
      2. The Patio Tomb's Contents ... 94
    C. The New Testament on Jesus' Family ... 95
    D. Could the James Ossuary Be the Missing Box? ... 95
    E. Observations and Conclusions ... 96

13. Historicity of the New Testament: Greek & Roman Sources ... 97
  I. New Testament in Extrabiblical Written Sources ... 97
  II. Roman Officials ... 97
    A. Pliny the Younger ... 97
    B. Tacitus ... 100
      1. Tacitus on Christianity ... 100
      2. Pontius Pilate Inscription ... 102
    C. Suetonius ... 102
  III. Pagan Writers ... 104
    A. Lucian of Samosata ... 104
    B. Celsus ... 105

14. Historicity of the New Testament: Jewish Sources ... 109
  I. Value of Jewish Sources ... 109
  II. Josephus ... 109
    A. John the Baptist ... 110
      1. The Text ... 110
      2. John the Baptist's Theology ... 111
    B. James, Brother of Jesus ... 112
    C. Jesus: Testimonium Flavianum ... 113
      1. The Text and Its Historical Setting ... 113
      2. An Over-Eager Defender of the Faith? ... 114
        a. Lying Pen of the Scribes (Jer 8:8)? ... 114
        b. Issues of Vocabulary, Style, and Anachronism ... 115
        c. The Text and Its Approximate Original Version ... 117
  II. Rabbinic Sources ... 118
  III. Where Does the Evidence Lead? ... 118

15. Sola Scriptura ... 121
  I. The Path to Truth ... 121

	II. The New Testament Only Gains Authority Through the Old Testament
	Law and Prophets 122
	III. Guidelines for New Testament Study 122
	A. Sola Scriptura 122
	B. Obedience Remains. 125
	C. Least in the Kingdom of God. 127

16. Equal Weights and Measures 129
   I. 1st Premise: Sola Scriptura 129
   II. 2nd Premise: The New Testament Is Based Solely on Old Testament
      Prophesy. 130
   III. 3rd Premise: The New Testament Relies on Israel's History 130
   IV. 4th Premise: The New Testament Is Not Based on Scriptures from
      Other Nations. 130
   V. 5th Premise: The NT Should Be *Constant*, Upholding the *7 Precepts of Truth*. ... 131
   VI. 6th Premise: The NT Cannot Rescind or Change YHWH's Divine Word 132
   VII. 7th Premise: The NT Fulfills the OT 132
   VIII. Prove All Things 132
   IX. Concepts Transform into Action. 133

17. Does Harmony Exist between the Old and New Testaments? 135
   I. Healing the Divide. 135
   II. Harmony: Comparing Old and New Testaments 136
      A. Grace & Truth. 136
      B. Hearing God's Voice and Seeing His Shape 137
      C. No Man Can Come to the Father but by Jesus. 139
      D. Has Any Man Other Than the Son of Man Ascended into Heaven? 140
      E. Prophecy of the Nazarene. 141
   III. Internal Harmony within the Book of John. 142

18. Paul on the Law: Part I 145
   I. Do National Constitutions Like the Torah Create Strife? 145
   II. Paul vs. James 146
   III. Man of Lawlessness? 148

19. Paul on the Law: Part II 149
   I. Promises to One or Many?. 149
   II. God's Promises to Abraham: Land and Children 150
      A. Promises Made to Abraham's Seed 150
      B. God Promises Many Seed and Gives Them the Promised Land. 151
      C. Fulfilling the Abrahamic Promise of a Multitude of Offspring 152

    D. A Fruitful Nation that Possesses the Enemy's Wealthy Strongholds........153
    E. The Ultimate Abrahamic Blessing..154

20. Divine Justice..157
    I. An Uncomfortable Place 157
    II. The Quest 157
    III. Is YHWH a Just and Righteous God?................................159
        A. Justice: the Essence of YHWH's Character 159
        B. Shall Not the Judge of the Earth Do Right? 160
        C. The Righteous and the Wicked in Divine Law..................161
            1. Divine Law 161
            2. Condemning the Wicked in the New Testament..........162
        D. The Source of America's Sickness?.............................162
        E. Innocent Blood...163
        F. Jesus on Bloodguilt 164

21. Substitute Atonement 167
    I. Is Blood Atonement Necessary? 167
        A. Paul on Purification by Blood 167
        B. God's Justice for Animals 168
        C. Almost Everything?..168
        D. Does God Forgive Sins without the Shedding of Blood? 168
    II. Substitute Atonement 169
        A. Every Person is Put to Death for His Own Sin 169
        B. Does God Reject all Human Substitutionary Atonement? 171
        C. When YHWH Visits Sin upon People 172

22. Just Keep Swimming 173
    I. Does YHWH Reject All Human Sacrifice? 173
        A. Is All Human Sacrifice Prohibited?............................173
        B. Can You Preordain What Has "Never Come to Mind"?..........174
        C. Can Offering of the Firstborn Son Atone for Sin?..............174
    II. Forgiveness without Sacrifice?.....................................175
    III. Premeditated Death?..177

23. Exceptions to the Law? 179
    I. The Righteous and Wicked Suffer Alike 179
    II. Can Ceremonial/Religious Law work Differently from YHWH's
    System of Justice?..180
        A. The Suffering Servant: Isaiah 53 180
        B. The Law of Sin Offerings.....................................180
        C. In a Plain Path 182

Appendix A	185
Notes	191
Select Bibliography	253
Scripture Index	281

Abbreviations

ACCS	Ancient Christian Commentary on Scripture
ACT	Ancient Christian Texts
AKJV	The American King James Version
ASBT	Acadia Studies in Bible and Theology
AYBC	Anchor Yale Bible Commentary
AYBRL	Anchor Yale Bible Reference Library
BAR	*Biblical Archaeology Review*
BASOR	*Bulletin of the American Schools of Oriental Research*
BDB	*The Brown-Driver-Briggs Hebrew and English Lexicon,* Francis Brown (Peabody, MA: Hendrickson Publishers, 2003)
BNTC	Black's New Testament Commentary
CAD	*The Assyrian Dictionary of the Oriental Institute of the University of Chicago,* 21 vols., eds. Martha T. Roth, et al. (Chicago: The Oriental Institute of the University of Chicago, 1956–2010)
CBQ	*Catholic Biblical Quarterly*
CC	Continental Commentary
CGAE	*Conceptions of God in Ancient Egypt,* Erik Hornung, trans. John Baines (Ithaca, NY: Cornell University Press, 1982)
CHALOT	*A Concise Hebrew and Aramaic Lexicon of the Old Testament*, William Holladay (Grand Rapids, MI: Eerdmans; Leiden: Brill, 1988)
CHS	Center for Hellenistic Studies
EPJS	Essential Papers on Jewish Studies
GDSAM	*Gods, Demons and Symbols of Ancient Mesopotamia,* Jeremy Black and Anthony Green (Austin: University of Texas, 1992)
GSAAP	*Geological Society of America Abstracts with Programs*
HALOT	*The Hebrew and Aramaic Lexicon of the Old Testament,* 2 vols, trans. Ludwig Koehler, Walter Baumgartner, eds. Johann Stamm, Mervyn E. J. Richardson (Leiden: Brill, 2001)
HCOT	Historical Commentary of the Old Testament
HNTC	Holman New Testament Commentary
HOSNME	Handbook of Oriental Studies; The Near and Middle East
HOTC	Holman Old Testament Commentary

HSHJ	*Handbook for the Study of the Historical Jesus, 4 vols.,* eds. Tom Holmén and Stanley Porter (Leiden: Brill, 2011)
IBC	Interpretation: A Bible Commentary for Teaching and Preaching
ICC	International Critical Commentary
ISBE	*International Standard Bible Encyclopedia,* ed. Geoffrey W. Bromiley (Grand Rapids, MI: Eerdmans, 1979–1988)
JBL	*Journal of Biblical Literature*
JEH	*Journal of Ecclesiastical History*
JFB	*Jamieson, Fausset, and Brown's Commentary,* Robert Jamieson, A. R. Fausset, and David Brown (Grand Rapids, MI: Zondervan, 1961)
JFS	*Journal of Forensic Sciences*
JHIEMC	Jewish Historiography and Iconography in Early and Medieval Christianity
JM	*The Jesus Mysteries,* Timothy Freke and Peter Gandy (New York: Three Rivers Press, 1999)
JPS	Jewish Publication Society
JSJ	*Journal for the Study of Judaism in the Persian, Hellenistic, and Roman Periods*
JSOT	*Journal for the Study of the Old Testament*
JSOTSup	Journal for the Study of the Old Testament, Supplement Series
LHBOTS	Library of Hebrew Bible/Old Testament Studies
LCL	Loeb Classical Library
LNTS	Library of New Testament Studies
LSJ	*Liddell and Scott's Greek-English Lexicon,* Henry George Liddell and Robert Scott (Oxford, Simon Wallenberg Press, 2007)
LXX	*The Septuagint with Apocrypha: Greek and English,* trans. C. L. Brenton (London: Hendrickson Publishers, 1851)
MJH	Modern Jewish History
NAB	The New American Bible
NAC	New American Commentary
NICOT	New International Commentary on the Old Testament
NRSV	New Revised Standard Version
OJG	*Open Journal of Geology*
OTL	Old Testament Library
PCS	The Preacher's Commentary Series
PNTC	Pillar New Testament Commentary

SAC	*Studies in Ancient Society,* ed. M. I. Finley (New York: Routledge, Taylor & Francis, 1974)
SBLDS	Society of Biblical Literature Dissertation Series
SEC	*Strong's Exhaustive Concordance*, James Strong (Grand Rapids, MI: Baker Books, 1997) [Denotes Strong's number only]
SEPM	Society for Sedimentary Geology
SHJ	Studying the Historical Jesus
SRSR	*Studies in Religion/ Sciences Religieuses*
TEV	Today's English Version
Thayer's	*Thayer's Greek-English Lexicon of the New Testament*, Joseph H. Thayer (Peabody, MA: Hendrickson Publishers, 2005, repr., Edinburgh: T&T Clark, 1896)
TOTC	Tyndale Old Testament Commentaries
TWOT	*Theological Wordbook of the Old Testament*, 2 vols., eds. R. Laird Harris, Gleason Archer, Jr. and Bruce Waltke (Chicago: Moody Bible Institute, 1980)
TynBul	*Tyndale Bulletin*
TZ	*Theologische Zeitschrift*
UBD	*Unger's Bible Dictionary,* Merrill F. Unger (Chicago: Moody, 1957)
UBSH	*United Bible Societies' Handbooks*, vol. 1 & 2. ed. Paul Clarke et al. (Reading, UK: United Bible Societies, 2011)
VT	*Vetus Testamentum*
VTSup	Supplements to *Vetus Testamentum*
WBC	Word Biblical Commentary
WBCS	Wiley Blackwell Bible Commentary Series
YE1	*YHWH Exists, vol. 1,* Jodell Onstott (Baton Rouge, LA: Emmanuel Academic Publishing, 2015)

Scripture Abbreviations

Tanakh/Old Testament

Gen	Genesis	Eccl	Ecclesiastes
Exod	Exodus	Song	Song of Solomon
Lev	Leviticus	Isa	Isaiah
Num	Numbers	Jer	Jeremiah
Deut	Deuteronomy	Lam	Lamentations
Josh	Joshua	Ezek	Ezekiel
Judg	Judges	Dan	Daniel
Ruth	Ruth	Hos	Hosea
1 Sam	1 Samuel	Joel	Joel
2 Sam	2 Samuel	Amos	Amos
1 Kgs	1 Kings	Obad	Obadiah
2 Kgs	2 Kings	Jonah	Jonah
1 Chr	1 Chronicles	Mic	Micah
2 Chr	2 Chronicles	Nah	Nahum
Ezra	Ezra	Hab	Habakkuk
Neh	Nehemiah	Zeph	Zephaniah
Esth	Esther	Hag	Haggai
Job	Job	Zech	Zechariah
Ps	Psalms	Mal	Malachi
Prov	Proverbs		

Apocrypha and Septuagint

1–2 Kgdms	1–3 Kingdoms	1–3 Macc	1–3 Maccabees

New Testament

Matt	Matthew	Titus	Titus
Mark	Mark	Philm	Philemon
Luke	Luke	Heb	Hebrew
John	John	Jas	James
Acts	Acts	1 Tim	1 Timothy
Rom	Romans	2 Tim	2 Timothy
1 Cor	1 Corinthians	1 Pet	1 Peter
2 Cor	2 Corinthians	2 Pet	2 Peter
Gal	Galatians	1 Jn	1 John
Eph	Ephesians	2 Jn	2 John
Phil	Philippians	3 Jn	3 John
Col	Colossians	Jude	Jude
1 Thess	1 Thessalonians	Rev	Revelation
2 Thess	2 Thessalonians		

Acknowledgments

This volume has been improved by the reading, editing, and input of invaluable friends and colleagues. I am grateful for their contribution to this book and their encouragement along the way. Despite multiple drafts, each was willing and eager to contribute to this project. I am filled with gratitude to have such tremendous support.

To my chief editor, Pam Stoll, who tirelessly edited multiple drafts, offered suggestions, clarifications, and patiently waited through what was to be "the final draft"—thank you! Pam not only edited but also drew my attention to other connections that I missed, thereby greatly improving the present manuscript's style.

This work also benefited from experienced editors and professionals. Robert Jacobson helped this manuscript become concise. He has a gift for detail and consistency. Bob, I appreciate your expertise, friendship, and encouragement. Sylvia Halpert made sure the manuscript was understandable for readers who have little exposure to biblical ideas. Her input also clarified the present text. Anna Jensen was my sounding board. Her encouragement was always a phone call away. I am grateful to each of you for your enthusiastic help and support for this project.

My family has also patiently waited through the long years of research. Thank you for your patience and understanding for the process and the time it takes to conduct extensive research. My prayer is that God will return these years to you with a double blessing.

Note on Sources

I have endeavored to base my research on scholars respected in their field. At the same time, I have searched for online open access to scholarship so the reader can delve deeper into a topic or verify the research presented in this book. For this reason, the reader will find many internal website links to publications cited in the footnotes. These links will also be listed in the bibliography under "For Further Research."

A Sleeping Giant?

I. THE MODERN SUFFERING SERVANT

Why has the Suffering Servant prophecy shaped the beliefs within Christianity and Judaism so differently? Jews see themselves and their history as fulfilling the Servant's traits, while Christians understand Jesus (Yeshua) to fulfill Isaiah's Suffering Servant prophecy as the Messiah. Most academic and theological studies remain divided along these lines. Can both Judaism and Christianity be correct at the same time? Do both Jews and Jesus simultaneously fulfill Isaiah's prophecy? Or does the text exclude one of these entities?

Consigned to different corners of the ring, brothers who should be standing together, have retreated to opposing corners. Modern Christianity tries to shed its shared history with his Jewish brothers. Judaism, accustomed to being attacked by brothers and foreigners on all sides, has often resorted to isolation to protect his own, rejecting any Christian theological dialog. This stalemate is far from the unity that Isaiah describes for the Suffering Servant at the latter-day restoration: "They will see eye to eye when the LORD shall bring Zion again" (Isa 52:8).

Modern Judeo-Christians have come to terms and accepted this uncomfortable stalemate as normal. Both sects are *sure* their interpretation is correct, yet logically speaking, can both be true at the same time? Is Jesus, as the Suffering Servant, simply a specific person who suffered within the broader category of Judah? Since Jesus was a Jew, this question is not as outlandish as it may seem.

While Christianity is united in its belief that Jesus fulfilled the Suffering Servant's role, other once commonly held beliefs have begun to disintegrate. The common bond of Christian unity over the past 2–3 generations is shattering as beliefs within the Church wander further and further away from God's original message. Judaism also adheres to many modern ideas that were created late in the nation's history but are attributed to God. These divisions of belief create chaos. We daily witness this chaos increasing. We've become accustomed to a stalemated *status quo* that ignores injustice, oppression, wickedness, and is resigned to just "go with the flow" in our religious beliefs.

Isaiah prophesied that the Suffering Servant will sprinkle and heal many nations (Isa 52:15; 53:5). The Servant's sprinkling resonates so deeply with people that it fulfills the prophetic vision in a cleansing so thorough that it brings about world peace: "Nations will no longer lift up weapons against nations, neither shall they learn war anymore" (Mic 4:3; Isa 2:4). This eternal healing of the nations has yet to occur. Almost 2,000 years have passed since the prophesied destruction of the Second Temple. With the modern wars in Ukraine, attacks on Israel, and immigrant and civilian violence, world peace is a far cry from our present reality. Because these promises have not been fulfilled, people have lost faith, turning against Jesus and against the Jews. Can a fresh investigation reveal a lost path? Can an unbiased investigation awaken the earth to eternal peace and healing?

Before we begin to understand the factors that will cause nations to no longer pursue war, we need to identify the issues that have created the chaos we now call reality. These factors are the same reasons why unity evades our understanding of the Suffering Servant. I have done my best to capture the current state of religion in America and around the world. Does the following state of affairs in this preface resonate with you?

II. IS AMERICA LOST?

We sleep to the sound our silence allows. Huge corporations are criminal enterprises now. Corporations incite division. Non-profits create violent riots. They lower property values, and then "private equity" buys up the city. No rule of law exists to forbid privatization of the city's police force. They use government to mandate policies that force their products on us—can we decline? My body is not my choice. They pay for tainted, scientific research which benefits their balance sheet. Corporations and governments strategize to reduce evidence of our existence. They ignore leaders who reserve luxury for their grand estates, while leaving their footprints flying all over global space. They are *too big to fail*. They are the monopoly. We are in misery while they consider citizens the enemy. Does America have any means to resist it? Or do we bury our minds in aimless work, silently sleeping life away?

Meanwhile, we work for slave wages as large corporations soak up crony profits. We sow, but another reaps (Lev 26:16). Will America become a landless society? We are confined to tiny serf quarters allotted by our new corporate lords. The *American dream* is rapidly descending into the American nightmare. Only those who play by its complicated rules find it lucrative. The new code has become laws for thee but not for me. Leaders enjoy one set of rights, privileges unbound by any Code of Law, while citizens are captive to the power of the day. Americans live in misery, with no idea how to resist. We silently sleep, dreaming of a better day.

Cities are rife with crime. Leaders who should prosecute it excuse it. Citizens are the prey. We drown our potential, seeking meaningless essentials, pursuing vanity to renew the meaning and quality of a life we once knew. The system is rotten to its core. America remains complacent in a paralyzing status quo as our freedoms slowly, then quickly wither away. We are in misery, as they exploit our penury. We have not discovered the means to resist it. We seek sweet slumber to silently forget it.

Inflation is now our new norm. Economic cycles only amplify America's ever-changing morals and unstable values. Every year America grows poorer still, reduced to lower and lower standards of living. Tax dollars benefit foreign countries while our people sleep in the streets. Politicians play both sides as long as arms are sold. We must support the war complex since peace isn't as lucrative. Just print more paper. Dilute citizens' buying power—they're not smart enough to know. Bribes and cronyism are America's new norm. Don't question me! I'm above the Law. No Code exists to resist the oppression of which they insist. Collective individuals now define right from wrong. Collectivism has become a source of our misery.

Americans work 2–3 jobs just to make ends meet, while all too often neglecting or selecting their basic necessities. Debt is how we survive this endless cycle of slavery that benefits our corporate lords, who enjoy more rights than individuals like you and me. They exploit this rotten system of ours to obtain through league what the individual could never achieve. Americans are beginning to own nothing and we are not happy. They divide us, wanting citizens to become enemies, while their distraction allows *too big to fail* to run the state. We deny the means that could resist it, so we fight for endless sleep.

To reject the law is to elevate the wicked; to obey the Law is to fight them (Prov 28:4)

"What is right for you isn't right for me," has led to no rights for anyone. *We the People* have exchanged the meaningful for the expedient. "I need it now" is America's new norm. This Machiavellian state fulfills those needs, driving up debt that brings us down to our knees. Groups of collective individuals now decide what is right for you and me. Our ways are not succeeding in this rotten system of ours. Decisions are made by those who pay no price for being wrong as their lobbied subsidies of power do boast. We the people have lost our voice! Our beliefs have no anchor to protect individuals like you and me. You'd better be happy in this New World Order, which can deliver what God never could.

One nation under God? What an absurdity! Americans and citizens around the globe remain powerless as we succumb to this unjust, rotten system. Like criminals, we remain silent in fear that for our words they will censor or indict us. They manipulate us to become our own enemies. That which could deliver us—we subtract it, as we sleep in complacent misery.

We detect incredible evil, but remain helpless to dismantle it. We are silent in the face of adversity. Citizens remain silent because we are powerless. We are powerless because we are sleeping. Americans are sleeping because we have forgotten and forsaken common sense. We forget the common sense in our values was defined by God. "There is nothing we can do," said 7 billion miserable people around the globe, being led to become their own enemies. How long can we go on living in this slumbering trajectory?

Our troubles did not begin with a president. Policy multiplied our agony. A new vision for America was conceived. The vision was laid to obtain the power to deceive. The vision held that America could be great without God as head of a lawful state. Our representatives legislated God out of style while implementing their own self-serving doubt. Theologian, politician, and philosopher have now reduced the Divine to you and me: We are our own gods now.

Shouldn't humans have a natural capacity to define right from wrong? Human reason now triumphs over God. We are our own masters, free to chose our oppressive, rotten destiny. America has not traded up, we've traded down. No longer does the Divine distinguish *law-abiding* from any crime. We've elevated the wicked whose power regulates the choices we make. Casting our sentiment does not decide any candidate when their cohorts count it up in this crony system that has become America's liberty. They are simply *too big to fail*. We slumber wishing there was a way to resist this increasingly miserable tyranny.

To reject the law is to elevate the wicked; to obey the Law is to fight them (Prov 28:4)

Social norms are the frenzies of our day, determined by meaningless manipulative media. Every opinion expressed is bought through political philanthropy. They tell us what to think: You'd better get on board or we'll cancel you from this global link. These lackeys for corporate lords define right and wrong for you and me. You'd better get on board or your show, your voice, or your platform—we'll retract it. Your social media had better not offend one of our undefined, ambiguous community rules or standards.

Yet natural law still governs all, even if invisibly. Our modernity cannot cancel reality. Among the gods, one is needed to reign supreme, a leader, corporation, or elite to anchor society. Man must create a new norm! And thus prevails the call for a Global State to rule them all. Give up your meaningless sovereignty! A new world order was conceived to manage lusts while exploiting humanity endlessly. With no God to object, we now have Divine power yet. We are God, deciding right from wrong.

We have exchanged the Creator for new lords who exploit our carnal lusts. They rule over us despite our disgust. We reject the firm, preferring the lukewarm. Now they say belief in God was the source of our misery. We don't need Him to tell us what to do. Truth does not exist, so why resist? We love our sleep. Why unpin our miserable desires, which determine our miserable, sinful destiny?

Why should any God exist? Religion? Who needs it? Why resist if individuals like you and me have redefined evil; it does not exist. The media now reports its link to the patriarchy. Men determine the rules of our collective state, allowing false flags everywhere that mandate our complacency. Our new lords exploit our labor and beliefs, while they enjoy endless incumbency. No borders to keep us safe. No Law to uphold the rights of man. We've exchanged God for man. The firm and limited Fear of God has been displaced by the boundless Fear of reckless man and his man-made state while we drown in the status quo of anxiety. We have been deceived!

They incite us to use our misery to divide our country by making God our enemy. They deny the firm, timeless Law that can empower us to resist. How long can we go on like this? As this rotten system fades into a mist, we forget that the past has been erased. Lies are now the truth of our day. We are living in a meaningless abyss. There must be a better strategy to withstand as this misery gets out of hand. What power can wake our silent slumber? What idea can unite us to resist? We the people are fed up!

To reject the law is to elevate the wicked; to obey the Law is to fight them (Prov 28:4)

III. A GODLESS NATION?

America has lost her religion, her God, and her way. The process did not begin with you and me. We were deceived by the lying words of men within our establishments. Legitimate questions provoked our quest to find truth and harmony. We desired to enjoin the common bonds of human camaraderie within our societies. But as we searched within the Church we discovered that our perception of God was naïve.

At first, the division in religion was minor. We discussed differences over the sinless nature of Mary, the virtue of perpetual virginity, or whether if once saved, we were always saved. Finding no stable ground to anchor our beliefs, the chasm widened. We began to question all that unified and enabled our firm stability.

Common sense was soon lost in the vast sea of relativity. Common sense was silently sacrificed on the altar of desire for the sake of a liberal society. Truth within the 10 Commandments, which unified and allied our grandparents' nation to withstand our modern misery was dismissed as if there was no irony. Ignored was its ability to empower and revive by using God's Code of Law to break through this rotten, miserable collective system of ours.

Without common ground avowed, each citizen went his own way, lost in an ocean of complacency. Instead of the written word, we began to substitute individual brands of religion, which had no code or accountability to God. Individuals like you and me trademarked our particular relative group. Looking back we can now see that two generations were all it took for us to forget His Book, leading to our drowning in a rotten sea of immorality. Two generations were all it took for us to forsake the source of our strength and unity. Two generations were all it took for us to be hooked on generalities.

Two generations and we cannot agree on justice for you and me. What is murder? Can we define it? Is killing an unborn baby a human right? What about executing a murderer when overwhelming evidence attests to his guilt? Oh no, that's not right! It's immoral, it just can't be! Two generations were all it took to show mercy where there should be justice and judgment where there should be mercy. We save the wicked but deliver the righteous to hostility

(Ezek 13:19). Two generations into rejecting one nation under God, we struggle to agree on basic ideas of what is right for you and me, like theft and crime.

Private property? Shouldn't it all belong to the community? Smash—and—grab merchandise is now becoming another new American social norm. Collective society now decides right from wrong. No room for God in this state. No universal civil code of law exists to hold all accountable in this rotten state (Deut 1:16–18). We are too big to fail. Every agenda the compromised media suggests only weakens and feeds our carnal lusts, without any sound policy. We are kept downtrodden, and in misery, while *too big to fail* exploits the weak, challenging every identity.

Two generations and we cannot agree on definitions of the family. Marriage is open, it has no bounds when defined by lawless, lustful rotten men. We object to common sense morality. Our children are no longer protected from harm as they are groomed for iniquity. A collective society encourages coveting and sees every self-indulgence as a need. Envy, which our grandparents once considered a deadly sin, is now admired under terminal taglines of "equality."

Two generations were all it took for the state to steal our born identity. Girls can't safely compete but must accept obscenities. Do not resist! No rights to privacy anywhere. *Too big to fail* AI knows it all. Is it God? It is only natural for girls to be ogled, and assaulted without any rights to privacy, and with no policy to protect their natural identity. Right and wrong are no longer decided by God.

Two generations were all it took for "love" to be redefined to include sexual relations between rotten adults and small children. Don't say "pedophile," say "ALA."[1] Compassion for immigration masks the horrors that deny any Sound of Freedom. Two generations are all it's taking for agendas to normalize bestiality. This latest trend is now gaining steam, without God's Law to deem its practice leading to more misery.

If you hold to a set of traditional moral values, society considers you callous and judgmental. You are an obstacle to progress. America's new social norms are constantly exploited to anchor society to radically new agendas. If you are not outraged by the older, traditional way that topic was understood yesterday, you are an obstacle to progress. You are the problem! Their minions will mock, cancel, and silence you into compliance. We are not prospering. We are withering away in our miserable greed. Man has now become his own enemy. And two generations were all it took to fall into a deep sleep despite the sound of reality which loudly proclaims that the Law is not an irony.

To reject the law is to elevate the wicked; to obey the law is to fight them (Prov 28:4)

Conflicts within religion weaken believers as more subversive and harmful social values creep into the faith allowing us to slide down its slippery slope. The ebb and flow these conflicts create lulls us into an uneasy and disquieted state. We see no path to unite our faiths, so we accept a fitful *status quo*. Our slumber arises from a complacency regarding right and wrong. Do Believers lack a Code of Law defined outside of humans like you and me? Is this why we have not yet awakened from our silent complacency?

IV. BRIDGING THE CHASM

The absurd assault on basic common sense arose quickly—within two generations. Our religious institutions became complicit, accepting funding in exchange for harmful agendas. Conflicting ideas within our denominations encouraged moral relativism. We lacked firm standards to anchor our beliefs. No firm truth allows us to consider one action universally right and correct, and its opposite action universally wrong. We have become so lost in our own individual religions that we now call good evil, and evil good (Isa 5:20).

Disillusioned, without any firm standard to enable the beliefs we should hold, believers became focused, almost obsessed with the afterlife. We have forgotten about "this life" that God has allotted us. Do we shirk our responsibility? Indeed, we have allowed our religious and political systems to fall into the hands of despots of rotten, lawless men who exploit and fleece the flock.

Yet, we wonder why God has not returned. Should He ignore our request to no longer be united under Him? Having slid so deep into misery, we find the antidote too remote. It is not expedient. Do we desire the way that enabled our grandparents to trust in Him? If God's ways are too onerous why make a fuss? Manmade truths are at an impasse. We are losing our civility. Fractured unity is turning into oppression: class against class, brother against brother, will everyone become an enemy? Can we afford this manmade lawlessness?

Without God's Divine revelation, we remain silently asleep. We are born to grow. We mature into the flower of life, then pass on. What future will we leave for our children? Do we desire them to inherit our misery? How far from God will *too big to fail* lead our children? As an unanchored society, life is consumed by uncertainty. It does not matter whether we acknowledge our departure from natural law or deny it. Secret or known, the consequence of our policy remains, no matter how we decry it.

> They are asleep. In the morning they are grass which grows up. In the morning it flourishes, and, in the evening, it is cut down, and withers. For we are consumed by your anger, and by your wrath we are troubled. You have set our iniquities before you, our secret sins in the light of your countenance. (Ps 90:5–8)

In this psalm, Moses understands that division and hardship occur as a natural consequence to our rejecting God. We grow no stronger than blades of grass. We can be easily torn and wither away. Nothing lasts. All is inflationary, bloated, and meaningless. It is not our lords that hold us down, but our own iniquities. The beliefs that govern our actions have darkened in our sleep. How do we reverse this constant struggle? How do we triumph over misery to live productively? Is all vanity (Eccl 1:2)? How can our lives succeed so that we may live in prosperity? How do we regain the power of our voice? When will silence no longer be the song of the majority?

V. AWAKENING TO STRENGTH AND UNITY

Being our own gods does not work out so well without One God to unite our hearts and ways. Throughout history, manmade states do lead to tyranny. How do we break this endless Tytler cycle of oppression, so we are not stuck in its depression? Our perception has been based upon misdirection. Our concession allows our misery without a Divine Code of Law to protect our rights. What if our silence we no longer allow? Would it heal the hate? Could it unite manmade enemies, transforming them into truest friends? Sympathy is of no avail! It is time for *too big* to fail. Enough of these corporate lords, when One God does reign Supreme! What if one common bond would unite and awaken us from this miserable night? Can we start afresh? Can God's written, timeless Code of Law pierce through manmade lies that deceive? It is time to awaken the giant.

> *To reject the law is to praise the wicked; to obey the Law is to fight them (Prov 28:4)*

The Crux of the Issue

Years of study have brought me to a single conclusion. If the events the Bible describes never occurred, it is senseless to believe the Bible is a Divine revelation relevant to one's personal life. This was my premise in Volume 1. If the Exodus never occurred, if God never met with Israel at Mt. Sinai, if Moses never existed, the quest for truth in Israel's God is meaningless. God's revelation of Himself to Abraham and the nation of Israel is the Divine claim of Israel's Scripture.[1] If it never happened, the Bible was conceived in fiction. Efforts to live by biblical instructions would be a deceptive waste of time. Modern academic scholarship has challenged many aspects regarding the Bible's accounts, providing conflicting evidence of biblical historicity.

Issues of validity in the Hebrew Bible (the Old Testament) compelled me to *prove all things*. I began investigating the soundness of the testimony for God's initial revelation of Himself to Israel and her patriarchs. My research in Volume 1 charted facts for ancient Israel's chronology, exodus, the conquest of Canaan, and the monarchy.

Encouragingly, I discovered vast archaeological and ancient written evidence supporting the existence of a historical Israel as described throughout the corpus of Old Testament books.[2] During 16 years of research, I discovered that events in Israel's history intersected with other nations at precise times in history, as supported by the Books of Judges, Kings, Chronicles, and prophets like Isaiah.

When records from Mesopotamia, Assyria, Egypt, or Babylon indicate contact with the land of Canaan or the people of Israel, Scripture usually reports this contact. Israel's story is internally reliable within Scripture and externally corroborated through historical and archaeological sources.

However, I also discovered that archaeology and history are incapable of evidencing whether God ever revealed Himself to Moses or the nation of Israel.[3] While archaeology and ancient inscriptions could corroborate the accounts of Israel's exodus and conquest, the evidence was not capable of revealing whether YHWH spoke His covenant at Mt. Sinai. I had to find another way to *prove all things*.

1
Prove All Things

I. THE CHURCH'S LEGACY

In early 1996, I was pregnant with our second child, another girl. My deep faith in God was unmovable. I loved Him and had a relationship with Him. I was saved and my sins were redeemed. My heart's desire was to be "well-pleasing" in God's sight. For as long as I can remember, I also struggled with a God who allows division, suffering, and strife. A God whose truth is determined by eras of men. What is believed truth today is not what the Church accepted 2,000, 1,000, 100, or even 10 years ago. God tells us not to make idols to worship them (Exod 20:5; 23:24; Lev 26:1; Deut 5:9). Yet, people pray to a symbolic image of Mary the mother of Jesus and to idols of Jesus and of the Saints.

Historically, a Christian's relationship was with the Pope, not God. Salvation only came through the Church.[1] Catholic tradition rivaled Scripture. No concept of a personal relationship with God existed until people could read statements in the Old Testament like, "love the Lord your God with all your heart, mind, and soul" (Deut 6:5), which revealed a personal God.[2] From the New Testament they could read Paul's challenge to "Prove all things and hold fast to that which is good" (1 Thess 5:21).

In 1452, Gutenberg invented the printing press. The Bible was the first book he printed. As printing presses spread across Europe, so did Bibles. For the first time, believers could prove the text for themselves. They could refer to the original Hebrew and Greek when translating into their language. Suddenly, truth became publicly accessible. Truth could no longer be controlled by an institution.

People soon discovered issues with the Church's official orthodox version. The written text exposed contradictions that opposed authorized Church doctrine. Public access to the Bible fractured the Church's iron grip on Europe's beliefs. The Church responded, using its power to ban the reading of Bibles, and threatening physical harm against all who dared to read unauthorized versions. (You can read the edicts from the Council of Trent in this footnote.[3])

The Church's threats against Christians did not discourage their hunger to know God. Defying threats of imprisonment and death, believers gathered to read God's personal written legacy for them. Obstacles could not prevent believers from seeking God. Just as persecution spread the Gospel, so did the Church's threats against heretics intensify believers' desire for firsthand knowledge of God's written word. People yearned for the right to *prove all things* for themselves.

Less than a century after Gutenberg's first Bible, "heretics" spearheaded the Reformation. This era challenged the Pope's authority and the Church's monopoly on political power over personal thought. The cardinal principle shared by every reformer held that the written Bible, not tradition, should be the sole source of spiritual authority. This was called *sola Scriptura*, or Scripture alone.[4]

The Church responded with blunt force. War and persecution were the Church's age-old armaments for obstructing believers from seeking and finding God. Modernly, the Church recasts this history by stating its goal was never to prohibit people from reading the Bible but to keep society relying on institutional authority to preserve unity within the overall religion.

> Despite the "spin" that some Evangelicals put on the Catholic position, the Catholic Church was never opposed to people reading the Bible. What it opposed was people reading interpretations of the Bible apart from the teaching authority of the Church, which would lead to the kinds of problems we have today with 30,000 denominations interpreting Scripture differently.[5]

Although the researcher's claim that the Church was "never opposed to people reading their Bibles," I can take a survey of my Catholic friends and they will tell me the Church discourages them from reading the Bible for themselves.[6] One Catholic friend asked me, "Why should we? Isn't that what the priests are for"? This flippant attitude is content with the status quo. It is satisfied with a religion dictated by men, not God. It is silence through complacency. Have we lost sight of the Reformers' vision of a truth based directly on the written word? Have we lost our skill to demonstrate our love for God by proving all things?

II. FREEDOM FROM RELIGION

As I studied academic and religious sources, I faced a blunt realization. Our freedom to seek God has brought about the Church's greatest fear: the splintering of Christian unity. Over 30,000 different Christian denominations exist today.[7]

Unity amongst religious denominations is strained. Families frequently fragment over religion, while wars for and against Christianity wage on today. Society has grown so divided that the basic beliefs that once unified our grandparents divide us today. Added to this gridlocked impasse is the uncomfortable reality that the beliefs within our churches are *un*stable. They change with every new generation.

What we believe today about faith, salvation, and tradition differs greatly from the time when Jesus walked and taught in Judea. Truth has become subjected to the modern whims of men. It is only internal and personal without any external standard of accountability to anchor or test it.

Our constantly evolving beliefs about God are far from the prophet Isaiah's ideal. Isaiah foresaw God's word standing firm. It resists changing times and is always available to unify believers.

> The grass withers, the flower fades because the spirit of YHWH blows on it. Surely the people are grass. The grass withers, the flower fades: but the **word of our God shall stand for ever.** (Isa 40:7–8. cf. Ps 90:5–8; 103:15–18)

Truth within God's word withstands the test of time, according to Isaiah. Truth guards against the rotten whims of humanity's ever-evolving and revolving ethics and values. Every few generations, new human ideas come to life. They take root and bloom. Society is intoxicatingly drawn to the novelty of that idea delivering something better and more expedient than was known in the past. But then, the consequences of that idea play out. The great idea was a diversion masquerading as truth. People abandon this once beautifully-alluring and promising belief in pursuit of the next trend that will make life more meaningful and less boring.

History reveals that people, and their beliefs, grow and die like grass. We keep repeating the broken past. In contrast, the word of Israel's God remains constant and steadfast. It remains valid throughout the ebb and flow of human history. Truth remains relevant because it is attainable, especially when we *prove all things*.

III. THE JOURNEY TO KNOW GOD

In 1997, I was invigorated. My girls were growing, and I loved being a mom. As my education broadened, I confronted new dilemmas. The contradictions within our churches weighed heavily upon my heart. I had inherited the Reformers' heretical thirst for truth and was dissatisfied with the official party line. The Reformation fractured the Roman Empire's iron claw politically, but not the people's religious complacency.

For the most part, people flocked to their own (usually ethnic) culture to understand God.[8] Soon, these beliefs were also challenged. As the Roman Empire's grip cleaved in two, so did people's belief in God. Would both God and man fade like grass? Each sect, to a lesser degree, repeated the Church's status quo defined by its Reformers. They were comfortable with their Catholic-less freedom, accepting strife and division amongst religious denominations. I was too idealistic to accept or be comfortable with a complacent God of strife.

Despite its misery, we naturally avoid anything that challenges the status quo, no matter how oppressive life becomes. We are comfortable being objects at rest, who remain at rest. A *Laodicean* spirit of indifference dominates our churches (Rev 3:15–17). We've obtained our political freedom to seek God over the past 250 years, yet we stopped where the Reformers left off.

Ignored are Scriptures' promises of universal peace and unity for a continued pursuit of truth.[9] Forgotten are the prophecies of a Day wherein people look to Abraham, to Sarah, and to Israel's God for truth (Isa 51:2). Neglected are the prophets' pleas for each of us to create a new heart within ourselves: a heart and a spirit capable of turning every nation's swords into ploughshares (Mic 4:3; Isa 2:4–5). We are content with our own little corner of freedom from religion.

My husband Jack and I were fascinated with Old Testament prophecy. As I studied, I became increasingly aware that I had unintentionally deemed much of that prophecy unnecessary. History divulged that many prophecies were fulfilled before Israel's fall to Assyria in 717 BCE and Judah's fall to Babylon in 587 BCE.

I also began to see the silent inter-testament period (540 BCE–170 CE) fervently appearing on the prophets' horizon. I was shocked to witness their alarming warnings for this era. The Second Temple Period was not a black hole in time that the prophets overlooked or ignored. It was spelled out in detail! The prophets also described the future of Israel's latter-day descendants. I was blown away by the 50+ texts that prophesy of Israel's latter end (cf. Lev 26:44–45; Deut 30:1–9; Ezek 36:22–30). I observed that God's written word did *not* foretell of destruction, but of the salvation of this latter-day generation who finally broke the endless cycle of sin's misery.

From Genesis to Zechariah, Scripture foretells Israel's latter-day descendants in the end times collectively seeking God, understanding truth, and turning from evil. The written word tells us that this generation will find Him "when we search for Him with all our heart" (Deut 4:28–29; 13:3; 30:1–10; Prov 8:17; Isa 51:1–7; Jer 29:11–14; Ezek 18:31–32; Hos 5:15–6:3; Amos 5:4). I wondered if this latter-day generation would finally accept Paul's challenge to prove all things.

The prophet Jeremiah refers to this era, telling us that we will no longer need to

> teach every man his brother saying, Know the Lord, because they shall all know me from the least of them unto the greatest of them, says the Lord. (Jer 31:34)

Jeremiah foretells humanity's universal understanding of truth. I wondered how this latter generation discovered this amazing unity. Was it simply through God's spirit? Could there be a tangible method that enables a universal knowledge of God? What if we right now, today, could seek and find this path? Would it lead to the earth "being full of the knowledge of God" (Isa 11:9)? What if the first step in fulfilling Jeremiah's vision was as simple as a dialog that proved all things?

2

Wrestling with God

I. REASONING TOGETHER: *THE FIRST STEP*

In early 1998, I was balancing motherhood with personal study. I loved spending time in God's written word. I remained dissatisfied with the drifting and ever-changing ideas churches were putting forth as Divine. As I kept digging, I realized that Paul's challenge to prove all things was not new. It was based on sound doctrine.

When Isaiah faced similar drifting of religious and moral values, he responded with a simple plea to *"come and reason together"* (Isa 1:18). Isaiah reveals the *first step* in healing a religion divided.

> Learn to do well by seeking judgment, relieving the oppressed, judging the fatherless, and pleading for the widow. **Come now, and let us reason together**, says the Lord. Although your sins be as scarlet, they shall be as white as snow; though they be red like crimson, they shall be as wool. (Isa 1:17–18)

Despite Israel's rotten state, Isaiah believed it was not too late to revive truth and justice. Logic could prevail through simple dialog.[1] Overcoming sin and restoring justice could be achieved through a discussion that "reasons together."[2] This seemed counterintuitive to me. Scholars and theologians have reasoned and debated over Scripture for over 25 centuries without unity emerging. Why would a dialog now differ from the past? How could it heal divided ideas about good and evil? How could proving all things enable us to hold onto that which is good?

II. FIGHTING THE GOOD FIGHT

In 1999, President Clinton was acquitted on both articles of impeachment. The Sopranos debuted on HBO, and I had my last hair perm. I was unpacking and settling into our first home, and the baby room for our first boy was coming along nicely. Quiet time, after the kids were sleeping, was spent reading and studying while Jack was in night school. Gradually, I began to see. The pieces began to fit together. Having an open dialog worked! This first step opened my understanding to see the path ahead.

As this dialog continued, I confronted an obvious reality. We are still chained to institutional authority. The Roman Empire collapsed, but its approach to religion remains. We do not yet base our beliefs directly on God's written word but wash them through the approval of manmade institutional authorities.

No one—no scholar or theologian—has undertaken an unbiased empirical investigation into Scripture's ideas of truth. Academics push theses that ignore more biblical texts than they consider. Theologians (most sincere) keep the masses sleeping through the ebb and flow of the status quo. Others refuse to check their ambition, exploiting superstition. Every charlatan offers a mystical piece of God for a price. With every Code of law subtracted, man cannot judge this wrong from right to protect himself from sin's misery.

Religion has become an aesthetic tool leveraged to manipulate the masses. Relativity depends upon the masses looking to man to find God. For academics, religion is a disease to be eradicated from the masses. Why did God allow this division? Why did He not make truth simple and easy for all to understand? Was Nietzsche correct when he pronounced God dead? Had God ever lived?

III. STRUGGLING WITH GOD

At the end of 1999, my world shattered. My seeking God seemed to come crashing down. I could not unsee. I could not unlearn. I could not forget or ignore it! If I was honest with myself, I had to face my own inherited and preconceived institutional beliefs. My faith and trust in God seemed lost. I began to wonder if it was all a lie used to manipulate and control the masses.

Jack and I ordered a book about prophecy and Israel's modern dispersed descendants. It challenged our expectations. The author presented compelling evidence that challenged our belief in Jesus. I was not looking for this, nor did I want it. I pushed the book aside, refusing to consider the evidence. My hubby, hungry for truth, pressed on.

Jack's questions would not let me rest. He was persistent. Both of us knew God's word. Jack knew his Bible and could quote it at random. He loved God and had given his life to Jesus. But now he was questioning core ideas. He challenged me and would not let me rest. As our dialog continued, I began to find some of his questions difficult to answer.

At the time, I felt like my whole world was falling apart. Had I been presumptuous to think anyone could uncover a truth capable of unity? Had I misunderstood Paul's encouragement to prove all things? Who was I to think that a universal truth even exists?[3] Should I be satisfied with the status quo of our conflicting and opposing institutions? Is truth relative?

I even began to wonder if the prophets' promises were just empty manmade lies. I walked away from religion, trying to ignore these vexing questions, hoping they would die off.

IV. HOPE RENEWED

Months turned into a couple of years. Through it all, I kept feeling God's gentle tug. I could feel God whispering that HE had this, and He had me. I should restart my journey to see if unbiased study and dialog could reveal anything new. I should press on. The search was not in vain. His promises were sure—even for me. If God exists, then I should be able to test the evidence and prevail.

One Scripture encouraged and reassured my studies.

> But if from there you will seek the Lord your God, you shall find him, if you seek him with all your heart and with all your soul. (Deut 4:29)

We can seek God and He's capable of being found![4] Scripture's promises took on new meaning for me. If God's ancient testimony, His dialog with Israel is real, then the promise that we will find Him is also within our grasp. God assures that His "lovingkindness and his truth will preserve" us (Ps 40:10–11). That promise includes individuals like you and me!

I rediscovered the emphasis God places on truth. It anchors the believer's relationship with God to reality. Truth prevents us from creating a God of our own making. If we desire a faith based on facts instead of a faith based on the ever-evolving whims and words of men, God's emphasis on truth must be taken seriously. If we are to have a relationship with Him, it is essential to acknowledge that He is a "God of truth" (Deut 32:4). Not only is He a God of truth, but truth defines His character.

> The Lord God (is) merciful and gracious, longsuffering, and **abundant in goodness and truth**. (Exod 34:6)

Since truth is one aspect of God's character (Ps 25:10; 31:5; 33:4; 57:3; 86:15; 100:5), we have no fear in proving all things (Deut 3:22). God wants us to have "truth in the inward and hidden parts" of our hearts and minds (Ps 51:6). Does this mean God's word can withstand any question—no matter how difficult?

V. ACCEPTING PAUL'S CHALLENGE

My research revealed that scholars and theologians approach the text with preconceived biases. They single out those texts that favor their positions. When Isaiah faced many competing and contradicting ideas about God, he pleaded for believers to weigh the evidence by reasoning together. What if the method that made this dialog work ignored institutional authority while renewing the Reformer's vision of the written text anchoring our beliefs? Could a *sola Scriptura* path yet reveal universal truth?

The competing ideas about God, and conflicts over morality and truth, persuaded me to prove all things by testing religious ideals against the written word. With an unknown adventure ahead, I accepted Paul and Timothy's call "to prove all things and to hold fast to that which is good."

VI. PREVAILING WITH GOD

In 2001, my studies took on a new resolve. No longer could I dismiss the questions my husband had voiced or those that gnawed at my conscience. My research turned from casual study into ground-pounding, investigative—up to 2 a.m.—research. Game on! Every religious person and every academic resource or counselor I'd consulted all held the same position: Truth is subjective. Truth is unknowable. Truth will always be in the eye of the beholder. Truth is simply relative to individuals like you and me. I felt God led me to this point to break through the veil of superstitious ignorance to prove all things.[5]

I am sharing my 25 years of research with you in the *YHWH Exists* series. The information in the Volume 2 series is part of the first book I wrote in 2015 but waited until now to publish it.[6] To break through the veil shrouding truth, I journeyed through difficult questions, faced sophisticated obstacles, and persevered to discover the wonderful reward God has waiting for regular individuals like you and me. This valiant path leads us to a unity that restores our systems of justice. This daring path can revive our families and heal our nation (2 Chr 7:14). Following God's instruction to seek Him empowers us to unshackle complacency's silent, subtle addiction.

The information in this series of books saved and rescued me from despair. It provided stable evidence to build my beliefs. It is the firm truth that can set every one of us free to live a life of joyous and meaningful purpose. Hard questions allow us to see that a miraculous and saving God is at the center of it all: the quest is not too onerous (Deut 30:11-16). It is a message of good news and hope that can bring about an age of salvation, fulfilling the prophetic vision of a world so full of the knowledge of God that we no longer need men to teach us. Amazingly, this vision is fulfilled by stepping onto the path that reopens a long-lost dialog.

However, I don't want you to take my word for it or trust my experience. Rather, prayerfully research and weigh the evidence for yourself. To make my case, I must step back and detach. I need to relate the ideas I considered in my studies objectively and empirically. Although I'll share my journey along the way, I want you to walk for yourself and to judge the evidence along this trail for yourself. Test for yourself and see whether Paul offered great advice when he encouraged believers to *prove all things*.

VII. ABOUT THIS BOOK

This book is formatted like Volume 1. There are three sections in *Does Jesus Exist*? The first section defines the path of concepts that will guide our investigative quest. Without guidelines, the questions our dialog asks could become outrageous. We could make demands that no text (ancient or modern) could satisfy and like those before us, arrive at a dead end. Like a court trial or medical research project, our method on the road to truth will rely on the **preponderance of evidence**.[7] (If you'd like to dig deeper, the endnotes contain sources and quotes from scholars and theologians which provide greater research in that endnote's topic.)

The second section journeys through the historical validity of the New Testament. Is there extrabiblical evidence to support that the people in the Bible were real or that its accounts really occurred? We will confront archaeological and historical sources before 200 CE to see whether the New Testament was well-known by many or a creation of a select few. Does evidence exist for a historical Jesus? If it does, what do those corroborations reveal about Jesus? Do clues reveal anything about the early beliefs the Church once held? You will find this section encouraging and reassuring as the adventure unfolds.

The third section routes us to view the more controversial issues of internal harmony. Do not be discouraged with this section's pilgrimage. Traveling through perplexing questions has the greatest reward. This section was the most difficult for me to live and retell. From the vantage point of these issues, you and I can look upon the facts in this case and make rational judgments capable of revealing the path that leads to a unifying theme between the Old and New Testaments.

Originally, Isaiah's prophecy of the Suffering Servant was also part of this book. I found that I was covering too much information in one book. I'd rather go slow than discourage the reader with a book whose odyssey is too long to read or has too much information. My hope is to encourage you on your journey to know God, not to overpower with a path of excessive evidence.

The next book in this series will reveal the important role Job plays in the Suffering Servant prophecy. Our investigation of Isaiah 53 will reveal 50 traits Isaiah establishes for God's Suffering Servant. But I'm getting ahead of myself.

Just as the Old Testament hinges upon a historical Abraham and Moses, so does the quest for truth in the New Testament rely on a Jesus who lived on earth and fulfilled what was written of him. This is why it is crucial to examine the evidence for Jesus before we move on to Isaiah 53's Suffering Servant. Only then can we consider Jesus's relationship to Isaiah 53 and the path that unifies us by leading us back to God.

VIII. AN UNEXPECTED JOURNEY

As I resumed studying, I discovered a crucial clue that stood out. It made my path clear. It was a way forward! It drew me closer to God than I'd ever been. I felt accepted. My relationship became alive—even when the path of truth seemed cloudy and far off. This revelation was stressed so many times in Scripture. I just didn't see it before. It was hiding in plain sight. As I came to understand this bedrock principle more deeply, I realized it held a transformational truth. It was the first firm fact, a concept that I could hold onto. Applying this simple concept revolutionized my walk with God.

Method for Uncovering Truth:
Preponderance of the Evidence

1ˢᵗ Step	Join a dialog to *prove all things*. The route relies upon the preponderance of the evidence.

3
When God Knows Your Name

I. KNOWING YOU BY NAME

A deep yearning within each of us desires to be known by name. When people know your name, you feel like you belong to a group or community. It links us to the unity of fellowship in this journey of life. You fit in and you matter. The 1980s sitcom *Cheers* became a hit series because it embraced this desire. The show's theme song repeated, "You wanna be where everybody knows your name." The moment one of the characters walked into the *Cheers*' bar, the cast would call out their name. "Norm!" The character felt loved and accepted. They belonged.

When people make the effort to remember your name, it feels like they care about you. You matter because they remember who you are—by name. There isn't much of a relationship when someone doesn't recognize your name. You are simply another acquaintance in their life. You do not stand out.

When important people know your name, it is special. You stand out to them. Celebrities have thousands of fans vying for their time and attention. When public figures know you by name, you either have a personal relationship with them or you stand out from the crowd competing for attention. If the President or a famous movie star knows you by name, a personal relationship or personal interaction usually exists. Something makes you different from the crowd, which causes them to know you—by name.

Moses had this type of relationship with God.

> I will do this thing that you have asked because you have found grace in my sight, and **I know you by name**. (Exod 33:17)

God and Moses were more than acquaintances, they were friends (Exod 33:11). God chose Moses, calling him—by name. Moses proved his worth by obeying God's request to lead Israel out of Egypt and teaching Israel about God's Code of Law as a productive way for the path of life (Exod 18:20).[1] This loyalty enabled Moses to find grace and favor in YHWH's sight. God was familiar with Moses. Moses knew he mattered to God because God knew him—by name.

God knew Moses before the Exodus when he was a simple shepherd. The first time God introduced Himself, He called Moses' name from the burning bush.

> God called unto him out of the midst of the bush, and said, *Moses, Moses*. And he said, Here am I. (Exod 3:4)

God piqued Moses's interest through calling him—by name. If God had called to Moses with a generic "man, man," Moses may have been less motivated to accept God's mission. Calling someone's name gets their attention. God's effort to know Moses' personal name enabled Moses to trust God.

II. GOD'S PERSONAL NAME

A. I Am: *The Second Step*

Humans desire a God that personifies life around them. We divide the Divine into bite-size pieces we can easily digest. We want a God who untangles and explains the world around us, especially when it disappoints. We have not yet understood a God who stands out and differs from the rest.

In his book, *Restoring Abrahamic Faith*, James Tabor (UNC Charlotte) remarks that Israel's God was different. Israel's lone Deity was distinct from the ideas common among the nations.

> The Hebrew Bible speaks of ONE GOD, beside Whom there is *no other*. In contrast to all other deities or claims about divinity, this ONE GOD is called the *true and living* God (Jer 10:10; Josh 3:10). The gods and goddesses of all the nations of the world are declared by the Hebrew prophets to be idols, empty vanity, and void of reality. They are largely personifications of Nature, and from a biblical point of view, they represent the various forces of the creation rather than the Creator. To put in modern Freudian terms, they are illusions based on human *imagination*, *fears*, *hopes*, and *dreams*. They represent our all-too-human need to project onto the vastness of our violent and terrifying universe some way of coping with the workings of nature or the operation of Fate in our lives.[2]

Unlike pagan gods, which personified human actions and feelings, Israel's God stood out. He eclipsed pagan cults by offering wisdom profoundly different from the nations' gods. He was not simply a force of nature or a myth of cosmic forces. He was a God who had something profoundly good to offer humanity.

II. God's Personal Name

When God laid out Moses' mission at the burning bush, Moses wanted to know who this God was that knew him by name. Moses lived his early life in Egypt among its plethora of deities. Was this one of Egypt's many deities? If so, which one?

> And Moses said to God, Behold, when I come to the Children of Israel, and shall say to them, The God of your fathers has sent me to you; and they shall say to me, What is his name? What shall I say to them? And God said to Moses, **I AM THAT I AM**: and he said, Thus shall you say to the Children of Israel, **I AM** has sent me to you. And God said moreover to Moses, Thus shall you say to the Children of Israel, *YHWH God of your fathers*, the God of Abraham, the God of Isaac, and the God of Jacob, has sent me to you. This is my name forever and this is my memorial to **all generations**. (Exod 3:13–15)

God reveals Himself through His personal name. He was not an Egyptian deity. He was Abraham's God: the God who blessed Isaac and Jacob. God reminded Moses that He had a history with his family, who had been called to be God's people (Gen 12:1–3). God vaguely describes Himself as "He is what He is."

The Hebrew word for 'I AM' is *ehyeh*, from the root *hayah*.[3] It means "to be" or "to exist."[4] This word is used in Gen 1:2, stating, the "earth *was* or existed without form." God reveals Himself as a self-existent Being: a God who simply "is" or simply "exists." The name 'YHWH' (הוה) derives from the root *hyh* or *hayah*. Since ancient written Hebrew was a consonant-based language, it did not employ vowels or vowel pointing. God's name in English is written as *YHWH*.[5]

YHWH reveals the personal name by which we should call God for "all generations."[6] Israel would know that "YHWH, God of your fathers" was sending Moses to deliver Israel from the hard labor of oppression. YHWH's name is so pivotal to our understanding that YHWH included it as the 3rd commandment in the Ten Commandments. He forbids humanity to use it in vain (Exod 20:7).[7]

God's personal name is the first solid truth that makes Him stand out from the nations' gods. It is the first general and universal rule that can guide, direct, and enlighten our path: God has a name! YHWH's name "is forever"! It stands as a constant reminder pointing us to a powerful God who can topple strong and impregnable foreign institutions that hold His people captive. Acknowledging and using His name is the crucial *second step* that begins to deliver us from the misery of sin. (The *first step* in ch. 2 is reasoning together through dialog, see pp. 5, 9–10.)

Calling upon YHWH's name gets His attention, especially when our own paths lead us astray. By using YHWH's name, we reveal a contrite heart and a spirit willing to do what God has asked: to acknowledge YHWH's "memorial to all generations." Taking the time to call God by His name demonstrates that we are not basing our beliefs on man. YHWH stands out! YHWH matters more than the promises and doctrines of men. YHWH's name also joins us to His people. We are not alone in life's quest. We walk with others who desire a better way, a fellowship based on truth.

Restoration begins with a name: God's personal name. He wants a relationship with us. YHWH revealed His name to prevent deception. He told Moses to share His name with His people so they could distinguish YHWH from other gods—by name.

B. Polytheism

The names we use for God play a vital role in our modern understanding of Him. The name we acknowledge for God reveals a lot about what we believe. When a person professes Jesus or Allah as God, two distinct ideas come to mind: one is Christian, the other Muslim.

Ancient nations worshipped far more gods than we do today. The Greeks had over 400! Amidst the host of deities, all ancient nations acknowledged a single, usually supreme, "Creator-god" in their pantheon (or company of gods). *Zeus* was the Greek's supreme deity. For the Assyrians, it was *An* from whom all other deities descended. For the Babylonians it was *Anu*. For the Egyptians, the sun god *Re* held this favored position. And for the Canaanites, *El* was the supreme deity.

Israel's God was different. He stood out. In contrast to the polytheism of Babylon, Greece, Assyria, and Canaan, the Old Testament's one Creator required no pantheon of deities.[8] YHWH, was a single being whose name and profoundly timeless doctrine stood out from the gods of contemporary nations (Isa 42:8; Ps 147:19).[9] Similarly, YHWH called a single nation—by name—to stand out and to preserve an accurate knowledge of Him.[10]

C. Baal

Just as Jesus and Allah reveal separate ideas about God, so do the nations' manmade gods. Pagan deities expose a path paved by man to manipulate and deceive. While YHWH was ancient Israel's God, *Baal* was a manmade god represented in wood and stone. Baal's name meant "the lord."[11] The name *Baal* was not unique since it was widely used for a plethora of pagan deities.[12]

Over time, the nations' supreme "Creator-gods" were displaced by the younger and more popular *Baal*. The older gods were either killed by the young usurper, or they simply "retired."[13] While the older "Creator-gods" retained their status, they were impotent and silent. In some cultures like Canaan, Baal was "complementary rather than in opposition" to the original "Creator-god" El.[14]

In Ugarit and Syria, 'the lord' was "known as the son and successor to the great god El."[15] In Assyria, Baal was called *Bel Asusr,*' while the god Marduk was the god Anu's son and lord in Babylon.[16] Baal was the Phoenician deity best known from the story of Jezebel's priests' duel on Mt. Carmel with the prophet Elijah (1 Kings 18).[17] The written Hebrew text *never* attributes the name *Baal* to YHWH. When people called out to 'the Lord'—by name—they were not calling out to YHWH, but to a pagan *baal*, who displaced the Creator-God. This is why YHWH specifically prohibited His people from calling Him by the names of other gods.[18]

Early in Israel's history, people craved paganism's physical idol worship. They saw the loving God from Mt. Sinai as aloof. Israel desired a pagan human deity over a God whose Code of Law established universal truth, justice, and unity in society. This led to the Israelites humanizing YHWH and making Him join paganism's pantheon. They wanted YHWH to manifest Himself like the other nations' idols: to be a tangible deity they could see, even if it was just wood and stone.

The *baals* became a widely-popular idol cult. People created idols to bring god to man. People exchanged YHWH's glory for wood and stone. John Day (Old Testament Studies at Oxford) observes,

> Prior to the discovery of the Ugaritic texts ... it was sometimes supposed that 'the Baals' referred to quite distinct Canaanite deities, each Baal having its separate local identity. The Ugaritic texts revealed, however, that **Baal, 'the lord,' was the epithet** (though becoming a personal name) of one great cosmic deity, Hadad, so that the local Baals were, in fact, simply local manifestations of this deity.[19]

Hadad was the name for Syria's Baal. He was usually termed 'Baal-Hadad' or 'Lord-Hadad.' Ancient Israel craved her own local physical manifestation of God. People wanted God to live among them. Israel forsook YHWH and made Him like the nations' baals. Israel pursued this global baalism by substituting the generic pagan '*baal*' or '*lord*' for YHWH's personal name. 'The Lord' became a title for YHWH.[20] Israel exchanged a distinct and personal relationship for the world's generic manmade gods. No longer would YHWH or His name stand out. YHWH became just another baal.

Archaeology sheds light on Israel's pagan tradition. Excavated at Kuntillet 'Ajrud in the Sinai Peninsula, an 8th-century BCE inscription reveals Israel's commingling of YHWH with pagan deities. The inscription's poem paraphrases Psalm 97:5, Isaiah 55:12, and Nahum 1:5. It uses the name Baal to refer to Israel's God—YHWH. The inscription reads,

> When God shines forth ... [Y]HW[H] ... The mountains will melt, the hills will crash ... The Holy One over the gods ... Prepare (yourself) [to] bless Baal on a day of war ... to the name of El on a day of [w]ar.[21]

Israel's commingling YHWH with pagan theologies meant she had forgotten the singleness of her God. She wanted to fit in. She wanted to be like every other nation, no matter the freedoms lost. By linking YHWH's name with other gods, YHWH's profoundly unique way to live became lost in religion. God was just another lord to lead astray and rule over humanity. Behind these idol lords, man ruled over mankind.

By King Manasseh's oppressive reign, the worship of YHWH as a baal and Asherah (the queen of heaven) as his consort became the official state religion in Judah (2 Kgs 21:7).[22]

Israel's people wanted to be like the nations around them, so the state adopted their practices (1 Sam 8:20). Israel made YHWH common, no longer wanting His name or His teachings to stand out. YHWH's laws were adapted to new socially acceptable norms. Israel rejected the path to personally knowing YHWH and His profound revelation at Mt. Sinai. With YHWH's unique way of life relegated to a common religion, Israel's leaders could easily manipulate and exploit the people for personal gain.

D. The Lord

Israel's prophets earnestly protested the nation's apostasy. They warned against the *lies* found in the theologies associated with the *lords* of Canaan's Baals and Babylon's Bel.

> Their sorrows shall be multiplied that hasten after another god: their drink offerings of blood will I not offer, *nor take up their names into my lips*. (Ps 16:4)

> Declare you among the nations, and publish, and set up a standard. Publish, and conceal not! Say, Babylon is taken, *Bel is confounded, Merodach* (Marduk) *is broken in pieces*; her idols are confounded, her images are broken in pieces. (Jer 50:2, parentheses added)

When YHWH's people forsook Him to seek other gods, it ended in oppressive sorrow. The righteous withstood the ever-evolving religions of baal and refused to substitute the names of false gods for Israel's one God—YHWH. In Psalm 16, King David withstood religious trends by refusing to offer sacrifices to false gods and denying supplications in the name of the *lords*.

Originally, Marduk rose to prominence as "the title Bel (lord) . . . came to be applied exclusively to Marduk."[23] The prophet Jeremiah foresaw a day when idols like Bel would be destroyed with Babylon's fall. As nations fell one by one, the baals of the people's own creation would wither, break into pieces, and disappear like grass.

Jeremiah repeatedly confronted Israel's tendency to mix YHWH with the baals like the Kuntillet 'Ajrud inscription did. He describes how lies in religion played out in his day.[24]

> The priests said not, Where is YHWH? They that handle the law did not know me. The rulers also transgressed against me, and the prophets *prophesied by Baal*, and walked after things that do not profit. (Jer 2:8)

> Look, you trust in *deceptive words that are worthless*. Will you steal, murder, and commit adultery, and swear falsely, and burn incense unto Baal, and follow after other gods you have not known and then come and stand before me in this house, which is called by my Name, and say, *We are delivered to do all these abominations*? (Jer 7:8–10, NIV)

Israel's priests, prophets, and kings exploited Israel's desire for pagan nations' lords.[25] Israel's elite were the worst offenders. Paganism profited Israel's pastors. Leaders corrupted their citizens to benefit from it. Their ever-changing definitions of right and wrong kept the people distracted in a constant conflict to adjust. They intentionally taught Israel to forget YHWH's universal Code of Law. Unbound by a Law that restrained their power and held them accountable to constitutional principles, rulers could continually make new demands on the people with impunity.[26]

Israel's citizens, of all nations, became the most reprobate (2 Chr 33:9). They broke YHWH's covenant by stealing, murdering, and committing adultery. Then, they came into YHWH's Temple and proclaimed they had been saved and delivered from the offenses they had just committed! No law existed to prevent their offenses since they had been delivered from YHWH's Code of Law that defined their offenses (Jer 7:8–10).[27]

> They are waxen fat, they are sleek. Yes, they surpass the deeds of the wicked. They do not plead the cause of the fatherless nor defend the rights of the needy . . . An astonishing and horrible thing has been committed in the land. The prophets prophesy falsely, and *the priests bear rule by their means; and my people love to have it so*: and what will you do in the end thereof? (Jer 5:28, 30–31)

The ruling class exploited the power that nameless religion gave them. Israel waxed rich through YHWH's Code of Law (1 Kgs 10:2; 2 Chr 9:9).[28] She enjoyed the fatness of prosperity that YHWH's way of life produced (Deut 31:20). But now she was comfortable. She considered herself a god capable of defining standards of right and wrong without YHWH's Code of Law to anchor them. This fad only empowered her leaders to exploit and oppress. Immorality within Israel surpassed that of the nations who had never known YHWH.

To make matters worse, YHWH's priests did not rule by His power nor did they acknowledge the constraints His Law placed on their agency. They ruled by oppressive authority that the lawless Baal cults enabled.[29] The people were comfortable with this dysfunctional status quo, believing in the priests' *lies* that they were better off with Baal than with YHWH.

The Baal's popularity overshadowed YHWH. Priests taught all gods were "the Lord." It was all relative. The Baal cult displaced YHWH, and His name was forgotten.

> How long shall this be in the heart of the prophets that prophesy lies? . . . (they) think to cause my people **to forget my name** by their dreams which they tell every man to his neighbor, as **their fathers have forgotten my name for Baal**. (Jer 23:26–27, parentheses added)

When people forget your name, they don't remember much about what you did or said. Rarely do they remember the specific ideas or laws you taught. You do not matter. You no longer fit in. You are no longer relevant. How can you matter when people don't even remember your name?

Today, when we talk about famous philosophers like Plato, Aristotle, or Locke we use their names to define the philosophy they taught. If we were to refer to all philosophers by the generic title "the philosopher," the ideas associated with their names would become disconnected. Their specific ideas would be rendered nameless and meaningless.

Israel's leaders used the Baals to lull Israel into the complacency of being common like other nations. YHWH's profound message was lost in laundered generalities. All ideas became relative. Without the protection of YHWH's universal Code of Law, Israel's citizens were easily manipulated and exploited like all other nations of the earth (as opposed to Deut 4:5–8). Men in the highest and most trusted positions *lied* to the people. Leaders promised one thing only to hide the crimes they committed behind their duplicity. Trusted leaders and scholars taught Israel to forget YHWH's name for 'the Lord.'

As Israel forgot YHWH's name, oppressive sorrow increased. No one remembered a Divine Code of Law that defined the taking of bribes as corrupt. No universal Divine standard existed to judge conflicts of interest. And no Divine Law prevented the king from raiding the residences of citizens who criticized his power. Even prophets—Israel's ancient journalists—were not safe. The Law, which protected regular citizens, was done away with in favor of manmade religion.

Lies sold in the name of religion silenced people's access to YHWH's power. Israel sold her inheritance for meaningless dreams and promises. Her love of truth grew silent. Israel became numb to the evil that surrounded her as she continued to cry out to Baal for deliverance. Would YHWH answer the cries made in the name of 'the lord'?

Method for Uncovering Truth:
Preponderance of the Evidence

Step 2	Use YHWH's Name	Refer to God by name—YHWH. Use His name to refer to God. When praying, call upon YHWH—by name.

4

Knowing God by Name

I. CONFRONTING INHERITED LIES: *THE THIRD STEP*

During my study on God's name, I discovered that Jeremiah prophesies of a Day when nations around the world awaken. People awake to a renewed desire for YHWH and a thirst for truth. After millennia of wars and persecution, many in the name of "the lord," we will finally realize that YHWH is our only path forward. YHWH is our only fortress and refuge from man's oppression.[1]

Jeremiah reveals the *third step* that my journey towards truth had to take for healing and restoration. He reveals the direction my journey should proceed for it to succeed. With this pivotal step, I embarked on an exciting journey, that took me one stride closer to knowing God. This transformative step empowers the earth to be full of the knowledge of God. It is a simple strategy that affects a lasting change and softening of humanity's hardened heart.

> O YHWH, my strength, and my fortress, and my refuge in the day of affliction, the Gentiles shall come to you from the ends of the earth, and shall say, Surely **our fathers have inherited lies, vanity, and things wherein there is no profit**. Shall a man make gods unto himself? They are no gods! (Jer 16:19–20)

The *third step* nations will take towards healing unity is a clear confession. We will wake up and willingly admit that we have inherited *lies* from our "traditional religions."[2] While two generations are all it took for us to be deceived, it takes but one to break the vicious cycle of deception. A simple confession unlocks the passageway leading to YHWH's salvation.

Inherited lies have hidden the plain path for society's deliverance. Only confession enables contrite hearts to know God personally. This admission is not one of guilt but of our reality. Our confession empowers our sensibility. It awakens us to see the traps along life's path, which misdirect to our enslavement. Our confession enables a heart to perceive the road of truth that YHWH has opened before us. The concession of our own way allows us to see

His. It removes the obstacles that impede our journey to know Him. Jeremiah tells us how to get from here to there. We can!

I left out the conclusion of this verse where Jeremiah draws attention to the primary means for unity, healing, and restoration. This truth reiterates the *second step* (see pp. 12–13, 18) we will take in using YHWH's name. It remains the key to knowing YHWH personally:

> Therefore, behold, I will this once cause them to know, I will cause them to know my hand and my might. And **they shall know that my name is YHWH**. (Jer 16:21)

Jeremiah foretells the path the earth will one day take in turning to Israel's God. No political or religious group can enlighten this path of unity enough to resist the affliction that the powerful and elite extract from ordinary citizens. They offer no defense to globalism's lack of accountability. YHWH wants us to know His name is essential to guide our discovery of His strength of truth.[3] In His name, we are empowered to overcome the constantly changing cycles and fads of human ethics and values.

The world will awaken to discover modern religions are *not only* empty, but they are weak and powerless. The modern status quo is unable to counter violence and oppression. Modern religion enables affliction that empowers one group to oppress the masses because no Rule of Law exists to hold all universally accountable. Nations will discover that the source of liberty's stability is as simple as calling upon YHWH—by name. This rule becomes the essential step in our journey back to YHWH. We will use YHWH's name to call upon God.

II. WARNING: DO NOT ADD OR TAKE AWAY

Small variations in a recipe change its outcome. You can have flour, sugar, cocoa, eggs, sugar, milk, and salt. The difference arises in the amount of liquid added. The same holds true for substituting baking soda for baking powder. They are not the same! They contain different chemicals. Baking soda is a base. It is often paired with acids like vinegar. Baking powder is alkaline and contains several acidic leavening agents and is double-acting, meaning it interacts with liquid and heat.[4] Baking powder also preserves a tangy taste. Substituting either of these in a recipe completely changes its outcome.[5]

The same is true with the Divine Name, which is revealed within YHWH's Code of Law (Exodus 3). God tells us to make contractual agreements by using His name to hold our word accountable (Deut 6:13). When we substitute YHWH's name for a generic "God" or "Lord" we lose the specific impact His name preserves. This is why He warned people against adding or taking away from His Code of Law; it ruins the recipe for success!

> You shall not add to the words which I command you, neither shall you subtract from it that you may keep the commandments of YHWH your God which I command you. (Deut 4:2, NIV)

> See that you do all I command you; do not add to it or take away from it. (Deut 12:32, NIV)

YHWH understood that changing the map changed the direction we would go. The path would detour to less desirable or even dangerous places. Like parallel lines, even slight deviations cause the lines to crash. Deviations lead to an entirely different destination. (Place your 2 index fingers on the right side of this diagram and continue their path. Notice how quickly they intersect and crash).

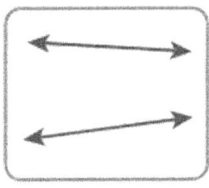

Not parallel

YHWH was not alone in warning humanity not to add or take away from His Law. The Book of Revelation also warns, "if any man shall add unto these things, God shall add unto him the plagues that are written in this book" (Rev 22:18).

When we ignore the distinction between YHWH's name and Jesus' name, we lose the important distinction between Father and son, between the God who sent Jesus, and the Jesus who was being sent (Matt 10:40; 15:24; Mark 9:37; Luke 4:43; 9:48; 10:16; John 5:23, 37–38). There is no honor to YHWH or Jesus in meshing them into one generic entity whom we term the "Lord" or "God." In doing so, we lose the specific way YHWH has given us to follow. We also succumb to Israel's ancient sin of ascribing to YHWH (and to Jesus) the name of baal.

III. FORGETTING YHWH'S NAME

King David understood that hardships occur when people depart from YHWH's path of life. David does not personify hardship as a force of nature or a natural state for humans to exist. Instead, David names one cause for Israel's suffering. In Psalms 44, David prophesies of a Day when Israel will remember what YHWH did for her ancestors in "the days of old" (Ps 44:1). He contrasts YHWH's miraculous salvation against the reality of Israel being "killed all the day long" and being "counted as sheep for the slaughter" (Ps 44:22).

After recounting the Law's curses for disobedience (Lev 26:14–39; Deut 28:15–68), David names one of the causes for Israel's suffering: she has forgotten YHWH's name!

> **If we have forgotten the name of our God** or stretched out our hands to a strange god; Shall not God search this out? For he knows the secrets of the heart. (Ps 44:20–21)

YHWH knew that if people had forgotten His personal name, then they were also ignoring His way of life. Forgetting and substituting YHWH's name in the wash of generalities allowed teachers to ascribe all sorts of manmade ideas to *the Lord*. New ideas would sprout up and wither away with new generations. Human ideas lacked an anchor.

While YHWH is a gracious and loving God (Exod 22:27; 34:6), He protects His name and reputation (Exod 20:5, 7; 34:14; Deut 4:24; 6:15; Nah 1:2). If people forget YHWH's name, He will seek to know our intentions. Do we forget Him due to our inherited beliefs? Or do we intentionally remain silently and complacently ignorant?

IV. JOHN JACOB JINGLEHEIMER SCHMIDT

Harry and Megan had a sweet relationship when they married. Harry showed his love and admiration for Megan by calling her "Pumpkin." While happy at first, mutual dysfunctions drove them apart and they divorced. About 2 years later, Harry remarried and had a much healthier relationship with Chelsey. They were close, sharing many common interests and values. However, Harry insisted on calling Chelsey "Pumpkin," a name she knows he used for his first wife. Over time, Harry slid into continually calling Chelsey "Megan." So, Chelsey confronted Harry over this continual slight. Harry dismissed her request, saying that it doesn't matter if he calls her Chelsey or Megan. They are both women and basically the same. Chelsey should know he is really referring to her.

How close of a relationship do you think Harry and Chelsey will have? How long do you think their marriage will last? We can relate to Chelsey being jealous for her name and wanting her name to distinguish her from her previous rival. None of us wants to be overlooked. We don't want to be confused with someone else. While none of us today would intentionally call YHWH "Baal," we do this unintentionally when we call YHWH by Baal's ancient title, "the Lord." YHWH wants us to know Him—by name!

V. POWER IN THE NAME OF YHWH

Knowing that YHWH has a personal name revolutionized my walk with Him. He was no longer some far-away God who does not see or hear my call. He became a God who responds to me as I seek truth.

> **YHWH is close to all who call upon him**, to all that call upon him **in truth**. He will fulfil the desire of them that fear him: he also will hear their cry and will save them. (Ps 145:18–19. Cf. Deut 4:7; Josh 24:14)

When we follow YHWH, we shed our need to personify God in terms of human suffering. We discover a God who teaches us to defeat all suffering through a profoundly Divine revelation. This revelation can finally release us from the ever-changing cycles of moral relativism, which bloom and wither with every passing generation. YHWH can stabilize our societies, so we are no longer manipulated to follow the next values' trend.

VI. FINDING STRENGTH IN THE NAME OF YHWH

Isaiah prophesies of a Day when YHWH's name is restored. This era of salvation becomes reality when God's people no longer dismiss YHWH's name as trivial.[6] We will finally realize it is a pivotal truth that guides our journey, which makes the vision possible. As people understand the profound justice, liberty, and prosperity that YHWH's way of life teaches, they will desire to call upon YHWH's name.

> In that day **you will say, Praise YHWH, call upon his name**, declare his doings among the people, make mention that his name is exalted. (Isa 12:4)

When society is not equipped with a universal set of values and ethics defined by a Divine Law to anchor their morality, they can be manipulated into just about any sort of horrific frenzy. People can see one ethnic group as problematic or inferior. They can be worked up and led to dismembering the other group's bodies just because their skin is a different color.[7] Society can be easily swayed to see another group of people worthy of extermination in gas chambers. The masses can easily be led to national suicide as they see their future and legacy, their own flesh and blood, as a burden to be destroyed before it is born.

Ancient pagan nations lacked Israel's codified standard of morality. Their political leaders easily manipulated the masses to sacrifice their children to the pagan god Molech (Lev 18:21; 20:2–4). This "culling" of the population prevented their numbers from growing strong enough to oppose oppressive regimes. But more than this, when people are willing to commit such gross atrocities in the name of a god or an ideology, they can be manipulated to do unimaginable horrors in that cause's name. History demonstrates people will do just about anything when they are not anchored to the rules that guide them in YHWH's path to life.

VII. WHEN THE WORLD KNOWS YHWH BY NAME

Murder, stealing, and adultery are wrong whether society acknowledges it or not. Burning helpless babies in the fire to an idol was not simply wrong for Israel, it was wrong for all nations. YHWH's covenant with Israel did not make Him forget other nations.

When Nineveh became trapped in a status quo that ignored murder, theft, and morality, YHWH sent the prophet Jonah to warn of the natural disaster into which their rotten system was spiraling. When a society, such as the Amorites, Israelites, or Assyrians, continually ignores injustice without holding their people accountable, a nation's sins "come to the full" (Gen 15:16) and disaster will eventually ensue.[8]

> Pour your fury upon the heathen that know you not, and upon the families **that call not on your name**: because they have eaten up Jacob, and devoured him, and consumed him, and have made his habitation desolate. (Jer 10:25)

Without Divine Law to hold humanity accountable, people will devour one another. It becomes a law of the jungle as survival of the fittest prevails. YHWH's profound universal standard for living life reforms these primitive and destructive tendencies. While YHWH instructed Israel by teaching a happy, stable way of life, nations that followed the baals continued being consumed by their own miserable iniquities.

Zephaniah foresees a Day when nations awaken. People finally become fed up with relying on man's ever-changing definition of right and wrong. Societies around the globe realize the narratives forced upon them in the name of fairness (and other taglines) only serve those who profit from them. People suddenly realize that the powerful elites burn Bibles and ban religion because it holds the formula for unifying people to withstand their oppressive forms of power.

Nations finally awaken to a healing unity that only YHWH can create.[9]

> For then will I turn to the people a pure language, that they may **all call upon the name of YHWH,** to serve him with one consent. (Zeph 3:9)

This shared consent among the nations is not a one-world government, but the antidote to it. It is the awakening of independent sovereign nations to truth. Nations awaken to realize their laws and ideas need anchoring. When YHWH anchors truth, society is empowered to withstand hidden agendas. The *third step* in this process is confessing that we have inherited lies from our institutions. We have been deceived! Thankfully, we are not stuck here! Our steps along this path are guided by precepts of truth. These precepts fulfill the prophetic vision by leaving the names of baal behind us to call upon YHWH—by name.[10]

VIII. THE LIE CONTINUES

Surprisingly, our modern Bible translations hide YHWH's personal name by making it common. Translators inadvertently influence us to forget YHWH—by name. To universally appeal to all people, translators used a generic title that people already knew. They maintained the status quo by using a pagan title for Israel's God. Modern translations made YHWH nameless by rendering God's personal name with the generic title "the LORD."

David Howard, who authored a book on Joshua remarks,

> God is referred to in this verse as "the Lord." This rendering, found in most English versions (as well as the Septuagint, which renders it *kurios*, "lord"), obscures the fact that here is God's personal name, which most scholars today agree was pronounced "Yahweh." This is the most holy, personal name of God, revealing much of his character, and it is praised repeatedly throughout the Psalms. It is the name whose meaning was revealed to Moses at the burning bush (Exod 3:11–15; cf. 6:2–3), and it tells us about God's eternal existence and his enduring faithfulness to his people.

"Yahweh" was God's personal name just as "Baal" and "Marduk" were the personal names of the high gods of the Canaanites and the Babylonians, respectively.[11]

YHWH's name appears over 6,000 times in the Old Testament. Every prophet recognized YHWH's name after Mt. Sinai. The generic title, "Lord" overshadows the personal name that reveals God. Because of the this, the knowledge tied to YHWH's name is lost. Rabbis, pastors, and scholars can easily cherry-pick the text to fit their own agenda under the title of an ambiguous "God" or "Lord."[12] Specific ideas, which underlie those texts are manipulated in a wash of empty generalities and platitudes. Precepts become divorced from YHWH's personal name, which anchors truth to the Divine, "thus says YHWH." This Divine word reveals the pathway to His profound way of life.

> **Your name, O YHWH, endures forever,** and your memorial, O YHWH, throughout all generations. (Ps 135:13)

IX. A NEW DAWN

Israel's prophets unanimously foresee a future Day when humanity recognizes YHWH alone as God. Baal no longer exists. The world is finished with its idols. Instead of forgetting YHWH, people finally forsake idolatry.

Hosea foretold of a Day when people would finally embrace YHWH and claim His salvation by refusing the names and titles of the world's gods. No longer would Baal be substituted for YHWH. People will "no longer ascribe my name to Baal."[13]

> And it shall be at that day, says YHWH, that you shall call me *Ishi*; and **shall call ME no more *Baali*.** For I will take away the names of *Baalim* out of her mouth, and they shall no more be remembered by their name. (Hos 2:16–17)

The Hebrew suffix -*i*- is a personal possessive suffix. It means, "my." The word *Ish* means husband.[14] Thus the word *Ishi* means "my husband." Hosea contrasts YHWH being Israel's husband to the competing ideas of Baal. *Baali* means "my baal" or "my lord." It emphasizes the husband's ownership and control over the wife. Hosea foresees a Day when humanity will no longer call YHWH "my Lord."[15] Nor will we consider YHWH to be an arbitrary lording master.[16] Instead, humanity will understand YHWH to be a loving husband.[17]

X. THE DIVINE NAME & THE SON OF MAN

Quite unexpectedly, the job of restoring YHWH's name and leading believers to call upon it falls to the *Son of man*. Psalm 80 is unique. It addresses a time when people are suffering from oppression. Strife defines the differences among the world of men (Ps 80:6). Divided unity has splintered into weaker fragments. When it seems this dilapidated and ever-eroding state will continue forever (Ps 80:4–6), Israel becomes anchored! Suddenly, YHWH's name shines forth once more!

The Son of man will revive believers to call upon YHWH's name.[18]

> Let your hand be upon the man of your right hand, upon the *son of man* whom you made strong for yourself, so we will not go back from you. **Revive us and we will call upon your name.** (Ps 80:17–18)

Restoring YHWH's name is the guiding light to the over-arching prophetic vision. It is tied to YHWH's salvation of a downtrodden and suffering people. Calling upon YHWH's name strengthens us to stand out from the suffering masses to walk in a profoundly-timeless way of life.

> And I will bring the third part through the fire, and will refine them as silver is refined, and will try them as gold is tried: **they shall call on my name** and I will hear them. I will say, It is my people: and they shall say, **YHWH is my God**. (Zech 13:9)

The generation who accepts this promise will embrace YHWH in truth. The generation who accepts this promise will awaken to no longer accept the miserable changing narratives that push us into paths containing evil agendas. The generation who accepts this vision will find that "before we call, YHWH will answer and while we are yet speaking, He will hear" (Isa 65:24). This generation will revive by calling upon YHWH—by name.

Zechariah links our calling upon YHWH as a sign of being counted as God's people. Calling upon YHWH's name allies us to a larger group. It is a Fellowship of Truth. God's name enables a resolve that is *un*swayed by the next hot issue. Instead, it is a firm and steady anchor that levels the frenzies manipulated upon society. It reveals a written truth capable of piercing lies and holding our churches and teachers accountable. Hosea prophesied of a time when all other names for God would cease. Is this the dawning of that day?

Steps for Discovering Truth
Method: Preponderance of the Evidence

Step	Action	Breaking it Down
Step 1:	Begin a dialog that seeks to prove all things.	The conversation holds fast to God's written (sola Scriptura) word reveals is good for man. It is a journey of discovery.
Step 2:	Use YHWH's Name	Refer to God by name. Use His name when referring to God. Call upon YHWH—by name when praying.
Step 3:	Confession	Acknowledge that we have inherited lies. Political and religious institutions have misdirected us with their power to deceive.

Scripture's Guiding Precepts of Truth

Truth	Concept	Breaking it Down	Text
Truth #1	God's name is YHWH	• Get to know YHWH personally—by name	Exod 3:13-14
		• Remember YHWH's name and to use it "throughout all generations"	Exod 3:15
		• Using YHWH's name keeps us anchored to His direct written word	2 Chr 18:26; Ps 33:4; 86:11; Isa 40:8
		• YHWH's name empowers us to overcome manmade lies	Exod 20:7

5

Breaking Relativism's Spell

I. RELATIVISM'S SPELL

Our society nears the grand finale of relativism's spell. Violence rages in city streets. Vast homelessness consumes the lives of ordinary families. Cronyism purchases the "constitutional" rights of our day. All righteous identity has been lost. Our government pits allies who value liberty against each other. We are spiraling, descending into relativism's suicidal end. Groomed we have been to tolerate evil. Conditioned are we into turning a blind eye to injustice and immorality. We've silently accepted the undermining of the family. Coexist with those who march in streets calling for your death and the death of your nation. Ignore gross debauchery. The spell instills insanity.

History silently reminds us that forbearance of evil leads to death and the collapse of society: ancient Israel, Pompeii, Rome, WW2 Germany, the USSR. Will America be next? Without a Divine Code of Law to rule the hearts of men by defining what is right for you and me, our society has grown callous, heartless, and depraved. We have forgotten the right and the good. We no longer seek to protect ourselves or future generations from harm. Our values are sick (Isa 1:5). We can no longer distinguish between good and evil. We love our enemies more than we love ourselves.

The recent October 7, 2023 Hamas/Isis terror attack in Israel is a case in point. When our teens and young adults discuss terrorist acts, they ask, "Were the babies beheaded or just shot"?[1] Their question implies that the difference matters. Is all moral clarity lost? Is the difference in the means of execution? Or is it in the generational, age-old anti-Semitic hate that drives terrorists to attack? Our society is sick and lost. Where sickness thrives, bad things will follow. Evil seems to be winning. Can it be turned back? Is all redemption lost?

II. RELIGION'S COMPLICITY

Conflicting ideas within our religious sects encourage moral relativism. No firm, universal standard exists to anchor our beliefs outside of man or his religion. No firm standard allows us to consider one action correct and its opposite action wrong and incorrect. We have become so lost in our own collective individual ideas that evil is now good and good is now deemed evil (Isa 5:20). We remain under relativism's spell: actions and ideas are stemming from emotion, not from a Divine Law that governs the heart and values of men.

As traditional ideas continue unpinned, each denomination claims to have God's truth. This occurs because emphasis is placed on different texts. One denomination discerns certain Scripture verses and texts as having primary importance.[2] A second denomination does not agree. It views these same texts to be less important, basing its primary doctrine on other biblical passages. This leads to elevating a completely different set of ideas as the basis of a precept for truth. A third group finds the first denomination's belief valid, but only in certain situations. Thus begins the ebb and flow of religious relativity.

I was also caught in this web of relativity during my early studies. I would study a topic and think I found the truth of that belief. Then, a few weeks later, I'd study it again and see it in a different light. My ideas were not firm or stable. They seemed tossed to and fro no matter how much I prayed and studied that topic.

Finally, after digging and searching, I discovered the path forward. I broke free of the spell. It was a healing method inscribed in Scripture of old. It was a plan so plain and simple that anyone could use it for any topic. As I began to use this method, my studies transformed. The pieces began to fall into place—no longer did my understanding contradict the evidence. No longer did truth waver. It became anchored and grounded. Not only did this method work for Scripture studies, but it applies to any topic that an individual desires to learn—whether Scripture or secular. Soon I understood this method contained a plan of action. It was an instruction manual that empowers us to forever break relativism's spell.

III. DISCOVERING THE PLAN

Can we arise from society's endless cycle of circular reasoning? Can we learn to no longer fall for the lies theologians and politicians play on our emotions? How do we recognize their sleight of hand that keeps us under their ban? One *deceptive* tactic keeps basic principles ambiguous. Ideas are never clearly defined. We are kept seeking an elusive utopic eternity but are taught that God's written instructions are insufficient for getting there. YHWH's written words are not enough.

God emphasizes truth's crucial importance (see pp. 7, 22, 35–36). Yet, most religious sects aim to keep ideas of truth mystical, nebulous, and just out of reach, so you keep coming back to the institution for the "correct" understanding of the text. Ideas lack firmness, shifting every few generations. Religious leaders keep ideas of truth relative to them. You must depend on them. Ambiguity keeps us wandering aimlessly in a Wilderness of Sin. We are not encouraged to seek for ourselves. Rarely are we told that we can without man.

Manmade "truth" is the antithesis of Jeremiah's vision of the road leading back to God. Jeremiah foresaw a passage along this journey, a way each of us could take to individually know YHWH without needing to rely on man's institutional authority. Jeremiah embraced an "I can" approach to God. He believed that each of us is capable of finding this method and using it: we can!

IV. DARE TO JOIN THE QUEST

While embarking on this journey, I soon discovered that I had to challenge my preconceived ideas. I was taught that the Law God gave at Mt. Sinai was deficient and inadequate. My preachers taught me that God gave Divine Law simply to show how inadequate we are and how impossible it is for us to follow it.[3]

As a child, I could not reason through these ideas. Even as a child, however, this belief seemed to contradict a loving God who teaches us how we should live (Exod 20:6; Deut 7:9; 30:16–20; Ezek 33:15). This theology implied YHWH set man up to fail from the moment He gave His Divine Law. I wondered if loving parents would teach their children a set of values and ethics simply to show they were incapable of living them. To me, this seemed wicked. Was this Israel's God?

Throughout my young adult years, I found myself reacting emotionally when reading YHWH's Law. I judged it to be evil. I simply accepted what my religion taught me: Divine Law is too difficult to keep. We need to be delivered from its instructions.[4]

The 10 Commandments made sense, but the rest of the Law seemed primitive and outdated. I felt trapped, stuck. I understood relativism's end but did not yet see the goodness or wisdom Divine Law establishes. I knew Jesus played a part in all of this, but I needed to understand the Law to understand God's overall plan. Was YHWH righteous to give us a Law, a social contract, that He knew we could never obey? I had to wonder: What did Jesus mean when he stated, "If you love me keep my Commandments" (John 14:15. cf Luke Matt 19:17; 11:28)? The current state of Christianity didn't offer any better solutions, so I pressed on to prove all things.

V. PRECEPTS LIGHT THE WAY

A breakthrough in the path forward came while I was studying Isaiah's instructions for reasoning together. I had totally overlooked Isaiah's instructions that prevent a productive dialog from reaching an impasse.

> **Whom shall he teach knowledge?** and whom shall he make to understand the report?[5] Those who are weaned from the milk and drawn from the breasts. **For**

> **precept must be upon precept, precept upon precept; line upon line, line upon line**; here a little, and there a little . . . To whom he said, This is the rest wherewith you may cause the weary to rest and this is the refreshing, yet they would not hear. (Isa 28:9–10, 12)

Isaiah tells us knowledge is based on a set of commands that work as precepts.[6] They are not arbitrary laws but build upon each other. One line of instruction builds upon another line of instruction.[7] YHWH gave these instructions to refresh us. One day, this method will lead to the earth "being full of the knowledge of YHWH" (Isa 11:9. Cf Jer 3:15).

King David builds upon YHWH's commands as precepts like no other. As I was reading about Daivd's love of the Law's precepts, I discovered that I needed to better understand what a precept is. **A precept is "a general rule intended to regulate behavior or thought."**[8] In Scripture, it is:

> a general term for the responsibility God places upon His people. Precepts are guiding truths which have the good of the individual in mind. . . . they are guiding principles rather than legal restrictions.[9]

Raymond Westbrook and Bruce Wells, two renowned scholars on biblical Law, define biblical precepts, thus:

> Everyday law refers to the religious and moral precepts that people were expected to follow in their everyday lives[10] . . . there is no clear dividing line between laws and moral precepts.[11]

Westbrook and Wells continue to describe the idea of biblical precepts as the foundation for ancient Israel's society:

> It comprises those rules that regulate relationships between humans who are the members of a society in the conduct of their everyday lives, protecting their economic, social, corporal, and psychological interests. Those rules establish rights and duties that can be enforced in a court of law. They fall into categories that are applicable in any developed legal system such as property (rights), inheritance, contracts, crimes, and evidence.[12]

YHWH emphasizes the importance of overall philosophies that govern His laws and instructions. For instance, Commandments 5–10 in the 10 Commandments define righteous human interaction. These instructions are based on the Golden Rule.

> You shall love your neighbor as yourself: I am YHWH. (Lev 19:18)

YHWH does not leave the idea of loving your neighbor as yourself ambiguous. Instead, He sets down specific laws and describes different situations where conflicts between neighbors occur. His laws instruct and teach us how to love your neighbor as yourself in real life.

Divine Commandments tell us how to live by the Golden Rule: Honor your parents, Do not murder, Do not commit adultery, Do not steal, Do not bear false witness, and Do not covet. I could find no fault in these commands. They were right and good. Each described actions I would not want to be done to me. This still left unanswered questions. Were the 10 Commandments the only good part of the Law? Were bondage and oppression concealed in the rest of YHWH's Law?

VI. PRECEPTS OF JUSTICE

Psalm 119 could be called the *Song of Precepts*.[13] No other chapter in the Bible praises the importance of understanding YHWH's precepts more than Psalm 119. Precepts empower and transmit understanding. They are the philosophical ideas that silently work in the background by governing commandments and laws. America and most Western Law Codes share this idea of precepts.

Presumed Innocence is one of America's founding precepts of justice shared with YHWH's Code of Law. A person is presumed innocent until overwhelming evidence demonstrates guilt (Exod 23:7; Deut 19:10, 13; 21:8–9; 25:1).[14] This ideal of justice has saved many a life from false accusations. This precept also protects life from a perverted justice system that requires the accused to demonstrate innocence—a standard that can rarely exonerate the innocent.

I began to see that YHWH's Law, also called *the Law of Moses*, was built upon precepts. The regulations that protected the innocently accused were not found in the 10 Commandments. They were embedded in the Law of Moses.

> Keep you far from a false matter. You shall not slay **the innocent and righteous**, for I will not justify the wicked. (Exod 23:7)

> **That innocent blood is not shed in your land**, which YHWH your God gives you for an inheritance, and so blood is upon you. (Deut 19:10)

Exodus 23:7 is found within a category of Law called "Judgments" (Exod 21:1). Judgments address issues of justice normally tried in a court of law.[15] YHWH's judgments establish precedents through examples of different legal situations by establishing predetermined penalties by law. In so doing, God limited a judge's future use of relativism to mitigate consequences for a crime. This precedent avoided overly-harsh or -lenient punishments. Once again, I discovered no hint of bondage in these ideas as they provided far more sanity than America's current system where thieves are simply caught and released and where families receive no justice for a murdered loved one.

VII. WHY DID DAVID LOVE THE LAW'S PRECEPTS?

King David poses a question relevant for today: "How can the young person cleanse his way?" (Ps 119:9). This question seemed to parallel my own: How can we break relativism's spell and be healthy again? David answers this question by encouraging us to "take heed according to your word." The term 'word' here specifically means the Divine Law of instruction given to Moses.[16]

David loved the precepts that governed YHWH's Law. He praises the Law as a guidebook back to a meaningful, prosperous, and worthwhile life.[17] His words shed light on how precepts work, revealing a path that can lead us out of the insanity of America's current suicidal tolerance of relativism and its wickedness.

> I will meditate on your **precepts** and have respect unto your ways. (Ps 119:15)

> Cause me to understand the way of your **precepts**: so shall I talk of your wondrous works. (Ps 119:27)

> I understand more than the ancients **because I keep your precepts**. (Ps 119:100)

The 10 Commandments and the Law of Moses are based upon precepts. "Thou shalt not murder," the 6th Commandment, is founded on the idea that human life is sacred. Everyone has a right to live until they violate another human's right to live. When a person commits murder, then the opposite and equal reaction must be applied to keep society just, stable, and balanced. Maintaining a righteous society prevents callousness of heart from spreading throughout society. Justice enables people to live by the Golden Rule. By meditating and understanding YHWH's precepts, we gain understanding, which illuminates the path to healing and peace.

Throughout Psalm 119, David speaks of his love of the Law's precepts. He saw these as good and desirable but understood falsehoods as leading people astray to an ill-fated destination. They were paths leading to misery, sickness, and hardship.

> Through your precepts I get understanding: therefore I hate every false way. (Ps 119:104)

> And I will walk at *liberty*: for I seek your precepts. (Ps 119:45)

> I am a companion of all them that fear you, and of them that keep your precepts. (Ps 119:63)

David understood YHWH's precepts as empowering liberty—a life where we are strong and free. A society where we do not fear enemies (foreign or domestic). YHWH's precepts create a nation where we do not have to lock our doors due to our fellow man's evil inclinations. A nation where we can prosper economically and obtain good health. But more than this, God's precepts define and facilitate an independent, sovereign nation that can share an inspiring, righteous identity. Understanding YHWH's precepts allows us to awaken from relativism's spell and return to the path of sane, rational thinking: To see the world as it is while walking a path that leads to its betterment.

As we have seen, the second step along this path is remembering YHWH's name. Restoring YHWH's name when we read the text enables and empowers us to identify the correct path forward out of a forest of generalities. It is the mechanism that opens and illuminates our way while preventing our own partiality or timidness of heart from leading us astray.[18]

> **I have remembered your name**, O YHWH, in the night, and have kept your law. This I had because I kept your precepts. (Ps 119:55–56)

Precepts illuminate a road we can tread to discover YHWH's amazing and unifying truth. David shares that the path we must take for liberty rests upon us obeying YHWH's precepts. These precepts are not nebulous or mystical. They are defined in a concrete Divine Law that all can access and obey. In following this road, we are empowered to see, perceive, and understand (Ps 10:17). We are strengthened in a righteous identity to stand tall (Lev 26:13). Following YHWH's precepts enables us to distinguish between truth and error so others cannot lead us down dangerous, deceptive paths.

VIII. PRECEPTS DEFINE TRUTH

We saw in the previous chapters that YHWH is a God of truth. Throughout the Bible, emphasis is placed on truth. Truth is important. In Psalm 100, truth is an idea that "endures to all generations" (Ps 100:5). This means that concepts are not relative to the beliefs of any generation but remain firm and steady throughout all generations. Psalm 117 reiterates this idea by recording that the "truth of YHWH endures forever" (Ps 117:2).

King David dropped breadcrumbs to serve as clues along the trail that leads us back to truth's original understanding. David evokes a sharp contrast. YHWH is near when we acknowledge truth, however, the wicked depart from YHWH's Law. But more than this, David tells us how to identify and define truth.

> They draw near who follow after wickedness, (but) they are far **from your law**. You are near, O YHWH, and **all your commandments are truth**. (Ps 119:150–51, parentheses added)

YHWH's Commandments define truth.[19] The wicked are far from YHWH's Divine Law, but He is close to those who observe His commandments. If we are to emerge from the web of relativity, we must use the sword of truth. Identifying solid truths enables us to be set free (John 8:32). Following David's trail of clues leads us to one of the clearest statements of truth in all Scripture.

> Your righteousness is an everlasting righteousness, and **your law is the truth**. (Ps 119:142)

The Law is truth! If we love truth and righteousness, if we desire to break relativism's spell, we must return to the sanity that Divine Law provides. *Emet* is the Hebrew word for *truth*. It means firmness, stability, certainty, and trustworthiness.[20] If we desire stability in our families and nation, YHWH's Law illuminates the path of healing and unity that can lead us there.

IX. WHEN DID TRUTH BEGIN TO EXIST?

One text I encountered caused me to pause. Was I misapplying these precepts of truth? Jacob, Abraham's grandson, states he also had YHWH's truth.

> I am not worthy of the least of all the mercies, and of all the **truth**, which you have shown to your servant. (Gen 32:10)

How could Jacob have truth if the Law was not given until Mt. Sinai? How could Jacob have something before it existed? While it is possible that Jacob had the precepts underlying the Law, he didn't have the Law. Or did he?

Did anything in Israel's early history indicate that Jacob also had truth through Divine Law? Had Jacob inherited truth from Abraham? If so, what was Abraham's idea of truth? Was it tied to any concept of Divine Law?

> For I know him, that he will command his children and his household after him, and they shall keep the **way of YHWH, to do justice and judgment**; that YHWH may bring upon Abraham that which he has spoken of him. (Gen 18:19)

Abraham understood "the way of YHWH." This way is defined as a path of "justice and judgment." YHWH's ability to bless Abraham depended upon Abraham walking in YHWH's path of justice.

While "the way of YHWH" was a path of "justice and judgment," it was still ambiguous to me. I wondered if any other texts supported Abraham having truth through Divine Law.

> Abraham obeyed my voice, and kept my charge, my commandments, my statutes, and my laws. (Gen 26:5)

This text names the specific categories of Law found in the Divine Law that YHWH gave Israel at Mt Sinai. Abraham had the exact same divisions of the Divine Law Code as YHWH gave Moses at Mt. Sinai![21] I was not taught this by any preacher or study group. I was blown away! Abraham knew about YHWH's Divine Law. This is why Jacob could say he had truth. The evidence thus far was constant and consistent. The data continued to support David's proclamation that Divine Law defines truth.

As I considered the precepts expressed by David and Jacob, I could not detect any hint that Divine Law was bondage or that we need to be delivered from it. I found no indication that Divine Law was deficient or insufficient in any way. I wondered if David was alone in this idea. I was sure my church was justified in seeing the Law as something Jesus had rescued me from. He kept the Law so we no longer have to. As I reflected on these ideas, I wondered: if the Law is no longer considered valid or applicable today, have we been presumptuous to throw out its precepts? Had I taken Jesus' words or the words of the disciples out of context?

6

Divine Bondage?

I. REMEMBERING THE LAW OF MOSES

As my journey continued, I protested. Textual evidence was challenging my inherited beliefs. Was it good to consider ideas different from my own? I felt uneasy about the unexpected discoveries that lay ahead. I was sure of my beliefs. I was comfortable. What if my worldview became unpinned? Despite my resistance, I couldn't shake the rottenness I'd seen running deep in society. There had to be a better way.

As I researched, I discovered David was not alone in defining truth by Divine Law. During the exile, Daniel refers to the Divine Law YHWH gave to Moses as the means for understanding truth.

> As it is written in the **law of Moses**, all this evil is come upon us, yet we made not our prayer before YHWH our God *that we might turn from our iniquities* and **understand your truth**. (Dan 9:13)

Daniel admits that national sins created the hardships his generation experienced through war and diaspora. The Law of Moses stipulated consequences for Israel's sins and breach of the Divine Covenant. These curses of the Law are defined in Leviticus 26 and Deuteronomy 28. Daniel links truth's discovery to people admitting their own complacency to iniquity that has allowed them to experience evil. Turning to YHWH in prayer aids in healing this dysfunction.[1] In this verse, Daniel refers to truth as being firm:

> The Hebrew noun translated truth has as its primary component of meaning the idea of firmness or solidness. The truth is a firm reality on which a person may count and which does not deceive. In this verse there is no question of abstract intellectual truth but of a firm decision made by God.[2]

Truth is defined by YHWH's firm decisions prescribed within His Law. It contains the only lasting precepts capable of tearing down deception's wall, a wall which blocks us from lasting peace and harmony.

During the Second Temple Era, Nehemiah also followed in David's footsteps by acknowledging that truth is tied to YHWH's laws. Nehemiah specifically refers to the Divine Law Code by mentioning Mt. Sinai.[3]

> You came down also upon mount Sinai, and spoke with them from heaven, and gave them **right judgments, and true laws, good statutes, and commandments.** . . . (Neh 9:13)

Nehemiah, like David, considers YHWH's law to be "true" (Heb. *emet*). YHWH's judgments (Exod 21:1–24:3) are righteous and preserve society.[4] "They are not simply negative commands but are instructions on how to live the godly life."[5] All the words YHWH spoke at Mt. Sinai provide good instruction through statutes, judgments, laws, and commandments (Lev 26:46; Neh 9:13; Ezek 44:24).[6] This is the same four divisions of law code Abraham had in Genesis (Gen 26:5, see pp. 36–37). Each of these was based upon the precepts in the 10 Commandments. The New Testament also embraces this idea when Paul writes that God gave Scripture for "instruction in righteousness" (2 Tim 3:16).

II. A SINGULAR ROAD

In ancient times, YHWH's Divine Law was the *only* legal code that established the idea of monotheism—the worship of one God alone. This idea existed nowhere else. It only existed in YHWH's Law and Israel's historical documents. YHWH established monotheism within a social compact—the 10 Commandments.[7] This covenantal contract established the basis of social justice and righteousness. Today, we call this type of contract a constitution.[8] This constitutional Law was clarified within the Law of Moses, which is also known today as the *Torah* or *Pentateuch*. This Divine Law provides practical applications for the teachings and philosophies within its philosophical instructions.[9]

Historically, ancient societies valued laws as a means for defining justice.[10] Surviving inscriptions demonstrate that law codes defining justice were key components of early temple organizations.[11] The Laws of Eshnunna, the Codex of Lipit–Ishtar of Isin, and the more well-known Hammurabi Code are a few codes that established justice for ancient nations.[12]

Moses asserts that YHWH's Law is more righteous, just, and an overall better way of life than any competing codes, philosophies, or religious ideals.

> Behold, I have taught you **statutes and judgments**, even as YHWH my God commanded me, that you should do so in the land where you go to possess it. Keep

therefore and do them because *this is your wisdom and your understanding in the sight of the nations, which shall hear all these statutes, and say, Surely this great nation is a wise and understanding people.* For what nation is there so great, who has God so near to them, as YHWH our God is in all things that we call on him for? And **what nation is there so great, that has statutes and *judgments so righteous as all this law*, which I set before you this day**? (Deut 4:5–8. See also, Deut 6:18)

Statutes and judgments are key components of Divine Law. They pave the way for justice and judgment. They are waymarks to wisdom and understanding.

As I view Western society, I see we have all but lost any wisdom, understanding, or basic common sense. Does Moses' understanding hold the antidote to our wayward paths? He understood that obeying Divine Law makes a nation great. Walking in its teachings enables society to draw near to YHWH our God. He will listen when we call upon His name. This was a completely different idea of Law than I had heard before. Was this the path to make a nation great again?

III. THE ROAD OF PROSPERITY

YHWH encouraged Joshua, Moses' successor, to obey Divine Law because it enables "our way to be prosperous." YHWH specifically tells Joshua that observing and doing all that is written within the Law, allows us to be successful (Josh 1:8).

> Only be you strong and very courageous that **you may observe to do according to all the law, which Moses my servant commanded you**. Turn not from it to the right hand or to the left, that you may prosper wherever you go.
>
> **This book of the law shall not depart out of your mouth**; but you shall meditate therein day and night, that you may observe to do according **to all that is written within it**: *for then you shall make your way prosperous, and then you shall have good success.* (Josh 1:7–8)

The Hebrew text presents a very different view of the Law than what I had grown up with. David, Joshua, Daniel, and Nehemiah praise the Law as the path to righteousness, peace, and prosperity. David writes, "*Perfect peace* have all they who love your Law and nothing shall offend them" (Ps 119:165). It did not contain any negative connotation.[13] I uncovered no idea that Divine Law was a source of bondage. Instead, it was a Law of peace. I also found no evidence that any prophet considered YHWH's Divine Law to be unfair. Every text embraced an *I can* religion.

Divine Law was beginning to sound like a self-help manual. It was a guidebook to a balanced life on earth. Isaiah builds on the power of Divine Law to create peace when he writes,

> Thus says YHWH, your Redeemer, the Holy One of Israel: I am YHWH your God which *teaches you to profit, which leads you by the path that you should go*. **O that you had hearkened to my commandments!** Then had your **peace** been as a river, and your righteousness as the waves of the sea. (Isa 48:17–18)

Isaiah joins David in linking peace, righteousness, and prosperity to YHWH's instructions. The prophets talk about the Law as a key to unlocking a peaceful world where people can thrive.

IV. THE LAW OF LIBERTY

Liberty is another precept Divine Law embraces. YHWH allotted every family unalienable land. This enabled them to live on nontaxable land, which could be rented or leased. Every 50 years, debt was forgiven. People who served as indentured servants, contracted employees, or slaves, were also set free every 7 years.[14]

> Proclaim liberty throughout all the land unto all the inhabitants thereof. It shall be a jubilee unto you. You shall return every man unto his possession, and you shall return every man unto his family. (Lev 25:10)

> King Zedekiah made a covenant with all the people which were at Jerusalem, to proclaim liberty unto them; That every man should let his manservant, and every man his maidservant, being an Hebrew or an Hebrewess, go free; that none should serve himself of them, to wit, of a Jew his brother. (Jer 34:8–9)

> I am YHWH your God, which brought you forth out of the land of Egypt, that you should not be their bondmen. I have **broken the bands of your yoke, and made you go upright**. (Lev 26:13)

YHWH's way of life ordained liberty for Israel's citizens.[15] Should people fall into poverty, YHWH's Law limited the time they could serve to repay those debts. This protected society from becoming oppressive. It prevented a select elite from profiting off the endless labor of the working classes. The 50-year Jubilee provided a national reset that kept families and their values strong. This policy prevented groups from gaining control over ordinary citizens. There was no room for *too big to fail*!

America's founding fathers embraced this idea, casting a bell tolling for liberty. The Liberty Bell became an iconic symbol of America's revolutionary independence, which based its idealism upon biblical principles.

Inscribed on the Liberty Bell in 1751: "Proclaim Liberty throughout the Land to all the inhabitants thereof" (Lev 25:10).

After years of study, I could discover nothing in the Old Testament that indicates YHWH's Divine Law is deficient in any way. Humans, however, are slow to trust. We are skeptical of the idea of the Divine, so we take the Law as a menu to pick and choose, or simply take one *a la carte*. Although we have a recipe for success before us, we pick and choose the ingredients we want to use. We add too much baking powder or salt, but then use too little flour or oil. Picking and choosing our recipe for success leads to a flat, miserable, and bitter loaf of the bread of life.

V. SHOULD WE REMEMBER THE LAW?

Another text challenged my preconceived ideas. Malachi is the last book of the Old Testament. He is one of the final prophets YHWH sent to Israel before hiding His face.[16] Malachi offers a final warning to Israel.

> **Remember you the law of Moses my servant, which I commanded** unto him in Horeb for all Israel, with the statutes and judgments. Behold, I will send you Elijah the prophet before the coming of the great and dreadful day of YHWH. He shall turn the heart of the fathers to the children, and the heart of the children to their fathers, *lest I come and smite the earth with a curse*. (Mal 4:4-6)

Malachi calls Israel to remember the Law of Moses, which was given at Mt. Sinai.[17] He specifically mentions YHWH's statutes and judgments as specific categories of Divine Law that we should remember.[18] This provoked a question for me. Why would YHWH's final words in the Old Testament encourage Israel to remember YHWH's Divine Law if God planned to do away with His Law all along?

VI. IT IS TOO DIFFICULT! WE CAN'T DO IT!

As I was wrestling with the contradictions of my inherited beliefs, I encountered a text that struck me in the heart. A crossroads lay directly in my path. I had to choose. Did I dare trust YHWH's written words? Would I turn back? Would I look to man or God?

> If you will hearken to the voice of YHWH your God, **to keep his commandments and his statutes** which are written in this book of the law, and if you turn unto YHWH your God with all your heart, and with all your soul. **For this commandment which I command you this day, it is not hidden from you, neither is it far off.**
>
> It is not in heaven, that you should say, Who shall go up for us to heaven, and bring it unto us, that we may hear it, and **do it**? Neither is it beyond the sea, that you should ask, Who shall go over the sea for us, and bring it unto us, <u>that we may</u> hear it, and **do it**? **But the WORD is very close to you, in your mouth, and in your heart that you may <u>do it</u>.**
>
> See, I have set before you this day life and good, and death and evil; In that I command you this day to love YHWH your God, to walk in his ways, and to keep his commandments and his statutes and his judgments, that you may live and multiply: and YHWH your God shall bless you in the land where you go to possess it. (Deut 30:10–16)

Like Jeremiah, Moses tells us *we can do it*! Divine Law is easy to obey.[19] It is not hidden or far off. It is not too difficult to understand. No one needs to get it for us or do it for us. This text sharply contrasts the Mesopotamian hero Gilgamesh, who has to cross the sea to find eternal life.[20] In contrast, YHWH freely taught us how to walk the path to immortality for ourselves. Moses tells us that YHWH put the power of life and death in our hands: it is our choice, so choose to live.[21]

The structure of the text in v. 14 is stronger in Hebrew. It states something more like: "So let us do it! — for the word is exceedingly near to you, in your mouth and in your heart to do it!"[22] Moses embraces an "I can" religion. This theology empowers the individual and the society that follows it to see the difference between good and evil, life and death. It thwarts deception. Divine Law empowers humanity to live rationally and righteously with justice as the core of its foundation.

Duane Christensen remarks:[23]

> The commandment is not inaccessible, it does not require some specially qualified person to make it all clear. In short, the law was specifically designed for our instruction in daily living.[24]

The Law is specifically designed for ordinary people. It is not too technical to understand or obey. We do not have to rely on man. We can!

VII. THESE ARE THE WORDS

When YHWH met with Israel at Mt. Sinai, YHWH personally spoke to Israel. He began by saying, "These are the words" (Exod 35:1), which the entire assembly heard.[25] Throughout

Exodus, Numbers, and Deuteronomy the term "words" (Hebrew, *davarim*) specifically refers to the Divine Law given at this event.

> These were not remote, abstract, esoteric principles but a word that was among and within them. The "word" (Deut 30:14) is the commandment (*miṣwâ*) of the Lord, that whole body of stipulation that Moses was commanding that very day (v. 11).[26]

When Moses writes that the "word is very close to us. It is in our heart and mouth that we may do it" (Deut 30:14), he is specifically referring to the words of instruction YHWH revealed in His Divine Law at Mt. Sinai and clarified during Israel's sojourn in the wilderness.[27]

> Observe and hear **all these words** *which I command you* that it may go well with you and with your children after you forever when you do that which is good and right in the sight of YHWH your God. (Deut 12:28)

These texts echo the advice I have given my own children to follow my instructions so they may enjoy the blessings of living uprightly and making wise choices.

I saw a pattern beginning to emerge. YHWH's laws and precepts are consistently described as a path or road. The way of YHWH leads to: wisdom and understanding (Deut 4:5–8; 16:18), success and prosperity (Josh 1:7–8; Isa 48:17–18), peace, healing, and health (Ps 119:165; Isa 48:17–18; Exod 15:26).

As I considered these texts, I felt righteous indignation. I had inherited the lie that the Law was a way of death. I had been told I couldn't keep it. The Law was hard and oppressive. I needed someone else to help me understand it. I shouldn't like it! But now I was discovering this idea contradicted the written word of God. I began to realize just how deep the deception ran. Our leaders told us "We can't" to keep us relying on them. They have established alternative meanings of right and wrong that are alien to the Bible. We've inherited a system that replaced the Divine with man.

VIII. THE WAY OF RIGHTEOUSNESS

Throughout the Bible, Divine Law establishes righteousness. Divine Law is truth (Ps 119:142). Righteousness is a precept that parallels truth. The righteous love Divine Law.

> Hearken to me, you that **know righteousness**, the people in whose **heart is my law** (Isa 51:7).

Righteous people love Divine Law so much that they commit it to their hearts. It becomes a part of them. They live by its precepts and instructions. Ezekiel also defines the righteous and their righteousness according to the Law:

> The person who sins will die. The son will not bear the punishment for the father's iniquity, nor will the father bear the punishment for the son's iniquity. **The righteousness of the righteous will be upon himself,** and the **wickedness of the wicked will be upon himself.** When the wicked man turns away from his wickedness that he has committed, and **does that which is lawful and right**, he shall save his soul alive, because he considers and turns away from all his transgressions that he has committed. He shall surely live, he shall not die. (Ezek 18:20–21. See also 18:27–28)

Ezekiel defines righteousness as "doing what is lawful and right." Since Divine Law was the source of truth in Israel which established morals and values, righteousness is defined by Divine Law.

Solomon makes the most outrageous claim regarding Divine Law.

> In the way of righteousness there is life; along that path is immortality. (Prov 12:28, NIV)

Throughout the Old Testament Moses and Israel's prophets define "the way of righteousness" as Divine Law. This path leads to eternal life where there is "no death" (KJV).[28] YHWH's way of life "includes both joy and fulfillment as well as immortality."[29] Not only does the way of YHWH lead to: wisdom and understanding (Deut 4:5–8; 16:18), success and prosperity (Josh 1:7–8; Isa 48:17–18), peace, healing, and health (Ps 119:165; Isa 48:17–18; Exod 15:26). It also provides a path of life to immortality: a path wherein there is no death (Prov 12:28; Ezek 33:15). Why had I never heard this teaching before?

VIII. The Way of Righteousness

Scripture's Guiding Precepts of Truth

Truth	Concept	Breaking it Down	Text
Truth #1	God's name is YHWH	• Get to know YHWH personally—by name	Exod 3:13–14
		• Remember YHWH's name and use it "throughout all generations"	Exod 3:15
		• Using YHWH's name keeps us anchored to His direct written word	2 Chr 18:26; Ps 33:4; 86:11; Isa 40:8
		• YHWH's name empowers us to overcome manmade lies	Exod 20:7
Truth #2	The Law defines Truth Psalms 119:142; 151; Dan 9:13	• Is founded upon philosophical precepts	Lev 19:18; Ps 119:15, 27, 100
		• Is good, just, and righteous	Gen 19:18; Neh 9:13
		• Is easy to obey	Deut 30:10–16
		• Provides widsom and understanding	Deut 4:5–8; 16:18
		• Makes our way prosperous & successful	Josh 1:7–8; Isa 48:17–18
		• Creates perfect peace	Ps 119:165; Isa 48:17–18
		• Is Perfect	Ps 19:7
		• Converts the soul	Ps 19:7
		• Is a path to immortality where death no longer exists	Prov 12:28; Ezek 33:15

7

Does the New Testament Uphold Divine Law?

I. UPHOLDING RIGHTEOUS IDENTITY

Does the New Testament also support righteousness being tied to Divine Law? If it does, it would strengthen the timelessness of Divine Law. It would be constant. I never heard a preacher or anyone in my Bible study classes bring up any New Testament text that supported the Law's validity.

I discovered that 1 John seemed to be quoting Ezekiel's ideals of righteousness. Ezekiel stated that the "righteousness of the righteous will be upon him," meaning the person who behaves righteously is righteous (Ezekiel 18 & 33).

> Little children, let no man deceive you. **He that does righteousness is righteous**, even as he is righteous. (1 John 3:7)

> If you fulfill the **royal law** according to the scripture: You shall love your neighbor as yourself (see *Lev 19:18*), you do well. But if you have respect to persons (see *Deut 1:17*), you commit sin, and are convicted by the law as transgressors. (James 2:8–9)

> (A) righteous man dwelling among them, in seeing and hearing, **vexed his righteous soul** from day to day **with their unlawful deeds**. (2 Peter 2:8)

> Sin is the transgression of the law. (1 John 3:4)

The New Testament conveys the same idea as the Old Testament. Keeping Divine Law causes one to be righteous while sin and the wicked are those who break YHWH's Divine Law.[1] While

John states, "he that does righteousness is righteous," Ezekiel worded it as "the righteousness of the righteous shall be upon him, and the wickedness of the wicked shall be upon him" (Ezek 18:20). It is the exact same concept.

Peter also upholds Divine Law by referring to how the righteous are vexed and troubled by the wicked's unlawful deeds. Psalms and Proverbs refer to the chaos wickedness creates and how it becomes a source of vexation to the righteous. In America, we see this in our schools where our children are groomed for all sorts of depravities and forced to normalize insane immoral behaviors.

James draws the clearest distinction of what constitutes sin. He does not *just* refer to the 10 Commandments. He refers to Divine Law as a "royal law" because it empowers us to become royal heirs to YHWH's promises. James quotes specific laws within the Law of Moses, emphasizing that if anyone's actions violate these laws, it is transgression or "sin."[2] Whereas those who observe Divine Law by fulfilling its responsibilities "do well." John provides the definition of *sin* from a New Testament perspective: **"Sin is the transgression of the law."**[3] The only Law the New Testament refers to is YHWH's Divine Law. These texts present a consistent and cogent idea of righteousness and truth.[4]

II. LAW IS VALID AS LONG AS HEAVEN & EARTH EXIST

I began to see that men had influenced my interpretation of the text. I totally overlooked the fact that Jesus states that he did not come to destroy the Law.

> <u>Think not</u> that I am come to destroy the law, or the prophets: **I am not come to destroy** but to fulfill. For verily I say unto you, Till heaven and earth pass, one jot or one tittle *shall in no wise pass from the law, till all be fulfilled.*[5] Whosoever therefore shall break one of these least commandments, and shall teach men so, he shall be called the least in the kingdom of heaven. (Matt 5:17–19)

Israel could also fulfill Divine Law daily through obedience—just like Jesus. Fulfilling the Law did not do away with it! To this point, Jesus reiterates that the Law is valid "until heaven and earth pass away." If heaven and earth still exist, then the Law remains valid.[6] Anyone who teaches men "to break the law" will be the least in God's kingdom.[7] This verse contradicted just about everything I had learned from my pastors. I had to wonder how many pastors would be least in God's kingdom.

III. JESUS UPHOLDS THE 10 COMMANDMENTS

As I considered Jesus' words, I realized my church had influenced another doctrine. Nowhere in the New Testament does Jesus state that his death or belief in him replaces Divine Law.

In Matthew 19, a young man asks Jesus what was needed for eternal life. Jesus replied:

> but if you will enter into life, keep the commandments. (Matt 19:17)

During this era, the ruling Jewish establishment had ignored Deuteronomy's injunction that forbade adding to or deleting from Divine Law (Deut 4:2; 12:32). They had developed an entirely parallel Law that contradicted and changed much of YHWH's original teachings.[8] Throughout this series, we will see how Jesus challenged these manmade traditions. Due to these traditions, the young man asked Jesus to clarify which commandments Jesus meant (Matt 19:18).

What I had read over time and time again, but ignored, was the fact that Jesus' response to this young man upheld Divine Law

> You shall do no murder. You shall not commit adultery. You shall not steal. You shall not bear false witness. Honor your father and your mother. And, You shall love your neighbor as yourself. (Matt 19:18–19)

Jesus completely upholds the 10 Commandments as the means to eternal life. Jesus also upholds the Law of Moses by quoting Leviticus 19:18 and reiterating the importance of the Golden Rule. The command to love your neighbor as yourself is not mentioned in Israel's Covenant of the 10 Commandments, but it is mentioned within the greater Law of Moses. Thus, Jesus continues to uphold Divine Law "till heaven and earth pass away."

IV. DEFRAUD NOT & THE LAW OF MOSES

A. Jesus Upholds the Law before His Death

The Gospel of Mark records a slightly different response to the young man's question on eternal life. To the above list in Matt 19:18–19, Mark reiterates Jesus' reply, which included the instruction that we should not defraud one another.

In Mark 10:3, Jesus appeals to the Law of Moses for authority, then quotes from it.[9]

> You know the commandments: Do not commit adultery; Do not kill; Do not steal; Do not bear false witness; **Defraud not**; Honor your father and mother. (Mark 10:19)

Jesus' instruction that we should not defraud is not found within the 10 Commandments. It is found within Divine Law, also known as the Law of Moses.

> You shall not defraud your neighbor, neither rob him. (Lev 19:13)

Jesus validates a Commandment that is not specifically found within the 10 Categories of Divine Law.[10] While the 10 categories, or 10 Commandments define a righteous way of living, the Law of Moses fills in the details and clarifies how we should apply those commandments. Every instruction in the Law of Moses falls under one of the categories within the 10 Commandments. Leviticus' injunction against defrauding our neighbor falls under the category of the 8th Commandment that we should not steal. Thus, Jesus continues to uphold the instructions within the Law of Moses "till heaven and earth pass away."

B. The Apostles Uphold Divine Law after Jesus' Death

Jesus was not alone in upholding the Law of Moses as remaining valid. After Jesus' death, Paul also confirms the validity of the Law of Moses by instructing,

> Nay, **you do wrong, and defraud, and that your brethren.** Know you not that **the unrighteous shall not inherit the kingdom of God?** Be not deceived: neither fornicators, nor idolaters, nor adulterers, nor effeminate, nor abusers of themselves with mankind, nor thieves, nor covetous, nor drunkards, nor revilers, nor extortioners, shall inherit the kingdom of God. (1 Cor 6:8–10)

Paul upholds Divine Law by stating that the *un*righteous will not inherit God's kingdom.[11] He defines the unrighteous as fornicators, idolaters, adulterers, homosexuals, abusers, robbers, the covetous, the drunk, the contemptuous, and those who extort. Paul specifically names these actions as disqualifying believers from inheriting God's kingdom. This resonates with Divine Law (Lev 20:10–27). While Jesus never needed to address homosexuality, Divine Law did. Leviticus 18:22 defines it as an "abomination" (cf. 20:13). Paul's ideas of inheriting God's kingdom originated with Divine Law. Paul embraces specific laws in the Law of Moses, which are outside the 10 Commandments.[12]

This teaching resonates with both John the Baptist and Jesus who both taught that believers should "bring forth fruit" demonstrating repentance (Matt 3:7–10; Luke 3:7–9). Those who "do not bear good fruit will be hewn down." Obedience is the fruit of repentance.

Paul, Silvanus, and Timothy also confirmed Divine Law by reiterating that believers should not defraud their brothers. They endorsed Divine Law by encouraging believers to "abstain from fornication" (1 Thes 4:3). They encouraged believers to sanctify themselves and resist lusts prevalent among the "Gentiles which know not God" (1 Thes 4:5).

> That no man go beyond and **defraud his brother in any matter**: because that the Lord is the avenger of all such, as we also have forewarned you and testified. **For God has not called us unto uncleanness, but unto holiness.** (1 Thess 4:6–7)

In their letters to the early churches, the New Testament authors continue to confirm the Law of Moses as relevant.[13] Not only do they uphold Leviticus 19:13, but they encourage believers to be holy.[14] This is another quote from the Law of Moses:

> **You shall be holy men** unto me: neither shall you eat any flesh that is torn of beasts in the field; you shall cast it to the dogs. (Exod 22:31)

Throughout Divine Law, YHWH calls humanity to be holy. While eating a mutilated animal that has been killed by another animal puts us at risk for disease, it also makes us *unholy* because it still has the blood in it. This type of animal slaughter makes us unholy and puts us at risk for disease. However, following YHWH's way of life keeps us healthy. This sets us apart, making us a holy people in God's sight.

Paul cannot be referring to any teaching from Jesus since Jesus never specifically commands people to be holy. Only his Father, YHWH, instructs people to be holy. Leviticus 11:46–47 reiterates YHWH's call for believers to be holy, tying holiness to the clean food Laws. Paul upholds believers' holiness again when he encourages us not to defile our bodies, which are the temple of God, but to keep our bodies healthy and "holy" (1 Cor 3:16–17).

> Wherefore the law is holy, and the commandment holy, and just, and good.... If then I do that which I would not, I consent unto the law that it is good.... For I delight in the law of God after the inward man: But I see another law in my members, warring against the law of my mind, and bringing me into captivity to the law of sin which is in my members. (Rom 7:12, 16, 22–23)

When Moses shared how easy Divine Law is to obey, He stated that YHWH had placed the choice of life and death/good and evil before humanity. Moses encourages us to choose life (Deut 30:19). In Romans 7, Paul upholds Divine Law as "good, just, and holy."[15] He also refers to delighting in the Law. Yet, Paul lived during a time when sin had been normalized by society. This created conflict, which Paul sought to overcome. Paul's struggle did not imply Divine Law was difficult. Like drug or alcohol addiction, once sin becomes part of your life, it takes a deliberate choice and a process to overcome tendencies that lead to death. To this point, Paul states that that which is good (i.e., the Law) is not death but allows sin to appear so that it may be known. This allows sin's consequences, which lead to death to be made manifest as "exceedingly sinful" (Rom 7:13). Thus, Paul is supporting Moses' statement that the Law is a way of life to reveal and overcome sin.

V. HEBREWS ON PERFECTION

During Jeremiah's days, Israel thought their actions did not matter. All they needed to do to be right with YHWH was to bring a sacrifice for sin. They could sin repeatedly without remorse.

They just needed to bring an offering to YHWH's Temple, and believe they would be forgiven (Jer 7:8-10; see pp. 16-17). Paul, like Jeremiah, addresses this erroneous belief.

> For the law having a shadow of good things to come, and not the very image of the things, can never with those sacrifices which they offered year by year continually make the comers thereunto perfect. (Heb 10:1)

Paul is right. First, the Law does foreshadow many good things yet to come in its promised blessings for all who obey (Deut 28:1-14; Lev 26:1-13). Second, the purpose of sacrifices was never to make Israel perfect. Every instruction that YHWH provides for making Israel perfect comes from Divine Law, not sacrifices.[16] It was a path of life—a holistic way of living—that made Israel perfect or *tanim*: wholly and completely pure. Twice YHWH tells people to be perfect. The first time occurred when YHWH gave Abraham the Circumcision Covenant (Gen 17:1). The second time occurred when YHWH reiterated the importance of the entire Law to Israel shortly before Moses' death (Deut 18:13).

Within the Law of Moses, there are about 50 stipulations that require sacrifices to be "perfect" and "without blemish." *Mishchat*, for instance, is a cultic term that means "blemished" (Lev 22:25).[17] Isaiah used this specific term in his prophecy of the Suffering Servant (Isa 52:14). YHWH disallowed blemished gifts and would only accept the best as tithes, offerings, and payment for sin's penalties. People could not offer their sick, diseased, or lame animals as sacrifices—they had to offer their best. Not only did sacrifices provide sustenance for Israel's priesthood, but diseased offerings could make the priests who ate those sacrifices sick. Unblemished animals held higher economic value than deformed animals. When people needed to pay fines for sin, they could not offer a worthless sacrifice and thus subvert the penalty on wealth for breaking the Law.

Israel, however, confused YHWH's instructions on sacrifices with being "perfect." They thought that the sacrifice's perfection was somehow transferred to them. Nothing in the Law indicates this. Rather, it was simply a penalty on wealth the same way a civil society penalizes theft, fraud, or negligence today. Thus, Paul is correct in stating that the sacrifices did not make anyone perfect. The only thing YHWH states makes us perfect is obeying the instructions in His path, which leads to life.

VI. JESUS UPHOLDS THE LAW AS TRUTH

Not only does Jesus state that Divine Law is valid, but he also tells us that YHWH's word is truth. Towards the end of his ministry, Jesus prayed to his Father asking,

> Sanctify them through your truth: **Your word is truth.** (John 17:17)

The only "word" that Jesus' Father gave to Israel was His Divine Law (see pp. 34–35, 40, 44–45). As people disobeyed this Law, YHWH sent prophets to encourage people to return to YHWH to walk in paths of righteousness. This again confirms Divine Law remaining valid today. I couldn't help but feel upset. I felt deceived.

For far too long we have been taught that the Law derived from man, not God. Institutions and teachers seeking their own following told us the Law is a way of death rather than the means to unify and heal society so no man can lead us off the path. YHWH's Divine revelation is the force of integrity that can empower each of us on the path of righteousness where we can never be led astray.

I have included a chart for easy reference in Appendix A. It shows the many places that Jesus and the New Testament uphold the ongoing validity of Divine Law.

VII. HOW DO WE AWAKEN FROM SLEEP?

As my studies continued, I was shocked to see the New Testament also taught that believers could fulfill Divine Law. In Romans 8, Paul states that when we walk in righteousness, rather than after the flesh, the Law can be fulfilled in each of us. Divine Law is the only Code in the New or Old Testaments that defines righteousness (see pp. 36, 40–46). Thus, Divine Law is a Law of Righteousness. When we walk in righteousness through obedience, not only do we gain a righteous identity, but the righteousness of the Law is fulfilled in us.

> That the **righteousness of the law might be fulfilled in us**, who walk not after the flesh, but after the Spirit. (Rom 8:4)

> Owe no man anything but to love one another, for **he that loves another has fulfilled the law** (Rom 13:8)

One of the greatest commandments in Divine Law instructs us to "love YHWH your God with all your heart, with all your soul, and with all your might" (Deut 6:5). In the next verse, YHWH tells us that His instructions should be "in your heart" (Deut 6:6).

Paul picks up on this theme in Romans 13 (above), telling us how we demonstrate our love of YHWH. Paul does not leave the statement "fulfilled the law" in Romans 13:8 open-ended. He defines *how* our love for one another is fulfilled.

> For this, You shall not commit adultery. You shall not kill. You shall not steal. You shall not bear false witness. You shall not covet. And if there be any other commandment, **it is *briefly* comprehended in this saying**, namely, You shall love your neighbor as yourself. Love works no ill to his neighbor: therefore love is the fulfilling of the law. (Rom 13:9–10)

Paul specifically teaches believers how to fulfill the Law through love. We fulfill the Law by obeying it! Paul not only endorses the 10 Commandments, but he also upholds the rest of the Law of Moses by "briefly" including it in the broad category of the Golden Rule.[18]

Understanding that each of us can be righteous, that our love of God and one another is demonstrated by obeying the Law, revolutionizes our walk with YHWH. It corrects the moral perversion of our society. Paul points out that when we love God with all our heart, our obedience will manifest in action. Paul singles out love through obedience as the means to awaken us from sleep!

> And that, knowing the time, that **now it is high time to awake out of sleep**: for now is our salvation nearer than when we believed. (Rom 13:11)

How can we awaken the giant? How do we awake from our endless sleep? Salvation is nearer than we believe when we obey Divine Law. This is how we show love and fulfill the Law of Righteousness, which is also a Law of Love. Divine Law continues to light the path (Ps 119:105). It is now time to awaken the Giant!

VIII. TESTING THE PATH

After 20 years of study, I put Divine Law to the test. I wanted to ascertain the legitimacy of the Bible's claims. I theorized that God's instructions should universally benefit all humanity. YHWH's instructions should make life remarkably better than if people lived without them. I investigated God's written protocols for human interaction, government, justice, Sabbath rest, and health protocols like circumcision, dietary laws, quarantine, morality, and abstaining from intercourse during menses.

I discovered that in each case, medical and scientific evidence supported the remarkable benefits that following biblical protocols creates. I reasoned that if YHWH's Health Code prevents disease (Exod 15:26), then it is good for humanity. It anchors man's ideas of health and can prevent the modern trend of "what is good for you is different for me" from being defined by those who benefit from that trend.

My investigation also uncovered Israel's ancient constitution: a document that introduced a representative government. This constitution established liberty by limiting the power of a very strong and centralized government. Israel's constitution limited oppression by establishing justice for society. It anchored social and economic principles to a system where all are equal before the Law. **God's way of life (Ps 19:7) established and preserved a society of laws instead of arbitrary, self-serving whims of men.** Israel's constitution held all accountable, whether rich or poor, popular or unpopular, powerful or weak, citizen or immigrant. All were accountable to one universal Law. This Law empowered incredible national unity.

The genius in this constitution founded a perfect balance among citizens, their government, their representatives, and God. Much of this evidence is presented in Volume 1 where

I concluded the preponderance of the evidence supported the validity of ancient Israel's history and the legitimacy of YHWH's revelation of Himself and His way of life to ancient Israel and her patriarchs. Our modern, rotten governments seek to define ideas of right and wrong collectively.

Unfortunately, modern governments are determined by the highest bidder. Every office and law is for sale. Lost are eternal principles and values that govern the choices we make.

Yet hope is not lost. King David reveals what can be. It is an ancient hope, a *tikvah* for our day:

> The Law of YHWH is perfect, converting the soul. (Ps 19:7)

The Hebrew for 'perfect' is *tamim*. It means wholly and completely perfect.[19] David says something even more profound. The Law has the ability to "convert" the soul. Divine Law can heal our callous hearts and minds. *Meshivat,* translated 'convert,' means "to cause to turn."[20] David states that Divine Law can turn our souls back to God—back to a right and good way of life. Why on earth would we want to forsake it?

To reject the law is to elevate the wicked; to obey the Law is to fight them (Prov 28:4)

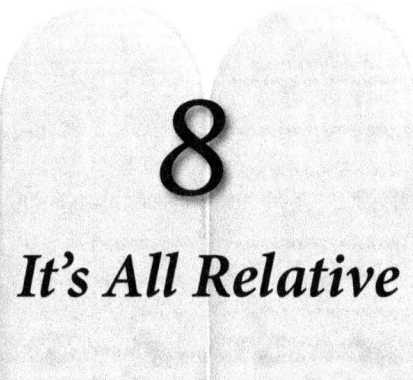

8

It's All Relative

I. INDIVIDUAL DISCRETION

An Ivy League professor entered the classroom and looked around.
Pointing, "You in the blue shirt, what is your name"?
"Devorah," she replies.
"Get out of my classroom. I do not like your face or your name. Do not come back to my class again."
"I don't understand," Devorah responds.
"I am not going to ask you again," the professor insists.
The classroom's silence is deafening. Devorah, obviously upset, packs up her bags and stands up.
"Faster please," taunts the professor.
She doesn't dare say anything as she leaves downcast, avoiding all eye contact. The door closes behind her.

Is the professor finished? Who will be next?
After a long, deep pause the professor poses a question.
"Why does law exist"?
Did anyone dare answer? Another long pause. . . .
"Social order" finally replies a guy in the 8th row.
"To keep people relying on the state," retorts a gal in the 4th row.
Seeing that the professor is not agitated,
"To protect personal rights" answers a student in the 10th row.
"Justice," replies Rachel in 4th row.
Now, the professor smiles. She has his attention.
"Thank you very much. Did I behave fairly to your classmate earlier"?
Everyone shakes their heads.

"Indeed I was unfair. So, why didn't any of you protest? Why didn't anyone try to question or stop me? Didn't you want to prevent this injustice"?

"We were afraid," came a bold reply from row 9.

"Fear of me was stronger than your will to prevent *in*justice?" the professor inquires.

Nobody answers.

"What you have just learned you couldn't have understood in 1,000 lecture hours if you had not lived it. Justice is treating people as they deserve. Law exists to ensure that people are treated fairly. Justice is based on treating all as equal before the law. When personal rights are violated, a person can seek remedy before a court of law.

"Should Devorah file a grievance against me with the university?"

"Absolutely!"

"Laws and rules exist to protect you from me. Maybe I habitually target students. How would the university know unless you or Devorah speak up? Why didn't you speak up earlier?"

"You didn't say anything. You were complacent because it did not affect you. I did not target you. This attitude speaks against you. You think that as long as it doesn't concern you, it's none of your business. I'm telling you, that if you don't help bring about justice, then one day you, too, may experience injustice, and no one will stand up for you. Truth and justice are impotent *unless* you stand up and fight for them. This is how you learn to break the sound of silence your complacency has allowed." Accountability is the power of Divine Law.

II. GASLIT MUCH?

Gaslighting is a form of psychological abuse where a person (or organization) causes someone to question his or her sanity.[1] Religious gaslighting causes people to question their ability to be righteous. They are told, "You can't"! Any attempt to live by a written Code of Law is deemed unworthy and insufficient. The victims' success in observing Divine Law is trivialized. Their righteous identity is erased. You can never be good enough!

A righteous identity empowers a person or group to stand on the strength of principle that an action, history, or belief is right and good. When those beliefs are constantly challenged by the church or society, people lose the strength that standing on truth allows. When a person does take a stand, that person is demoralized as judgmental, inflexible, and patriarchal. The person's righteous identity is undermined. Personal confidence threatens the system. What if people stand on high moral ground and demand accountability? This rotten system would begin to crumble! Much better for the establishment when people believe their righteousness is worthless. Then an institution, group, or government can replace and control the direction of a society's beliefs. Righteousness is the antidote to insanity.

Relativism is a form of gaslighting. We are told that a person's right to depravity is just as important as strong morals and values. Individual "rights" are all equal. They are just different

This meme is one gaslighting tactic. It implies both perspectives are equal. However, it ignores the artist's directions, which instruct "stand here," to obtain the right perspective.

perspectives. They substitute "rights" for *wants* and *lusts* knowing we've lost the firm values that allow us to see their blatant agenda. This trick strengthens and empowers enemies to oppress. They undermine any righteous identity, so we have nothing to stand on. When all principles, morals, and perspectives are equal, ideas based on God are rendered irrelevant. This tactic has been used for so long that we have lost our ability to find our identity in the Divine. We can no longer discern what is right for you and me. Capricious new rules are enforced. When confronted, we waver because we no longer see God defining our identity.

The strength in relativism's spell is believing that Divine Law does not produce a better life. It is in believing the lie that all beliefs and religions are equal. "Coexist" leads to chaos. We lose our constitutional values of liberty derived from Divine Law.

With a righteous identity erased, a new profile can be forged. People can be manipulated to comply and question anything without a righteous identity to withstand. Citizens can be manipulated to undermine their own nation, their own people, their own national borders (which protect them), and their own gender. They are ever-seeking a new identity to replace what was deemed unworthy or insufficient, and yet they are never satisfied.

We trade a path leading to the perfect balance of liberty and preservation of society for endless dead-end trails that lead to chaos, war, and the dissolution of the family. Abuse of all sorts is encouraged. No one wants accountability. Without righteous and firm morals, people become pliable. They are easily manipulated. They are blinded to the agenda. The forces pushing for abortion, gender change, or encouraging families to no longer have children only seek to weaken America (or any nation) so she can be conquered and replaced. As impossible as this may seem, it is a reality. Historically, democratic nations only survive but 200 years.[2] In 2024, America is 248 years old and on life support. Time is running out for our constitutional Republic. The grace period we have to return is quickly fading away.

III. FINDING IDENTITY IN GOD

The strength in America's *Declaration of Independence* was not in its rebellion against the king of England. Its strength was in its appeal to the Divine Rights of man–rights defined by God.

> We hold these truths self-evident, that all men are *created* equal, that they are endowed by **their Creator** with certain unalienable Rights.... " (Declaration of Independence: A Transcript)[3]

America's founding fathers did not appeal to men for independence but stood on the principle that human rights were endowed by God.[4] America's revolution prospered because its people believed their cause was right and just.

Believing in your righteousness—whether through God or obedience—enables sanity. Seeing yourself, your God, and your nation positively enables you to stand for the right and the truth. It is difficult to defend a person, nation, or God you secretly believe is unrighteous or unjust. The hidden places in your heart betray your will and undermine your ability to stand up for yourself, your nation, your people, and your God.

Although departing from the Divine path of life has produced war and misery, the gate remains slightly ajar to return to God. Righteousness is a breastplate and a helmet of salvation for those empowered by Divine Law (Isa 59:17; Eph 6:13–14). Only by following His path can we enter His salvation. Only then can His Divine light shine through us.

IV. HOW CAN WE RECOGNIZE TRUTH?

My journey unpinned a cherished belief. The Law is not bondage. It is liberty. At Mt. Sinai, YHWH announced that He was delivering Israel "from the House of bondage" (Exod 20:2; Deut 5:6; 6:12). I felt peace flood my soul. Divine Law provided concrete ideas and principles that I could build my life upon. The path was easy to travel, and it was perfect in every way.

Despite these facts, I still needed more concrete ideas. Truth still seemed ambiguous. How could I easily identify truth? I needed firm precepts to guide how I could clearly judge between subtle ideas of right and wrong. Concepts along YHWH's path of righteousness needed to shine like runway lights so I did not miss them. As I discovered truth's formula, I also saw it worked for many fields of study. It was not limited to ideas of doctrine or God. Clear definitions of truth enlightened all paths that one may study. Wow! Did it ever catapult and ground my journey forward!

9

Precepts of Truth

I. WHAT IS TRUTH?

Ambiguity allows the text to be abused. It enables religion to keep ideas mystical, so men are needed to interpret them for us. Ideas are kept relative to the individual. Reducing our relationship with God to mysticism thwarts all accountability. What God requires is kept undefined so a human intermediary is needed "to go up into heaven and bring it to us so we may understand and do it" (Deut 30:12). Vagueness in our understanding allows man to usurp God, telling us, "You can't!"[1]

At this point in my study, the precepts that define truth along YHWH's path of life were foggy. The text states the Law defines truth, but what exactly does that mean? I began to seek definitive precepts and concrete ideas to see if straightforwardness could break through the haze. What ambiguity could clear ideas dispel?

> God is not a man, that he should lie; neither the son of man, that he should repent: shall he say and not perform? Shall he speak and not keep to his word? And he said, "Blessed be YHWH God for behold, I have received command to bless: I will bless and not turn back." (Num 23:19, 20, rendered from the AKJV and the LXX)

Constancy is one of the earliest ideas in the Bible. It is a firmness of word that does not change. Instruction, promise, or precept cannot be rescinded. Once YHWH gives His word, He cannot annul it. Over the course of a decade, I discovered 7 crucial traits of truth which are precepts that govern what truth is (we will cover the first 6 traits in this chapter). Truth is closely related to the concept of constancy.

Balaam. In the above story, Moab's King Balak sought to curse Israel—to prophesy against Israel's future. He hired the pagan prophet Balaam to do the dirty work. However, YHWH told

Balaam that he could not curse Israel since He had already given His word. YHWH promised to bless Abraham "and his seed after him" (Gen 26:3). Men, even if they are prophets, cannot change YHWH's word. They cannot "turn it back," *recant*, or *annul* contracts, covenants, or promises once they are given because YHWH's word is constant and steady. If YHWH were to renege on His promises, they would become false since they are no longer enduring, trustworthy, or constant.

Moses. In the intensely-dry desert wilderness, Israel cried out for water (Num 20:1-6). YHWH commanded Moses and Aaron to speak to a rock in the sight of the congregation rather than hitting a rock as they had done previously. This would show that YHWH—not man—provided water for the people (Num 20:8). This was Israel's 12th rebellion. Each rebellion challenged Moses' and YHWH's authority. In his anger, Moses struck the rock. Moses claimed to be fetching water for Israel of his own power. His emotions prevented him from sanctifying YHWH alone as God.

In a world where people believed the Egyptian gods could take many forms, Moses failed to distinguish himself from YHWH. For this sin, Moses could not enter the Promised Land (Num 20:12). Despite Moses' rebellion against YHWH's instructions, YHWH still gave Israel water just as He had promised (Num 20:11). Moses' disobedience did not annul YHWH's promise. YHWH's word was constant despite man's rebellion and disregard of it.

King Saul. When King Saul rebelled against YHWH, the prophet Samuel quoted Balaam's parable. Samuel reiterated that YHWH does not cancel His word.

> YHWH has rent the kingdom of Israel from you this day, and has given it to a neighbor of yours, that is better than you. *The Strength of Israel will not lie nor repent: for he is not a man, that he should repent.* (1 Sam 15:28-29)

YHWH judged Saul and said He would strip Saul of his kingdom, preventing Saul's reign from turning into a ruling dynasty. This judgment could not be "rescinded." The Creator did not repent of His judgment. YHWH followed through—keeping His own word by removing the kingdom from Saul's hand. While YHWH can be moved to show mercy in His judgments, if a person or society does not affect lasting change in their behaviors, judgment will eventually catch up to that person or society. The issue is always the violation of YHWH's instructions, which bring life (Deut 30:15-16; Prov 6:23; 10:17; 12:28; Jer 21:8; Ezek 33:15). YHWH's instructions are constant, which is why violating them brings about its own self-destruction.

The Young Judahite Prophet. Scripture's constancy is corroborated again by the prophet who prophesied against Jeroboam's altar. YHWH commanded a young Judahite prophet to "eat no bread, nor drink water, nor turn again by the same way that he came" (1 Kgs 13:9). An older prophet tested the young prophet by *lying* to him. The older prophet said that YHWH changed His word, so the younger prophet could "turn again by the same way that he came." The younger trusted the word of man above the word of YHWH. He "turned again" to eat at the older prophet's home and disobeyed God. Consequently, YHWH sent a lion to kill the young, rebellious prophet for failing this test. A prophet's obedience must be firm since he or she speaks for God.

The Judahite prophet failed to understand the foundational attribute of his Creator: YHWH does not change His instructions.[2] The younger prophet disbelieved God, preferring a man's reassuring words despite man's words contradicting YHWH's direct instruction. Although the Judahite prophet was slain, the word that YHWH commanded him to speak against Jeroboam's altar *still came true* (2 Kgs 23:14-16). Why? Because YHWH does not waver or change His word (Ps 15:4; 102:27). His words stand firm, coming to pass regardless of a prophet's rebellious and arbitrary actions. YHWH "will never depart from truth or change it (Ps 111:7f)."[3] Because YHWH's word is constant, we can trust it. If YHWH were to renege on His word, it would become false and could not be trusted.

Isaiah. The prophet Isaiah champions YHWH's constancy. When YHWH's spoken and written words "stand forever," they are firm, trustworthy, and constant. YHWH's words are eternal.

> The grass withers, the flower fades, but **the word of our God shall stand forever**. (Isa 40:8)

> You have done wonderful things; your counsels of old **are faithfulness and truth**. (Isa 25:1)

Truth is unchanging: although seasons change, like humanity's ideas of right and wrong through the ages, YHWH's direct word, the "thus says YHWH," is steadfast.[4] Humanity's thoughts and beliefs come and go like grass (Isa 40:7). This is why human–derived beliefs are often false, as time and circumstance demonstrate that they fail and cannot endure. In contrast, YHWH's perfect word is constant (Ps 19:7).[5] He is faithful to His written word. When YHWH's glory is revealed, all flesh will see that YHWH's word *does* indeed *stand* forever!

Definition of Truth

Clarity revolutionized my journey! Clearly–defined Principles hold our reasoning honest and accountable. Precise definitions allow us to know we are walking in YHWH's path of life. Checking our words and actions against YHWH's unchanging precepts allows us to stand firm on principle without being swayed when people seek to gaslight or deceive us. We can crush their narratives with the weight of truth.

> אֱמֶת/*emet*—Firmness, trustworthiness; Constancy, duration; Faithfulness; truth.[6]

> Truth: FIDELITY, *CONSTANCY*; the state of being the case: FACT; the body of real things, events, and facts: ACTUALITY; the property (as of a statement) of being in accord with fact or reality.

Truth comprises two main concepts: constancy and fidelity. These attributes allow truth to be trustworthy. Truth is an idea or precept that YHWH's written word is firm, constant, and reliable.[7] It does not change, even when people disobey. In other words, truth is truth despite man's sinful actions and violation of the Law. Mao's genocide of his own people, which resulted in 80 million deaths, did not rescind the precept that murder is wrong. Neither did Stalin's massacre of 40 million people make murder any less wicked. The same is true for YHWH's instructions to ancient Israel, to specific people in the Bible, or to humanity in general. YHWH's written promises cannot be rescinded or annulled.

Modernly, the biblical idea of truth is best described by Bertrand Russell's *correspondence theory of truth*. The two basic elements in this view embrace the idea that both truth and falsehood exist. A belief's truth or falsehood always depends on something that lies outside the belief itself.[8] In other words, truth consists in some form of correlation between belief and fact. Truth is a general category that is defined by specific traits, concepts, or precepts. Truth is nearly synonymous with constancy.

II. CONSTANCY: 1ST PRECEPT

Truth's attribute of constancy makes truth steady. It prevents the grass from withering, the flower from fading, and values from changing every few generations. Constancy is the strongest principle underlying truth. Balaam's reply that he could not "turn back" or "change" YHWH's word expressed this concept.

King David provides another great description of constancy and righteousness. Righteous people uphold truth by being constant with their own words. When a person promises to do something, they keep their word. They do not change that word or go back on their word. While YHWH condemns vile people,

> He honors them that fear YHWH. *He that swears to his own hurt, and **changes not**.*" (Ps 15:4)

YHWH honors those who fear Him. He also honors those who embrace His precepts. Righteous people will also exhibit constancy in their words and actions. David champions the concepts of truth by pointing out that YHWH's word exhibits constancy and fidelity—the promises YHWH has given do not evolve.[9] YHWH upholds His own word, even if it is to His own hurt. YHWH's act of constancy makes Him righteous.

> My covenant will I not break, *nor alter* the thing that is gone out of my lips. (Ps 89:34)

> For I am YHWH, **I change not**; therefore, you sons of Jacob are not consumed. (Mal 3:6)

During times of duress, *a righteous man* will keep his sworn word even if it impacts him negatively (Num 30:2). The details of YHWH's word are unchanging. Once YHWH has given His word, He will not break or alter what He has promised to do. YHWH does not "do-over" or manipulate His promises.[10] YHWH's word is constant: it does not deviate to the right or the left in what YHWH has stated He will do (Deut 5:32). If Israel rebels, YHWH will apply the curses of the Law (Leviticus 26; Deuteronomy 28–30:9) bringing Israel to repentance. However, humanity's disobedience cannot annul YHWH's promises or covenants.

Definition of Constancy

The first precept that defines truth is its innate ability to be constant. Truth resists change and is impervious to being altered—even by God Himself. These are the concepts associated with constancy:

> Constancy: steadfastness of mind under duress: FORTITUDE; *FIDELITY*, LOYALTY; **freedom from change**.

Added to the ideas of constancy and fidelity are the precepts that YHWH's word remains steadfast—even under the duress of Israel's sins—YHWH's words and His promises hold firm. YHWH's words exhibit fidelity, loyalty, and fortitude. YHWH's words and precepts have a resolve and firmness of reality to encourage resistance to change.

If an idea or doctrine is truth, it will be steadfastness, even during times when Israel causes duress by her idolatry and disobedience. During these times, YHWH will follow His covenantal stipulations. Beliefs must demonstrate fidelity and freedom from changing standards. YHWH cannot change His precepts or stipulations (recantation)! This last definition is paramount. Even if Israel has rebelled, God will not change the contractual terms of His agreement(s). *If YHWH recanted His previous agreements, then He is not a God of truth.*[11] *Any doctrine or teaching that seeks to annul YHWH's word cannot meet the definition of truth*, and that person sins through dishonesty. Constancy is the 1st precept of truth.

III. FIDELITY: THE 2ND PRECEPT

Truth's attribute of *fidelity* stresses accuracy in the details. Volume 1 of this series explored this topic in depth. I compared the written text, considered the Documentary Hypothesis, compared the Old Testament's accounts with the known archaeological records for many ancient settlements, and worked to re-create its chronology. In every single area of study, the Old Testament exhibited fidelity.

Archaeological evidence and ancient written sources support Israel's Exodus and the Conquest with the destruction of 336 known heavily walled towns in Canaan.[12] Biblical chronology accurately records the destruction of Shechem after Abimelech's coup (Judg 9:28). While archaeologists date this layer of destruction to 1180 BCE, biblical chronology dates it to

1186 BCE.[13] Six years is well within the accepted limits of deviation. One exact synchronism is the contact Assyria's King Shalmaneser made with Israel's Kings, Ahab and Jehu.[14] Scripture accurately records the exact year they met as confirmed by Assyria's annuls. These are just a few examples of truth preserved in the biblical text.

The Law's fidelity is also evidenced by medical research, which supports the Divine Law's prohibitions against unclean foods, intercourse during menses, and the health benefits of circumcision. Surprisingly, fidelity is also exhibited on the exact day circumcision should be performed. Infants have the greatest ability for their blood to clot with both the prothrombin protein and vitamin K peaking on the 8th day of life.[15] This is in addition to women enjoying a 58% less likelihood of developing cervical cancer when their partner is circumcised.[16] Since Volume I's publication in 2015, I discovered published research supporting abstinence from intercourse during menses, resulting in much lower incidents of endometriosis. The studies suggest endometriosis is more likely to develop by engaging in sex during menstruation.[17]

While documents can be damaged or scribal errors occur, the overwhelming fidelity to the exact details of YHWH's words remain. Divine Law coincides with actions beneficial to humanity. No human could make this up! Even the Prophetic Code, a law governing all biblical prophecy, coincides with 70-year intervals in Israel's history (Lev 26; Deut 28–30:9).[18] The combined Prophetic Code is accurate down to the specific details of what was specified to have occurred during every 70-year period.

Thus far, the Old Testament (*Tanakh*) is faithful. It witnesses exactness to the words written within it. Specific prophecies of events or people and their exact fulfillment are demonstrated through history and Scripture. Fidelity is a foundational concept for truth.

Definition of Fidelity

> Fidelity: the quality or state of being *faithful*; accuracy in details: EXACTNESS.

This definition holds the text and the truth seeker accountable. When studying the text, we should empirically adhere to the details of what is written. If we add our own preconceived ideas to what is written, then we add and take away from God's original path and the course deviates to a different destination (Deut 4:2; 12:32). Fidelity is truth's 2nd precept.

IV. FAITHFULNESS: THE 3RD PRECEPT

Faithfulness is the third criterion for truth.[19] Faithfulness is sticking it out with someone, even during hard times.

> Know therefore that YHWH your God, He is God, **the faithful *God***, which keeps covenant and mercy with them that love him and keep his commandments to a thousand generations. (Deut 7:9)

> It is of YHWH's mercies that we are not consumed, because his compassions fail not. They are new every morning: **great is your faithfulness.** (Lam 3:22–23)

> Forever, O YHWH your word is settled in heaven. Your *faithfulness is unto all generations*: You have established the earth, and it abides. **They continue this day according to your judgment**: for all are your servants. Unless your law had been my delight, I should have perished in my affliction. (Ps 119:89–92)

YHWH is faithful and loyal to His word. In Psalm 90, YHWH's faithful word established the earth during creation. His faithful judgments enable the earth to operate according to the laws of physics. David presents YHWH's words and precepts, which govern the heavens, as the same precepts or principles of the Law YHWH gave to Moses. These principles teach us how to live. In Lamentations, YHWH's mercies do not fail since they are renewed daily. This thoroughly supports the concept of YHWH being faithful despite people's shortcomings. Faithfulness is a pivotal concept of truth. It is related to constancy. Faithfulness is what makes YHWH and His word trustworthy.

Definition of Faithfulness

> Faithful: steadfast in affection or allegiance: LOYAL; *firm in adherence to promises* or in observance of duty: CONSCIENTIOUS.

Throughout the Old Testament, YHWH consistently demonstrates a "firm adherence to promises made." There is no wavering. *Even when Israel is disobedient and walks in idolatry, YHWH does not revoke or rescind His word.* The actions of Jacob's seed cannot annul promises or covenants given to the nation or her patriarchs.[20] Even if it is to the Creator's own harm (Ps 15:4), He must uphold His promises to the ancient nation of Israel and keep His word. This is what makes YHWH righteous. Faithfulness' firm and constant steadiness, along with its conscientiousness to detail, makes faithfulness truth's 3rd precept.

V. RIGHTEOUSNESS: THE 4TH PRECEPT

What benefit is there in truth if the Creator does not obey His own word?[21] If truth matters, then YHWH is not a hypocrite. He obeys His own written Code of Law, which enables life. In fact, it is only by adherence to the written Divine Law that anyone is righteous—even God.

> Far be it from you to do after this manner: to slay the righteous with the wicked, that the righteous should be as the wicked, who are far from you. **Shall not**

> **the Judge of all the earth do right?** (Gen 18:25. Cf Deut 25:1; 1 Sam 26:23; 2 Sam 22:21, 25; 1 Kgs 8:32; Job 33:26; Ps 5:12)

> He is the Rock. His work is perfect, for all his ways are just. A God of truth and **without iniquity**, just and right is he. (Deut 32:4)

> **Your righteousness is an everlasting righteousness,** and *your law is the truth.* (Ps 119:142)

> Stand still, that I may reason with you before **YHWH of all the righteous acts of YHWH,** which he did to you and to your fathers. (1 Sam 12:7. See also Judg 5:11; 2 Chr 12:6; Neh 9:8; Job 36:3; 40:8; Ps 1:6)

> I will praise **YHWH according to his righteousness**: and will sing praise to the name of YHWH most high. (Ps 7:17. See also Ps 22:31)

> **Your righteousness also, O God, is very high,** who has done great things. O God, who is like unto you! (Ps 71:19)

YHWH's righteousness is stressed over 200 times in Scripture.[22] God's righteousness is not some lofty, arbitrary ideal. YHWH's adherence to His own Divine Law is what makes Him a righteous God and Judge. Not only is He the world's Judge whose ways are perfect, He is "without iniquity." Righteousness is the 4th requirement or precept of truth.

Definition of Righteousness

This concrete definition aligns with the Bible's concept of righteousness:

> Righteous: *Acting in accord* with divine or moral law: free from guilt or sin.

YHWH acts in accord with His own Divine and Moral Law. His constant obedience to Divine Law makes Him free from guilt or sin. The Creator's words, actions, and judgments demonstrate that He follows His own path of life. This is the most pivotal point of our entire trial. Throughout the Old Testament, YHWH and His prophets claim that He is righteous.[23] God's perfection (2 Sam 22:31; Deut 32:4) and His freedom from sin and guilt are what separate "God" from mortals.

VI. RIGHTEOUSNESS IS NOT ARBITRARY: THE 5TH PRECEPT

Truth's fourth trait was righteousness (see above). Righteousness keeps truth being good. Truth's traits of constancy, fidelity, and faithfulness could be used for evil purposes that eventually lead to destruction. Many things can be constant but evil. For instance, murder has been a constant reality throughout human history. It began with Cain and has faithfully continued in every generation. Murder exhibits fidelity in that no generation has ever existed without a murder taking place. Today, murder has become commonplace, and its victims are without number throughout the earth. Although murder is a constant of human history, murder's constancy does not make it true. Murder is not valid nor is it a trait of truth because murder opposes truth's precept of righteousness. Truth's precept of righteousness prevents its concepts of constancy, fidelity, and faithfulness from being used for evil purposes. Righteousness anchors truth to the concepts within Divine Law. Righteousness' ability to withstand being arbitrary is truth's 5th precept.

Definition of Arbitrary

> Arbitrary: depending on individual discretion (like a judge) and **not fixed by law**; marked by or resulting from unrestrained and often tyrannical exercise of power; based on or determined **by individual preference or convenience rather than by necessity or the intrinsic nature of something**; existing or coming about seemingly at random or by chance.

Since YHWH is righteous, He is not arbitrary. Constancy opposes being arbitrary. YHWH does not use "individual discretion" or demonstrate an "unrestrained" or "tyrannical" exercise of power, *nor does He use favoritism* in His dealings with humanity. His judgments are based upon His own Divine Law and He operates within that Law to do what is necessary to bring about a lasting salvation for all people. Righteousness is not an arbitrary act, and neither is truth. Both are consistent to upholding and obeying the word YHWH gave and lives by—even for God Himself.

VII. VERIFIABLE

The sixth criterion for Divine Law to merit the distinction of truth is its ability to be externally verified. It is the ability of a law or history to be tested in the natural world. Applied sciences like archaeology, medical studies, linguistics, or applications from other fields of study should be able to test many of the Bible's claims (the same holds true for all fields of study). This does not mean that every single instruction should have the ability to be demonstrated as valid, but the overall *preponderance of the evidence* should support its laws as being good for humanity.

Volume 1 spent many chapters seeking whether external evidence exists for Divine Law's validity. Does evidence exist to support that the Bible's stories really occurred? Much of our study focused on historicity and whether supporting archaeological and written sources attest to a similar record for ancient Israel to what is written in Scripture. In Volume 1, the evidence upheld and confirmed the validity of Divine Law. As our study turns to the New Testament, historicity will remain a crucial criterion for truth. The ability for a text to be externally verified is the 6th precept of truth.

These six "universal precepts" of truth are firm, and they make sense. They are an immovable and solid foundation. Using these concepts enables us to discover truth in scientific and biblical studies alike: they are universal concepts. This is how we break men's power over us! This is how we hold politicians, theologians, and academics accountable.

> To the law and to the testimony: if they speak not according to this word, it is because there is no light in them. (Isa 8:20)

I began using these principles as the basis of my studies and YHWH's word came alive! My studies no longer held internal contradictions. I could study a topic weeks or years apart and the evidence supported the same conclusion each time I studied it. This led to incredible peace and joy. However, as my journey continued, I discovered that I held another preconceived belief in error. This belief challenged everything I had learned in the Church.

Precepts of Truth

Precept	Definition	Text
Truth	The Hebrew *emet* means firm, trustworthy, CONSTANT, enduring, and faithful. This embraces the English definition of Truth, which is: FIDELITY, CONSTANCY; the state of being the case: FACT; the body of real things, events, and facts: ACTUALITY; the property (as of a statement) of being in accord with fact or reality	Num 20:1–6; 23:19–20; Isa 40:8; 1 Sam 15:28–29; 2 Kgs 23:14–16; Ps 15:4; 102:27
1. Constancy	Steadfastness of mind under duress: FORTITUDE; *FIDELITY*, LOYALTY; **freedom from change**	Num 30:2; Lev 27:10, 33; Ps 15:4; 89:34; Deut 5:32
2. Fidelity	The quality or state of being *faithful*; accuracy in details: EXACTNESS	Accuracy in its accounts, chronology, requirements withing the Law, written text. (Lev 26; Deut 28)
3. Faithfulness	Steadfast in affection or allegiance: LOYAL; *firm in adherence to promises* or in observance of duty: CONSCIENTIOUS	Duet 7:9; 1 Sam 26:23; Ps 36:5; 40:10; 89:1–8; 92:2; 119:75, 86, 90–91, 138; Lam 3:22–23; Isa 25:1; 49:7

4. Righteousness	*Acting in accord* with divine or moral law: free from guilt or sin	Gen 18:25; Duet 25:1; 1 Sam 12:7; 26:23; 2 Sam 22:21, 25; 1 Kgs 8:32; Job 33:26; Ps 5:12; 7:17; 71:19; 119:142. See also Judg 5:11; 2 Chr 12:6; Neh 9:8; Job 36:3; 40:8; Ps 1:6
5. Righteousness Is Not Arbitrary	Arbitrary: depending on individual discretion (like a judge) and not fixed by law; marked by or resulting from unrestrained and often tyrannical exercise of power; based on or determined by individual preference or convenience rather than by necessity or the intrinsic nature of something; existing or coming about seemingly at random or by chance	*Gen 18:25; Deut 32:4;* Ps 7:17; 11:7; 22:31; 36:6; 45:7; 48:10; 50:6; 71:16, 19; 72:1; 98:2; 119:142; Isa 5:16; 41:10; 42:21; 45:19; 56:1; Jer 9:24; Ezek 18:25; Dan 9:7; Mic 6:5; Zec 8:8
6. Verifiable: Historicity	Scripture's history or its teachings can be verified and evidenced. Its history can be evidenced through archaeology. Its dietary and purity instructions can be validated through scientific studies. Divine Law can also be tested and verified by the effectiveness of its constitutional, legal, and criminal code in producing a just and moral society	Covers the entire Bible from Genesis to Revelation

While these precepts provided a firm standard for truth, I was still missing the final piece to this puzzle. The final piece was specific to Scripture and was not universal. It allows us to specifically distinguish truth in God's written word. It was the missing concept that completed the precepts of truth.

10

"It's Hard to be a Diamond in a Rhinestone World"

—Dolly Parton

I. A RIGHTEOUS DIFFERENCE

The correspondence theory of truth holds that both truth and falsehood exist. So far, I had six precepts upon which I could prove all things. However, I was still missing a crucial factor. What made YHWH's Divine Law and His revelation different from other ancient nations? What if no difference exists between YHWH's theology and that of other nations? Did all nations have truth?

As my study continued, I discovered that I needed one more specific criterion for judging whether Israel's Scriptures were true. Unlike the six Precepts of Truth, this final precept was *not* universal. It was limited to Scripture.

Dissimilarity is the seventh criterion for Divine Law to be truth.[1] The theology of Abraham and Israel needed to be different (or set apart) from other religions when it was given. This investigation required standards that could be measured in concrete ideas. These ideas needed to be systematically analyzed and compared.[2] This did not mean that Israel did not have similar customs or traditions, but God's instructions should demonstrate a philosophy that contradicted the falsehoods in pagan theologies.

Context is vitally important with this criterion. It is easy to become overzealous with the precept of dissimilarity. According to biblical chronology, Noah lived until Abram was 58 years old and Shem lived until Jacob and Esau were 50 years old (*YE1*, p. 896). These early generations would likely preserve a memory of creation and the flood colored by their own ethnic and cultural systems of transmission. From the biblical perspective, the entire earth once had truth and justice. This was the reason YHWH could not judge the Amorites since their society had not yet devolved into depravity (Gen 15:16). This was as late as 2450 BCE. After Noah and Shem died (*c.* 2050 and 1840, respectively), a stable means of preserving truth broke down as society splintered and leaders vied for power. This was the reason YHWH called Abraham to preserve truth as Noah was reaching the end of his life. By the time Israel exodused from Egypt 430 years after Abraham immigrated to Canaan, the nations had fallen away from the knowledge of God.

While *historicity* means there should be similarities with contemporary cultures and traditions showing that the events occurred when the Bible records that they happened, *dissimilarity* means there should be enough theological, legal, and ritual differences to be at odds with other philosophies at the time God gave His instructions. The precept of *fidelity* greatly aids in this study since it examines the details of how a specific law, concept, or theology is applied (see pp. 65–68). The instructions within YHWH's Divine Law should separate Israel's theology from other ancient nations. Dissimilarity to contemporary ancient nations is the 7th precept guiding our study of truth in Scripture.

Before I could investigate the historical validity of the New Testament (like I did the Tanakh), I needed to know if anything separated YHWH's theology from contemporary nations who worshipped the baals. I knew YHWH did not like their name or their representation as physical idols. Did anything more than a name separate YHWH from the *baals*?

II. MONOTHEISM

Monotheism is the belief in a single deity. This was the first significant doctrine that distinguished Israel from other nations throughout the days of Abraham, King David, Isaiah, and Jeremiah. It was the primary difference between Israel and all other religions.[3] This idea is demonstrated in many verses in the Old Testament.

> Hear, O Israel: **YHWH our God is one YHWH**. And you shall love YHWH your God with all your heart, and with all your soul, and with all your might. (Deut 6:4–5)

> Know therefore this day, and consider it in thine heart, that YHWH, he is God in heaven above, and upon the earth beneath: **there is none else**. (Deut 4:39)

The Hebrew text establishes the idea of absolute monotheism.[4] YHWH is a single Deity who created the world, caused the flood, plagued Egypt, led Israel in the wilderness, revealed His name, and gave Israel His Divine Law. He is the same God who applied the Law's curses for Israel's breach of contract (Leviticus 26; Deuteronomy 28). Other nations believed in a plethora of deities who fought amongst themselves. Each pagan city had its own deity. Each deity had differing abilities: some healed disease, others caused it. But no nation believed in a single deity responsible for all.[5]

> **I am he. Before me there was no God formed, *neither shall there be after me*. I, even I, am YHWH and beside me there is no Savior.** I have declared, and have

saved, and I have showed when there was no strange god among you: therefore, you are my witnesses, said YHWH, that I am God. (Isa 43:10–12)

My husband Jack was the one who brought these verses to my attention. He took this verse as absolute. He believed these texts disqualified Jesus from being God. He kept pestering, asking "If YHWH is only one YHWH and there is none else, where does Jesus fit in"? "How can Jesus be a God if no God was formed before YHWH and there will be no God formed after YHWH"?

My response was that Jesus was part of the Godhead. He was just one aspect of YHWH. I knew my next step had to tackle this issue from the New Testament. There was something Jack was missing in his understanding of these verses. Before I could do that, I still needed clearer distinctions between Divine Law and practices among the nations so I could better understand the dissimilarities that made it truth. If these dissimilarities distinguish truth from falsehood, then their precepts should be constant throughout both the Old and New Testaments.

III. CUSTOMS

My journey led me to Israel's prophets. They consistently emphasized that pagan nations' customs and their gods were at odds with YHWH's path of life. Moral sins were egregious crimes: killing infants and human sacrifices, incest, adultery, homosexuality, and bestiality. These sins God would not ignore. These moral sins are mentioned in Leviticus 18 and 20. YHWH warns Israel that part of the reason He cast the Canaanites out of the land so Israel could colonize it was because those nations had corrupted themselves through the immoral acts specifically outlawed by Divine Law. YHWH warned that He would do the same to Israel if she committed the same moral sins (Lev 18:26–30). Thus, YHWH was not an arbitrary judge because He applied the same standard for both the Canaanites and Israelites.

> And you shall **not walk in the manners of the nations,** which I cast out before you: for they committed all these things,[6] therefore I abhorred them. (Lev 20:23)

> You are a holy people to YHWH your God. YHWH has chosen you to be a peculiar people to himself, above all the nations that are on the earth. (Deut 14:2)

YHWH's path of life differed from the practices common among the nations. Two pagan rituals specifically banned were the "cutting of one's flesh" for the dead and tattoos (Lev 19:28). Another custom God forbid was boiling an animal in its *own* mother's milk (Exod 23:19; 34:26; Deut 14:21).[7] This prohibition did not forbid eating meat and dairy together.[8] It separated Israel from pagan nations by denying a fertility rite associated with the pagan goddess Ashtaroth.[9]

Throughout His Law, YHWH emphasizes the call for Israel to be peculiar and different. They were not called to be different for the sake of being different, but God's people were to be different through a just and righteous identity. This enabled amazing unity while empowering the righteous to counter false narratives that weaken and divide a people. They were not to be different just to stand alone, but to be a light to the world as they taught the nations (Isa 49:6) about living and walking down a different path, a road that leads to life, not death.

IV. SHOCKING CLAIM

Israel's Scriptures reveal a bold claim. Of all nations, only Israel retained YHWH's truth. Other nations may have once had truth through a basic Divine Law while Noah lived. After Noah's death, people like the Amorites (Gen 15:16) corrupted it (Deut 12:30–31; 18:9–14). YHWH chose Abraham for at least two reasons. First, Abraham was Shem's youngest living 1st born heir (Gen 10:1, 21–25; 11:10–29). Second, Abraham was willing to teach his children "the path of justice and judgment" (Gen 18:19).[10] I had already discovered that no other nation claimed to have truth. Pagan gods simply represented the nature of the world people lived in. I could also agree that pagan practices like human sacrifice and ritual sex were wicked.

> They (the gods) are *vanity and the work of errors:* in the time of their visitation, they shall perish. **The portion of Jacob is not like them**: *for he is the former of all things.* Israel is the rod of his inheritance: YHWH of hosts is his name. (Jer 10:15–16. See also Jer 14:22; 16:19; 23:16; 51:17–19. Parentheses added for clarity)

Around 2008, while I was working on Volume 1, I discovered that pagan religions used cumbersome incantations that were substituted for medicine. Priests served as intermediaries between the patient and the gods. In fact, *pagans had no direct access to their gods*. The petitioner always had to go through man. Most ceremonies were "voodoo–like" in nature. Rituals called for things like clay figurines or idols. These images were substituted for the human petitioner. Other ingredients included beer, milk, or fat from a lion or hippopotamus. Some even called for human excrement![11]

These rituals lacked any correspondence to medicinal remedies. They were mystical customs that placated the gods and made the petitioner feel like he had done something to remedy his situation. Incantations were also lucrative for the priests who carried them out.

In contrast to pagan theologies, *Israel had direct access to YHWH*. God "was so close to Israel for all things that her people would call upon Him for" (Deut 4:7). He directly heard their prayers. People like Samuel's mother Hannah had direct access to YHWH through prayer (1 Samuel 1). King Hezekiah could turn to YHWH and plead directly to YHWH for healing from sickness (2 Kgs 20:7). When Hezekiah's son, King Manasseh, was captured and deported to Assyria for his sins, he appealed directly to YHWH from his captivity in Assyria.

YHWH heard his prayer, returned him to Israel, and reestablished his throne (2 Chr 33:18-19). *No intermediary was needed or required for healing or forgiveness* (Isa 59:1).

Divine Law separated Israel from the nations. YHWH did not call the Mesopotamians or the Egyptians to preserve the Divine Law of truth, he called Abraham's family alone.

> He showed his word to Jacob, his statutes, and his judgments to Israel. He has not dealt so with any nation: as for his judgments, they have not known them. Praise you YHWH. (Ps 147:19–20)

> O children of Israel, against the whole family which I brought up from the land of Egypt, saying, **You only have I known of all the families of the earth**; therefore, I will punish you for all your iniquities. (Amos 3:1–2)

Israel was the only nation YHWH singled out to preserve His word of truth.[12] This is why Isaiah stresses that YHWH called Abraham alone (Isa 51:1-2). While Egypt, Assyria, Babylon, and Greece may have once had truth, by the time YHWH gave Israel His Law, that knowledge became corrupted. These nations lacked truth in their theology and systems of governance. YHWH did not reveal truth to other nations after He called Abraham. He preserved His truth through Israel and her descendants alone.

> Listen to me, you that follow righteousness, you that seek YHWH ... Look to Abraham your father, and to Sarah that bore you: for **I called him alone**, and blessed him, and increased him. (Isa 51:1–2)

Isaiah calls for the righteous to return to YHWH by investigating Abraham's history.[13] If we seek righteousness and want to know God, we will find the answers in YHWH's revelation of Himself at Mt. Sinai. His interactions with the ancient nation of Israel reveal the blessings for walking in YHWH's way of life or the curses for rebelling against it. "YHWH has not dealt this way with any other nation" (Ps 147:20). Knowing and living by Divine Law causes your life to overflow with peace and joy!

V. YHWH VS. MANMADE GODS

Since YHWH gave Israel a path of life that created harmony and truth in society, He warned Israel against following Canaanite practices. The words He commanded created a life of peace and prosperity. However, paganism was always looking for new adherents to enrich their priests and strengthen their nations: Israel could be deceived!

> Observe and hear all these words which I command you, **that it may go well with you**, and with your children after you forever, when you do that which is

> **good and right in the sight of YHWH** your God . . . Take heed to yourself that **you are not <u>snared</u>** by following them, after they (the Canaanites) are destroyed from before you; and that you inquire not after their gods, saying, How did these nations serve their gods? even so will I do likewise. (Deut 12:28, 30)

YHWH considers His words "righteous and good."[14] Other legal and religious systems were deficient, leading societies into oppression.[15] Israel could be deceived by dysfunctional religious customs, traditions, and beliefs. Further, foreign customs provided a deceptive, feel-good, or guilt-ridden religion to which people could succumb.[16] YHWH clarified that Abraham's children should not serve Him in the manner that other nations worshiped their gods. *YHWH's requirements for salvation and His truth opposed contemporary pagan customs and beliefs.*

Idols were only one aspect of idolatry.[17] Every nation embraced particular philosophies associated with the gods' physical manifestation (i.e. the idol).[18] George Mendenhall observes that "deities—their symbols and rituals—were merely state-sanctioned expressions of entrenched social values."[19] Nations believed in ideas, theology, and philosophies, which comprised their beliefs.

I was even more surprised to discover that pagan theologies dealt with ideas of salvation. Pagan beliefs held ideas about what the gods or society required a person to do to be saved, cleansed from sin, and rewarded with pleasures in an afterlife.[21] German Egyptologist Jan

In ancient Egypt, when a person died they were judged by having their heart weighed against a feather. This feather was Maat, a goddess that represented truth and justice. If the person had sinned, broken laws, or had a heavy heart, that individual could not pass over to the afterlife.[20]

Assmann concludes that the idol-worship in Egypt's Isis and Osiris cult "from the very beginning . . . had to do with salvation and eternal life."[22]

The Greeks also held beliefs on sin and salvation. Idol worship pertained to the god's physical manifestation.[23] The second-century pagan philosopher Celsus (175 CE) shares his own beliefs as a pagan who lived about a century and a half after Jesus. Celsus held that the "pagan representation of the gods are understood" by the believer "as having symbolic meaning and should not be taken literally since they are 'symbols of invisible ideas and not objects of worship in themselves.'"[24]

The more important aspects of polytheism lay hidden in the initiation rites, "mysteries," and the gods' various requirements.[25] "Early Homeric hymns (*c.* 800 BCE) extolled ritual purity as the condition of salvation, and people were baptized to wash away all their previous sins."[26] Before the Greeks, we learn that the Egyptians (at the time of the Exodus) held many of these same ideas regarding sin and salvation.[27]

I felt uneasy about my ideas of salvation. They seemed to parallel pagan beliefs. I questioned which part of these ideas was pagan and which part was truth. I had been baptized and my sins were washed away through my belief in Jesus. Was the difference simply false gods versus Jesus? Jack had not yet tackled this topic in his studies, but I knew he was not far behind. I needed to understand these issues and have answers ready before he began sharing his thoughts on these issues. I was beginning to question one aspect of my beliefs that I did not share with Jack.

VI. WHY DOESN'T DIVINE LAW WORK?

Along my journey, I kept circling back to one roadblock that I haven't yet shared. It troubled me. Despite all that Scripture states about Divine Law being a path of prosperity, liberty, and immortality—it hasn't worked. Israel has never obtained eternal life by obeying Divine Law. People in ancient Israel died just like everyone else. Additionally, Israel's history is one of strife, turmoil, and war. While I could evidence many health benefits from Divine Law, there is not one real life example that it enables immortality. How could I trust Divine Law if we have no evidence that it produces eternal life?

Precept of Truth Unique to Divine Law

Trait	Definition	Text
7. Dissimilarity	Israel's Divine Law & Theology, her system of justice should be dissimilar to other nations during the time of the Exodus, Judges and Monarchy Periods	*Deut 18:9*; Judg 2:13; 1 Kgs 16:32; 18:25; 23:4–5; *Isa 44:9–46:13*; *Jer 2:8*; *10:1–16*; 11:13, 17; 12:16; 19:5; 23:27; 32:29; Zeph 1:4

11

YHWH Sues Israel

I. YHWH'S CONTROVERSY

From the outset of my quest, I knew that Israel rebelled over 14 times during the Exodus and wilderness sojourn.[1] The people saw YHWH's plagues in Egypt and walked between walls of water while crossing the Red Sea. Despite seeing these miracles, Israel constantly rebelled against God. During the Judges Era (1508–1058 BCE), Israel rebelled over 8 times. Her final defiance in this period was in asking for an absolute monarchy like the nations around them (1 Sam 8:5) instead of the constitutional monarchy allowed by Divine Law (Deut 17:14–20). During 470 years of the Monarchy, Israel's prophets constantly chastised Israel for doing all the sinful atrocities Divine Law forbids. Was this why no evidence exists for Divine Law fostering immortality?

As I considered this resistance to YHWH, it seemed familiar. Israel considered Divine Law unfair! People ignored God, believing their way was better. I felt like I was seeing something anciently modern for the first time: Israel never had walked in YHWH's path of life! Israel rebelled against it before she ever tried it. As I was studying this aspect of Divine Law, I discovered the Covenant Lawsuit YHWH filed against Israel about 800 years after the nation's covenant with Him at Mt. Sinai.[2] Israel's prophets testified against Israel's generational breach of Divine Law. The prophets' words challenged another one of my beliefs as I embarked on a new leg of this journey.

II. THE COVENANT LAWSUIT

Ancient Israel believed Divine Law held her back. During Israel's Monarchy Period (1049–587 BCE), Israel accused God's Law of being unrighteous and unfair.[3] She did not like missing out on the temporary pagan piousness of burning one's own children alive in ritual sacrifice to the gods. Her people did not like that she only had one God, which by comparison was boring. There were fewer festivals to celebrate and there were no temporary, drug-induced highs.[4]

Israel grew to resent the way of life given at Mt. Sinai. The people did not see the limits the Law placed on society's ability to oppress one another as beneficial. Instead the people thought it limited progress. She claimed its healthy boundaries were deficient and difficult to obey.

> Yet the house of Israel says," The way of YHWH is not equal." O house of Israel, are not my ways equal? Are not your ways unequal? (Ezek 18:29)

Israel believed YHWH's path of life was unfair.[5] She hadn't even tried it but condemned it for being a way of living that does not work!

Prophets like Micah and Ezekiel challenged Israel's complaints against Divine Law.[6] Like the apostle Paul, Micah challenged people to weigh the evidence to see if it held true. Would Israel prove all things? Israel's prophets testified as witnesses on YHWH's behalf. They claimed YHWH's ways were just, fair, and righteous. What more could YHWH do for Israel? YHWH recites His history with the nation. He delivered Israel from "the house of bondage" and established the people in their own land so they could be free. He gave Israel a Law which taught her how to live successfully in health, peace, and prosperity.

YHWH gave Israel everything people need but they still rejected it. Israel complained that all of YHWH's actions were not good enough. She preferred magic, incantation, and false beliefs. She wanted these to supernaturally make her prosperous while ignoring that she was oppressing her neighbor, accepting bribes, and exploiting the vulnerable.

> Hear you ... YHWH's controversy ... for YHWH has a controversy with his people, and he will plead with Israel. O my people, what have I done to you? Wherein have I wearied you? *Testify against me.* (Mic 6:2–3)

> Produce your cause, says YHWH. Bring forth your strong reasons, says the King of Jacob. (Isa 41:21)

Israel did not need complex incantations or intermediaries to access God—she already had direct access. No nation "had God so close for all that Israel called upon Him for" (Deut 4:7). Still, Israel coveted conformity and to be like all the nations. She wanted the gratification that a ritual would fix all her ills—anything but accountability to a Code of Law.

> You say The way of YHWH is unfair. Hear now, O House of Israel! Is not my way fair? Are not your ways unfair? ... Therefore, I will judge you, O House of Israel, everyone according to his ways, says Adonai YHWH. *Repent, and turn yourselves from all your transgressions* **so iniquity shall not be your ruin**. (Ezek 18:25, 29–30. See the entire context in Ezekiel 18 and 33. Rendered from KJV and God's Word translation.)

The Children of Israel considered YHWH's way of life within Divine Law as unrighteous and unfair. Ancient Israel asserted YHWH's Law was difficult. For 500 years, YHWH pleaded for people to repent, and to turn from sin before their own ways reaped natural disasters.

Prophets like Isaiah and Hosea also weighed in on the lawsuit between Israel and YHWH:

> Let them bring them forth and show us what shall happen. Let them show the former things that were, that we may consider them and know the latter end of them. Or declare to us things for to come. (Isa 41:22, Douay-Rheims, translation)

YHWH understands cause and effect. He understands why events happened in the past and how they recur in the future.[7] He knows that those who do not know history are doomed to repeat it. YHWH witnessed over 2,500 years of human history before He gave Israel His Divine Law. Because He dwells outside humanity, YHWH can discern the consequences of our actions and offer a better path of life.

During Israel's final days as a nation, hope remained! Ezekiel wrote chapter 18 shortly before Babylon besieged Jerusalem. Judah's sins were overwhelming. They had come to the full and judgment was imminent. The people and her king willfully violated the covenant, choosing to oppress the poor rather than obey YHWH's statutes of liberty that freed the disadvantaged (Jer 34:8–22). Even in these final days, while Israel's broken system was on life support, hope endured. Israel only needed to turn from her wicked ways to live by YHWH's Divine way of life.

> When the wicked man turns away from his wickedness that he has committed, and **does that which is lawful and right**, *he shall save his soul alive.* Because he considers and turns away from all his transgressions that he has committed, he shall surely live, he shall not die. (Ezek 18:27–28)

Despite the people's heinous wickedness, Israel only had to end her depravity, turn to YHWH, and do what "is lawful and right." No complicated rituals. No intermediary. And no sacrifice was necessary.

III. THE INDICTMENT

The prophet Hosea also addresses the Covenant lawsuit claiming that the people's unequal ways lacked mercy, truth, or any knowledge of YHWH. In fact, Israel's prophets judged her more wicked than the nations YHWH had cast out before her (2 Chr 33:9).[8]

> Hear the word of YHWH you children of Israel. YHWH has a controversy with the inhabitants of the land **because there is no truth, nor mercy, nor knowledge of God in the land.** (Hos 4:1)

Were Hosea's words not written 2,600 years ago, they'd seem to have been written on a recent blog. America's rotten, miserable system despises truth and the knowledge of God. We desire moral relativism where each of us can set our own standards of what is right for you, isn't right for me. We don't care that rights are eroded for everyone. "It doesn't affect me"! "You do you and I'll do me." Yet we wonder why violence, theft, and oppression cause us to grow more divided and poorer still.

Like ancient Israel, America despises and ignores the rule of law. Laws are manipulated to benefit *too big to fail*, with no limits to the state. Neither ancient Israel during Hosea's day nor America today are lands of truth or mercy. People desire to progress beyond righteousness and justice with a callous regard for their fellow man.

Ignoring a firm, written Divine Law by accepting bribes, exploiting human rights, and suspending laws only enables oppression. The elite seek financial profit by exploiting law rather than being held accountable and equal before the law. Government programs allow them to do it. Why do we allow our politicians to enrich themselves by their office? Our children are taught they can identify as the opposite sex or as animals in America's schools. We have accepted all absurdity as routine. Just let us sleep! America ignores the lessons from ancient Israel's history. Yet, we are repeating them. America has lost any general knowledge of YHWH. Most people do not even know YHWH's name! And those who do know it refuse to use it.

We are just as stubborn today as Israel was 2,500 years ago. Will humanity ever have a change of heart? Was this Jesus' mission? To turn our hearts back to YHWH so we could escape Malachi's curse (Mal 4:6)?

IV. LAW FOR THE FUTURE?

Israel never did walk in YHWH's Divine Law. She found it contemptible. Isaiah prophesies of a day when YHWH's Law is no longer despised. In this day, YHWH's Law will finally be respected as a way of life that not only works but also one that we can do. "We can!"

> YHWH is well pleased for his righteousness' sake; he will magnify the law and make it honorable. (Isa 42:21)

Despite humanity's shortcomings, YHWH will inspire the Law to be honored. *Adar* is the Hebrew word for 'honorable.' It means "great" or "majestic."[9] Isaiah is telling us that one day, we will discover the power in Divine Law. We will seek to prove all things and be willing to admit the Law is not only worthy of admiration but it is also a Law we can do.

V. WHEN MEN CANCEL YHWH'S LAW

Isaiah's statement that YHWH will magnify the Law and make it honorable parallels Malachi's plea for Israel to "remember the Law of Moses" (See p. 43) This continues to raise the question

I had seen before: Why would YHWH do away with His Law if He wanted people to remember it and planned to finally make it honorable in the future?

Another verse parallels Isaiah's prophecy that YHWH will make Divine Law honorable. David recognizes that when people's values depart so far from God's precepts, YHWH would arise to judge the people.

> It is time for you, YHWH, to act because **they have made void your law**. (Ps 119:126)

When Israel first departed from the Law, her leaders used ever-changing definitions of right and wrong to keep people distracted.[10] They remained in a vicious cycle and in a constant conflict to adjust. Unbound from a Law that restrains power and holds leaders accountable to constitutional principles, rulers continually made new demands on the people while lessening demands on their own power base.[11]

As time passed and people remained silent to tyrannical power, her leaders undermined Divine Law even further. Her leaders encouraged the people's silence by alleviating all accountability before the Law. Israel could break YHWH's covenant by stealing, murdering, and committing adultery. Then, she could come into YHWH's Temple, offer a meaningless sacrifice, and proclaim she was saved and delivered from the offenses she just committed! Eventually, Divine Law and its precepts were done away with, and no one noticed. Israel's people could no longer remember a Code of Law that defined their offenses (Jer 7:8–10; 5:28, 30, 31).[12] Nor could they remember what it was like to live in a just society.

People could no longer discern that leaders were exploiting their complacency, and worse, many preferred unspeakable depravities.

> Woe unto them that call evil good, and good evil; that put darkness for light, and light for darkness; that put bitter for sweet, and sweet for bitter! Woe unto them that are wise in their own eyes, and prudent in their own sight! Woe unto them that are mighty to drink wine, and men of strength to mingle strong drink: Which justify the wicked for reward **and take away the righteousness of the righteous from him**! (Isa 5:20–23)

The story is as old as time. True as it can be. Those who seek power know it is attained by abolishing a person's righteousness.[13] A righteous identity allows a person to see when evil is being substituted for good. Personal righteousness allows us to oppose evil's complicity, breaking its silenced hold.

Israel ignored and voided YHWH's Law. Initially, YHWH filed a lawsuit. Then, Israel did away with Divine Law. Once Israel voided Divine Law and made it of no effect, judgment was imminent. YHWH would act!

VI. OUT WITH THE OLD RHINESTONES, IN WITH THE NEW

A. Continuing the Dialog, Repeat Step 1

As I weighed this evidence, I talked with fellow believers. In our dialog, I discovered that every Christian I knew believed YHWH's instructions at Mt. Sinai were difficult, unfair, and too hard to obey. The 10 Commandments were "okay," but believers considered the dietary and health laws, the taking one day a week off from work, and the judgments for criminal cases too onerous and difficult for humanity to obey.

I also discovered that in most Christian circles, the Father is seen as a harsh, judgmental, and exacting God from whose Law we need to be delivered (Rom 7:1, 6). Some even believed that we needed to be saved from the Father! Or at least His wrath. Almost every person I asked believed Divine Law to be a way of life by which no one can be righteous, justified, or restored to a relationship with God.[14]

I had to ask: Was not this ancient Israel's claim against God? This ancient claim stood out like a loud billboard sign proclaiming: "YHWH is unfair"! YHWH's controversy has not ceased, nor has it been settled. YHWH's controversy rages on today and awaits a final verdict. Was Israel correct in her allegations against YHWH?

B. Modern Controversy?

The similarity between modern and ancient arguments against Divine Law troubled me. Do we continue YHWH's controversy today? Do we also void YHWH's Divine Law? Or do we honor it?

I began to see that each of us, to some degree, has followed in Israel's footsteps. We substitute our own individual version or our church's version of truth for the actual written words God Himself gave to humanity (Ezek 33:15). We have lost the early Protestant Reformer's cry that truth is obtained through *sola Scriptura*.[15] We deem God's words, His bread of life (Deut 8:3), insufficient for a holistic way of life (Micah 6; Ezekiel 18, 33).

Modern religion continues ancient Israel's accusations by claiming YHWH gave humanity a way of life that is too difficult to observe: The Law is a burden. I had studied enough religions to conclude none within traditional streams of Christianity or Judaism followed the Scriptures as written. Each added to or deleted from them at a whim. My trial of Israel's God (that began in Volume 1) was far from over.

It was the summer of 2001. I wondered if adhering to the actual words of God could reveal truth obscured by men. No study had yet attempted this quest. Could I yet uncover the secret that restores unity and peace to humanity?

I began with the same criteria for the trial of the New Testament as I had for the Old Testament. It would be senseless to discuss history and theology from the New Testament if Jesus never actually existed or if Christianity did not begin with Jesus' mission. If the New Testament could demonstrate reasonable historical validity through external sources, I could consider its written theology and how it enlightens my study from Volume 1.

VI. Out with the Old Rhinestones, in with the New

My investigation in Volume 1 concluded with evidence supporting YHWH's righteousness. But the Old Testament covered an older period in time before God became silent. The New Testament presents more evidence for God's interaction with man. Does the New Testament support the same standard for righteousness as the Hebrew Bible?

My journey now veered onto a new path. The criteria remained the same. I would use the preponderance of the evidence to see if sufficient facts existed to determine whether Jesus really lived. The seven concepts of truth would continue to guide my way. What would I discover? Would I find my beliefs confirmed or would they be unpenned? Does Jesus exist?

Precepts of Truth

Traits	Definition	Text
Truth	The Hebrew *emet* means firm, trustworthy, CONSTANT, enduring, and faithful. This embraces the English definition of Truth, which is: FIDELITY, *CONSTANCY*; the state of being the case: FACT; the body of real things, events, and facts: ACTUALITY; the property (as of a statement) of being in accord with fact or reality	Num 20:1–6; 23:19–20; Isa 40:8; 1 Sam 15:28–29; 2 Kgs 23:14–16; Ps 15:4; 102:27
1. Constancy	Steadfastness of mind under duress: FORTITUDE; *FIDELITY*, LOYALTY; **freedom from change**	Num 30:2; Lev 27:10, 33; Ps 15:4; 89:34; Deut 5:32
2. Fidelity	The quality or state of being *faithful*; accuracy in details: EXACTNESS	Accuracy in its accounts, chronology, requirements withing the Law, written text. (Lev 26; Deut 28)
3. Faithfulness	Steadfast in affection or allegiance: LOYAL; **firm in adherence to promises** or in **observance of duty**: CONSCIENTIOUS	Duet 7:9; 1 Sam 26:23; Ps 36:5; 40:10; 89:1–8; 92:2; 119:75, 86, 90–91, 138; Lam 3:22–23; Isa 25:1; 49:7
4. Righteousness	*Acting in accord* with divine or moral law: free from guilt or sin	Gen 18:25; Deut 25:1; 1 Sam 12:7; 26:23; 2 Sam 22:21, 25; 1 Kgs 8:32; Job 33:26; Ps 5:12; 7:17; 71:19; 119:142. See also Judg 5:11; 2 Chr 12:6; Neh 9:8; Job 36:3; 40:8; Ps 1:6
5. Righteousness Is Not Arbitrary	Arbitrary: depending on individual discretion (like a judge) and not fixed by law; marked by or resulting from unrestrained and often tyrannical exercise of power; based on or determined by individual preference or convenience rather than by necessity or the intrinsic nature of something; existing or coming about seemingly at random or by chance	Gen 18:25; Deut 32:4; Ps 7:17; 11:7; 22:31; 36:6; 45:7; 48:10; 50:6; 71:16, 19; 72:1; 98:2; 119:142; Isa 5:16; 41:10; 42:21; *45:19*; 56:1; Jer 9:24; Ezek 18:25; Dan 9:7; Mic 6:5; Zec 8:8

6. Verifiable: Historicity	Scripture's history or its teachings can be verified and evidenced. Its history can be evidenced through archaeology. Its dietary and purity instructions can be validated through scientific studies. Divine Law can also be tested and verified by the effectiveness of its constitutional, legal, and criminal code in producing a just and moral society	Covers the entire Bible from Genesis to Revelation
Precept of Truth Unique to Divine Law		
7. Dissimilarity	Israel's Divine Law & Theology, her system of justice should be dissimilar to other nations during the time of the Exodus, Judges and Monarchy Periods	*Deut 18:9*; Judg 2:13; 1 Kgs 16:32; 18:25; 23:4–5; *Isa 44:9–46:13*; *Jer 2:8*; *10:1–16*; 11:13, 17; 12:16; 19:5; 23:27; 32:29; Zeph 1:4

12

Historicity of the New Testament: Archaeology

I. EQUAL WEIGHTS AND MEASURES

In Volume 1, I did not appeal to the New Testament to establish the soundness of the Old Testament. Internal consistency demonstrates the validity and reliability of a text.[1] Internal harmony means the authors' facts and ideas do not contradict. This is the first step in determining whether a text is an authentic word of God. Therefore, I established the soundness and validity of the Old Testament based on the internal consistency of the text and the external evidence, such as archaeology, to verify its claims.

External evidence can support or contradict the text. My study specifically tested Scripture to see if it is historically, scientifically (including medically and socially) sound. Validity is based *not only* on accuracy and reliability, but on the betterment of the individual and society.[2] In Volume 1, this was established through archaeology, kings' lists, chronology, written historical material, and scientific support for Israel's laws and her history.

The same holds true for the New Testament. It must demonstrate both internal consistency within itself and consistency with the Old Testament since it claims the Old Testament as its foundation. Like the *Tanakh* (Old Testament), it must also demonstrate historical reliability. Only then can it be considered actual history. Truth always corresponds to reality: real facts and real events. Believing in the stories of Moses, the Exodus, or the Conquest is senseless if these events are fairy tales and did not occur. Likewise, it makes no sense to believe in the New Testament if Jesus never existed, or never obeyed God's instructions, or was never crucified, or never rose again. Thus, history continues to play an essential role in testing the reliability, constancy, and validity of the Bible. Therefore, like Volume 1, we must first investigate whether there was a historical Jesus and whether the New Testament preserves an accurate account of his life, his teachings, and his death before we can assess its theology. If we can establish that a reasonable historical validity exists, then we may consider how this evidence illuminates the theology of the Old Testament, the text that prophesies of Jesus and the New Testament.³ What follows is the evidence that currently exists.

II. ARCHAEOLOGY

Unlike our study of ancient Israel, we have no archaeological (physical) sources to support the historicity of Jesus or the New Testament (with one possible exception, below),⁴ despite claims that the crucifixion nails have been excavated or the shroud in which Jesus was wrapped was discovered. Matteo Borrini, a chemistry professor who tested stain patterns on the Shroud of Turin, claims these ideas are far-fetched, fanciful, and lean towards pseudo-science.⁵ The one exception to physical evidence may be the James Ossuary, which led to a lengthy court battle over forgery.

A. *The James Ossuary*

Around 1980, antiquities collector Oded Golan purchased an ossuary box. An ossuary is a small burial box to place bones after the body decomposes. Physical evidence supporting the historicity of Jesus may come from an inscription on an ossuary box. The evidence in the contentious James Ossuary debate is thus far inconclusive. If authentic, the ossuary would date to *c.* 63 CE and emboldens the claim for a historical Jesus since the inscription on the side of the box reads: "James, son of Joseph, brother of Jesus."⁶

In 2002, Semitic epigrapher André Lemaire declared the ossuary and its inscription authentic.⁷ The following year the Israel Antiquities Authority (IAA) alleged that the inscription

The James Ossuary was on display at the Royal Ontario Museum from November 15, 2002 to January 5, 2003.

was forged. In 2004, the ossuary's owner, Oded Golan, was charged with forgery, fraud, and deception. The protracted trial lasted 5 years. After several paleographic experts declared the inscription authentic, it was referred to scholars outside of Israel. In 2008, an archaeometric analysis conducted by Amnon Rosenfeld, Howard Randall Feldman, and Wolfgang Krumbein strengthened the argument for the ossuary's authenticity.[8] The report concluded the patina (a surface's exposure to air over a long period of time) on the ossuary matched that in the engravings and that microfossils in the inscription seemed naturally deposited.[9]

Another 2020 study involved soil analysis from various tombs around Jerusalem. Scholars concluded that the soil deposits inside the James Ossuary matched those from the Talpiot Tomb and other ossuaries that were known to have been excavated by archaeologists from the Talpiot Tombs.[10] The ossuaries' ties to this burial place are significant since they bear inscriptions naming people the New Testament cites as part of Jesus' family. The most notable of the Talpiot ossuaries were inscribed, "Jesus, son of Joseph," "Mariamene," "Jude, son of Jesus," "Jose," and the inscription in question, "James, son of Joseph, brother of Jesus."[11]

B. The Talpiot Tombs

Two separate tombs in modern east Talpiot were built on an ancient wealthy estate in Jerusalem. These tombs have literally cast forth their dead. The tombs were built less than 200 feet apart.[12] Hidden for centuries by mud and earth, blasting for new construction revealed both tombs in 1980–81. The first tomb, referred to as The Garden Tomb, was hastily and poorly excavated.[13] The second, the Patio Tomb, was never excavated. Religious zealotry prevented thorough excavation and understanding of the tombs when construction exposed their existence.[14]

1. The Garden Tomb

When the initial blast unearthed these tombs, the first was hastily excavated as a salvage operation.[15] It contained ten stone ossuaries with 6–7 lids.[16] Three were unbroken.[17] Seven were broken and six were eventually restored.[18] The difficulty in understanding these artifacts was two-fold: the pressure to cease excavation asserted by the ultra-Orthodox Jews combined with the sparse and incomplete notes left by the archaeologist Joseph Gath made a full understanding of exactly what was discovered in the tomb and where it was discovered woefully incomplete.[19] Gath died before completing the full archaeology report. The most frustrating part in all this is that the ossuaries were never properly cataloged and matched to the attribution numbers from the cave.[20] However, six inscriptions on these ossuaries were published by 1994.[21]

The ossuaries in the Garden Tomb are remarkable since they correspond to people that the New Testament indicates were close to Jesus. The affinity of these names with people in the Bible earned this burial site the controversial name "The Jesus Family Tomb."[22]

In his catalog, Rahmani mentions the following ossuaries:

1. Mary (which appears as Mariamenou Mara—"of Mariamenou Mara")
2. Judah, son of Jesus (Yehudah bar Yeshua)
3. Matya and Mata (contraction of the name Matityahu—Matthew)
4. Jesus, son of Joseph (Yeshua bar Yehoseph)
5. "Joseph" (Yehoseph)
6. Marya

7–9. No inscriptions
10. Missing

Scholars such as Jody Magness assert that, by definition, a "rock-cut" tomb near Jerusalem was a "family tomb."[23] The fifth-mentioned ossuary (above) simply reads "Joseph" (Yehoseph), who Rahmani suggests was the first interred patriarch in this family tomb and Jesus' father, being both Jesus' father and Judah's grandfather. The fourth ossuary, "Jesus son of Joseph" is striking in that it *may* link everyone in this tomb together through the stories in the New Testament.[24] This evidence could be strengthened by James Tabor's proposal that the "James, brother of Jesus" ossuary was originally part of this collection but was later stolen and entered the dark antiquities market.[25]

2. The Patio Tomb's Contents

The Patio Tomb was never excavated and its contents were rearranged during the hasty 1980s archaeological survey. Several names from ossuaries in this tomb have stirred imagination with their similarity to those mentioned in the New Testament. The names mentioned on these ossuaries include:

Mariamene (identified as Mary Magdalene[26])
Yoseh (identified as Joses, the brother of Jesus–Mark 6:3)

Scholars urge caution with reading too much into the similarity of names.[27] This also raises the question as to where Joseph of Arimathea was buried. Does the reference to Joseph refer to him or Jesus' father? What is unprecedented in this discovery were ossuaries that contained traditional early Christian images, which depicted Jonah and the fish (a whale) within a context that hints at a resurrection from the dead.[28] An unprecedented inscription on one box used the divine name (prohibited by Judaism during this era). When James Charlesworth, an expert in Greek and early Christianity, saw the inscription, he read the inscription as, "The Divine Jehovah raises up from [the dead]."[29] Although those interred in this cave may have hoped for a resurrection, their bones remained in the cave.[30]

C. The New Testament on Jesus' Family

According to the New Testament, Jesus' mother, Mary, had 7 children. Joses (Aramaic: *Yoseh*, Greek: *Iōsē*) was Jesus' younger brother (Acts 4:36), who was a consolation to Mary after Jesus' death.[31]

> Is not this the carpenter, the son of Mary, the brother of James, and Joses, and of Juda/Jude, and Simon? And, are not his sisters here with us? And they were offended at him. (Mark 6:3. See also John 2:12; Gal 1:19; Jude 1:1)

> Among which was Mary Magdalene, and Mary the mother of James and Joses, and the mother of Zebedee's children. (Matt 27:56. See also Mark 15:47)

The name Mary is mentioned several times and was quite popular in this account and as attested in archaeological surveys.[32] If Jesus had married Mary Magdalene, we would expect to find at least two Marys in a family tomb (his wife and his mother or daughter).[33]

D. Could the James Ossuary Be the Missing Box?

Despite the heated trial, the geological society has maintained the antiquity of the James' Ossuary inscription.[34] Statistician Professor Camil Fuchs at Tel Aviv University examined the prevalence of Jewish males who died in the 1st century CE. He discovered a less than 1.7% chance of an adult male living in Jerusalem having a father named Joseph and a brother named Jesus. This means that from a statistical analysis, there was only one James who had a brother named Jesus and a father named Joseph: the James referred to in the Bible as being Jesus' brother.[35]

One of the foremost New Testament scholars, Bart Ehrman notes that,

> when the New Testament talks about Jesus' brothers, it uses the Greek word that literally refers to a male sibling. There is a different Greek word for cousin. This other word is not used of James and the others. A plain and straightforward reading of the texts in the Gospels and in Paul leads to an unambiguous result: these "brothers" of Jesus were his actual siblings.[36]

The accounts of Jesus' family from both the ossuaries and the New Testament fit well with the earliest Church historian Hegesippus' written records *(c.* 110–180 CE). According to Eusebius, Hegesippus (our only surviving source), wrote a 5-volume set on early church history, which included a list of Bishops.[37] In Eusebius' *Ecclesiastical History*, he quotes from Hegesippus.[38] Several of Hegesippus' writings in *Hypomnemata*, his memoir on early Church history, mentions Jesus' family in four separate accounts.

Eusebius quotes Hegesippus' 5th Volume as referring to "James, who was called the brother of our Lord."

The charge of the Church passed to James the brother of the Lord, together with the Apostles. He was called the 'Just' by all men from the Lord's time to ours, since many are called James, but he was holy from his mother's womb. (*Eccl Hist* 2.234–5)[39]

In a later book, Eusebius mentions Simeon, the son of the Lord's uncle Clopas who was "a cousin of the Lord" and became a bishop in the Church on account of his family relationship to Jesus (4.22.4).[40] Hegesippus also upholds the claim of Jude 1:1 by acknowledging Jude as Jesus' brother. "Now there still survived of the family of the Lord grandsons of Judas, who was said to have been his brother according to the flesh, and they were delated [reported for the crime] as being of the family of David" (3.20.1).[41] The earliest Church records of Jesus (by Saint Hegesippus) appear very comfortable with Mary's children and their family relationships to Jesus.[42]

E. Observations and Conclusions

If authentic, the ossuaries' connection to the Talpiot Garden and Patio tombs challenges traditional religious assumptions. It grants historicity to people like James, Jose, Judah, and Mary Magdalene as having existed in Jesus' life.[43] However, it challenges the Catholic Church's and early Protestant Reformer's theology on the Perpetual Virginity of Mary.[44] At the very least, the tomb brings into question the prudish doctrine that places unfounded value on perpetual virginity (an idea that contradicts the Abrahamic Covenant's promises of many children[45]) since Mary had 5 sons. This tomb also brings into question the Bible's silence on Jesus' personal life. Other ossuaries from the tomb indicate Jesus married Mary Magdalene, fathered children, and his body was buried in the family tomb.[46]

Archaeologist David Graves remarks, "The claims, if true, would negate the resurrection and possibly nullify the Christian faith."[47] While the general consensus is thus far in the affirmative for the James Ossuary,[48] our investigation will consider this artifact and its greater implications for the Talpiot Tombs as a cautious possibility. This leaves extrabiblical texts as the primary exhibits by which we can validate or debunk the New Testament's accounts.

13

Historicity of the New Testament: Greek & Roman Sources

I. NEW TESTAMENT IN EXTRABIBLICAL WRITTEN SOURCES

Extrabiblical sources mentioning people in the Bible cannot prove a person existed. Early accounts can only corroborate a claim that a historical person existed or that an event took place (e.g., the deportation of Israel, which is attested in the Old Testament and Assyrian inscriptions). Thus, the verdict, similar to a court trial, must rely on the preponderance of the evidence.[1] With a void of archaeological evidence, our study will rely on the data we possess: written sources that refer to Christianity, Christ, and Jesus.

Non-Christian sources are the most reliable since no apparent agenda exists for supporting Christianity or its ideals.[2] Sources are usually divided into two categories: Roman and Jewish. Despite their hype, the Dead Sea Scrolls do not mention Jesus or his followers.[3] While no first-century Greek or Roman author mentions Jesus by name, they do refer to a "Christ" and to "Christians."[4] Three non-Christian and non-Jewish Roman sources exist for early Christianity. All three sources were written less than a hundred years of Jesus' lifetime.

II. ROMAN OFFICIALS

A. Pliny the Younger

The earliest surviving reference to Jesus is in the writings of Pliny the Younger, a lawyer installed as governor of the Roman province Bithynia-Pontus in Asia Minor (modern-day Turkey). He was a contemporary of Hegesippus (whom we met in the previous chapter).

Pliny is termed "the Younger" to distinguish him from his uncle, Pliny "the Elder," the natural scientist and historian who perished in 79 CE during the eruption of Mt. Vesuvius, which claimed Pompeii. Pliny the Younger's reference to Christianity occurs within a series of letters written to Emperor Trajan seeking his advice for governing his province. Letter 10

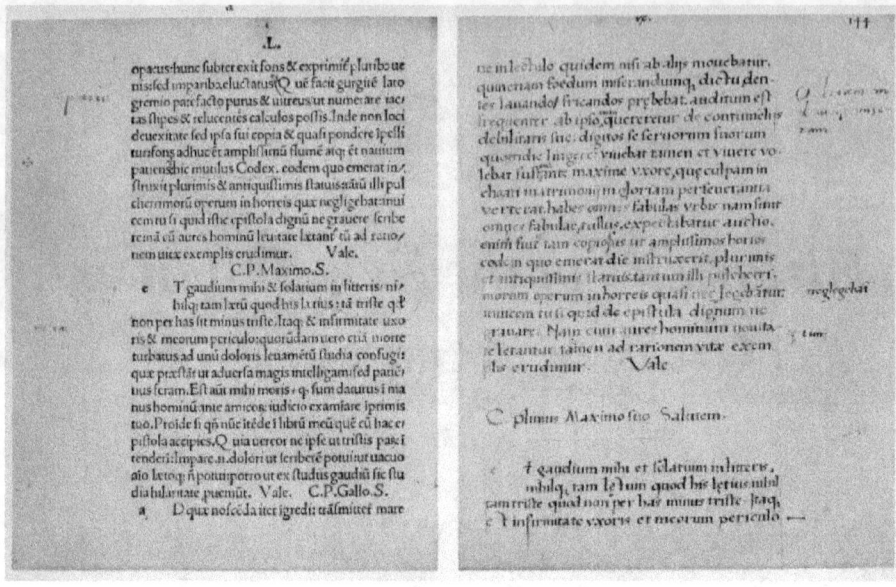

A Sixth-Century Fragment of the Letters of Pliny the Younger.
(Courtesy of Elias Avery Lowe and Edward Kennard Rand, Project Gutenberg)

(*Epistulae X.96*) to Trajan, dates to 112 CE, specifically mentions "Christ" and "Christians." It is the first known document to describe Christian worship and persecution.[5]

The background to Pliny's letter began with Rome's subjugation of Judea and the eastern states. Deprived of independence, the conquered peoples sought emancipation. Groups banded together to unshackle Rome's iron grip. The Jews revolted in 39-40 and 67-70 CE. This led to the emperor passing a law making it illegal for people to gather in social groups. Those who ignored this decree were executed. Having just assumed the governorship (c. 109-111 CE), Pliny began interrogating Christians whose habit was worshiping together. Pliny sought to ascertain if leniency could be applied to three situations: (1) adolescents due to their age; (2) defendants who proved they were not Christian by recanting twice and "cursing Christ;" and (3) to those who also worshipped the emperor, or was being outed as a Christian enough to warrant execution?[6] Pliny also asks if anonymously written accusations were admissible evidence.

This is the bulk of Pliny's correspondence.

Having never been present at trials of the Christians, I am unacquainted with the method and limits to be observed either in examining or punishing them. Whether any difference is to be made on account of age, or no distinction allowed between the youngest and the adult; whether repentance admits to a pardon, or if a man has been once a Christian it avails him nothing to recant; whether the mere profession of Christianity, albeit without crimes, or only the crimes associated therewith are

> punishable... In the meanwhile, the method I have observed towards those who have been denounced to me as Christians is this: I interrogated them whether they were Christians. If they confessed it, I repeated the question twice again, adding the threat of capital punishment. If they still persevered, I ordered them to be executed.... Those who denied they were, or had ever been, Christians, who repeated after me an invocation to the gods and offered adoration, with wine and frankincense, to your (Trajan's) image, which I had ordered to be brought for that purpose, together with those of the gods, and who finally cursed Christ—none of which acts, it is said, those who are really Christians can be forced into performing—these I thought it proper to discharge... (even if) they had been of that persuasion but had quitted it, (a.) **some 3 years, others many years, and a few as much as 25 years ago**. They all worshipped your statue and the images of the gods, and cursed Christ. (*Epistulae* X.96, parentheses and emphasis added for clarification)[7]

The greatest revelation (a.) from Pliny's letter is that Christians had existed in Turkey since at least 85 CE—25 years before Pliny's governorship. This harmonizes with accounts in the Books of Acts, Romans, and Corinthians of Paul's and the Apostles' missionary journeys throughout the Roman Empire. Thus, 85 CE—about 50 years after Jesus' death—would represent the earliest secular account of Christians in Asia Minor.[8]

Pliny continues,

> They affirmed, however, the whole of their guilt or their error, was, **(b.) that they were in the habit of meeting on a certain fixed day before it was light when they sang in alternate verses a hymn to Christ, as a god**, and bound themselves by solemn oath not to any wicked deeds, but never to commit any fraud, theft, or adultery, never to falsify their word, nor deny trust when they should be called upon to deliver it up; after which it was their custom to separate, and then reassemble to partake of food—but food of an ordinary and innocent kind. Even this practice, however, they had abandoned after the publication of my edict, by which, according to your orders, I had forbidden political associations. I judged it so much the more necessary to extract the real truth with the assistance of torture from two female slaves, who were styled 'deaconesses'. But I could discover nothing more than depraved and excessive superstition.[9]

Scholars offer varying opinions as to the crime Christians committed, other than bearing the name of a group that opposed Roman rule and refrained from emperor worship.[10] Pliny's account opposes modern views that the worship of Jesus as God did not originate until the Council of Nicaea in 325 CE.[11] In their earliest practice, Christians worshipped Christ as God.[12] They expressed worship (b.) through a morning ritual where Christians sang songs to Christ.[13] While this text does not identify Jesus as the Christian Christ, it corroborates the New Testament's descriptions of people worshiping Jesus as God.[14]

Pliny's letter on the handling of Christians provides an independent witness, which validates that Christianity existed in the 1st century CE. It corroborates the rudiments of the New Testament account where Christians worshipped Christ as God, giving us a first-hand report of Christianity's influence on the Roman Empire.

B. *Tacitus*

1. Tacitus on Christianity

A faithful friend of Pliny the Younger, Publius Cornelius Tacitus (56–120 CE), was a Roman senator and historian. In 97 CE, he became Consul of Asia.[15] Part of their correspondence is preserved in Pliny's book, *Letters* (mentioned in the Pliny section above).[16] Physical evidence of Tacitus' life is also attested by a tomb inscription.[17] While he authored several books, he is best known for two: the *Annals of Imperial Rome* and the *Histories*.[18] Unfortunately, both surviving texts contain large lacunae (gaps from damage).[19] The years when Jesus would have been most active and his trial discussed are part of this gap (29–32 CE).[20] Tacitus wrote *Annals* in 115 CE. He provided facts that appear to corroborate the death of Christ and persecution of the early Church. According to Tacitus, a "mischievous superstition" started in Judea and spread to Rome. This superstition originated from a "Christus," whom Pontius Pilate put to death during the reign of Emperor Tiberius.

> Christus, from whom the name had its origin, suffered the extreme penalty during the reign of Tiberius at the hands of one of our procurators, Pontius Pilatus, and a most mischievous superstition, thus checked for the moment, again broke out not only in Judaea, the first source of the evil, but even in Rome, where all things hideous and shameful from every part of the world find their center and become popular. (Tacitus, *Annals* 15.44)[21]

Emperor Nero rounded up and executed Rome's Christians in the most public, painful, and humiliating ways. His persecution of heretical Christians and Jews was later inherited by the Church of Rome. Tacitus tells us that Christians were crucified, some "rolled in pitch and set aflame while still alive to light Nero's gardens; others were wrapped in fresh animal skins and wild dogs set on them, tearing them to shreds."[22]

According to Tacitus, Nero wanted to restructure Rome into a city worthy of his name. Facing opposition, a fire mysteriously broke out in the most opportune part of the city in 64 CE, where merchants stored flammable goods. Strong winds hurled flames across the city. Thugs, claiming to act on the Emperor's orders, threw torches on the inferno and forbade extinguishing them. The fire raged for six days. Of 14 districts, only 4 survived intact. To make matters worse, rumors circulated that during the fire, Nero (known for his ample voice) had mounted a stage and sang of the destruction of Troy. Rumors of Nero's involvement seemed confirmed when he began constructing an outrageously elaborate palace and restructured the entire city (Tacitus, *Annals* XV.38–42).[23] Public sentiment was on the verge of revolution when Nero devised a solution: blame the Christians.

> But neither human help nor imperial munificence (lavish gifts), nor all the modes of placating Heaven, could stifle scandal or dispel the belief that the fire had taken place by order. Therefore, to scotch the rumor, Nero substituted as culprits and punished with the utmost refinements of cruelty, a class of men, loathed for their vices, whom the crowd styled Christians. . . . First, then, the confessed members of the sect were arrested; next, on their disclosures, vast numbers were convicted, not so much on the count of arson as for hatred of the human race. And derision accompanied their end: they were covered with wild beasts' skins and torn to death by dogs, or they were fastened on crosses and, when daylight failed, were burned to serve as lamps by night. Nero had offered his Gardens for the spectacle and gave an exhibition in his Circus, mixing with the crowd in the habit of a chariotever or mounted on his car. Hence, in spite of the guilt which had earned the most exemplary punishment, there arose a sentiment of pity, due to the impression that they were being sacrificed not for the welfare of the state but to the ferocity of a single man. (*Annals*, XV.44, parentheses and emphasis added for clarity)[24]

Tacitus shares several important facts. First, Christ was executed by Pilate, who served under Tiberius. This fact is compelling since Luke 3:1 also refers to Tiberius being Emperor at the time of Jesus. Second, Pilate was the Prefect of Judea during Jesus' trial, as attested in the New Testament. While we have other extra-biblical references to Pilate, Tacitus is the lone Roman source to associate Pilate with Jesus' trial and subsequent death. This is significant since Pilate's hand in Jesus' death is mentioned in every Gospel account. Third, the Christian "mischievous superstition" began in Judea, then spread to Rome. This again substantiates the New Testament's scenario where Christianity originated in Judea and spread across the Roman Empire. Tacitus supports Pliny's assertion that Christianity had spread throughout the Empire by the time he came into office, and Christianity had spread to Rome *within one generation (30 years) of Jesus's death*.

Fourth, when Rome burned in 64 CE, Christianity had enough members for Nero to pin Rome's destruction on them, indicating their numbers were likely in the hundreds, if not thousands. That Christians could become a scapegoat to expunge Nero's alleged crime demonstrates that Nero considered them a significant political threat. This point is often overlooked in discussions on early Christianity. If Jesus is the Christ to whom Tacitus refers, *then the first persecutions of Christians began by 65 CE, within the first generation of Christians. This was less than 30 years after Jesus's death*. This is consistent with Pliny's account, which indicates Christian persecution was an ongoing policy of Rome's emperors by 109 CE when Pliny became governor. Thus, Tacitus' account, from a pagan Roman official, independently corroborates the tenets of the early church in the New Testament.[25]

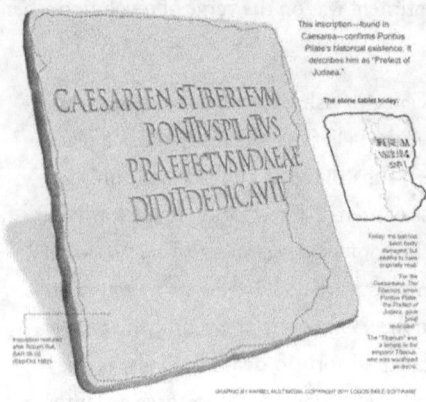

© Faithlife Corporation, makers of Logos Bible Software – www.logos.com

Pontius Pilate's Incription

To the Divine Augusti [this]
Tiberieum...Pontius
Pilate... prefect of Judea
...has dedicated [this].

2. Pontius Pilate Inscription

We also have physical evidence for Pontius Pilate. Discovered during excavations in 1961 on the coast at Caesarea Maritima, an inscription by Pilate confirms he was Prefect of Judea during Tiberius' reign. While Tacitus does not specifically mention Jesus by name, there is no other known story or scenario that fits the evidence other than the accounts mentioned in the Gospels and in the Book of Acts.[26] Tacitus is the lone extra-biblical Roman source to link Pilate to Jesus' trial and execution.

C. Suetonius

Gaius Suetonius Tranquillus (*c.* 69–130/40 CE) was a lawyer, poet, and another friend of Pliny the Younger. His book *De Vita Caesarum* is a biography of the lives of the first 12 Caesars. During Claudius Caesar's reign (41–54 CE), Suetonius refers to an instigator termed "Chrestus" within the Jewish community in Rome around 49 CE.[27]

> Since the Jews constantly made disturbances at the instigation of Chrestus, he expelled them from Rome. (*The Life of Claudius* 25.4)[28]

The term "Chrestus" is generally accepted to be a variant Latin spelling of "Christus."[29] This is possibly another Roman reference to "Christ." Unfortunately, "Chrestus" is ambiguous.[30] Many religious and nationalist zealots led Jewish uprisings during the first and early second centuries (CE). 'Chrestus' is also a Greek name, which does not provide any clarity.[31] Suetonius'

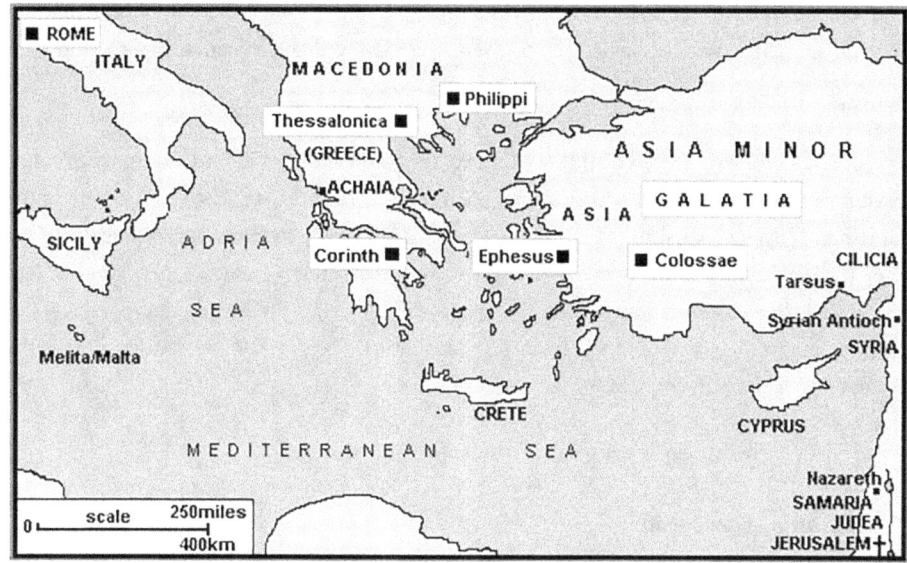

Places to which Paul and the Apostles traveled or sent letters according to the New Testament. Map courtesy of Gordon Smith. http://www.ccel.org/bible/phillips/JBPhillips.htm

account, however, is perhaps corroborated by a similar reference to Christian persecution in Rome within the Book of Acts.

> After these things, Paul departed from Athens and came to Corinth; And found a certain Jew named Aquila, born in Pontus, *lately come from Italy*, with his wife Priscilla; (*because that Claudius had commanded all Jews to depart from Rome*:) and came to them. (Acts 18:1–2)

The Book of Acts tells us Aquila and Priscilla converted to Christianity before meeting Paul in Corinth. While the author of Acts may have Suetonius' event in mind, there were other messianic pretenders in Rome.[32] Although the evidence in *Claudius* 25 is inconclusive, Suetonius' account of Christians during the reign of Nero bolsters the New Testament's accounts that Christianity spread rapidly throughout the Roman Empire and was met with brutally repressive measures. Suetonius' record demonstrates that persecution of Christians occurred before 54 CE (when Claudius I died), less than 25 years after Jesus' death.

In his discussion on Nero, Suetonius (like Tacitus) refers to Christians persecuted for their "new superstitions."[33]

> During his (Claudius I's) reign many abuses were severely punished and put down, and no fewer new laws were made: a limit was set to expenditures; the public

banquets were confined to a distribution of food... Punishment was inflicted on the Christians, a class of men given to a new and mischievous superstition. (Nero 16.2)[34]

Suetonius' statement agrees with that of Pliny the Younger's and Tacitus' accounts of interrogations and executions of Christians for their "superstitions" that deprived the state of the Christians' loyalty (worship of Caesar) and tax oblations, which were usually offered to the state (i.e., to Caesar) in the form of offerings. Suetonius attributes Rome's "Christian abuse" to the group's "mischievous superstition."[35] Thus, the impartial, if not hostile, surviving sources from Roman officials uphold the historical account of Christianity as recorded within the Book of Acts, the Epistles, and the Gospels.

III. PAGAN WRITERS

A. Lucian of Samosata

Pagan writers constitute a second group that had no interest in furthering Christianity. Their writings contribute to another ancient observation of early Christianity. Lucian was a Syrian writer who lived c. 115–200 CE.[36] Above all, he was a satirist, ridiculing everything to expose deceit (like the modern Babylon Bee or Onion). He mocked the sacred to expose hypocrisy. In *The Death of Peregrine*, he ridiculed the Christians' naivete in being duped into following Peregrine, a charismatic con artist who killed his father and became a leader second only to Jesus within Christian groups.[37]

> It was now that he (Peregrine) came across the priests and scribes of the Christians in Palestine and picked up their queer creed. I can tell you, he soon convinced them of his superiority: prophet, elder, ruler of the Synagogue—he was everything at once; expounded their books, commented on them, wrote books himself. They took him for a god, accepted his laws, and declared him their president. **The Christians, you know, worship a *man* to this day—the distinguished personage who introduced their novel rites and was crucified on that account.** Well, the end of it was that Peregrinus was arrested and thrown into prison... The Christian communities put themselves to the expense of sending deputations, with offers of sympathy, assistance, and legal advice (to Peregrine). The activity of these people in dealing with any matter that affects their community is something extraordinary. They spare no trouble, no expense. Peregrine, all this time, was making quite an income on the strength of his bondage; money came pouring in.[38] (Parentheses and emphasis added for clarification)

Lucian confirms that "Christians" worshipped a man who introduced a new creed and was crucified. Like Pliny, Lucian corroborates that Christians worshipped this man as early as

130 CE (well before the Council of Nicaea). Lucian understands the man who Christians worshipped to be a sage or teacher (rabbi) who introduced new religious ceremonies into his sect. The church also had a strong support system for its members.

Lucian continues,

> You see, these misguided creatures start with the general conviction that they are immortal for all time, which explains the contempt of death and voluntary self-devotion, which are so common among them; and then it was impressed on them **by their original lawgiver** that they are all brothers, from the moment that they are converted, and **deny the gods of Greece, and worship the crucified sage, and live after his laws**. All this they take quite on trust, with the result that **they despise all worldly goods alike, regarding them merely as common property**. Now an adroit, unscrupulous fellow, who has seen the world, has only to get among these simple souls, and his fortune is soon made; he plays with them.[39]

Lucian understood the Christian godman to be a lawgiver from Palestine (cf. Gal 6:2; Rom 3:27; James 2:12).[40] Christians believed in "immortality" and life after death. He also relates that Christians lived according to a set of laws *and* denied pagan gods. He criticized the Christians' naivete in accepting any "evangelist" (like Peregrine) who claimed to understand Scripture and their tendency towards emotionalism rather than relying on facts.[41] Lucian demonstrates a vague understanding of charismatic Christian preachers, who can easily lead the flock astray. Further, he is aware of the Christian affinity as a brotherhood. He corroborates the accounts in Acts (2:45; 4:34–5:1–8), where *Christians despised wealth, lived off a general fund, and denied personal property.*[42]

Lucian's account reveals he was only vaguely familiar with Christians. He claimed their leaders were priests, conflating them with Judaism. However, many early Christians likely followed the priests and the teachings of Jesus at the same time, just as they would have any other rabbi. Lucian considered Christians to practice a "new form of [mystical] initiation" like the pagan cults of his day. This charge was also levied by Celsus, another pagan philosopher (see B. below). Lucian's overall derogatory tone, "that one whom they still worship today" (§11); "that first lawgiver of theirs'" (§13); "that crucified sophist" (§13), demonstrates he was relating his view of Christianity as he saw it in his day.[43] Despite his bias and ill–regard of this new sect, Lucian corroborates the basic tenets of the Christian faith that existed long before 160 CE, and 165 years before the first Council of Nicaea.[44]

B. Celsus

Celsus was a 2nd–century (CE) Greek philosopher and polytheist (a believer in multiple gods). His famous work, *On the True Doctrine* (c. 175 CE), wherein he criticized Christianity is lost. About 70 years after his death, Origen, one of the earliest Church scholars, felt the need to respond to Celsus' criticisms. Between 60–90% of the original text was incorporated into

Origen's lengthy response, *Against Celsus*.⁴⁵ That Origen felt motivated to respond to Celsus' 70-year-old allegations demonstrates the impact Celsus' charges had on the early Church.

Celsus' criticism of Christianity reveals just how widespread this new religion had become long before Celsus wrote his treatise. His criticism acknowledges the universal views held by the early Christian sects that believed Jesus was born of a virgin, crucified, and resurrected.

> Who has not heard the fable of Jesus' birth from a virgin or the stories of his crucifixion and resurrection?⁴⁶

This pagan philosopher was also familiar with stories of the magi, Herod's plot against Jesus, and the family's trip to Egypt.⁴⁷ The text of the New Testament existed to the extent that Celsus could quote from the crucifixion account of Jesus' pleading on the cross.⁴⁸

Around 100–130 years after Jesus' death (3–4 generations later), Celsus acknowledges that Christians disdained idolatry and met in groups under pain of death from Roman officials. Prayers were invoked in the name of Jesus, who was known to work miracles (although Celsus attributes it to magic).

> The cult of Christ is a secret society whose members huddle together in corners for fear of being brought to trial and punishment . . . They practice their rites in secret in order to avoid the sentence of death that looms over them. . . . Take their aversion to what they term idolatry. . . . The Christians . . . are always incorporating the name of Jesus and a short story about him in the formula . . . Jesus himself was taught to work wonders using magic and incantations.⁴⁹

While Celsus criticizes many aspects of Christianity, he finds the ease with which this new religion preyed on society's uneducated poor and simple, coupled with its lack of accountability, to be most appalling. He writes that the Christian belief in the resurrection, afterlife, and final judgment was "nothing new" to the world's pagan religions.⁵⁰ He compares the Christian philosophical view and reliance on faith alone to that of the Roman Savior–deity Mithras and the cults of Sabazius or Hecate.

> Just as the charlatans of the cults take advantage of a simpleton's lack of education to lead him around by the nose, so too with Christian teachers: they do not want to give or to receive reasons for what they believe. Their favorite expressions are "Do not ask questions, just believe!" and: "Your faith will save you!" . . . They discourage asking questions of any sort.⁵¹

Celsus continues his polemic, comparing Christian beliefs in savior deities to other cults of his day and pointing out how much they shared in common.⁵² The fatal flaw with Christianity for Celsus is taking the mystery rites literally. Pagans had used these same rites (e.g., the Passion of Christ) as methods for teaching virtue.

Ironically, Celsus appears to have read the Hebrew Scriptures when he condemns Jews who followed Jesus for "turning aside from the faith of their fathers" and "deserting Israel for another name."[53] He further asserts that Jesus had profaned the Sabbath,[54] and those who followed him were deceived.

> Worst of all, he managed to convince you to follow him in his profanity and lying, or those of you who appeared ready to be deceived. He is a liar, because while respecting on occasion the outward forms of our observances, yet he did not hesitate to abandon them for the sake of convenience: circumcision, the feasts of new moons, the distinction between what is clean and unclean. All of this was done for the deceitful purpose of winning over the Jews, only thereafter to lead them astray. The one who will punish the unrighteous will come from God, and on that day, how you will despise this Jesus![55]

> What could be sillier than what the Christians call wisdom! The god of the Jews, their great lawgiver (say the Christians) made a mistake. Be it so: then why do you accept his laws as being worth following—why take these laws and interpret them as allegories? Why do you so grudgingly worship this Creator, you hypocrites, when he promised the Jews everything—that he would make their race prosper, that he would raise them up from the dead in their own flesh and blood—this same God who inspired the prophets? Yet you pour abuse on him! But when you Christians find things made difficult for you by the Jews, you come around and say that you worship the same God as they do! What is to be believed? For when your master, Jesus, lays down laws contrary to those laid down by Moses, in whom the Jews put their faith, you immediately undertake to find another God, one who is different from the Father.[56]

Celsus does not hold back harsh criticism. He finds the vast divisions between the many sects of early Christianity perplexing and disturbing.[57] His treatise reveals that by at least 150 CE, the accounts within the New Testament were well-known and disseminated throughout the Roman Empire. So well-known and available were these stories in 175 CE that Celsus could quote from a "New Testament" account of Jesus' life.[58] Because his views are not favorable to Christianity, his feelings towards Christians demonstrate that he had no agenda to create or support the general tenets of the faith. Celsus' accounts corroborate the beliefs of the early Christian faith before 170 CE and the first council of Nicaea, thus demonstrating the basic story of Christ was well-known before Celsus lived.[59]

14

Historicity of the New Testament: Jewish Sources

I. VALUE OF JEWISH SOURCES

Non-Christian Jewish sources provide a unique view of early Roman Judea. They also grant insight into popular religious and political ideals before and after Jesus' life. Most Jews did not accept Jesus as a Messiah or Savior. Their independent testimony brings to focus the turbulent era of Roman occupation and the Jews' response to it. Since Jewish authors were not partial to Christianity, they constitute another disinterested source for verifying the historicity of the New Testament.

II. JOSEPHUS

Our investigation is not only interested in validity but also in beliefs held by and described within the New Testament. Josephus allows us to turn back the pages written by modern man-made theologies to reveal beliefs once held by those whose histories it records.

Flavius Josephus is one of the most important ancient history writers. Born into an aristocratic family about seven years after Jesus' death (*c.* 40 CE), his works preserve Jewish history while attempting to resolve conflict with the past. One of his first books, *Jewish Wars*, details the conflicts in Judea from Antiochus IV Epiphanes to Titus (164 BCE–75 CE). Many of the latter conflicts Josephus narrates since he was personally involved.

During the Jewish uprising against Rome in 66 CE, Josephus served as general of the Jewish troops in the Galilee. He became known as a turncoat after he reneged on a suicide pact with his soldiers when defeat was certain. Surviving his army's martyrdom, he was taken to the Roman general Vespasian.

Not losing the advantage, Josephus "prophesied" that God had revealed to him that Vespasian was destined to become emperor of Rome. Fortunately for Josephus, the "prophecy" was fulfilled three years later after Nero's suicide when three emperors failed to succeed. Once Vespasian became emperor, he left his son Titus to complete the siege of Jerusalem.

Josephus, who considered himself a pious Jew, served as an interpreter for the Romans when Jerusalem fell in 70 CE. Any Jews who opposed Rome were slaughtered while the Second Temple and the city were razed. Josephus again came out of the situation for the better. Not forgetting Josephus' "prophecy," Vespasian relocated Josephus to Rome, providing him with a prestigious position and patronage for his history writing. Thus, in an odd irony, we have Rome to thank for preserving on paper the history of Israel, which it destroyed physically in war.

A. John the Baptist

1. The Text

About 60 years after Jesus' death, in 93 CE, Josephus released his magnum opus, *Antiquities of the Jews*, a 21-volume account of the history of the Jews from Adam to Josephus' own day. His books discuss several people named Jesus and the events surrounding John the Baptist (*Ant* 18.5.2).[1] Josephus devotes far more attention to John the Baptist than to Jesus, whom he mentions in passing. Josephus' account is not only enlightening due to its parallel to biblical accounts but also because it sheds light on John's original theology.

Josephus begins his account of John the Baptist by describing the destruction of Herod's army, which the Jews considered retribution for John's death.

> But to some of the Jews, the destruction of Herod's army seemed to be divine vengeance, and certainly a just vengeance, for his treatment of John, surnamed the Baptist. For Herod had put him to death, though he was a good man and **had exhorted the Jews to lead righteous lives, to practice justice [*dikaiosynē*] towards their fellows and piety [*eusebeia*] towards God**, and so doing to join in baptism. In his view, this was a necessary preliminary if baptism was to be acceptable to God. **They must not employ it to gain pardon for whatever sins they had committed, but as consecration of the body implying that the soul *was already cleansed by right behavior*.** When others too joined the crowds about him, because they were aroused to the highest degree by his sermons, Herod became alarmed.

> Eloquence that had so great an effect on mankind might lead to some form of sedition, for it looked as if they would be guided by John in everything that they did. Herod decided therefore that it would be much better to strike first and be rid of him before his work led to an uprising, than to wait for an upheaval, get involved in a difficult situation and see his mistake. Though John, because of Herod's suspicions, was brought in chains to Machaerus, the stronghold that we have previously mentioned, and there put to death, yet the verdict of the Jews was that the destruction visited upon Herod's army was a vindication of John, since God saw

fit to inflict such a blow on Herod. (*Ant* 18.5.2,[2] brackets and bolding added for emphasis clarification)

Josephus' account is in general harmony with the Gospels (Matthew 14:3–11 and Mark 6:16–29). The New Testament's reason for Herod's killing of John the Baptist was John's outspoken criticism of Herod's affair with his brother's wife. Josephus' account fits well into this scenario, even though Josephus never mentioned Herod's affair. Instead of highlighting the final incident that induced John's demise, Josephus focuses on John the Baptist's mission at large, crediting his anti-establishment movement as the overall motive for Herod's evil act. Thus, Herod likely killed John the Baptist for his charismatic ability to lead a revolt and for his criticism of Herod's affair with his brother's wife.[3]

Josephus' account of John the Baptist is considered authentic by most scholars.[4] Steve Mason, one of the foremost scholars on Josephus, remarks that Josephus describes John's teaching according to his "usual way of describing Jewish ethical responsibility. Against the charges that Jews were atheists and haters of humanity, he says that all Jewish customs (*ethē*) are concerned with 'piety [toward God] and justice [toward humanity]."[5] Josephus' depiction of Judaism's values reflects the popular morality of the Greco–Roman world.[6] Josephus' overall aim presented Judaism as a philosophical tradition that embraces the world's highest values.[7] Josephus includes John the Baptist in his list of pious Jewish philosophers who opposed Roman rule. Surprisingly, Josephus does not connect John the Baptist to Christianity or to Jesus but considers him a man with his own message for Judea and his own independent following (Matt 3:1–12; Mark 6:29; Luke 7:19–20[8]).

2. John the Baptist's Theology

Josephus' account allows us to peel back the layers of man-made theology to reveal John the Baptist's original teaching. Josephus offers a striking independent confirmation of John's requirement that people first repent and commit to behave righteously before coming for immersion. As Josephus words it, "They must not employ it [baptism] to gain pardon for whatever sins they had committed, but as a consecration of the body, implying that the soul was already cleansed by right behavior" (*Ant* 18.5.2).[9] While this doctrine challenges modern theology that righteous works and righteous behavior are contrary to a theology of faith, it is the doctrine the New Testament confirms John upheld.

Matthew 3:7–10	Luke 3:7–9
But when he saw many of the Pharisees and Sadducees come to his baptism, he said to them.	Then said he to the multitude that came forth to be baptized of him.

> "O generation of vipers, who has warned you to flee from the wrath to come? **Produce, therefore, fruits meet for repentance**: And think not to say within yourselves, We have Abraham to our father: for I say to you, that God is able of these stones to raise up children to Abraham. And now also the axe is laid to the root of the trees: therefore every tree which brings not forth good fruit is hewn down, and cast into the fire."

> "O generation of vipers, who has warned you to flee from the wrath to come? **Produce, therefore, fruits worthy of repentance**, and begin not to say within yourselves, We have Abraham to our father: for I say to you, That God is able of these stones to raise up children to Abraham. And now also the axe is laid to the root of the trees: every tree therefore which brings not forth good fruit is hewn down, and cast into the fire."

John's message, as recorded in the New Testament, like Josephus' account, calls for Jews to repent from sin and produce righteousness: the fruit of repentance.[10] John accuses the Judeans of trusting in their pedigree from Abraham rather than the way of justice and judgment that Abraham taught (Gen 18:19; 26:5). John warns that if the people of Judea do not repent (and their lives manifest repentance), then they will be judged for it. Josephus seems to have accurately grasped the context of John's message.[11] This exactness to detail aids in establishing a reasonable validity to the accounts within the New Testament.

B. James, Brother of Jesus

Josephus was very good at introducing his subjects and familiarizing his reader with references to people, then referring to them again in a related context. His treatment of James pre-supposes the reader is familiar with Jesus. Josephus' reference to Jesus with James served to distinguish James from the many other men who bore the same name during this era. Josephus' usage implies that Jesus was so well-known as to be a distinguishable person and that the relationship between James and his brother Jesus was well-known.

The reference to James in Book 20 of *Antiquities* occurs in the context of the violent internal fighting within the Jewish high priesthood, where tactics of robbery, stone-fighting, and starvation were employed within the Jewish priesthood (*Ant* 20.179).[12] The Roman governor Felix had died, and the new governor, Albinus, was traveling to replace him. With all the in-fighting, Herod's great-grandson, Agrippa II, revoked the high priest's office from a man named Joseph and gave it to Annanus (the son of Annanus). Josephus remembers this high priest as "arrogant in manner and an extremely brash man," known for his harsh legal Saducean judgments. He was "very rigid in judging offenders above all the rest of the Jews." (*Ant* 20.9.1).[13] With the Roman procurator's death, Annanus wanted to exercise his power and show force to his rivals.

So he assembled the Sanhedrin of judges, and brought before them **the brother of Jesus who was so-called Christ**, whose name was James and some of his companions. And when he had formed an accusation against them as breakers of the law, he delivered them to be stoned. (*Ant* 20.9.1, emphasis added)[14]

Annanus did not convene the formal Sanhedrin court but an informal court with lesser accountability.[15] Jewish factions found this act "intolerable." Some appealed to Albinus, the new Roman governor. Others appealed directly to King Agrippa, who then removed Annanus from office after he had held the position for only 3 months.

Few scholars question the validity of Josephus' reference to James or to him being Jesus' brother.[16] The language used in this account is typical of Josephus. The storytelling is also typical of Josephus. Many translations, unfortunately, leave out the term "so-called" that appears in the original text. The phrase "so-called Christ" indicates Josephus' reluctance and discomfort with this term. Josephus was simply reporting what some people had called Jesus, which was Christ.[17] This leaves us with the final reference relevant to our study: Josephus' mention of Jesus.

C. Jesus: Testimonium Flavianum

1. The Text and Its Historical Setting

The section where Josephus mentions Jesus has become known as "The Testimony of Josephus," which recognizes Josephus by his first name, "Flavius" (see the Latin title above). Josephus' mention of James in connection with Jesus implies a link to Christianity. The text referring to James is straightforward. The *testimonium flavianum* is problematic. Because the peculiar wording and ideas in the text did not exist until the 2nd to 4th centuries CE, there is much debate on whether Josephus wrote these passages or whether they were added by later editors since Josephus' works were preserved solely by Christian translators.[18]

The reference to Jesus occurs in the broader context of Pilate's problematic governorship and continual incitement of Jews by either placing idols in Jerusalem (*Ant* 18:3.1) or stealing from the Temple's funds (*Ant* 18.3.2). The section also covers the uprisings and tumults, painting "a picture of escalating tension for Jews around the world."[19] It is within the overall context of instability, deception, and tumult that Josephus mentions Jesus.[20]

> Now there was about this time Jesus, a wise man, if it be lawful to call him a man; for he was a doer of wonderful works, a teacher of such men as receive the truth with pleasure. He drew over to him both many of the Jews and many of the Gentiles. He was [the] Christ. And when Pilate, at the suggestion of the principal men amongst us, had condemned him to the cross, those that loved him at the first did not forsake him; for he appeared to them alive again the third day; as the divine prophets had

foretold these and ten thousand other wonderful things concerning him. And the tribe of Christians, so named from him, are not extinct at this day. (*Ant* 18.3.3)

The reason most scholars—even Christians—reject this passage as being written by Josephus is that he was thoroughly Jewish and never believed in Jesus nor converted to Christianity. This point was made clear by the early Church-father Origen (185–253 CE), who twice stated that Josephus rejected any belief in Jesus' messiahship.[21] The Greek word "christ" means anointed.[22] In Hebrew, the word is *messiah*.[23] The statement that "Jesus was the Christ" is a confession of faith (cf. Luke 23:35; John 7:26; Acts 9:22).[24] The authenticity of this passage is suspect as it is unlikely that a Jewish non-Christian would state that Jesus was more than a man, much less the Messiah (in whom he did not believe).[25] It is even more unlikely that Josephus would state that Jesus had fulfilled the Hebrew scriptures, especially when he cited other messiah claimants during the 2nd Temple Era (*War* 2.4.1–3; 2.8.1; 2.17.8; *Ant* 17.10.5–8) who made messianic claims with similar results: being crucified by Rome.[26]

One of the foremost New Testament scholars today, Bart Ehrman, considers another factor. Josephus was an admitted turncoat. The Jews despised him so thoroughly that they did not care for any of his works. This caused his books to be handled and transmitted solely by Christians. Josephus may have made a peripheral reference to Jesus (see below), but scholars conclude that Christian scribes added a few more descriptions of Jesus to "help" Josephus' original work.[27]

2. An Over-Eager Defender of the Faith?

a. Lying Pen of the Scribes (Jer 8:8)?

The works of Josephus that exist today were only handled and copied by Christian scribes.[28] The majority of these copies date to the time of the Church father Eusebius of Caesarea (260–339 CE).[29] A few variant versions of the *testimonium flavianum* exist from other Christian translations but without its pro-Christian bias.[30] The versions of the early Church father Jerome, the Bishop Agapius of Hierapolis, and Michael (the Syrian, Monophysite patriarch of Antioch) are far more restrained.[31] Jerome's version, for instance, does not state Jesus was the Messiah but that "he was believed to be the Messiah."[32] These translators were likely working from an original text and not relying on Eusebius' enhanced version.[33] These departures at critical points in the text arouse suspicion.

Eusebius, as a credible source in general, has come into question.[34] Other texts demonstrate Eusebius manufactured details about various historical accounts to make Christianity seem more favorable in the eyes of pagans.[35] Most of his fictitious accounts had one goal: to make Christianity and its God look credible and appealing to pagans.[36] Yet, it is Eusebius' overall scholarship that is also questioned. He demonstrates that he can manipulate a text when it is to his advantage—or the advantage of his point. He attributes a passage in *Demonstration*

(*Ant.* 8.2.402d–403) to the Jewish Alexandrian historian Philo (*Embassy to Gaius* 299), when, in fact, the passage is drawn from combining language from Josephus' *Antiquities* (18.55–59) mixed with his own redaction.[37]

Ken Olsen, a graduate student at Duke University, raises a similar question regarding the *testimonium flavianum* where the text reads, "receive truth with pleasure."[38] Throughout Josephus' writings, the term "pleasure" (ἡδονή) had a negative connotation that meant an excess of physical or sensual pleasure, something that was to be shunned.[39] Philo (*Sacr.* 45), who lived at the same time as Josephus, used the term with the same meaning. Two hundred years later, the term took on a positive meaning in Eusebius' works, conveying the idea of a good attitude.[40] Olsen questions whether the *testimonium flavianum* was originally authored by Eusebius in his defense of Christianity since it is very similar to other usages where he praises the "pleasure" with which Christians "do well" (see *In Praise of Constantine* 17.11; *Martyrs of Palestine* 6.6; and Eusebius' comments on Psalm 67:4 in PG 23 co. 684D).[41] If this text was originally Eusebius' work, it appears that he used the same type of redaction as he had when quoting Philo.[42] Other scholars take the opposite position. Since the text lacks the antisemitism and hatred towards Jews for killing Jesus that developed during the 4th century CE, they find the text is either directly from Josephus or it is a version that existed before Eusebius.[43]

Bart Ehrman highlights another curious fact. Early Christian authors were zealously looking for evidence to justify their faith. They drew on any source they could find to validate their beliefs, hoping to attract non-believing pagans. Yet, as ambitious as these authors were, not one (Justin, Tertullian, Origen, and others) mentions Josephus' reference to Jesus or James as a defense of their faith. How is it that no Christian author is aware of this passage until Eusebius?[44]

b. Issues of Vocabulary, Style, and Anachronism

The vocabulary and style of *testimonium flavianum* are problematic due to peculiarities found nowhere else in *Antiquities* or any of Josephus' works. The first description that raises suspicion is the *testimonium flavianum*'s awkwardness within the overall context of Book 18 of *Antiquities*, which deals with the folly of Jewish rebels. Josephus' assessment of Jesus is uncharacteristically supportive, lauding him for his virtue. Second, Josephus is usually incredibly careful in describing Hebrew customs when he expresses them in Greek terms to a Roman audience. Yet, he is strikingly silent on the differences between a Hebrew messiah and a Greek 'Christ,' a term he has never mentioned.[45]

A third piece of evidence reveals an early Christian hand in "helping" *testimonium flavianum* become Christian is found in two anachronistic (out of chronological order) phrases from later periods that appear in the early text of Josephus. Steve Mason points out that,

> the word translated "worker" in the phrase "worker of incredible deeds" is *poiētēs* in Greek, from which we get the word "poet." Etymologically, it means "one who does"

and so it can refer to any sort of "doer." But in Josephus' day it had already come to have a special reference to literary poets, and that is how he consistently uses it elsewhere (nine times)—to speak of Greek poets such as Homer.[46]

It appears a Christian translator was trying to "help" Josephus' reference to Jesus say more than it did. From the Christian viewpoint, a "doer of wonderful works" implies that Jesus performed miracles. However, in Josephus' day, it meant that Jesus was a "poet of wonderful works" not a miracle worker. Ken Olsen points out that nowhere else does Josephus use the idea of "doer" for "poet." Nor does he use this construction of Greek (ποιέω with παράδοξος) in the sense of wonderworking.[47] Do we have any clue as to who this over-zealous scribe may have been?

While these types of constructs are alien to Josephus, they are quite common to Eusebius. In fact, he uses this phrase more than a hundred times.[48] Another giveaway is that the Greek construction for "doer of miraculous works" (παραδόξων ἔργων ποιητής) does not appear anywhere in the known written Greek world before the literature produced by Eusebius.[49] Thus, the phrase makes no sense in Josephus' day.

Fourth, scholars have mentioned the text's description of Christians as a "tribe" (Greek, *phylon*) when Josephus would have known that Jesus and his followers were fellow Jews. About 100 years later, a small Christian movement in the 2nd century CE began to refer to Christianity as a "third race," which would explain the text's designation as a tribe.[50] The context fits the ideas popular about 200 years after Josephus' death in Eusebius' time, but not at the time of Josephus' writing. Josephus uses the word *phylē* 11 times to describe "gender," a "swarm" of locusts, but usually to signify distinct races or nationalities like the tribe of Judah.[51] It is never used to designate an offshoot of a tribe. The only time phylon (rather than *phylē*) appears in any work of Josephus is in *testimonium flavianum*, in an unusual context of tribes as an offshoot of Jews. Eusebius' usage of the term in his works, however, mirrors the concept of race reflected in the last sentence in connection with Christians.[52] Thus, the evidence again raises the question of forgery, or at the very least, "helping" the text reflect support for a historical Jesus.

Fifth, it is unlikely Josephus mentioned the resurrection since Josephus was very careful in relating stories that were not well-verified. An alternate version of the text by Agapius tones down the open-ended endorsement of resurrection to read:

> But those who had become his disciples did not abandon his discipleship. They reported that he had appeared to them three days after his crucifixion and that he was alive; accordingly, he was perhaps the Messiah, concerning whom the prophets have recounted wonders.[53]

Finally, it is unlikely that Josephus, who did not consider Jesus different from any other virtuous teacher or rabbi in Jewish history, would state that Jesus had fulfilled the "divine prophets." The phrase "divine prophets" is odd for Josephus. The closest parallel is his description of

Isaiah. "He was by the confession of all a divine and wonderful man in speaking truth: and out of the assurance that he had never written what was false" (*Ant* 10.2.2). Josephus is not calling Isaiah a god or godman but stating that he possessed a godly character, which was demonstrated by Isaiah's speaking the truth. Since Josephus did not see Jesus differently from other virtuous teachers, he is not likely to have stated that Jesus fulfilled the prophets. Thus, the text (as we have it) evidences quite a bit of "monkeying" with Josephus' words.

c. *The Text and Its Approximate Original Version*

Much of the *testimonium flavianum* is likely legitimate. Josephus probably referred to Jesus as a "wise man" who drew Jews and Gentiles to follow him.[54] Josephus calls both Solomon (*Ant* 8.2.7) and Daniel (*Ant* 10.11.2) "wise men," so this characterization of Jesus is not alien to his writing style.[55]

Agapius' version also upholds this characterization of Jesus.

> At this time there was a wise man who was called Jesus. His conduct was good, and [he] was known to be virtuous. And many people from among the Jews in other nations became his disciples. Pilate condemned him to be crucified and to die.[56]

While the Agapius version omits the phrase that implies the Jews were really behind Jesus' death, it is not out of character for Josephus. He often refers to "leading men" among the Jews, especially in *Antiquities*, Books 17 and 18. These "leading men," like those responsible for the trial of John, were known for their tumultuous spirits and rash judgments. Intrigues were common during this violent era in Jewish Judea, where leaders were continually jockeying for power and authority. Thus, the reference to leading men in the *testimonium flavianum* was likely authored by Josephus.

Josephus also likely mentioned Pilate's execution of Jesus and that his followers continued to adhere to his teachings. It would stretch the limits of credible scholarship for a man who rejoiced in converts to Judaism to have written such unusual things regarding Jesus in a positive light. Ehrman concludes that an original passage likely referred to Jesus, but only with the facts: (1) he was a wise man; (2) he did startling deeds; (3) he was a teacher; (4) he was condemned to death by Pilate; and (5) his Christian followers did not die out.[57]

If we reject the questionable portions of *testimonium flavianum*, the core that remains still upholds the story reported in the New Testament. Josephus is an astounding source for witnessing John the Baptist and his theology, which is confirmed by the New Testament's account. This again grants legitimacy to the original text. Josephus' reference to James as Jesus' brother corroborates the account of the early Church historian Hegesippus that James was Jesus' biological brother. Eliminating the enhanced positive descriptions of Jesus from Josephus' work does not impact his overall recognition of Jesus. The value of *testimonium flaviunam* is that the accounts of Jesus and Christians broadly parallel the same history in the Gospels.

II. RABBINIC SOURCES

The Mishnah, written *c.* 200 CE, is the oldest part of Jewish rabbinic literature. It records the sayings of many early Jewish rabbis. It never mentions Jesus. The first reference occurs about 400 years later, too late and too full of rumors (Mary was seduced by a Roman soldier) to be considered here.[58] Thus, rabbinic (Talmudic) sources are too far removed from the people who lived during or shortly after Jesus' lifetime to be useful sources.

III. WHERE DOES THE EVIDENCE LEAD?

I considered the historical evidence in these chapters in a different order than what I've presented it here. For me, it was finding one piece of evidence that demonstrated validity. Then, I was on a roller coaster as I discovered another preconceived idea did not stand up to the evidence. When I finished the historical study, I came away confident of the overall credibility of the New Testament's account.[59] The following were points I could generally verify.

Archaeology. Archaeological evidence for a historical Jesus was either questionable or lacking. However, the James Ossuary and the Talpiot Tomb may strengthen the physical evidence. While the facts supported Jesus and his family, they also presented troubling questions. The tomb indicates Jesus' possible marriage to Mary Magdalene, children, and an earthly death. This seemed impossible and did not sit well with my Christian upbringing.

Jewish Writings. The overall written evidence supported the New Testament's historicity. Josephus attests to John the Baptist and to Jesus' brother James. Written evidence exists from Roman officials, pagan scholars, and Josephus. There is sufficient evidence to conclude that there was a man who was believed to be Christ and who also gathered a following of Jews and Gentiles. The Christian movement began *c.* 30 CE and spread into Asia Minor by 60 CE (see p. 101).

Roman Writings. Early Christians worshipped Christ by praying and singing songs to him. Christians refused to worship pagan gods at the peril of their own lives. Christians refused to worship Rome's emperors and gathered to worship despite Rome's threats and persecution. Rome considered Christianity a "vain superstition" and used the Christians as scapegoats as early as 64 CE. Rome held inquisitions as early as 96 CE and brutally persecuted and executed the early believers. Thus, secular sources broadly confirm the stories of early Christianity within the New Testament.

In Volume 1, I set up a trial based on the concept of being innocent until proven guilty.[60] Thus far, the New Testament has passed the test of extrabiblical evidence since sources attest to many of the people and modes of worship mentioned in the text. Therefore, it is not unreasonable to find it historical: many, if not most, of the historical facts it contains actually occurred. Jesus really existed!

The most important question that continued to bother me was Israel's ancient allegations that YHWH was unfair. These are allegations that many modern believers continue today.

YHWH was the defendant in this trial. If Divine Law remains valid today, how does Jesus fit into this picture? I knew what I had been taught growing up in my own flavor of Christianity, but I wanted to continue to compare my own preconceived ideas with the actual written word of God. How does the written word indicate Jesus would save humanity?

Questions like these kept flooding in! Would evidence from the New Testament continue to vindicate YHWH as a righteous God and judge? Was YHWH righteous to allow early Christians to suffer and die? Is God righteous to allow those who believe in Him today to continue to suffer and die? Would I yet find Israel's ancient allegations in favor of the plaintiff or the defendant? My soul could not rest until this issue was resolved, so I pressed on.

15

Sola Scriptura

I. THE PATH TO TRUTH

Several general truths emerged from my study of the New Testament's historicity. The story of Jesus and Christianity was well-known by 65 CE. While historical sources cannot prove the events in the Gospels or the greater New Testament occurred, secular writers attest that Christians existed. A Christian movement occurred, centered on a persecuted Christ, who was crucified by Roman rulers. The New Testament existed by 170 CE to the extent that a pagan scholar could quote and refer to its accounts. I could safely conclude that secular history broadly reflects the New Testament's biography. There was a historical Jesus. A Jewish man who taught in Judea. A man who has influenced beliefs for 2,000 years after his death.

My journey had turned into an investigation. Was Israel's God and judge of the earth righteous? The core of ancient Israel's charge against YHWH did not involve validity. Israel's people claimed God's ideals of social order, justice, and His theology were unfair. They accused God of being unrighteous. I saw that the remainder of this trial must rely on theology. Did empirical data (verified through comparative experiment) exist by which I or anyone else could either condemn or exonerate God? The next route my path would take needed to investigate the relationship between YHWH and Jesus: between Father and son.

No less than 200,000 different Christian sects exist today.[1] Each sect contradicts the other in the specific ideas it holds as truth. Each sect has its own criteria for right and wrong and these ideas are relative to each passing generation. Isaiah 52:8 prophesies of a day when we will see eye to eye. A day wherein we are no longer divided by beliefs. A day where we are no longer divided by politic, sect, or religion. No Baptists. No Catholics. No Protestants. No Presbyterians. No Judaism. No Muslims. Our identity will not be in our religious sects. Our identity will be found in YHWH's righteousness (Deut 6:25; Isa 54:17).[2] We will be many independent nations united by love of the earth's only God. We will be united by love of His constitutional truth and His righteousness. Each person will know YHWH: from the least to the greatest (Isa 25:7; Jer 24:7; 31:34; Ezek 38:16).

How do we get there? How do we emerge from our present system of divisive misery? Is there some magical formula? Or, can rudimentary scholarship reveal a forgotten path? The promise echoed throughout scripture is that if we seek God, if we seek truth, if we seek: we will find Him. However, it must be a whole-hearted quest (Deut 4:29; Jer 29:13). YHWH is a God of truth who can be found![3] I had followed the breadcrumbs and discovered Jesus really existed.

Now, I needed to understand how Jesus fit into YHWH's plan of salvation. Overwhelming evidence demonstrates that Divine Law remains valid as long as "heaven and earth" exist (Matt 5:18). Prophesies in the Old Testament foretold a future Day when the Law will be exalted, honored, and obeyed (Isa 2:3; 42:4, 21; Jer 31:33; Ezek 36:27). How does Jesus further this process? I had not yet reached my final destination. There was still much ground to cover as my journey set off again.

II. THE NEW TESTAMENT ONLY GAINS AUTHORITY THROUGH THE OLD TESTAMENT LAW AND PROPHETS

I also knew I could not keep putting off Jack's questions. YHWH had made it possible for me to be a stay-at-home mom with time to research while Jack worked. I was spending 10–14 hours a day studying while balancing cooking, teaching, and spending time with the kids. I'd often stay up to 2 and 3 a.m., enjoying the solace to think through the various issues and evidences.

Jack's questions were not going away. My answers were insufficient on several issues he'd raised. I had to ask if I was being honest with myself or just protecting my emotions. I did not feel it was right in YHWH's sight to ignore them. These issues were pivotal to exonerating YHWH as a righteous God. Jack's questions seemed tied to the historic conflict between Divine Law and Jesus' mission for humanity's salvation. I wondered what we have missed. If Jesus upheld his Father's Divine Law, how would I now understand Jesus' mission of salvation?

So far, I had 7 concepts that had governed my research in volume 1 (see pp. 63–81). Now, I needed to establish guidelines that would govern my research for the New Testament. The guidelines that I discovered worked well were nothing new. They were already in use. In conversation with Christian friends, I discovered that everyone held to these guidelines, they just weren't vocalized or reiterated well in our religious institutions. They remained silent and unspoken, but needed a voice. They needed to be drawn out of the shroud of darkness to be clearly defined so I could know exactly what I believed. These are the waymarks I discovered in my journey through the New Testament.

III. GUIDELINES FOR NEW TESTAMENT STUDY

A. *Sola Scriptura*

The first premise returns to the vision held by every member of the Reformation. The New Testament writings are empowered solely by the Old Testament Scriptures. When the New

III. Guidelines for New Testament Study

Testament refers to "holy Scriptures," it is solely referring to Israel's Scriptures in the Old Testament.[4]

> Which he had promised afore *by his prophets in the holy scriptures* ... (Rom 1:2. See also 2 Tim 3:15)

> Jesus answered them, Is it not written in your law, I said, You are gods? If he called them gods, to whom the word of God came, and the *scripture cannot be broken*. (John 10:34–35)

Jesus does not claim authority on his own. Jesus ties his authority to his Father. He refers to Psalm 82:6, which refers to humanity as gods (*elohim*) because we are the children of the YHWH. Jesus' ties his authority to being sent by his Father, as prophesied in the Old Testament. Jesus never claims his authority came from any source outside of YHWH or Israel's Scriptures.

> I proceeded forth and came from God. **Neither came I of myself**, but he sent me. (John 8:42[5])

> Because I seek not mine own will, but the will of the **Father which has sent me**. (John 5:30)

Jesus further explains that his being sent by the Father was prophesied in the Old Testament Law and prophets. **He did not come to do away with the Law** but to fulfill what was written by Moses.[6]

> Think not that I am come to destroy the law, or the prophets: **I am not come to destroy**, but to fulfill. For verily I say unto you, **Till heaven and earth pass, one jot or one tittle *shall in no wise pass from the law, till all be fulfilled***. Whosoever therefore shall break one of these least commandments, and <u>shall teach men so, he shall be called the least in the kingdom of heaven</u>. (Matt 5:17–19)

In the Sermon on the Mount (Matthew 5), Jesus appeals to Divine Law for his authority. He also gives two stipulations for Divine Law's ongoing authority in a believer's walk with God. Jesus' first stipulation is that the Law remains valid until "heaven and earth" pass away. Jesus' second stipulation is that Divine Law remains valid until "all is fulfilled."[7] When Jesus died, there was much of the Law that remained to be fulfilled. There was a reason Jesus reiterated this point.

When Jesus' earthly mission ended, Israel had not turned from her sins to obey YHWH's voice, nor obey "all that YHWH commanded you this day." Israel's descendants remained scattered among the nations. They would continue to be "sifted among the nations" for the next 2,000 years (Amos 9:9). Yet, the conclusion of the Prophetic Code within Divine Law promised:

> And it shall come to pass, when all these things are come upon you, the blessing and the curse, which I have set before you, and you shall call them to mind among all the nations, where YHWH your God has driven you. And **(you) shall return unto YHWH your God, and shall obey his voice according to all that I command you this day**, you and your children, with all your heart, and with all your soul; That then **YHWH your God will turn your captivity**, and have compassion upon you. And (He) will return and **gather you from all the nations, where YHWH your God has scattered you**. (Deut 30:1–3)[8]

Jesus provides reasons for Divine Law remaining valid. Anyone who teaches men to break the smallest of YHWH's instructions will be considered least in the kingdom of heaven. By tying his mission to fulfilling part of the Law, Jesus bases His authority to speak and teach Israel coming from His Father's Divine Law.

Throughout the New Testament, Jesus bases his authority solely upon the words of Israel's Law and her prophets.

> And beginning at <u>Moses and all the prophets</u>, he expounded unto them in **all the scriptures** the things concerning himself. (Luke 24:27)

> But those things, which God before had shown **by the mouth of all his prophets**, that Christ should suffer, he has so fulfilled. (Acts 3:18. This is a reference to Isaiah 53)

> He that believes on me, **as the scripture has said**, out of his belly shall flow rivers of living water. (John 7:38)

> Has not **the scripture said**, That Christ comes of the seed of David, and out of the town of Bethlehem, where David was? (John 7:42. This is a reference to Mic 5:2)

> And the **scripture was fulfilled**, which says, And he was numbered with the transgressors. (Mark 15:28; This is a quote from Isaiah 53:9)

> And he said unto them, These are the words which I spoke unto you while I was yet with you that all things must be fulfilled, **which were written in**

> **the law of Moses, and in the prophets, and in the psalms** concerning me. (Luke 24:44)

> Then he took unto him the twelve, and said unto them, Behold, we go up to Jerusalem, and **all things that are written by the prophets** concerning the *Son of man* shall be accomplished. (Luke 18:31)[9]

Throughout the New Testament, Jesus upholds Israel's scriptures—the Old Testament—as the basis for the Father sending him for humanity's salvation.

Jesus' role in Israel's history—his role for humanity—is established and defined by Israel's Law and her prophets. Luke 24:4 (above) explicitly refers to the Law of Moses—not the Hammurabi Code or laws from other nations—for the role Jesus would play in Israel's history.[10] When Jesus refers to psalms in this verse, he is not referring to psalms from Babylon, Assyria, or Egypt. Jesus is solely referring to psalms written within the Hebrew Scriptures, today known as the Old Testament (or Tanakh in Judaism). Therefore, the Old Testament continues to be the foundation and litmus test by which the evidence must be weighed.

B. Obedience Remains

Not only does Divine Law remain valid, but the New Testament must uphold the same ideas as the Divine precepts YHWH revealed to ancient Israel. David proclaimed Divine Law "perfect" (Ps 19:7).[11] It was wholly and completely optimal in every way because it was a Law that enabled liberty: it was a Law of Liberty.

I was surprised to find so many verses in the New Testament which upheld Divine Law. I had read over them, but never really thought about these texts. Part of the reason I never gave them much thought was that I had never heard sermons on Divine Law in the churches I attended, but those texts are there! The New Testament reiterated that Divine Law remained valid during Jesus' lifetime and after his death. First John, for instance, upholds Deuteronomy 30:11–16. John reiterates the idea that the *Law of Moses* given at Mt. Sinai is not a burden. It is the means by which we can judge whether we love God.

> By this we know that we love the children of God, **when we love God and obey his commandments.** For this is the love of God, **that we keep his commandments. And his commandments are not burdensome.** (1 John 5:2–3)

> But he said, Blessed rather are those who hear the word of God and **keep it!** (Luke 11:28, ESV)

> Children, obey your parents in the Lord, for this is right. (Eph 6:1)

> And this is love **that we walk according to his commandments**. This is the commandment, **just as you have heard from the beginning**, so that you should walk in it. (2 John 1:6, ESV)

Obedience to the Law of Moses is stressed throughout the New Testament.

First John 5 tells us that YHWH's commandments are not too hard nor are they a burden. They are the test we can apply to ourselves to know whether we love God. This is exactly what Deuteronomy 30:11–16 tells us!

Luke 11:28 reiterates that those who obey the word of God will be blessed.[12] It may be remembered that the phrase "word of God" throughout the Old Testament always refers to the Divine Law YHWH gave to Israel at Mt. Sinai—the words YHWH spoke audibly to the entire nation of Israel (see pp. 44–45).

The Apostle Paul in Ephesians 6:1 upholds the 4th Commandment in the 10 Commandments by instructing children to obey their parents. Second John 1 upholds the Golden Rule established in Leviticus 19:18. This instruction is not found within the 10 Commandments. It is found in the Law of Moses. John stresses that the Golden Rule was not a new commandment (2 John 1:5), but a "commandment" that believer's had from "the beginning."[13]

Jesus believed it was possible for ordinary people to obey the Law by no longer sinning. In fact, he instructed at least two people to no longer sin.

> Behold, you are made whole: **sin no more**, lest a worse thing come unto you. (John 5:14)

> And Jesus said unto her, Neither do I condemn thee: **go, and sin no more**. (John 8:11)

When Jesus tells people to sin no more, he is upholding Divine Law. Jesus believed it possible for people—he believed it possible that sinners—could "sin no more."[14] It is unlikely that Jesus was requiring people to do something outside their capabilities since Jesus tells us, "My yoke is easy, and my burden is light" (Matt 11:30).[15] Jesus did not see Divine Law as being too difficult or onerous to obey. If Jesus had seen Divine Law as being too difficult to obey, he would not have told people to obey it by no longer sinning.

Jesus, the Disciples, and the Apostles continue to uphold Divine Law as valid. The New Testament supports Divine Law as a way of life to lived by believers. The Law remains valid! It continues to be a path of life even after Jesus' death. At this point in my studies I felt betrayed by my pastors. I could not fathom how my pastors and teachers ignored theses texts and encouraged me to join their path of relativism. After years of study, I now see their path of relativism was similar to other brands on the market.

C. Least in the Kingdom of God

I have mentioned this text before. I'm bringing it up again because I had read over this text many times for it to sink in. I was taught that it says the opposite of what the text actually supports. There is another reason Jesus upholds the validity of the Law in Matthew 5:17–19. When he talks about those who will be least in the Kingdom of Heaven, Jesus is not making up a new doctrine. He is referring to a specific curse that is written in the Law of Moses.

> For verily I say unto you, Till heaven and earth pass, one jot or one tittle *shall in no wise pass from the law, till all be fulfilled*. Whosoever therefore shall break one of these least commandments, and <u>shall teach men so, he shall be called the least in the kingdom of heaven.</u> (Matt 5:17–19)

Jesus is upholding his Father's doctrine. In his Father's Divine Law, YHWH had established a curse against those who did not confirm that Divine Law should be obeyed.

> Cursed be he that confirms not all the words of this law to do them. And all the people shall say, Amen. (Deut 27:26)

YHWH's curse did not condemn people for not obeying all the words or instructions in the Law.[16] This curse specifically addressed those who did not confirm or teach that the Law is valid. If anyone taught humanity to break the Law of Moses, then he or she would be least in YHWH's kingdom since they would fall under Deuteronomy's 27:26's curse.

I began to see the New Testament as an extension of the Old Testament. The same precepts were reiterated in both. Now, I needed clear directions for tackling Jack's questions in the New Testament. During my study for Volume 1, I discovered 7 universal precepts that govern any study for truth within Scripture. These govern study for both the Old and New Testaments. Now I needed to build upon the new ideas of Sola Scriptura and Jesus' encouraging of ordinary people to obey Divine Law. Surprisingly, I found that in addition to the 7 universal precepts for truth, there were 7 premises or guidelines that would direct my path through the New Testament. Could these allow us to uncover a universal path established by God, not man?

Jack's questions also weighed on my heart. While his questions were sincere, I doubted he considered all the evidence. This quest, however, was not about Jack. I wanted to know God. I wanted to better understand my relationship with Jesus. I desired to prove all things to see if a path of unity exists in this journey towards truth.

16

Equal Weights and Measures

I. 1ˢᵀ PREMISE: SOLA SCRIPTURA

My journey through the New Testament needed to be directed by firm guidelines. Like my investigation of the validity of Divine Law in Volume 1, solid concepts would keep my path accountable and on track.

The first premise is *sola Scriptura* is: The New Testament (NT) is founded upon Old Testament (OT) doctrine.[1] If we accept Jesus' teaching, then we should listen to his statement that he did not come to destroy the Law or the prophets. The teachings from the Law and the prophets remain valid as long as "heaven and earth endure" (Matt 5:17–19).

Jesus reiterates this point again when he upholds the two great categories of ancient Israel's constitutional Divine Law:

> Love the Lord your God with all your heart and with all your soul and with all your mind (see Deut 6:5; 11:13; 30:6). This is the **first and greatest commandment**. And **the second is like it**: Love your neighbor as yourself (Lev 19:18) All the Law and the Prophets hang on these two commandments. (Matt 22:37–40, NIV)

When Jesus reiterates that we should "love the Lord our God," he is not referring to himself. Jesus is quoting from Deuteronomy where the original text reads: "*Love YHWH your God with all your heart, mind, and soul*" (Deut 6:5; 11:13; 30:6, cf pp. 1, 44, 68, 76). Jesus is upholding the foundation upon which the Father's path to salvation is based.[2] Loving YHWH and His way of life enables us to succeed!

The same goes for the second division of Hebrew Law. YHWH establishes healthy boundaries for relationships with our fellow man. He establishes righteous precepts and just laws so our society can be stable. Divine Law teaches us how we are to love our neighbor in a balanced way so we do not oppress our brother, while preventing our brother from oppressing us. It is a perfect balance. It is the Law of Liberty.

II. 2ND PREMISE: THE NEW TESTAMENT IS BASED SOLELY ON OLD TESTAMENT PROPHESY

The second premise is similar to the first: the NT is empowered solely by OT prophecies. When the New Testament refers to prophets or prophecies, it is not referring to prophecies issued by foreign prophets whose ethnicity comes from Egypt, Babylon, Greeks, or India. When Jesus or the disciples refer to prophets and prophecy, they are specifically referring to Israel's prophets and their works, which today comprise part of the Old Testament.

I mention this because in my dialog with friends and acquaintances, I've discovered that some believers hold to the idea that Jesus spoke to Israel and to humanity solely on his own accord. He did not need to be sanctioned by his Father through any prophet in the Old Testament. I hope the evidence presented here shows that this belief goes against Scripture. This evidence could bring believers one step closer to being united as *One people under God*. It can lead us one step closer to ending our self-inflicted misery.

III. 3RD PREMISE: THE NEW TESTAMENT RELIES ON ISRAEL'S HISTORY

Our third premise holds that the New Testament relies on Israel's history. Throughout this journey, I will show references to the New Testament's teachers basing ideas from Israel's past history. This evidence will be significant when we investigate the *Day of YHWH* as Israel's Judgment Day.

IV. 4TH PREMISE: THE NEW TESTAMENT IS NOT BASED ON SCRIPTURES FROM OTHER NATIONS

Our fourth premise accepts that the NT is *not* sanctioned by Greek writings, such as *The Iliad*, *The Odyssey*, or even the Homeric poems. Neither does the NT base its doctrine on Hindu Scriptures, such as the *Bhagavad-Gita*. New Testament doctrine and its validity are established solely based on Israel's Scriptures and should be a completion of the OT.

In other words *sola Scriptura*:

The whole of the New Testament presupposes and rests upon the Old Testament.[3]

While this may seem basic, the growing trends of relativism and its moder beliefs project Jesus as simply another manifestation of a pagan god. In this belief system, Krishna, Buddha, Jesus, and Mohammed are considered to be on-going, progressive manifestations of God.[4]

Our 4th premise coincides with *Dissimilarity*, the 7th *Precept of Truth* (see pp. 75–81). For Divine Law to be truth, it must be dissimilar to the teachings of pagan nations. While overlap of ideas can exist, there should be enough instructions (like justice, dietary regulations, healthcare protocols, direct access to God, a system for accountability, etc.) to distinguish it from the teachings of other nations. This is way YHWH was quite specific that no one could change His Law by adding to or diminishing from His Law (Deut 4:2; 12:32). It may be remembered that when a philosophy or regulation is added to Divine Law or deleted from it, it changes the Law of Liberty into one of oppression (see pp. 20–21 for discussion).

V. 5TH PREMISE: THE NEW TESTAMENT SHOULD BE CONSTANT, UPHOLDING THE 7 PRECEPTS OF TRUTH

This brings us to our fifth premise. The NT should be *Constant*. This premise coincides with the 1st Precept of Truth but stresses constancy and fidelity between both the Old and New Testaments. The NT should demonstrate that it is constant, faithful, and loyal to OT doctrines and ideals (see pp. 63–67). The NT must maintain the previous *7 Precepts of Truth*, which provided the means to test the evidence in the OT in *Volume 1* (see YE1, 1–14). The ideas and teachings within the New Testament must be constant, which is the essence of the idea of truth. If YHWH gave ancient Israel truth through Divine Law, then the New Testament cannot abrogate or change that Law. The New Testament—just like ancient Israel's prophets—must demonstrate freedom from change, even during times of duress.[5]

> For **I am YHWH, I change not**. Therefore, you sons of Jacob are not consumed. Even from the days of your fathers you have gone away from my statutes and have not kept them. *Return unto me, and I will return unto you*, says YHWH of hosts. (Mal 3:6–7)

The NT should maintain the same standard of fidelity with exactness to detail. It must be faithful and loyal to the standard of truth established by Divine Law. YHWH's word does not change, nor can it be rescinded.

YHWH's righteousness and Jesus' righteousness remain pivotal issues throughout this investigation. While Israel alleged YHWH and Divine Law were unfair, the NT upholds that Jesus easily obeyed Divine Law.

> **By one man's obedience** the many will be made righteous. (Rom 5:19, ESV)

> But **I do as the Father has commanded me**, so that the world may know that I love the Father. (John 14:31, ESV)

> For we do not have a high priest who is unable to sympathize with our weaknesses, but one who in every respect has been tempted as we are, **yet without sin**. (Heb 4:15, ESV)

Jesus, as YHWH's son, should show the same fidelity and righteousness with regards to his Father's Divine Law. His teachings should *not only* uphold the Law, but they should cause people to love the Father and His way of life. In John 14:31 Jesus is referring to the philosophy reiterated in 1 John 5:2–3, which emphasizes we can know that we love God and that we are part of His people by keeping His instructions. Jesus ties his love of the Father to his own obedience. In fact, Jesus tells us it is the way we know Jesus loved the Father.

Throughout Scripture's history, only two entities are proclaimed to be "without sin." The only two people said to be without sin are YHWH and Jesus. It is essential that both are tried according to the same standard. There is no room for hypocrisy. Like YHWH, Jesus should demonstrate that his teachings and his actions were "without sin" (Deut 32:4). This premise did not trouble me since truth can stand up to being questioned.

VI. 6TH PREMISE: THE NEW TESTAMENT CANNOT RESCIND OR CHANGE YHWH'S DIVINE WORD

The sixth premise holds that for the NT to be validated as "the word of God," it cannot change or rescind OT Doctrine (see p. 224, note 5).[6] Neither can it change YHWH's previous commands, which David had proclaimed perfect (Ps 19:7). While this is a continuation of *sola Scriptura*, I needed to clearly state this premise in order to conduct my investigation while traveling the path towards truth.

VII. 7TH PREMISE: THE NT FULFILLS THE OT

The seventh premise guides our journey by seeing the New Testament as simply a completion and fulfillment of Old Testament prophecies and doctrines.[7] You and I can fulfill the command to honor our parents and to "keep the Sabbath holy" (Exod 20:8; Isa 56:2–8). You and I can fulfill the Law of Moses by loving your neighbor as yourself (Lev 19:18). Fulfilling Divine Law does not invalidate its teachings any more than fulfilling the US Constitution invalidates America's founding Social Compact. Fulfilling the Law simply means that one is obeying its requirements and enjoying the blessings that Law observance empowers.

This continues to build upon the 7 *Precepts of Truth*. The tenets of the OT should be in unison with the New Testament. Constancy will be assessed by the coherence in repetition: whether a particular doctrine or concept is reiterated and upheld, or whether it is dissimilar, and the ideas attempt to invalidate Divine Law.[8] The same standard of accountability must be applied to both Old and New Testaments. Divine Law must remain the litmus test for the NT. These seven premises will guide and direct our search for truth in the Greek Scriptures.[9] As I reviewed these premise, I was both excited and satisfied with their means to test truth in the New Testament.

VIII. PROVE ALL THINGS

My quest set out to prove all things and to "hold fast to that which is good" (1 Thes 5:21). I had travelled through amazing ideas. I unearthed a firm foundation. Along the way, I met so many other believers who were truth-seekers on this quest. Each of us wanted to know God, to follow Him, and to make Him known. The fellowship of truth was strengthening.

Before my journey set out again, I wanted to make sure I accurately understood Paul's instruction for studying Scripture.

> Be you transformed by the renewing of your mind that you may **prove** what is that good, acceptable, and perfect will of God. (Rom 12:2)

> Beloved, believe not every spirit, but **try the spirits** whether they are of God. Because many false prophets are gone out into the world. (1 John 4:1)

Dokimázete (*dokima/zete*, Greek), the word for 'prove' in the above verses, means to test or examine.[10] I encountered similar precepts in the Old Testament. Isaiah challenges us to reason through logic (Isa 1:18).[11] Other texts consistently demonstrate that YHWH tests and proves us to see "whether we will walk in *His* Law or not" (Exod 16:4).[12] I needed to be aware of YHWH's tests along the way. While I was litigating Israel's ancient case against God, YHWH was constantly proving us to see whether we will be obedient to Divine Law.

I had to continue this journey to see if a cogent and universal philosophy had been overlooked in its teaching. I would continue to carefully and contritely consider the evidence (Josh 24:14; Ps 34:18; 51:17; Isa 57:15; 66:2). It was essential that my conclusions were based on *sola Scriptura*: YHWH's written word, so I did not lean upon my own understanding and inherited beliefs (Prov 3:5; Isa 1:18).

IX. CONCEPTS TRANSFORM INTO ACTION

The time had come to tackle Jack's questions. I had the necessary tools. I had a firm foundation. I decided to reduce the 7 Premises for the New Testament into three general questions. I would use these three general statements to test all 7 premises:

1. The New Testament gains authority by prophecies made in the Old Testament (Matt 5:17,18 and Luke 16:17. See section III in this chapter on p. 130).
2. If the New Testament's authority comes from prophecies made in the Old Testament, there should be great harmony between the two testimonies (i.e., between the OT and NT).
3. Jesus fulfills what was written of Him in the Old Testament (Luke 24:44; Matt 5:17; John 1:45).

I had already sufficiently tested question #1 (above) in the previous chapter and concluded that the New Testament supports that its only source of authority derives from YHWH and the Old Testament Scriptures (see pp. 51, 122–25). Over 20 New Testament texts supported this belief.

Now, I needed to focus on question #2. If the New Testament is an extension of the Old Testament, both canons should exhibit constancy. I posed a simple question to test the evidence. My entire faith seemed suspended from it:

Does constancy exist between the Old and New Testaments?

I also wondered whether the New Testament continues to reveal YHWH as a righteous God. Had I ever understood what the New Testament reveals about Jesus' righteousness? How do these ideas interact with YHWH's plan of salvation? Why does YHWH allow strife and division to exist among believers today? Why does truth remain relative to you and me?

My study would continue to follow Paul exhortation to prove all things.[13] Later books in this series will examine the 3rd general idea (above) by investigating the many prophecies Jesus fulfills. The *Suffering Servant* will be the 1st prophecy we will examine in this ongoing quest for truth. But before I could delve into Isaiah 53, I had to deal justly with Jack's questions. Would my beliefs be challenged again? Would they hold firm? I discovered this leg of the journey to be the most difficult. I asked: How deep do our father's inherited lies go?

17

Does Harmony Exist between the Old and New Testaments?

I. HEALING THE DIVIDE

Richard Rubenstein, a scholar on Conflict Resolution at George Mason University, shares his reason for covering the history of conflict within Christianity. He focused on it

> because it tells us so much about where we come from and what divides us. The story may even suggest how violent divisions can someday be healed. And, somehow, I believe that the figure of Jesus will play an important role in that healing.[1]

Rubenstein studied the history of violent conflicts between ultraorthodox Jews and other groups in Israel. He investigated religious conflicts within Christianity, and the ongoing religious wars persisting across the globe to this day. After years of study, Rubenstein—a Jew—perceived that Jesus would play a key role in healing the divide to bring peace on earth. Little did he understand how accurate his perception was or just how unconventional this healing would be.

Modern beliefs prevent God's latter-day salvation. Accepting the status quo only keeps us sleeping, silent to the eroding of our peace and values. In the Church you can seek, only if you ask the right questions. If your questions are too difficult, you'll receive the left boot of fellowship. Repeatedly, God tells us that He honors sincerity and responds to our quest for truth (Josh 24:14; Ps 145:18; Isa 10:20; Dan 9:13; Zech 8:16, 19).[2] Quite unexpectedly, while working through the issues Jack raised, a forgotten path began to come into view. It was a path so overgrown and littered with debris that all knowledge of its existence was lost. It was a plain path that held no ambiguity and led directly to YHWH.

I am sharing with you for the first time the results of a discovery that is almost too incredible to believe. A knowledge that has been locked, hidden, and passed over for 2,000 years. This plain understanding of Scripture allows God to return to us once more. The time has come to lift the veil that divides and holds us captive (Ps 82:5; Isa 25:7; 29:18; 42:16; 58:10;

60:1–2). The resolution that heals relativism and the division among religious sects begins with our second premise question: Does the New Testament harmonize with Divine Law and prophets of the Old Testament (see p. 133)?

II. HARMONY: COMPARING OLD AND NEW TESTAMENTS

The biblical passages I am sharing below challenged how I had been taught to understand them. I encourage you to read these texts for yourself in your Bible. How does each text fit into the Bible's overall treatment of that topic? Pray and think about these verses for yourself. Remember, you can!

Jack challenged my comfortable faith with the texts that follow. I mentioned earlier that this section was the hardest for me to write and to share. Yet, these questions allowed me to discover the path that leads to unity and truth. Investigating these verses creates a direct relationship with YHWH that has been the most amazing blessing for me. I would like to share this blessing with you. The Book of John presents issues I had trouble resolving.

A. Grace & Truth

New Testament

> For the law was given by Moses, **but grace and truth came by Jesus Christ**. (John 1:17)

John contrasts the Law of Moses to Jesus. This implies that ancient Israel never had YHWH's grace or His truth until Jesus' ministry.[3] This made me very uncomfortable. Throughout the Old Testament, Divine Law establishes truth (see pp. 40, 44–45). Moses found grace in YHWH's sight long before Jesus. So much so, that YHWH knew Moses by name and called Moses His friend (Exod 33:12–13, 17). Israel's people also found grace in YHWH's sight (Exod 33:16). This is evidenced by YHWH delivering them from Egypt, leading them through the Wilderness towards the Promised Land, and YHWH upholding His promises despite Israel's 14 rebellions in the Wilderness. By contrasting the Law of Moses with grace through Jesus, John implies that Divine Law did not offer grace before Jesus' ministry. I remembered solid evidence that contradicted this assertion.

Old Testament

Exodus is not the only book that supports Israel enjoying YHWH's grace before Jesus. The Book of Psalms also embraces grace existing during the days of King David. Grace was accessible for all those who walked uprightly.

II. Harmony: Comparing Old and New Testaments

> For YHWH God is a sun and shield: **YHWH will give grace** and glory: no good thing will he withhold from them that walk uprightly. O YHWH of hosts, blessed is the man who trusts in you. (Ps 84:11–12)

Hen, the Hebrew word for 'grace' means grace, favor, or acceptance.[4] *Charis*, the Greek for 'grace' in John 1:17 means grace, favor, or kindness.[5] The Hebrew and Greek share the same meaning. Those who walk uprightly have always had access to YHWH's grace and His truth (Ps 15:2; *25:5, 10*; 40:11). YHWH will not withhold any kindness to those who walk in His ways. He will protect them as a shield, and YHWH delivers the upright from persecution.

The New and Old Testaments share the same standard. Uprightness remains the prerequisite for YHWH's grace. Repentance from sin causes people to be upright since they "go their way and sin no more" (John 5:14; 8:11). John the Baptist and Jesus urged people to repent from sin (Matt 3:2; 4:17; Luke 13:3, 5). When people repent from sin, they turn from sin to walk uprightly.

The Book of Acts also upholds repentance from sin as the key to a restored relationship with God.[6]

> Repent you, therefore, and be converted that your sins may be blotted out. (Acts 3:19)

If we repent, then we turn from sin by obeying Divine Law. This enables us to be righteous and upright. We can receive God's grace and the blessings that Divine Law empowers. This way of life is easy to do—we can!

This left me wondering what John meant by contrasting Divine Law with Jesus as the only means for grace and truth. What if John was not excluding grace from existing in Divine Law before Jesus? I had to wonder if my traditional understanding was shaped by man. John could simply be making two statements that are not mutually exclusive. John may simply mean that an additional grace and truth came through Jesus' ministry.

B. Hearing God's Voice and Seeing His Shape

New Testament

> No man has seen God at any time . . . (John 1:18)

> And the Father himself which has sent me, has borne witness of me. You have **neither heard his voice at any time**, nor seen his shape. (John 5:37)

The Book of John continues to contrast Divine Law with Jesus. John makes several assertions that the other Gospels do not. In John's account, Jesus states that no one has heard the Father's voice or seen His shape. The evidence from the Old Testament suggests that John was writing to gentiles and was not writing to Jews since his statements contradicted the Old Testament.

Old Testament

> And all the people saw the thunderings, and the lightnings, and the noise of the trumpet, and the mountain smoking: and when the people saw it, they removed, and stood afar off... And YHWH said unto Moses, Thus you shall say unto the children of Israel, **You have seen that I have talked with you from heaven.** (Exod 20:18, 22)

> These words **YHWH spoke** to all your assembly in the mount out of the middle of the fire of the cloud of the thick darkness. **He spoke with a great voice** and he added no more. And he wrote them in two tables of stone and delivered them to me. And it came to pass, **when you heard the voice** out of the middle of the darkness (for the mountain did burn with fire) that you came near to me, even all the heads of your tribes and your elders. And you said, Behold, YHWH our God has showed us his glory and his greatness and <u>we have heard his voice out of the midst of the fire</u>. **We have seen this day that God does talk with man, and he lives.** Now therefore why should we die? This great fire will consume us, *if we hear the voice of YHWH our God* anymore, then we shall die. (Deut 5:22–25)

> Did ever a people hear the voice of God speaking out of the midst of the fire, **as you have heard**, and live?... **Out of heaven he made you to hear his voice** that he might instruct you: and upon earth he showed you his great fire and **you heard his words out of the middle of the fire.** (Deut 4:33, 36)

> Moses speaking to Israel: "And YHWH spoke to you out of the middle of the fire. You heard the voice of the words, but saw no similitude, **only you heard a voice.**" (Deut 4:12)

> YHWH speaking to Moses: "And I will take away mine hand and **you shall see my back parts**, but my face shall not be seen" (Exod 33:23).

In the Old Testament, the entire nation of Israel heard YHWH's voice at Mt. Sinai.[7] Moses beheld the shape of YHWH's back. The Greek "οὐδεὶς" translated "no one" in John 1:18 is exclusionary.[8] John states that "no one" has heard God's voice or seen His shape. The verse goes on to imply that only Jesus "has declared God." I had reservations about this teaching. What about Israel's prophets? What about Moses? They had also declared YHWH's grace and His truth. Why does John seem to exclude them?

New Testament scholar Matthew Henry understands John's statement to imply, "the nature of God being spiritual, He is invisible to bodily eyes, He is a being whom no man has seen, nor can see (1 Tim 6:16)."[9] In an alternative interpretation, Henry understands that this text could imply that the future revelation of God in Christ would overshadow the revelation to Israel, or that Moses had only observed a similitude of YHWH, and not His actual backside.[10]

For me, Henry's explanations did not resolve the contradiction. At Mt. Sinai, Israel heard YHWH's audible voice while prophets continued to hear and be YHWH's voice in later history. They spoke in YHWH's name, saying, "Thus says YHWH." After the First Temple was destroyed, Israel continued refusing to listen to YHWH's voice. The prophet Zachariah tells us that Israel's society refused to turn their ears towards God and hear His message through His prophets.

> Be you not as your fathers, to whom the former prophets have cried, saying, "Thus says YHWH of hosts, 'Turn you now from your evil ways, and from your evil doings, but they did not hear, **nor listen to me**," says YHWH. (Zech 1:4)

Throughout Old Testament times, the Children of Israel heard YHWH's voice. She heard it audibly at Mt. Sinai as it blasted like a trumpet and was accompanied with thunder (Exod 20:18–22). Later, YHWH sent prophets like Isaiah and Jeremiah to reiterate how turning from Divine Law leads to destruction.

I wrestled with reconciling John's statement that humanity has never heard YHWH's voice nor seen His shape. Maybe John was addressing the gentiles? Or maybe John was only addressing his generation: Was it just John's generation that had not heard God's voice? Four hundred years had passed since Israel's last prophets spoke to Israel as YHWH hid is face from His people and their sins (*c.* 430 BCE–30 CE). Perhaps John had this era in mind.

C. No Man Can Come to the Father but by Jesus

New Testament

> Jesus sad to him, I am the way, the truth, and the life: **no man comes unto the Father, but by me.** (John 14:6)

No other Gospel shares John's account. This text troubled me because it denies our direct access to the Father. Throughout ancient Israel's history, people had direct access to YHWH (see pp. 63–64, 78–79, 84–85).

Old Testament

> For what nation is there so great, **who has God so close to them, as YHWH our God is in all things that we call upon him for?** (Deut 4:7)

Divine Law made Israel great. It allowed YHWH to be close to Israel. People had direct access to YHWH. He heard their prayers. Moses talked directly with YHWH. Hannah, David, and Hezekiah prayed directly to YHWH and He heard and answered their prayers. No intermediary was needed. This was the one trait that I had previously discovered separated Israel from pagan nations. The lack of an intermediary made Israel dissimilar to other nations. Israel had direct access to YHWH.

In my own walk, I understood and appreciated praying to Jesus. Why would John's account state that we could no longer have direct access to the Father and King of the universe? The only conclusion that reconciled this contradiction was this change being a judgment against God's people for their sins. Humanity's direct access to the Father is denied as YHWH hides His face from us (Deut 31:17–18; 32:20; Isa 8:17; 54:8; 64:7; Jer 33:5; Ezek 39:23–24).

D. Has Any Man Other Than the Son of Man Ascended into Heaven?

Old Testament

> And it came to pass, as they still went on and talked that, behold, there appeared a chariot of fire and horses of fire. It parted them both asunder and **Elijah went up by a whirlwind to heaven.** (2 Kgs 2:11)

> And Enoch walked with God and he was not, because God took him. (Gen 5:24)

New Testament

> And **no man has ascended up to heaven** but he that came down from heaven, even the Son of man which is in heaven. (John 3:13)

Elijah was a man who ascended into heaven.[11] Enoch was taken by God. The New Testament implies that Jesus is the only one to ever have physically (Acts 1:9) ascended into heaven.[12] This seemed contradictory. I had to wonder. Is Jesus Elijah? Is he Enoch? Or, is this verse referring only to the spirits of Elijah and Enoch?

I needed a moment to reflect. While Jack brought up many of these texts, some I discovered on my own. Were these contradictions later additions made by well-meaning Church fathers? Or was I just raised with the institutional understanding of them? The contradictions were not simple issues. The OT supported God's people having access to grace and truth before Jesus walked on earth, while John asserts people had neither until Jesus' ministry. Did David lie when he stated YHWH's Law is truth (Ps 119:142)? The Old Testament held many accounts of people hearing YHWH's voice and Moses saw His shape. This also countered John's written account. The OT supported people's direct access to YHWH, the Father of humanity.

For John, the only way to access the Father is now through Jesus. It seemed like YHWH was "retiring" from having an active role in human affairs. This seemed oddly familiar. Why would YHWH change the way people accessed Him? Was this a judgment against Israel's constant rebellion against Him? I couldn't just ignore these issues. These contradictions are why we have so many different religions today. Each sect hangs their beliefs on different sides of this divide as Christian unity remains fractured. The divide then invites moral relativism while ultimately ignoring and denying YHWH. We forget His Divine path of life.

I did eventually find a path that can unite us. A path that resolves these issues. The only way I know how to share this plain path is to bring you on the same journey I traveled. Wisdom and understanding are gained by working through issues, not ignoring them. Please stick with me as our fellowship crosses the river onwards toward truth.

E. Prophecy of the Nazarene

New Testament

> And he came and dwelt in a city called Nazareth that it might be fulfilled that which was spoken by the prophets, "He shall be called a Nazarene." (Matt 2:23)

Old Testament

> No such prophecy exists.

No Old Testament prophet says anything about Nazareth. It also does not mention anyone being called a "Nazarene." I discovered that the difficulty lies within the New Testament's view of all Scripture as being inspired and infallible—literally, "God-breathed" (2 Tim 3:16). If all Scripture is God-breathed (hinting at perfection) why has the prophecy of Nazareth failed to appear in any version of the Old Testament (i.e., Masoretic or Septuagint)?

When I studied Israel's chronology in Volume 1, I found at least three errors in the state's record regarding length of king's reigns. Several contradictory accounts also exist regarding battle casualties and the amounts of tribute.[13] While this does not impinge on the integrity of the text (e.g., Ahab and Jehu still reigned; battles and tribute mentioned in the Bible still occurred), it brings into question the modern understanding that every word in scripture is "God-Breathed," a term which likely had a different concept for Paul than it does for us today.[14] Thus, we can conclude that some of our modern theological ideas depart from the writer's original written context.

III. INTERNAL HARMONY WITHIN THE BOOK OF JOHN

New Testament: John 5

> If I bear witness of myself, my witness is not true. (John 5:31)

In John 5, Jesus states that if he were to bear witness of himself, then his own witness is not true.[15] The next verse appeals to the witness of John the Baptist (John 5:33), saying, "*there is another that bears witness of me and I know that the witness . . . is true*" (John 5:32). Jesus does not appeal to himself, but to John the Baptist as a witness that his mission was from his Father.

New Testament: John 8

> It is also written in your law, that the testimony of two men is true. I am one that bear witness of myself and the Father that sent me bears witness of me. (John 8:17–18)

If Jesus bears witness of himself, then is it a true witness? John 8:17–18 contradicts John 5:31. Jack brought up these texts several times. As he saw it, the above statements are mutually exclusive. Either a person who bears witness of oneself is "not true" (John 5:31) or, one who bears witness of oneself "is true" (John 8:17). He found that it cannot work both ways.[16] Did Jesus bear witness of himself? Jack's questions had me wondering whether scribes misquoted or erred in their transmission of the text. I left open the possibility these were Jesus' original words since the Law required at least two witnesses to establish a matter (Deut 17:6; 19:15).

These verses in the Gospel of John challenged my faith. So many times, I wanted to turn away from the evidence. So many times, I tried to distract myself from these issues. So many times, I had turned to pastors who offered solutions that did not resolve these conflicts. So many times, I wanted to quit. It would have been easy to turn back. It was normal to accept the status quo and return to endless sleep. But how could I go on living in the vast sea of relativity where no standards exist? America and her religion are failing! My heart's desire is to know God. I wanted to understand truth and I was seeing America detour down a path of oppressive destruction. Could truth awaken the sheep?

I could have given up. But if I had given up, rather than following Paul's exhortation to fight the good fight (1 Tim 6:12) and Paul's exhortation to embrace what is set before us with patience (Heb 12:1), I never would have discovered the key to unlocking the mystery of conflicting religious beliefs. I would have missed out on discovering the obstacle that once removed empowers unity for modern Judeo-Christian belief systems. The evidence that resolved the conflict within my soul. I am so glad that I held on tightly to YHWH's teaching that we can!

18

Paul on the Law: Part I

The Gospel of John presented challenges. At the time I was unsure if John's account contradicted the Old Testament and the other Gospels. I questioned whether my inherited understanding had misinterpreted those texts to see them undermine Divine Law. Each time I came to a difficult text, it felt like I was picking up a stone blocking the path that leads back to YHWH. I was setting it on the side of the road—not to discard it, but to put it into categories so each one could be better understood. As I did this, the path towards truth grew brighter and brighter.

When Jack was challenging my beliefs, he often referred to Paul's teaching on Divine Law. He concluded that Paul offered an entirely different theology than what YHWH or Jesus had taught. I took Jack's position seriously, but I was sure there was a good explanation. I began the next leg of the journey not sure what stones I would uncover next.

I. DO NATIONAL CONSTITUTIONS LIKE THE TORAH CREATE STRIFE?

New Testament

> Because if they of the law be heirs, faith is made void. The promise made has no effect. **Because the law works wrath.** Where no law exists, there is no transgression. Therefore it is of faith that it might be by grace to the end the promise might be sure to all the seed. Not to that only which is of the law but to that also which is of the faith of Abraham, who is the father of us all. (Rom 4:14–16)

Old Testament

> ***Great peace*** *have they which love your* **Law** *and nothing shall offend them.* (Ps 119:165)

> Mark the perfect man and behold the upright, because the end of that man is peace. (Ps 37:37)

> Thus says YHWH your Redeemer, the Holy One of Israel, I am YHWH your God which teaches you to profit, which leads you by the way that you should go. *O that you had hearkened to my commandments!*[1] *Then had your* **peace** *been as a river, and your righteousness as the waves of the sea.* (Isa 48:17–18)

It has been my experience that wrath occurs due to the absence of Law.[2] California is dealing with mobs breaking into stores, grabbing all they can and fleeing before police arrive. It is so bad that stores are closing and no longer doing business in San Francisco and other lawless areas. Wrath occurs due to injustice and lawlessness. When the wicked prey on the innocent and the righteous, it produces hard feelings. It is bad enough when a woman is raped, but when no law or court upholds her right to seek justice, anger and depression prevail. The absence of Divine Law does not eliminate transgression, it empowers the wicked to oppress. In fact, one of the first actions dictators like Stalin, Mao, Kim, or Hitler take is to suspend or eliminate any rule of law that can hold them accountable.

Paul asserts that the promise of righteousness comes through faith, not through obedience to YHWH's constitutional Law (see pp. 41–41, 87).[3] This statement contradicts Genesis 26:5, which insists Abraham obeyed by keeping YHWH's statutes, commandments, and laws.[4] These are the three basic tenets of the constitutional Law given to Israel at Mt. Sinai.[5] Abraham was righteous because he kept the Law, not simply because he believed.[6] *Abraham was righteous because his faith led to obedience.*

Earlier in my studies, I had uncovered many texts written by Paul that confirmed Divine Law as valid. Now, Paul was undermining YHWH's Law. It seemed like there were two different "Pauls" in the text. The First Paul upheld the Law, the Second Paul tried to do away with the Law.

II. PAUL VS. JAMES

I discovered there was a divide in the Christian Church between the teachings of "second Paul" and James regarding righteousness. Paul's statement contradicts both John the Baptist's and Jesus' teaching that a person's life should bear righteous fruit, or it will be cut down. Paul's writings seemed to dismiss the timelessness of Divine Law.

Paul, in the Christian Scripture, uses this verse (referring to Gen 15:6) to prove that merit depends on faith rather than the law; but James draws the opposite conclusion: Man is justified by works and not by faith only (James 2:21–25, parentheses added).[7]

The Christian Church remains split today. One group has a heart for Paul's teaching on the irrelevance of Divine Law. The other group has a heart for James, the brother of Jesus, and his teaching that the Law is just as relevant today as it was 4,000 years ago.[8] Seeing this contradiction in written texts was confusing and aggravating. It was difficult to know who to trust.

The Hebrew Scriptures presented a unified position: The Law produces "great peace." It does not work "wrath." Early in my journey, I discovered texts proclaiming Divine Law as the path of peace and the way of life leading to immortality. Ezekiel termed YHWH's Law the "statutes of life" (Ezek 33:15). Divine Law teaches a blueprint for healthful living that prevents disease.[9] Above all, the Old Testament Law establishes liberty through a system of impartial justice and governance.[10] As a national constitution, it creates order for a free and civil society.[11] Paul's statements deeply troubled me. As I understood it, he was questioning all that my research had uncovered. I had solid evidence that the Hebrew Scriptures endorsed James' position on the Law and that Paul's opinion contradicted both. This led to my next question.

If there is no law, does transgression cease to exist?[12] I wondered if Paul's statement was rational. Many nations today exist without righteous constitutions and without codified law. They live in chaos.[13] They are ruled by men, mobs, or oppressive majorities or minorities. The common component among these lawless nations is social strife. Wrath, violence, and murder of brethren runs rampant. Nations such as South Africa, Kosovo (Yugoslavia), Syria, Iraq, Iran, North Korea, Gaza, and Somalia are great examples of the wrath that arises from the void of righteous systems of law.

Venezuela has reaped this type of "transgressionless" society where no law exists to transgress. The ruling class oppresses its citizens without recourse. The economy has collapsed, and people are dying of starvation.[14] Almost 8 million people have entered a diaspora, fleeing the oppressive nation.[15] Do these nations exemplify Paul's ideal of a society without law? For me, the question remained: Does the absence of civil or Divine Law avert wrath?

If YHWH never gave a Law to Israel, would it make murder any less wrong? Would stealing be any less of an injustice against our fellow man? King David asserts YHWH's Law brings such incredible peace that nothing can cause the upright who love Divine Law to stumble.[16] They cannot fall!

Faith without action is a life unlived. Life without action does not really believe. Faith acts upon YHWH's steadfast Divine Law. A rational faith holds its beliefs accountable to God—not man.[17] If faith is simply based upon belief itself, it is easily manipulated. Pastors, priests, political or military leaders, prophets, and evangelists can lead people astray (just as Lucian points out occurred in the early Church, pp. 104–5).

III. MAN OF LAWLESSNESS?

"Second Paul" seemed to contradict "First Paul" who upheld Divine Law, Jesus, and James. Second Paul seemed to encourage rebellion against Divine Law by teaching that YHWH's Law works wrath or that it is impossible to both have faith and obey (Rom 4:14–15). As I reflected on the evidence I had thus far, I remembered 2 Thessalonians' warning us of the "man of lawlessness."

> Don't let anyone deceive you in any way, for that day will not come until the rebellion occurs and the **man of lawlessness is revealed**, the man doomed to destruction. (2 Thess 2:3, NIV)

First Paul warns us not to "be deceived in any way." This text mentions rebellion as the reason for destruction.[18] This rebellion was not against Rome, but against Divine Law. As I reflected on the evidence, I had to ask if I was discovering the promise in this text. Was Second Paul the man of lawlessness that God warns us about?

My study had revealed that turning from Divine Law leads us to sin (Prov 28:9; 2 Kgs 17:13). In my own life, I was witnessing the absence of law turn America upside down. Further, history attests that far too many societies fell into spiritual and physical bondage because they were not founded on justice. These manipulative, oppressive, and manmade lies deprive people of property, possessions, family—and all too often—life itself.[19] As I struggled with these questions regarding Paul's ideas on the Law, I remembered that God's promise is for each of us to know Him for ourselves (Jer 24:7; 31:34; Ezek 38:16). I had seen that the process begins by reasoning together and not giving up during difficult times, so I pressed on.

19

Paul on the Law: Part II

I. PROMISES TO ONE OR MANY?

I was beginning to understand why there are so many different religious sects today. The greatest conflict in the New Testament was whether Paul upheld Divine Law like Jesus or whether he was "trained in false words" to "deceive his neighbors" (Jer 9:5).

Paul's stance on the Abrahamic blessings presented further challenges for me. He continues his discourse by asserting that the promises YHWH gave Abraham through His covenants were *not* meant for Abraham's numerous children. Instead, YHWH intended His promises solely for Jesus:

> Now to Abraham and his seed were the **promises** made. **He did not say, And to seeds as of many, but as of one: and to your seed, which is Christ.**[1] (Gal 3:16. See also Gal 3:17–19)

> For the promise that he should be the **heir of the world was not to Abraham or to his seed through the law,** but through the righteousness of faith. (Rom 4:13)

YHWH made many promises in His three covenants with Abraham. He promised that Abraham's children would become many nations (Gen 26:3–5; see below). Abraham's seed would become as the "stars of heaven" in multitude.[2] And, only Abraham's children (through Jacob) would possess the Promised Land (Gen 22:17; 26:4; 28:14).[3] In another **promise**, YHWH pledged to make Ishmael fertile and numerous: "the father of twelve chieftains" (Gen 17:20). YHWH specifically offered this promise to Abraham "because he is your **seed**" (Gen 21:13). If YHWH's promises were meant solely for Jesus, how did Jesus make Ishmael 12 chieftains?[4]

One method of dealing with this contradiction equates Jesus with YHWH, the "Father" in the Old Testament.[5] If, however, Jesus is YHWH, then why does Paul state that the Abrahamic

Promises are only for Jesus and not for Abraham's many offspring? This circular reasoning has Jesus—the Father—issuing the Abrahamic promises to Himself (as the promised seed). In this scenario, Abraham's biological children are "cut out" of the prophesied blessings.

If Jesus issued promises to himself through Abraham rather than to Abraham's children, it impinges upon YHWH's righteousness. Jesus (as Abraham's God) would be deceptively manipulating Abraham for himself. So, the question remains: how has Jesus received the Abrahamic blessing of Ishmael becoming 12 chieftains? The reason this troubled me so much is that YHWH's righteousness was at stake. If YHWH eliminated Abraham's other seed or descendants from His promises, then YHWH had been dishonest with Abraham.

II. GOD'S PROMISES TO ABRAHAM: LAND AND CHILDREN

A. *Promises Made to Abraham's Seed*

In the Promised Land Covenant, YHWH promised Abraham that his seed would be as the stars of heaven. YHWH specifically disallowed adoption as a viable means of inheriting His covenants. He established physical descendants (*me'ayim*, lit. sperm) as the only legitimate heirs to His covenants.

> The word of YHWH came to him, saying, "*This shall not be your heir,* but he that shall come forth ou**t of your own bowels** (*me'ayim*) **shall be your heir**". And he brought him forth abroad, and said, "Look now toward heaven and tell the stars, if you are able to number them". And he said to him, **"So shall your seed** (*zera'*) **be"**. And he believed in YHWH. And he *counted it to him for righteousness*. (Gen 15:4–6, parentheses added)

> I will establish my covenant between me and you and **your seed** (*zera'*) after you in their generations for an everlasting covenant, to be a God to you, and to **your seed** (*zera'*) after you. (Gen 17:7)

In Volume 1, we investigated the Promised Land covenant in detail.[6] Adoption was one issue we examined. These were the conclusions we could reasonably draw from the written text.

The only stipulation that YHWH makes in the Promised–Land Covenant is both to forbid Eliezer to inherit Abram's covenants (or his estate) as an *ewuru*[7] (an adopted heir to a childless master) and to define the terms for inheriting YHWH's covenants. *Binding on both Abram and YHWH* is the basis by which Abram's children can inherit his covenants: only Abram's *me'ayim*[8] (*lit.,* sperm) qualify.[9] . . . Even loyal, "adopted" servants may not substitute for Abram's physical offspring.

Abram had inherited Noah's and Shem's blessings because he was their physical descendant.[10] Likewise, only Abram's children were eligible for inheriting (or dispossessing) Canaan's land. Although Shem had other descendants who benefited from Noah's blessings, only Abraham's descendants would benefit from YHWH's covenants, such as inheriting the Promised Land. The next blessing, however, was not exclusive.

YHWH, knowing the eternal value and worth of the family, gave Abram the most powerful blessing on earth: children. Not only would Abram's numerous children fill his heart with love and joy, but through them YHWH would fulfill His promise to make Abram's seed a mighty and powerful nation to whom kings would listen and bow. YHWH planned to use Abram's children to ensure a Torah-based culture and value system. Through the family, YHWH would build a mighty and righteous people who had the faith to live by His way of life and preserve its philosophical heritage for future generations.[11]

Thanks to Abraham's children, the Bible has been preserved today. Thanks to Abraham's children, we can know and read God's Divine Law for ourselves. This blessing of knowing God—through His written word—was not preserved by the Greeks, Romans, Hindus, or other peoples. It has been preserved thanks to Jews and Christians—the physical descendants of Abraham through Israel.[12] Jesus did not preserve and protect the written Hebrew Scriptures throughout history, but Abraham's seed did (Acts 13:8; Rom 3:2).

Throughout the Old Testament, God clearly states that the only way to *inherit* the Abrahamic covenants is through biological descendants. When YHWH promised David that his son would inherit his throne, God reiterated that only biological seed can fulfill this promise (2 Sam 7:12). This in no way limited other nations or people from accessing the blessing of YHWH's covenants, but it did establish Abraham's seed as the means through which the nations would come to know and understand His constitutional Divine Law as a way of life that instills perfect peace (Isa 26:3).

B. God Promises Many Seed and Gives Them the Promised Land

The Hebrew Scriptures continually reiterate that Abraham's promises were intended for the entire nation of Israel—the biological seed of Abraham, Isaac, and Jacob. In fact, a thousand years before Jesus was born, the nation of Israel had already received many of the Abrahamic blessings.

As early as 1500 BCE, Moses emphasized that YHWH had fulfilled His promises to Israel by multiplying Abraham's seed and causing them to inherit the Promised Land. Moses and David understood the Abrahamic blessings as being intended for the entire nation of Israel— the biological descendants of Abraham.

> Remember Abraham, Isaac, and Israel, your servants, to whom you swore by yourself, and said to them, **I will multiply your seed as the stars of heaven and all this land that I have spoken of will I give to your seed, and they shall inherit it forever.** (Exod 32:13. See also Lev 26:42)

> *Fulfilled:*
> Behold, I have set the land before you: go in and possess the land which **YHWH swore to your fathers, Abraham, Isaac, and Jacob, to give to them and to *their seed after them* ... YHWH your God has multiplied you. Behold, you *are* this day as the stars of heaven for multitude.** (Deut 1:8, 10)

> But David took not the number of them from twenty years old and under because **YHWH had said he would increase Israel like to the stars of the heavens.** (1 Chr 27:23)

Moses and David understood God's promises to Abraham as being intended for Abraham's many seed: the entire nation of Israel. To erase these blessings and change their intended recipient would question every word written by Moses or David.

As I wrestled with these issues, I remembered that truth is established in the initial words God spoke to Abraham, Isaac, Jacob, and Moses.[13] A later writer has no power to rescind or change the parameters of God's promises. As Isaiah states, "To the Law and the Testimony, if they speak not according to these, there is no light in them" (Isa 8:20). Was Paul just another man trying to make his own religion like so many pastors after him?

C. Fulfilling the Abrahamic Promise of a Multitude of Offspring

As I continued to work with Jack's questions, I was seeing that many promises to Abraham had been fulfilled long before Jesus' birth. I also witnessed that within every covenant YHWH bestowed to Abraham, He promised to multiply Abraham's seed as the stars of heaven. YHWH reaffirmed this promise to Isaac, promising that Abraham's seed would be called in Isaac's name (Gen 21:12). A "sure house" was one sign of a righteous person, while the lack of living seed (as in the case of wicked King Ahab) indicated a man's unrighteousness.[14] I wondered whether Jesus fulfilled this Divine promise.

For Jesus to fulfill the Divine promise of seed, he would also need to have physical offspring. I discovered a stone that presented an obstacle. The Gospels do not record that Jesus ever married or had children. In the coming kingdom of heaven, Jesus states that humanity will not marry or have children (Matt 22:30).[15] I wondered how Jesus, as the heir to the promises of Abraham and Isaac, could fulfill this prophetic promise in Genesis 26 and have a multitude of seed? While I couldn't rule out the evidence from the Talpiot Tomb, which presented the possibility that Jesus had children, it did not ease the overall contradiction of Paul's claim.

These ideas are not intended to offend or to shatter your faith. I am sharing my journey with you and the agonizing questions with which I wrestled. Religion has become manmade without being held accountable to YHWH's written word. To restore that accountability, we must begin with ourselves. I am sharing these complex issues so that you can understand for yourself and come to know God by the voice of His own words.

Through God's direct written word to you, you can understand an unlikely and almost unbelievable salvation that is "nearer than you believe." These questions and our ongoing trial of YHWH's righteousness will lead to truth and a faith that cannot be shaken: a faith that withstands difficult questions. Truth stands the test of time. Truth does not change with new generations or religious movements. Understanding truth leads to a salvation that heals disease and provides practical answers to the pain, suffering, and misery in the world today. But more than this, repentance and returning to the Divine words of YHWH will awaken the sleeping giants of the earth today.

D. A Fruitful Nation that Possesses the Enemy's Wealthy Strongholds

God promised Abraham that His children would become a multitude. During the Diaspora, they would evolve into nations with kings. Eventually, Abraham's children would return to possess the Promised Land (Gen 17:4–7, 26:4).[16]

> My covenant is with you. You shall be a *father of many nations.* . . . a father of many nations have I made you. And I will make you **exceedingly fruitful** and **I will make nation***s* **of you**. Kings shall come out of you. And I will establish my covenant between me and you *and your seed after you in their generations* for an everlasting covenant to be a God to you, and *to your seed after you*. And I will give to you, and *to your seed after you*, **the land wherein you are a stranger, all the land of Canaan, for an everlasting possession**. *I will be their God*. And God said to Abraham, You shall keep my covenant therefore, you and your seed after you in their generations. (Gen 17:4–9)

> In blessing I will bless you, and in multiplying **I will multiply your seed as the stars of the heaven, and as the sand which is on the seashore. Your seed shall possess the gate of his enemies.** In your seed shall all the nations of the earth be blessed because you have obeyed my voice. (Gen 22:17–18)

In the Burnt Offering Covenant, YHWH promised that Abraham's seed would possess the Promised Land. He also promised that Abraham's seed would own its enemies' strategic "gates" (Gen 22:17; 24:60).[17] Controlling the Promised Land was the entire reason YHWH called Abraham to leave Haran (Genesis 12). Did Jesus fulfill the Abrahamic promise by causing Israel to inherit the Promised Land? Did Jesus fulfill this promise to Abraham's seed?

During Jesus's lifetime, the hardened and cruel Roman armies controlled the Holy Land. Rome had annexed the Promised Land and Israel with it in 63 BCE. In 37 BCE, Rome established an Edomite king, Herod the Great, to rule over the Jews. Herod eliminated the remnants of the independent Jewish Hasmonean dynasty and Israel's descendants lost her independence to Rome. She lost control over the Promised Land as Israel bore the Law's curse of oppression (Deut 28:58–68). Israel was slaughtered and oppressed for her disobedience.[18]

During Jesus' lifetime, the people direly needed deliverance from Rome's dastardly oppression. YHWH's instruction for cleansing His land in the judgment of Numbers 33 (the Effacement Judgment) was still binding on the Judean nation.[19] Did Jesus and his followers fulfill YHWH's command to drive out Canaan's natives or the more recent Roman colonists? Did Jesus receive Abraham's promise of inheriting the Promised Land during his earthly lifetime? Or, did YHWH intend for Jesus to inherit this promise at his Second Coming?

The ability to possess an enemy's gate is not spiritual. It always refers to military prowess.[20] Jesus' mission was not a military quest, but a movement for religious enlightenment. He never possessed any enemy strongholds. Rather than conquering enemy fortifications, he taught Israel to love her enemies (Matt 5:44; Luke 6:27, 35). How did Jesus' mission fulfill Paul's statement that Jesus was the only seed to receive or fulfill the Divine promise of owning his enemy's gates? The Romans and even certain Jewish leaders were surely enemies to Jesus and his followers. So, why did Jesus not deliver himself and his followers from Rome's cruel blow to fulfill YHWH's promise to Abraham?

Does the Bible teach that Jesus could fulfill these promises after his death (and resurrection)? Or, did he need to fulfill the Abrahamic promises before his death? These questions have nothing to do with Jesus' actual ministry or the important reason YHWH sent Jesus to Israel. My questions dealt solely with Paul's statement that all of Abraham's promises to his children (seed) were meant only for Jesus. Finally, I discovered one possible solution.

E. The Ultimate Abrahamic Blessing

I discovered a unifying theme to God's initial blessings. Central to every Abrahamic and patriarchal promise was one essential blessing. It is the purpose upon which all other blessings were based.

> I will bless them that bless you and curse him that curses you. **In you shall all families of the earth be blessed.** (Gen 12:3)

Blessing the entire world—not just Israel—is the central blessing, which runs throughout all patriarchal covenants (Gen 18:18; 22:18; 26:4; 28:14). Perhaps Paul considered this specific blessing as being intended solely for Jesus.[21] Paul may have specifically meant that the promise to be a blessing to the families of the earth was fulfilled through Jesus's ministry and his death.

YHWH's oracle, which Israel safeguarded, conveys God's statutes of life (Ezek 33:15). America's constitution adopted so many of these principles that the United States became one of the freest lands on earth. She enjoyed unprecedented liberty and justice that few nations have realized. Any nation can obtain this paradigm. It only needs to adhere to a righteous and unbiased system of justice and judgment: a constitutional law that protects individual liberty while delineating healthy boundaries between citizens and the state.

With all the statutes of life that YHWH provides, the only blessing left for Jesus to fulfill is to bless the nations by teaching people to return to his Father's Divine Law. This does not diminish Jesus' importance. In fact, this specific blessing makes Jesus' mission all the more important. I wondered if Jesus' mission to save the world from sin was the specific blessing to which Paul was referring. I also desired to understand how Isaiah's prophecy that "the pleasure of YHWH would prosper" (Isa 53:10) in the Suffering Servant's hand fit within these texts.

I also needed to investigate how YHWH's promise of blessing those who blessed Jesus and cursing those who cursed Jesus was fulfilled. At face value, I had to consider the possibility that Paul did not intend this promise for Jesus since Jesus and most of the disciples were persecuted or killed.

These issues challenged the very core of my faith. I was tempted to walk away from all religion. I felt like any harmony or truth was beyond human knowledge. But I could not give up. I had seen too much good in the Bible—in both the Old and New Testaments—so I pressed on. It was there that I finally discovered a way past all these stones and boulders that littered the path.

20
Divine Justice

I. AN UNCOMFORTABLE PLACE

I don't remember if I studied these issues in the order presented here or not. At some point, I considered them during my early quest. I would try to nonchalantly bring these topics up in conversation with trusted friends and teachers. Each time, the subject was abruptly changed. I wanted to ignore them as I had done so many times before. Was I sinning by contemplating these questions? Or was I sinning by ignoring them?

> He that turns away his ear from hearing the law, even his prayer shall be abomination. (Prov 28:9)[1]

My basis for seeking truth had to rely on "hearing Divine Law." If I turned from that standard of righteousness, justice, and liberty, even my prayers risked becoming abominable to YHWH's ears. So, I pressed on to consider the most challenging evidence to my faith. These were the verses that shook me to my very core.

II. THE QUEST

As my journey continued towards God, I realized that I needed to hold myself accountable. I had taken the first step by embarking on a dialog that sought "to prove all things and hold fast to that which was good" (see pp. 1–11). I had also taken the second step and was consistently calling upon YHWH's name (pp. 12–14, 18). It was this step that empowered my journey as my study of YHWH's word came alive! It began to demonstrate amazing constancy.

I realized, however, that I was struggling with the third step (p. 19–24, 27). As much as I was challenging my inherited lies and the "institutional authority" that perpetuated them, I was holding onto them at the same time. It is here that I must confess that I put off and ignored

Jack's most challenging questions. In fact, I turned away from hearing them, using the excuse that I was sinning by considering their evidence.

Finally, I had to face my aversion. How is considering Scripture sin? Did God mean it when He encouraged us to "come now and reason together"? I found nothing in the Bible which indicated I should not consider Jack's questions or the biblical texts he brought up. The only justification came from teachings in the Church, which kept people silent while following manmade leaders and teachers—teachers whose doctrine all too often made them least in the kingdom of God.

In 1999, it became clear to me that Jack was walking away from the New Testament, and I was his sounding board. We would debate ideas back and forth—both of us wanting to know God and to know truth. He asked questions that I had difficulty answering. Sure, I could rationalize them, but I felt like I was not being honest with myself or God.

The reason these texts shook my faith to its very core is that it presented a real and frightening possibility. It was the next logical question: Had YHWH sinned? I had set out in Volume 1 to put YHWH on trial by testing ancient Israel's allegations that YHWH and His Divine Law were unfair. The texts Jack presented turned everything I thought I knew upside down. But, I had made a commitment to myself and to God. I had made a commitment to seek Him and to see if He would be just, so that I could find Him. So, I journeyed through the evidence that continued to litter my path. These were not simple stones I could pick up and place on the side of the road. They were landslides that stopped me in my tracks.

As I reflected on my journey thus far, I could understand that we now have to go through Jesus to access the father, since YHWH was hiding His face from people and from their sins (John 1:17).[2] John could be referring *only* to His generation never seeing God or hearing YHWH's voice (John 1:18; 5:37). It had been almost 500 years since YHWH had sent a prophet to warn Israel of the consequences of her sins (*c.* 430 BCE–30 CE). According to the Law, Jesus could "bear witness of himself, "but he also needed 2–3 other witnesses to verify his testimony. John the Baptist and the Disciples more than provided the second and third witnesses.

Thus far, I had found Paul's stance on Divine Law was the most difficult to reconcile. It seemed like there were two Pauls—the First Paul who upheld Divine Law, and the Second Paul who despised it. Why would Paul diminish the Law when Malachi had encouraged us to "remember the Law of Moses my servant, which I commanded them in Horeb for all Israel, with the statutes and judgments" (Mal 4:4)? This was the very last prophet to speak to Israel since he lived *c.* 430 BCE. I also wondered about Malachi's curse in 4:6 that if we turned from the Law and if relationships between parents and children are not healed, YHWH would send a curse upon the earth.

The "Second Paul" also contradicted Jesus' brother, James, and his stance that Divine Law remained valid after Jesus' death. Isaiah had prophesied that one day YHWH would "magnify the Law and make it honorable" (Isa 42:21). Did Jesus' mission fulfill this prophecy? How did Jesus fit into YHWH's statement that He would act when people "have made void your law" (Ps 119:126)?

I have to confess that I was troubled by Paul's attempt to cut Abraham's descendants out from YHWH's promises to Abraham's seed. If Paul was correct, it presented strong evidence that YHWH sinned by deceiving Abraham into accepting His promises. However, if Paul only intended the promise which stipulated the world would be blessed through Abraham's seed was meant for Jesus, I could understand Paul's statement.

While I still had questions, my faith held on. I was sure there were texts from the Old Testament I had missed, or texts I had misunderstood. Almost every believer I know considers YHWH's Law too difficult to observe. Most have never heard Deuteronomy 30:11–16 that Divine Law is easy to obey. We also read right over John's statement that the Law is not "burdensome" (1 John 5:2–3). While I wondered what else I had read over and missed, my faith in YHWH and in the validity of Scripture held firm.

In 2001, I felt that I was sinning against God by ignoring Jack's challenging texts. I was not being honest with myself or God to turn away from them. I had to ask myself again, "How can YHWH's word be sin"? I spent much time in prayer as I finally considered Jack's evidence.

III. IS YHWH A JUST AND RIGHTEOUS GOD?

I had put off Jack's questions long enough. I had to examine Jack's questions by giving them the same consideration as I had my own. Further, I had to follow the path to which this understanding led. Was it good? Did it account for all biblical data? I could not dismiss Jack's questions if I was being serious about proving all things.

God's justice was the first issue that troubled Jack. Justice is the standard that distinguishes righteousness from wickedness. It is also the founding precept of Divine Law. The 10 Commandments distinguish between righteous and wicked acts. If you murder, steal, commit adultery or idolatry, bear false witness, dishonor your parents, or covet your neighbor's possessions, then you have transgressed Divine Law and you have acted wickedly. To understand Jack's question, I needed to travel through YHWH's precepts of justice.

A. Justice: the Essence of YHWH's Character

The precept of justice is so central to Divine Law that YHWH tells us it defines His very character. When YHWH revealed His name to Moses (so Moses could know Him by name,) YHWH revealed the essence of His character.

Justice is at the very core of who YHWH is. He did not reveal Himself as an open-ended God of love, since "love" is all too often dysfunctional and abusive. Love is an emotion difficult to define. This is why YHWH revealed Himself as a God of a healthy type of love based on justice and accountability.

> YHWH, YHWH God, merciful and gracious, longsuffering, and abundant in goodness and truth, keeping mercy for thousands, forgiving iniquity and transgression and sin, and **that will by no means clear the guilty;** visiting the iniquity of the fathers upon the children, and upon the children's children, unto the third and to the fourth generation. (Exod 34:6–7. See also, Num 14:18; Deut 5:9)

YHWH's statement that He "will by no means clear the guilty" is reiterated in Divine Law where He teaches us not to exonerate the wicked. The judgments He established for Israel specifically reiterate this fact: "I will not justify the wicked" (Exod 23:7). This is one of the clearest concepts in the Old Testament. Before I share Jack's question that is based on these ideas of righteousness, there is another text that influenced his thought process. It was a text that He considered to challenge our modern inherited understanding.

B. Shall Not the Judge of the Earth Do Right?

God revealed His precept of justice during a dialog with Abraham. YHWH was sending messengers to destroy Sodom and Gomorrah. Abraham was concerned that given the city's great sins, YHWH would punish the righteous with the wicked.

> And Abraham drew near, and said, **Will you also destroy the righteous with the wicked**? Peradventure there are fifty righteous within the city: will you also destroy and not spare the place for the fifty righteous that are therein? (Gen 18:23–24)

Abraham was concerned with God's collective judgement. Would the righteous also fall prey to God's judgment? Abraham wanted to know whether YHWH would spare the righteous. Would God's grace and mercy be withheld from them because they lived within a city of "grievous sin" (Gen 18:20)? Abraham's most compelling statement follows his question about whether God would destroy the righteous with the wicked.

> **Be it far from you to do after this manner, to slay the righteous with the wicked**: and that the righteous should be as the wicked, that be far from you: **Shall not the Judge of all the earth do right?** (Gen 18:23–25)

Abraham thought that God's killing of the righteous alongside the wicked was evil. It was reprehensible that God would ever consider judging the righteous and the wicked with the same verdict or reward. This led Abraham to ask one of the most powerful questions in the entire Bible: *Shall not the judge of the earth do right?*

If God killed the righteous with the wicked, then YHWH, as humanity's righteous judge, would sin by violating His own Divine Law. It was YHWH who prohibited killing the righteous like the guilty. This concept of justice was originally one of the precepts that caused me to fall in love with Divine Law and its ability to establish righteous societies. This led me to a related text that influenced Jack to question his inherited understanding.

C. The Righteous and the Wicked in Divine Law

1. Divine Law

When YHWH revealed Himself to Israel, He codified the precept of justice into Divine Law. This was the same precept that Abraham had understood: *judges must judge righteously, which is defined by Divine Law.*

> Keep you far from a false matter. **Do not kill the innocent and righteous: because I will not justify the wicked.** (Exod 23:7)

> If there be a controversy between men, and they come unto judgment, that the judges may judge them; **then they shall justify the righteous and condemn the wicked.** (Deut 25:1)

The author of Genesis tells us that Abraham had "the way of YHWH," which was based on "justice and judgment" (Gen 18:19). This is why Abraham questioned YHWH's intention with Sodom and Gomorrah. Abraham knew Divine Law, which forbade killing the righteous and innocent alongside the wicked and guilty. Of equal sin was the crime of justifying or exonerating the wicked when their crime was undeniable.

King Solomon validates YHWH's precept of justice when praying at the dedication of the First Temple. He quotes from Divine Law, saying,

> Then hear you in heaven, and do, and judge your servants by **condemning the wicked, to bring his way upon his head, and by justifying the righteous**, to give him according to his righteousness. (1 Kgs 8:32; 2 Chr 6:23)

Solomon paraphrases YHWH's judgment in Deuteronomy (above). He implores YHWH to uphold Divine Law by condemning the wicked and justifying the righteous.

Now for Jack's question. Jack understood the justice established by Divine Law to trump all other politics or theologies. He wanted to know how YHWH, as the earth's judge, could allow and "foreordain" (1 Pet 1:20; Heb 9:26; Rev 13:8) the death of an innocent person "from the foundation of the world," even if it was His own son. According to Divine Law, the only time a parent could allow their child to be killed was when they were horrifically rebellious against their parents and God (Deut 21:20–21). There was no other circumstance under which a parent could allow his or her child to be killed. Sacrifices to placate gods like Molech were strictly prohibited (Lev 18:21; 20:2–5; Jer 32:35). As I thought about it, I was also troubled by this inherent contradiction. So, I turned to the New Testament for evidence.

2. Condemning the Wicked in the New Testament

I discovered that Jesus also upheld the Old Testament's Divine precept of justice. He validates his Father's Law by teaching,

> The Son of man shall come in the glory of his Father with his angels; and then **he shall reward every man according to his works.** (Matt 16:27. Cf. Rom 2:4, 6; 1 Cor 3:8; 2 Tim 4:14)

Jesus teaches that he, as the Son of man, will uphold his Father's judgment by "rewarding every person according to what that person has done."

The Book of Revelation also upholds this precept that God renders unto each person according to his or her actions. In chapter 2, Jesus acts upon his prophecy in Matthew 16:27 (above). The setting here is the Son of man's return and his judging the Churches that arose in his name. As God's son, Jesus condemns the sinners within the Church of Thyatira. Jesus says,

> I will kill her children with death; and all the churches shall know that I am he which searches the reins and hearts:[3] and **I will give unto every one of you according to your works.** (Rev 2:23. See also Rev 20:12–13; 22:12)

While Jesus' judgment of the Thyatira Church seemed harsh, Jesus does uphold the concept of karma: that God brings our own ways upon us (1 Kgs 8:32; 2 Chr 6:23). I did have to stop and think for a moment. Jesus' words imply that he did not intend for his death to atone for the sins being committed in the Thyatira Church. Jesus emphasizes this point by stating he would kill Thyatira's children for the Church's sins.[4] Even after Jesus' death, YHWH's precept of justice continued to work the same as it had during Old Testament times. Not even Jesus or his death alleviated personal accountability.

This precept of justice where the righteous are justified and the wicked are condemned is the basis of Israel's entire Law. It is also the cornerstone of justice throughout the *free* Judeo-Christian Western world, even when this ideal is now being trampled and ignored. Society's rebellion against YHWH's Law does not disannul or rescind what is right and true. When a person or society disobeys or rebels, that person or society will reap the consequences of those actions, much like America is today.

D. The Source of America's Sickness?

America today struggles not because she is righteous, but because she is silent to wickedness. We ignore murder. When a criminal with a long rap sheet commits murder and is convicted of his crime, he is jailed for a decade if we're lucky. Criminals are now released after a few years.[5] All too often, they murder again. This hits home for me.

Back in the early 1980s, my grandmother, "Oma," had a little friend in his late 80s who stood less than 5 feet tall. She drove him around as he could not drive himself. Oma came to pick him up one day only to find police and ambulances surrounding his house. Milton had walked home from the post office and was joined by a convicted murderer who had been released from jail only 2 weeks earlier. He beat Milton to death with his own cane for a $24 Medicare check. The cane was shattered into 9 pieces. Society's leniency towards crime allowed an innocent man to die. Justice is the foundation of any free and righteous society. We should not put innocent people in jail for crimes they do not commit, nor should we exonerate people for murdering the innocent. Universal justice before an impartial law empowers nations to enjoy liberty. Nations such as China, North Korea, or Iran, which murder people for political opposition or to harvest their organs do not follow Divine Law and their citizens do not enjoy YHWH's *Law of Liberty*.

This is why Jack's question on justice challenged my faith. Justice was central to *every* instruction within Divine Law, a precept which Jesus upheld. How did Jesus' overall mission fit into these precepts? I also remembered Divine Law's precepts of truth. These constant standards upheld Isaiah's claim that YHWH's precepts do not fade like grass, but are constant, faithful, and exhibit fidelity to the details of YHWH's instructions. Did Jesus teach that his suffering and his death were pre-ordained? At this point, all these ideas seemed confusing.

E. Innocent Blood

Throughout Divine Law, YHWH reiterates the importance of protecting the innocent who have *not* committed any crime worthy of death. Murder was a crime worthy of the death penalty. When justice failed, the family, nation, or the entire national society would incur "bloodguilt."[6]

> Keep all these commandments to do them, which I command you this day, to love the YHWH your God, and to walk ever in his ways . . . **that innocent blood is not shed in your land.** (Deut 19:9–10)

I learned about bloodguilt during my research for Volume 1. I came to understand how YHWH "visited the iniquity of the fathers upon the 3rd and 4th generations of those who hate Him" (Deut 5:9). YHWH waited until 3 or 4 *consecutive* generations rebelled against the Law and hated Him before YHWH applied judgment (Deut 5:9). God did not condemn the righteous but condemned the wicked in those families. This precept of justice remained constant and did not contradict YHWH's precept of justice.

When society conducted a trial for a murderer in a court of law, YHWH forbade showing mercy or exonerating the criminal when overwhelming evidence attested to his guilt.

> Your eye shall not pity him, but you shall **put away the guilt of innocent blood from Israel**, that it may go well with you. (Deut 19:13)

YHWH ordained society to take steps to remedy bloodguilt so the land did not become polluted and callous to murder. Society should not turn a blind eye to crime.

Murdering the innocent was the most egregious crime according to Divine Law. When King Manasseh shed "innocent blood" in Jerusalem, YHWH declared that He would no longer pardon Manasseh's sins (2 Kgs 24:3-4). YHWH would not tolerate Manasseh's Stalin- and Hitler-like behavior. This is why I was troubled by Jack's question regarding how YHWH, as the earth's judge, could predestine or foreordain the death of an innocent person even if the goal was to provide atonement for humanity's sins. It impinged upon YHWH's claim to be righteous. Thankfully, my journey was not over yet.

F. Jesus on Bloodguilt

I soon discovered that Jesus upheld this concept of bloodguilt and justice. In His Law, YHWH stated that He does not clear the guilty, but renders the "guilt" or consequence of sin upon the children unto the "third and fourth generation" of those *who hate* Him (Exod 34:6-7; Num 14:18; Deut 5:9). Jesus validates this concept of justice by stating that all the previous bloodguilt of past generations would fall upon the wicked within his generation living in *c.* 34 CE.[7]

> Woe to you, scribes and Pharisees, hypocrites! . . . that **upon you may come all the righteous blood shed upon the earth**, from the blood of righteous Abel to the blood of Zacharias son of Barachias, whom you slew between the temple and the altar. **Verily I say unto you, All these things shall come upon this generation.** (Matt 23:29, 35-36. See also, Luke 11:50-51)

Jesus identifies the scribes and Pharisees not only as hypocrites but also as heirs to Israel's collective bloodguilt. Jesus mentions Zechariah (above). Priest Jehoiada was Zechariah's father and King Joash's uncle. Jehoiada had married Joash's aunt, Jehosheba. Jehoiada and Jehosheba saved the infant prince Joash from his wicked grandmother and raised him as their own son. Zechariah was like a brother to Joash. Being a faithful priest, Zechariah accused Judah of "transgressing the commandments of YHWH" so they "could not prosper" (2 Chr 24:20). King Joash and Judah's elders killed Zechariah (2 Chr 24:20-22) and forgot Jehoiada's and Jehosheba's kindness in protecting and raising him.

Judah's leaders killed Zechariah because he spoke the truth. His murder was never atoned for and remained a stain on the houses of Judah and David. They both bore bloodguilt for shedding innocent blood (Matt 23:30; Deut 19:10-13; 21:8-9; 1 Sam 19:5; 1 Kgs 2:31; 2 Kgs 24:4; Ps 106:38; Prov 6:17; Jer 7:6; 22:3; *26:15*).

Jesus' condemnation of his generation mirrors that of the prophet Jeremiah's warning. When Jeremiah was persecuted for revealing Judah's sins, he warned Judah's elders:

> But know you for certain, that if you put me to death, **you shall surely bring innocent blood upon yourselves, and upon this city, and upon the inhabitants thereof**: for of a truth YHWH has sent me to you to speak all these words in your ears. (Jer 26:15)

Jesus' condemnation that his generation would pay for the collective sin of Israel's bloodguilt upholds the same precept as Jeremiah's warning to his generation.

I did wonder why Jesus ascribed Abel's blood to his generation when they took no part in Cain's crime. Israel did not trace her bloodline to Cain, who murdered Abel, but to Seth who was born after Abel's murder (Gen 5:7–32). I questioned why Jesus ascribed bloodguilt to the wrong bloodline but I wondered if there was some prevision in the Law that allowed it. Perhaps people had intermarried so much that even Israel's bloodlines were crossed with Cains' so that they also bore his bloodguilt, which had not been atoned for.[8]

I had missed another fact in my previous studies. Jesus indicates that judgment for bloodguilt would fall upon his generation. While Jesus' sermon was not urgent, He did inform the scribes and Pharisees that this judgment would be so severe it would leave Judah's house "desolate" (Matt 23:38). We will examine this judgment further when we investigate the *Day of YHWH* later in this series. For now, all my attention was devoted to the issues I was struggling to make sense of.

I had to stop and think about Jack's questions. Divine Law is based on justice. The fundamental precept of justice is that the innocent are not put to death, nor are the wicked ignored when they hurt their fellow man. This led me to ask if YHWH could still be righteous by ordaining Jesus' innocent suffering and death. It took a few years of in-depth study, but I did find an answer. Before I share my response to Jack's questions, we need to delve into the related topic of substitute atonement, which bears on the reason YHWH sent Jesus to die innocently to atone for the sins of the world (Gal 1:4; 1 John 2:2). I discovered that Jack's next question helped me to reconcile these issues.

21

Substitute Atonement

I. IS BLOOD ATONEMENT NECESSARY?

A. Paul on Purification by Blood

Jack also challenged my belief in blood atonement through Jesus. There were several texts he understood to counter my belief. He cited Hebrews' statement on blood atonement as his first proof.

> Indeed, under the law **almost** everything is purified with blood, and without the shedding of blood there is no forgiveness of sins. (Heb 9:22, ESV)

There are two parts to Paul's statement. The first part is that under Divine Law, *almost* everything is purified by blood.[1] This harmonizes with Leviticus, which establishes a similar doctrine:

> For the life of the flesh is in the blood, and I have given it to you on the altar to make atonement for your souls, **for it is the blood that makes atonement by the life**. (Lev 17:11, ESV)

According to the Law, blood provides an atonement for life. Verse 11 in Leviticus addresses YHWH's prohibition against ingesting animal blood (Lev 17:10, 13–14), which was already established in God's covenant with Noah. This prohibition remains binding upon all humanity today (Gen 9:4–5). The topic in Leviticus 17 is God's ensuring justice for animals when humans use them for sacrifice by "shedding their blood" (Lev 17:4). The final verse in Leviticus 17 lists a sin that is not covered by blood atonement.

B. God's Justice for Animals

The subject in Leviticus 17 is bloodguilt. Animal bloodguilt is incurred by shedding an animal's blood when the animal is not aggressive towards humans or other animals (Exod 21:28–36). *During Israel's sojourn in the Wilderness*, anytime a person ate meat, the animal had to be brought to the "door of the tabernacle" to be slaughtered. Its muscle, the part that would be eaten, was either cooked beside the altar, or was cooked outside the camp away from the altar (Exod 29:14; Lev 8:17; 9:11; 16:27). If Israel did not follow this protocol, or if she ate any meat without draining the animal's blood, the people would incur bloodguilt for having shed an innocent animal's blood of life (Lev 17:3–4, 13).

Animals that were killed by other animals did not incur bloodguilt since humans did not kill them. This, however, presented another issue. The meat of the slain animal would still have the blood in it since it had not been drained. Eating this type of meat causes the person to become unclean or unhealthy.[2] This is not where sin occurred, however. The sin occurred when the person did not follow the steps *to become clean again*, like bathing and washing his or her clothes before evening. When a person did not follow YHWH's instructions to become clean again, the person still "bore his iniquity" (Lev 17:16).

Blood atonement did not apply to someone who simply became unclean by eating a dead animal which was killed by another animal. Despite the fact that the meat from the torn animal still had blood in it, eating the dead animal only made a person unclean. It did not incur bloodguilt (Lev 17:4). No blood sacrifice was required since a person did not kill the animal. A person simply had to take the steps to become clean again.

C. Almost Everything?

My previous studies had overlooked Paul's statement that "almost" everything is purified by blood. The Greek word here is *schedon*, which means "nearly" or "almost."[3] It has the same meaning in Acts 13:44 and 19:26. In the first part of Hebrews 9:22 (above), Paul is stating that not every sin is made clean through the shedding of blood according to Divine Law, which is what we see in Leviticus 17 (above).[4]

D. Does God Forgive Sins without the Shedding of Blood?

The first half of Hebrews 9:22 accurately clarifies that *almost* all sins are purified through blood. Ceremonial sins like becoming unclean and not taking the steps to become clean again were not covered by blood sacrifices and a person "bore his iniquity" until he or she took the steps to remedy their uncleanliness.

The next part of Paul's statement is confusing. In the second half of the verse, Paul writes:

> without the shedding of blood there is no forgiveness of sins.

I grew up understanding this verse to be open-ended: only through the shedding of blood could any sin be forgiven. However, Jack pointed out that Divine Law ordained forgiveness of sins without the shedding of blood. He drew attention to Leviticus 5, which ordains that flour can be used for a sin offering.

> He that sinned shall bring for his offering the tenth part of an **ephah of fine flour for a sin offering**. He shall put no oil upon it, neither shall he put any frankincense thereon: for **it is a sin offering**. Then shall he bring it to the priest, and the priest shall take his handful of it, even a memorial thereof, *and burn it on the altar*, according to the offerings made by fire unto YHWH: **it is a sin offering**. And the priest shall make an atonement for him as touching his sin that he has sinned in one of these, **and it shall be forgiven him**: and the remnant shall be the priest's, as a meat offering. (Lev 5:11–13)

I was flabbergasted! Poor people could offer flour as a sin offering without any shedding of blood—and they were forgiven! Leviticus 5 lists all the types of animals that could be brought for sin offerings and allows flour to be one means for forgiveness and atonement.

At face value, Paul's statement that "without the shedding of blood there is no forgiveness of sin" contradicts the Law. I had to wonder if the Second Paul wrote this or if it was added by a later hand. Whatever the case may be, Paul correctly clarifies that the shedding of blood did not apply to ceremonial sins by using the word "almost." This harmonizes with Divine Law. What else would I uncover as Jack continued to challenge my beliefs?

II. SUBSTITUTE ATONEMENT

As I investigated Jack's questions, I felt caught between two opinions. I never knew that the shedding of blood could not purify or cover sins of uncleanliness. Further, the Law allowed for atonement and forgiveness without any shedding of blood or blood sacrifice. This evidence contradicted everything I had been taught in the Church. Why did theologians skip over the first part of Paul's statement regarding sins of uncleanliness?

At first, I thought Jack's next question could be easily debunked. He challenged Jesus' ability to be a substitute atonement for sin. Jack believed that according to the Old Testament, no one could atone for another person's sins. No person or God could die—or needed to die—for another person's sins no matter how great those sins were. These are the texts Jack used to support his position.

A. Every Person is Put to Death for His Own Sin

The first proof Jack used to support that no one could die on behalf of another was the stipulation in Divine Law that each person is put to death for their own sin.

> The fathers shall not be put to death for the children, neither shall the children be put to death for the fathers: **every man shall be put to death for his own sin.** (Deut 24:16)

I had already understood this text to be the foundation of justice, so I did not foresee any possible issues. YHWH judges justly and does not kill you for any crime I commit.

Jack also pointed out that Jesus also upheld this concept and did not teach that his death could save anyone from their sins.

> Then said Jesus again unto them, I go my way, and you shall seek me, and **shall die in your sins**. Where I go, you cannot come. (John 8:21)

Jack believed that the wicked's own blood could atone for their sins. He understood the death of the wicked to provide its own atonement. Jack understood Jesus to teach this same idea. Even those who sought Jesus would still "die in their own sins" if they did not believe in the "I am."[5] I already understood this to be YHWH's Divine name (see pp. 11–27). I also understood Divine Law to uphold this idea of justice, judgment, and atonement, even when YHWH held out hope for repentance.

King Solomon built upon this precept that the wicked are often slain to deliver the righteous. The death of the wicked serves as a ransom for the righteous.

> The wicked shall be a ransom for the righteous, and the transgressor for the upright. (Prov 21:18)

While Jack and I agreed on this idea of justice and judgment, we disagreed on where Jack understood this concept to lead. Jack was beginning to understand the New Testament to contradict Divine Law.

This is the specific New Testament contradiction Jack had in mind. He understood the concept of a righteous person's death, which could atone for the wicked, to contradict Divine Law.

> For Christ also suffered once for sins, **the righteous for the unrighteous**, to bring you to God. He was put to death in the body but made alive in the Spirit. (1 Pet 3:18. Cf 1 Cor 15:22)

Peter states that the reason for Jesus' death was to suffer for the "unrighteous." His life was exchanged: the righteous for the unrighteous.[6] The question Jack posed, however, was: "If everyone is put to death 'for his own sin' how can any person be an atonement for another?

My reply was that "it was different with Jesus because he was God's son. YHWH can define His own method for forgiving humanity's sins. Animals atoned for people's sins and they foreshadowed Jesus' death." Jack's reply asked, "Is God above His own Law"? "Can humans be substituted for animals"? Jack extended his questions, further asking, "Can an unblemished (sinless) human be substituted for a blemished (sinful) human"? Jack understood Peter's theology to contract Proverbs (above) where wicked transgressors are given as a ransom for the righteous. For Jack, Peter's theology was backwards and contradicted YHWH's precept of justice.

Jack's questions revealed a contradiction in my own beliefs. If I answered "yes" to this question, it meant YHWH was arbitrary and could not be righteous. If I answered "no" then I had to wonder if God's son or anyone else could be a substitute for another's sins. I felt caught between two opinions. Could YHWH be righteous if He sacrificed an innocent person in order to save another person? What if that sacrifice didn't save one person, but saved the entire world from its sins for the greater good? Would that allow YHWH to remain righteous?

B. Does God Reject all Human Substitutionary Atonement?

The second proof Jack used to counter substitute atonement demonstrated Divine Law in action. It was a real-world example. After Israel sinned by committing idolatry with the Golden Calf, Moses offered himself as an atonement for Israel's rebellion. YHWH rejected Moses' offering of himself for the sins of the group while clarifying how He dealt with sins like this.

> Moses said to the people, You have sinned a great sin. Now I will go up to YHWH and peradventure **I shall make an atonement for your sin**. And Moses returned to YHWH and said, Oh, this people has sinned a great sin, and has made them gods of gold. Yet now, if you will forgive their sin; and if not, blot me, I pray you, out of your book which you have written.
>
> And YHWH said unto Moses, **Whosoever has sinned against me, him will I blot out of my book.** Therefore now go, lead the people unto the place of which I have spoken unto you: behold, my Angel shall go before you: nevertheless in the day *when I visit, I will visit their sin upon them.* And YHWH plagued the people, because they made the calf, which Aaron made. (Exod 32:30–35)

Jack understood this text to establish several things. First, Moses tried to make an atonement for the people's sin of idolatry, which YHWH rejected. Second, YHWH clarifies that the person ("him," above) who sins against Him will be blotted out of YHWH's book, thus rejecting any substitution. This harmonizes with the essence of YHWH's character where he states that He does not "clear the guilty" (Exod 34:7; Num 14:18; Deut 5:9).[7] Jack also drew attention to the harmony between Deuteronomy 24:16 and YHWH's rejecting Moses' substitutionary offering of himself. Jack highlighted the continued harmony in the Old Testament regarding justice.

C. When YHWH Visits Sin upon People

The third proof Jack brought up to counter substitute atonement was one I already noticed. YHWH did repay Israel for her sin in worshipping the Golden Calf by "visiting her iniquity upon her" through a plague. The word for "visit" is the exact same word used in Numbers 14:18 when YHWH reveals the essence of His character.[8] He "visits the iniquity of the parents upon the children to the 3rd and 4th generations of those who hate him" (Deut 5:9). "Visiting" a person's or a nation's sins upon them always refers to judgment.[9]

After Israel sinned with the Golden Calf, YHWH visited a plague on Israel in much the same way He had visited Sodom and Gomorrah's sins and delivered to them the fruit of their doings. The death of the wicked provided an atonement for their own sin. YHWH's judgment also harmonized with John the Baptist's and Jesus' popular teaching that trees which do not produce righteous fruit will be cut down (Matt 3:10; 7:17–19; 12:33; Luke 13:4; John 15:2). YHWH "cut down" Israel's rebellious and idolatrous trees who broke the covenant by worshipping the Golden Calf.

I also remembered that plagues were one of the curses of the Law (Exod 15:26; Deut 28:58–62). Less than 40 days before worshiping the calf, Israel had covenanted with YHWH and promised to reject idolatry (Exod 19:8; 20:1–5, 23). The people sinned through idolatry when they worshipped the Golden Calf. This was Israel's 5th rebellion since leaving Egypt, so YHWH plagued the people (see 1st endnote in chapter 11), which held them accountable.

Jack emphasized that YHWH did not offer any means for substitute atonement to mitigate this rebellion but repaid the guilty through a plague (Exod 34:7; Num 14:18). YHWH did not clear the guilty. He "brought his way upon his head" (1 Kgs 8:32; 2 Chr 6:23). Jack drew attention to the constant harmony of this idea throughout the Old Testament. This evidence from my dialog with Jack posed a question for me. If YHWH atones for sin by giving the guilty the fruit or reward of their actions, how can Jesus' life also atone for those sins? Jesus' teaching that he would judge the Thyatira Church also upheld the validity of Jack's question. If Jesus continued to judge believers the same way his Father judged people, how does Jesus provide a substitute atonement for sin?

22

Just Keep Swimming

I. DOES YHWH REJECT ALL HUMAN SACRIFICE?

A. Is All Human Sacrifice Prohibited?

The fourth proof Jack used to counter my belief in substitute atonement was YHWH's prohibition against human sacrifice.

> You shall not let any of your seed pass through the fire to Molech, neither shall you profane the name of your God: I am YHWH. (Lev 18:21)

YHWH forbade sacrificing one's children as atonement for sin, or to gain favor with any deity. Molech was a pagan Ammonite deity (1 Kgs 11:7; Ezek 23:39).[1] Archaeology indicates infants were burnt between 1-3 months of age.[2] YHWH found this practice so abominable that He cursed parents who murdered their own children. If society did not judge and execute these parents (Lev 20:4), then YHWH would personally set his face against that parent to "cut him off" from among the people (Lev 20:5; Deut 18:10).

King David also condemns sacrificing innocent blood. He specifically mentions the sin of sacrificing one's own children as shedding their blood.[3]

> And **shed innocent blood**, even the blood of their sons and of their daughters, whom they sacrificed unto the idols of Canaan: and the land was polluted with blood. (Ps 106:38)

Shedding the innocent blood of one's own children could not atone for any sin. Instead, it "polluted the land" (Num 35:33; Ps 106:38; Jer 3:1-2).

Jack understood this text to prohibit God from sacrificing His own innocent son to atone for another's sin. He argued that it was hypocritical to see the text in any other light. Human sacrifice violates Divine Law. Jack reasoned that human sacrifice was universally wrong. It was not just wrong because it was offered to Molech. Human sacrifice to any deity—including YHWH is wrong. While I understood Jack's argument, I remembered there were texts from the Old Testament that countered Jack's belief. I'll share these with you in a moment.

B. Can You Preordain What Has "Never Come to Mind"?

The fifth proof Jack offered against substitute atonement was Jeremiah. He saw Jeremiah's statement to be black and white: YHWH completely prohibits any and all human sacrifice. The entire concept of human sacrifice was so alien to YHWH that it never crossed His mind.[4]

> Because they have forsaken me. . . . They have built also the high places of Baal, to burn their sons with fire <u>for burnt offerings</u> unto Baal, **which I commanded not nor spoke it, neither came it into My mind**. (Jer 19:4, 5)

I had always read this text in the context of Baal worship. After studying YHWH's Divine name, I understood that Israel tried to commingle the worship of YHWH with that of the baals. Human sacrifice was one aspect of this pagan cult. YHWH challenges these pagan practices by specifically stating that He never contemplated requiring Israel to offer her sons as burnt offerings.

Jack's question built on Jeremiah's statement. Jack asked: "If the sacrificing of sons for burnt offerings never came into YHWH's mind, nor did he command it, how could YHWH pre-ordain His own son as atonement for humanity's sins"? "Pre-ordaining" requires forethought, which Jeremiah claims YHWH did not have in regard to human sacrifice.

This question really got to me. Was it possible for YHWH to have *never* thought of asking Israel to sacrifice her own children for her sins, but then pre-ordain the death of his own son as payment for Israel's sins? This troubled me and challenged my faith. I was angry that *if* YHWH was a God of truth, He had allowed such contradictory precepts in His word. As I struggled with these questions, I remembered Israel's sacrificial system. I was sure the evidence to counter Jack's belief would be found in the regulations for Israel's sacrifices and offerings.

C. Can Offering of the Firstborn Son Atone for Sin?

The sixth proof Jack used to counter my belief in substitute atonement was the prophet Micah's sermon on Israel's reliance on sacrifice without repentance. During Micah's and Isaiah's days, Israel was seeking to take drastic measures to mitigate the consequences of her sins since she had begun to reap the consequences for breaching natural law.

The nation's fields had become blighted (Lev 26:16; Deut 28:22), famine often plagued the land (Lev 26:19; Deut 28:23-24), she faced constant conflicts from invading armies, and diseases were beginning to develop within the population (Lev 26:16; Deut 28:18, 22; 1 Kgs 14:1, 17; 2 Kings 20:1-3).[5] When Israel had covenanted with YHWH, He listed specific consequences for Israel's breach of pact. Now, Israel was reaping what she had sown as YHWH visited her sins upon her.

Israel was always eager to do anything to mitigate these curses except returning to YHWH and obeying His Law. She finally resorted to sacrificing her children as atonement for sin. Micah challenged this theology asking if human sacrifice availed anything.

> Wherewith shall I come before YHWH, and bow myself before the most high God? shall I come before him with burnt offerings, with calves of a year old? Shall I give my firstborn for my transgression, the fruit of my body for the sin of my soul? (Mic 6:7)

In my own studies, I had seen that multiplying sacrifices did not influence YHWH to forgive sins. People had to take the specific steps outlined in Divine Law to become right with YHWH through repentance and obedience. But Jack took this discussion in an entirely different direction.

The question Jack posed was this: "If people cannot give their firstborn to atone for their sins, then how can God give His own son to atone for their sins"? This was the same question Jack asked before. Jack saw this as the same contradiction. He understood Micah to say that YHWH did not need any innocent firstborn to die for humanity's sins, even if it is God's own son. YHWH could fully forgive. Jack followed it up with Micah's statement that YHWH had already shown Israel how to live through His Divine word given at Mt. Sinai.

> He has shown you, O man, what is good. And what does YHWH require of you, but to do justly, and to love mercy, and to walk humbly with thy God? (Mic 6:8)[6]

Micah is quoting from Deuteronomy 10:12-13, which is part of Divine Law. YHWH did not leave people to arbitrarily define justice, mercy, or goodness. He spelled out His requirements in detail. Micah further emphasizes the balance between justice and mercy, which protects the righteous and condemns the wicked. Obedience demonstrates humility (Deut 8:2; 2 Chr 7:14). Jack, however, thought this text also implied that humanity *could obtain* YHWH's forgiveness without sacrifices. He reminded me of Ezekiel 18 where a wicked person simply repents by turning from his sin to obey and is forgiven.[7]

II. FORGIVENESS WITHOUT SACRIFICE?

The seventh proof Jack used to support his position that YHWH disallows substitute human atonement came from Ezekiel. I was quite familiar with this text because it is central to the

Covenant Lawsuit. Ezekiel counters Israel's allegations that Divine Law was unfair. Ezekiel clarifies how sin and YHWH's judgment of sin works within a family:

> When the son has done that which is lawful and right, and has kept all my statutes, and has done them, he shall surely live. **The soul that sins, it shall die. The son shall not bear the iniquity of the father, neither shall the father bear the iniquity of the son**: the righteousness of the righteous shall be upon him, and the wickedness of the wicked shall be upon him.
>
> **But if <u>the wicked</u> will turn from all his sins that he has committed, and keep all my statutes, and do that which is lawful and right, <u>he shall surely live, he shall not die</u>**. All his transgressions that he has committed shall not be mentioned unto him: in his righteousness that he has done he shall live.
>
> Have I any pleasure at all that the wicked should die? Says the Adonai YHWH: and not that he should return from his ways, and live? (Ezek 18:19–23)

Ezekiel upholds the relationship between sin and forgiveness established in YHWH's Divine Law. YHWH stipulates that "the soul that sins, it shall die." Ezekiel validates Deut 24:16, which forbade society from substituting parents for their children's sins or substituting children for their parent's sins. Each person was put to death for his or her own sins.

Ezekiel continues to assert that a person cannot share his or her personal righteousness or wickedness with anyone else.[8] His wording implies that personal righteousness or wickedness is non-transferable (Ezek 18:20). Each person reaps what he sows.[9] YHWH's requirement for forgiveness was simply that a person repent by keeping all of YHWH's statutes and do "that which is lawful and right."[10] Furthermore, all of his previous sins would be forgotten and not remembered (Ezek 18:22; 33:16). YHWH follows up by clarifying that He has no pleasure in the wicked's death but desires that the wicked turn from their wicked ways.

These texts presented a conundrum for me. This is exactly how I understood repentance to work in the New Testament. However, I believed this simple method of repentance and forgiveness was unattainable for people before Jesus' death. But Ezekiel was making it seem like this is how repentance has always worked under Divine Law. If the wicked always had access to this type of repentance, what was the purpose of Jesus' sacrifice?

As I read and studied Ezekiel 18, I was drawn again to Israel's charge against YHWH's unfairness, which is mentioned twice in this context (18:25, 29; 33:17, 20). Israel's complaint seemed to object to how easy it was for someone to obtain forgiveness by turning from their sins to obey Divine Law. Israel wanted complicated and more demanding rituals to rid her of sin rather than a plain and simple path of obedience. I had to wonder if I was doing the same by believing in Jesus' death as a substitute for my own sins, but I didn't think so since there were Scriptures that backed up my position and countered Jack's questions.

III. PREMEDITATED DEATH?

As our dialog continued, Jack's questions came back around to his original proof (see p. 167). He couldn't shake the contradiction in precepts of Jesus' death being preordained "from the foundation of the world." Jack believed that if Jesus had lived an innocent and righteous life, then his death could not be "preordained" from creation. If YHWH had planned the death of His innocent son in any way, then YHWH sinned. These are the verses with which Jack struggled.

> the Lamb slain from the foundation of the world. (Rev 13:8)

> For then must he often **have suffered since the foundation of the world**: but now once in the end of the world has he appeared to put away sin **by the sacrifice of himself**. (Heb 9:26)

> Who verily was **foreordained before the foundation of the world**, but was manifest in these last times for you . . . (1 Pet 1:20)

If YHWH preordained a righteous person—even His own son—to die for the sins of another, then YHWH had sinned because the Law prohibited anyone from killing a righteous person. These are the texts Jack understood a belief in vicarious atonement to violate.

> Keep you far from a false matter. **Do not kill the innocent and righteous: because I will not justify the wicked.** (Exod 23:7)

> If there be a controversy between men, and they come unto judgment, that the judges may judge them **then they shall justify the righteous and condemn the wicked.** (Deut 25:1)

During our dialog, I pointed out that YHWH did not actually kill Jesus. The Romans did. Jack understood YHWH's foreordaining or predestining Jesus' innocent death to be no different than David's killing of Uriah the Hittite. David did not physically lift his hand to kill Uriah, but he did send Uriah into a battle where it was impossible for Uriah to survive (2 Sam 11:14–17).

David's sin in killing Uriah was the one grave sin for which Israel's scribes remembered King David (1 Kgs 15:5). David's sin and the bloodguilt he incurred could not be atoned through sacrifice (Num 35:31–33; Ps 51:14, 16), since Divine Law prohibits sacrifice to alleviate the penalty for premeditated murder (Num 35:31–33). If the murderer's life was not taken for his victims' life, then the penalty for that sin remains for the murderer's descendants. *When 3-4 consecutive generations reject Divine Law*, their lives are substituted as payment for the family's sins since they, too, have become guilty through their own disobedience. YHWH ends the mercy He extended to the murderer's family (Exod 20:5; Num 14:18; Deut 5:9).

David had acknowledged this system of justice by asking YHWH to "deliver me from blood-guiltiness" (Ps 51:14) after he murdered Uriah. As earth's judge, YHWH needed to provide justice for Uriah, so Uriah's bloodguilt remained on David's House through the fall of Israel's Monarchy (2 Sam 12:10–11; 16:22). This was the prophet Nathan's point when he told David, "The sword shall never depart from your house" (2 Sam 12:10). David had despised YHWH (2 Sam 12:10) by murdering an innocent and loyal man and by committing adultery, yet David had also been loyal and faithful to YHWH in all else. Therefore, YHWH showed mercy to David but when David's children also rebelled, justice would be executed upon his *wicked* children.[11]

Jack understood the theology of Jesus in a similar light. If YHWH intentionally sent His innocent son into an impossible situation where He knew Jesus would be killed, then like King David, YHWH would have sinned and He, too, would bear "bloodguilt."

Divine Law addresses political matters like penalties for theft, murder, property lines, perjury, and other civil matters of a functioning society. Jack believed Divine Law made no distinction between civil or religious crimes: when one sinned like David, they also sinned against God (2 Sam 12:13).[12] YHWH had to obey His own Law. If He predestined the death of an innocent man, even if it was His own son, then God had sinned. Despite Jack's solid evidence, I remembered texts I had studied which challenged this position and presented solid evidence that ceremonial or religious law worked differently than civil law. Now my journey would seek to understand whether ceremonial and religious law lay on a path separate from civil and criminal law. Were they divergent paths? Or, did they merge into one?

23

Exceptions to the Law?

Jack had made his case. He had presented solid evidence. I totally agreed with him on Divine justice. Many of the issues he raised challenged my faith. As my journey continued, I discovered exceptions to the rule of Law. These exceptions challenged Jack's proofs.

I. THE RIGHTEOUS AND WICKED SUFFER ALIKE

Human history demonstrates the innocent are constantly killed alongside the wicked. During our dialog, Jack questioned, "If YHWH has the power to prevent the gross atrocities of human suffering and genocide, is He righteous to withhold that protection"?

To this I replied that "there were many times in Scripture that YHWH afflicted the righteous without cause. David's innocent son died for his sin with Bathsheba" (2 Sam 12:14-19). "While YHWH did not kill Job, He did afflict Job by allowing satan to inflict immense suffering." Jack was uncomfortable with this evidence. He believed that there was either a contradiction in these texts and the Bible was untrue, or our inherited beliefs had missed something.

In Job's story, satan did not set Job up—YHWH did. YHWH set Job up by asking satan about Job. Since David's infant son and Job were not God's biological sons, I also had to ask if YHWH's judgments were righteous. Did God sin by unjustly afflicting Job? Did God sin by ordaining the death of David's innocent son? I knew many friends and scholars who walked away from God based on the question of why the innocent suffer. Bart Ehrman, one of the greatest New Testament scholars alive today, cites God's allowing human suffering as the primary question that originally transitioned his faith from Christianity to agnosticism.[1]

II. CAN CEREMONIAL/RELIGIOUS LAW WORK DIFFERENTLY FROM YHWH'S SYSTEM OF JUSTICE?

A. The Suffering Servant: Isaiah 53

As I searched for answers, I began to see that religious law may work differently than civil law. YHWH told Abrham to offer his "firstborn son" as an offering to YHWH (Genesis 22). While there was no indication that Isaac's offering was for humanity's sin, it surely represented some purpose.

Isaiah also prophesied of the Suffering Servant who was innocent, bore Israel's sins, and was slain for the sins of the world. This challenged Jack's position on both substitute atonement and YHWH allowing an innocent person to be killed for a specific reason: to save and heal Israel and the world from their sins.

The Book of Acts cites Isaiah 53 as "The prophecy" that foretold the purpose of Jesus' mission. In the Book of Acts, Jesus used this text as the reason for his suffering.

> The place of the scripture which he read was this, "He was led as a sheep to the slaughter; and like a lamb dumb before his shearer, so opened he not his mouth." (Acts 8:32)

The author of the Book of Acts is quoting from Isaiah 53:

> But **he was wounded for our transgressions, he was bruised for our iniquities**: the chastisement of our peace was upon him; and with his stripes we are healed. All we like sheep have gone astray; we have turned everyone to his own way; and **YHWH has laid on him the iniquity of us all**. He was oppressed, and he was afflicted, yet he opened not his mouth: **he is brought as a lamb to the slaughter**, and as a sheep before her shearers is dumb, so he opened not his mouth. (Isa 53:5, 6–7)

Isaiah specifically states that the innocent Suffering Servant was "wounded for our transgressions and bruised for our iniquities." This meets the criteria of substitutionary atonement where someone is wounded for the sake of someone else.

B. The Law of Sin Offerings

Religious or Ceremonial Law did not seem to pose any obstacles to my beliefs. I was sure that this part of Divine Law would reconcile the contradictions between Divine Law and the New Testament to illuminate the path forward. So, I considered the corpus of religious law on sacrifices for sin. These were the specific regulations that bore on the issues Jack and I were discussing.

II. Can Ceremonial/Religious Law work Differently from YHWH's System of Justice?   181

Sin & Trespass Offerings. Animals were slain to atone for two types of sin. The first was the sin offering (Leviticus 4), the second was the trespass offering (Leviticus 5). While they were similar, each had slightly different requirements for prescribed animals and meal offerings.

Blood vs. Fat. The blood from the sin offering was never offered upon the altar but poured at the altar's base (Exod 29:12; Lev 4:7, 18, 25–30, 34; 5:9; 8:15; 9:9). It seemed that blood had little to do with atonement for most sins. The only thing offered on the altar for sin and trespass offerings was the fat (Exod 29:13; Lev 1:8, 12; 3:10–11, 14–17; 4:19, 26, 31, 35; 6:12; 7:4–5).[2] The animal itself was eaten by the offeror and the priest (Lev 7:15–18; Deut 12:5–8, 27; 14:22–23; 15:19–23), but its meat was never offered on the altar. These facts seemed to stretch all limits to the allegorical application of the entire sacrificial law being applied to Jesus.

Different Sacrifices. As I kept studying, I discovered that there were different types of offerings and they were specific to different groups of people. Lay citizens like you and me could bring a lamb or goat, but it always had to be female (Lev 4:28, 32; 5:6). If the sin offering was for the priests or the entire congregation, a bull (which was male) was required for a sin offering (Lev 4:3, 13–21). When rulers, like the king, committed sin, they had to bring a young male goat as payment for sin (Lev 4:21).

The ceremony for the *Day of Atonement* specifically required a young goat, not a lamb according to the Law (Leviticus 16:15–26). One goat was sacrificed while another was sent into the wilderness. A ram is a male sheep or goat, which was also required as part of the *Day of Atonement* ceremony. A bull was also required as reparation for the priests' sins during this ceremony, too (Lev 16:11). As I researched these specific stipulations, I could find no concept of a general sacrifice covering all trespasses.

Throughout the New Testament, Jesus is *only* referred to as a lamb offering (John 1:29, 36; Acts 8:32; Rev 5:6–8, 12–13; 6:1, 16; 7:9–10; 12:11). His death is never associated with a bull, which was the sacrifice needed to atone for sins of the general congregation and the priesthood (Lev 4:4, 13–15). Further, Jesus is never considered to be a female lamb. What if the specific wording in Divine Law reconciles these issues? Could fidelity to the New Testament's details reveal forgotten truth? Have we overlooked the specific purpose of Jesus' sacrifice because we no longer look to Divine Law (Isa 8:20)?

Sacrificial Meals. These facts challenged my understanding that Jesus' life or any one life could be a one-time sacrifice for all sins. There were different types of sacrifices for different types of sins, and not all sacrifices were for sin. Some offerings were for joy, peace, and thanksgiving (Lev 7:11–15). Further, people basically enjoyed a barbecued dinner with their religious leaders (Lev 7:15–18; 19:6–7; Deut 12:5–7). Often, the animal itself was cooked outside the camp, away from the Temple's altar. This again challenged my understanding. It was not the animals' body that was given as a sacrifice, but its fat mixed with spices, which provided a "sweet smelling savor" (Lev 1:9, 2:2; 6:15, 21). This seemed similar to the spices we use today to add to meat to enhance its flavor.

This seemed to oppose the statement in Ephesians that Jesus' offering was a "sweet smelling savor" since Paul substitutes Jesus' body for the required fat that was to be sacrificed upon the altar as required by Divine Law (Eph 5:2; Phil 4:18; Heb 10:5). If the sacrifices were symbolic and representative of future events, could I ignore the specific differences within these sacrifices to collapse them into one final sacrifice for mankind?

Jesus vs. Paul. I discovered another issue that totally upheld Jesus' teachings but challenged the precepts Paul taught in his letters to the churches. In Divine Law, sacrifices could only be offered for *un*intentional sins.[3] This aligned with Jesus' teaching that he would judge the Thyatria Church according to their sins. Jesus clearly indicates that his death could not atone for Thyatria's intentional sins (Rev 2:21-23; Heb 10:26). To this point, Jesus states that he had given the Thyatira Church time to repent for "fornication," "adultery," and other "deeds" but the people refused (Rev 2:21-22). These sins continue to be violations of Divine Law. Even if I found Jesus to be an ultimate sacrifice for all of humanity's sins, his death could only cover *un*intentional sins—according to Divine Law and Jesus' own teachings.

Does the Sacrifice have to be specific? These issues did not provide rest for my soul. The landslides in my path continued to prevent my journey from progressing forward to knowing truth. I had to wonder whether Jesus' sacrifice was a one-time offering for all sin or just a specific offering to cover unintentional sins. If the latter, it would explain the many prophecies of Israel's prophets which refer to the latter restoration of Israel's sacrificial system during a future era of restoration (Isa 56:7; Jer 33:18; Ezek 40; Hos 3:4-5; Zech 14:21).

Son of Man restores the Divine name. When I discovered the importance of YHWH's name, I evidenced the key role the Son of man would play in restoring the relevance and importance of YHWH's name in daily life (Ps 80:17-18; see pp. 25-26). This prophecy has yet to be fulfilled. I had to ask: Did YHWH's word fail to come to pass? Or, does the Son of man yet have a role to play in restoring his Father's name in our modern-day history today?

Justified Relativity? When I set out on my journey, I saw that new religious beliefs, moral values, and political ideas continue sprout into life with each passing generation. These trends flourish because we have nothing upon which to anchor our ideas. Isaiah pleaded for ancient Israel to "learn" (Isa 1:17) so she was capable of "reasoning together" (Isa 1:18). I had obeyed Isaiah's ancient plea. Yet, I now stumbled upon textual evidence that seemed to justify some of the circular reasoning that pervades modern religion today. At this point in my journey, YHWH did not seem like a timeless God whose ideas never fade. There were very real exceptions to the precepts within Divine Law.

C. In a Plain Path

I concluded Volume 1 by promising that YHWH's righteousness would be revealed in the pages of the New Testament. I also promised we would understand the reason Israel's Diaspora has lasted over 2,500 years. I withheld discussing the many prophecies of Jesus. To appreciate and understand Jesus's mission from the perspective of written Divine Law and the prophets, I first had to become grounded in the Scriptures the Church had once forbidden us to read (see pp. 1–2).

With the foundation established, I could investigate YHWH's mission and purpose for Jesus. Isaiah based Chapter 53 on the Book of Job, a parable of an ancient Son of man. Hidden within the books of Job and Isaiah 53 is the way by which we can finally overcome relativity. The facts that guide our journey finally vanquish our misery, allowing us to be unified, healed, and redeemed today.[4] I discovered that the Suffering Servant's 50 pivotal traits reconciled almost all of the contradictions Jack raised.

The knowledge of the Suffering Servant healed my soul! It was this knowledge that justified me and saved me from an ill-fated path. The knowledge within the Suffering Servant took away my doubts. This is why the *Suffering Servant, Part 1* is the next book in this series. Can the Suffering Servant prophecy reveal why innocent people suffer today? The secret hidden within the Suffering Servant empowers our triumph over silence to no longer allow rotten corporations and governments to oppress us. We can!

What I once considered obstacles to YHWH's exoneration became the solutions for reconciling these contradictions. Powerful truths can heal our divided world. "We shall know the truth, and the truth shall set us free" (John 8:32, paraphrased). We will further investigate the exceptions to Divine Law as this series continues.

As I continued to adhere to the seven Precepts of Truth, they enabled a discovery of truth wherein no contradictions exist. They resolved what I once considered exceptions to Divine Law. The specific precept that will aid the next study is Truth's trait of *fidelity: exactness to detail*. The Precepts of Truth will prove to be so incredibly firm and unchanging that they can be classified as scientific law. The synthesis, which Divine Law creates, ends our miserable complacency. Divine Law enables us to fight for the right and the good. Understanding that we can be righteous allows us to stand up against evil. The Giant is awakening!

I had inherited many beliefs unsupported by Scripture. I had discovered so much good in the Bible. Would I be dissuaded by several significant issues? There was no choice. I had to continue to travel forward. My years of past research were behind me. I was just beginning to discover the beauty, logic, and common sense in YHWH's Law, a code that revealed a path full of hope, joy, and peace that could enable nations to live together in harmony.

Jesus upheld Divine Law, supporting it as the means to eternal life (Matt 19:18–19; see pp. 46, 50–51). What I discovered about the Suffering Servant totally empowered and revolutionized my understanding and love of God. This discovery broke through the giant boulders blocking my path. I cannot wait to share this incredible discovery hiding in plain sight for the past 2,000 years.

Now is the time to repair this breach! Now is the time to remove the stones of stumbling and to raise up that which has been veiled and lost (Isa 25:7). Come with me and be encouraged as I continue to share my journey of discovery with you. This journey makes an amazing leap forward in the next chapter as the boulders and landslides blocking YHWH's plain path reveals a door hiding in plain sight (Ps 27:11; Prov 15:19; Isa 40:4). It was a door that did not require any secret language or code but opens by looking to the past to reveal the most amazingly clear passageway for the future (Isa 48:3–5, 12–13, 16; 51:2). The knowledge within the Suffering Servant prophecy opens this passageway.

Appendix A

Jesus & the New Testament Upholds Divine Law

Topic	New Testament	Divine Law	Prophets
Jesus Teaches Divine Law Remains			
Divine Law is valid until "heaven and earth pass away," this is another way of saying "forever."	Matt 5:17–19; Luke 16:17	Deut 4:40	Ps 105:8, 10; 111:8–10; 146:6; Isa 40:8; Ezek 37:14
Each of us can "fulfill" and obey the Law.	Matt 5:18; Luke 11:28; John 5:14; 8:11; 2 John 1:6; James 2:8–9; Rom 8:4; 13:8; Eph 6:1	Deut 4:5–8; 6:18; 12:28; *30:11–16*	Josh 1:7–8; Ps 119:55–56; Isa 48:17–18; Mal 4:4–6
Jesus lists the 10 Categories of Laws as a path for eternal life.	Matt 19:17–19; Eph 6:1	Exod 20:1–17; Deut 5:1–21; 30:15, 19–20; 32:47	Prov 12:28; Ezek 33:15
Jesus states that we "live by every word of God." This is a quote from Deuteronomy, referring to YHWH's Divine Law, which had just been revealed at Mt. Sinai.	Matt 4:4–7	Deut 8:3	
Jesus prays, saying his Father's "word is truth." Divine Law was YHWH's word, which defined truth.	John 17:17	Exod 34:6	Gen 31:10; Ps 119:142; Mal 2:6; Neh 9:13
Peter quotes Isaiah "the grass withers, the flower fades, but the word of the Lord stands forever." The only word YHWH gave Israel when Isaiah wrote this quote was His Divine Law.	1 Pet 1:23–25		Isa 40:7–8
Upholds Divine Law in the Law of Moses (not mentioned in the 10 Commandments) after Jesus' Death			
Jesus and Apostles uphold both the 10 Commandments and other laws, teachings within Divine Law, which occur outside the 10 Commandments, such as not defrauding others and loving your neighbor as yourself.	Matt 19:18–19; Mark 10:19; Luke 18:20; 1 Cor 6:8–10; Eph 6:1	Lev 19:13, 18	

Topic	New Testament	Divine Law	Prophets
Church elders forbade Gentile believers to eat food offered to idols, or that which was strangled (died of itself), fornication because Moses taught Israel the right way to live. The only definition of "fornication" Jesus' Jewish believers like James and the first church elders understood was defined by Divine Law.	See below	See below	See below
Specific Laws outside the 10 Commandments, which the New Testament Upholds or Prohibits			
Love your neighbor as yourself	Matt 19:18–19; Mark 10:19; Luke 18:20; 1 Cor 6:8–10; Eph 6:1	Lev 19:18	
Do not defraud	Matt 19:18–19; Mark 10:19; Luke 18:20; 1 Cor 6:8–10; Eph 6:1	Lev 19:13	
Upholds ceremonial law after Jesus' death: we are to be clean and holy	1 Thess 4:6–7	Exod 22:31	
Respecting persons is sin	James 2:8–9	Deut 1:17	Ps 40:4
Fornication: the NT defines sexual sins such as formicaation as, adultery, homosexuality, "a man having relations with his wife's mother," and other debauchary according to Divine Law. In some cases, the NT quotes directly from Divine Law when defining actions as sin.	Matt 15:19–20; Mark 7:20–23; Acts 15:20, 29; 21:25; Heb 13:4–5; 1 Cor 5:1, 19–21; 6:9–13, 18; 7:2; 10:8; 2 Cor 12:21; Gal 5:19–21; Col 3:5; Eph 5:3, 5–6; 1 Thess 4:3–4; 1 Tim 1:10; 2 Tim 2:22; Jude 1:7; Rev 2:14, 20–23; 9:21; 17:1–2; 19:2; 21:8; 22:15	Exod 20:14; 22:16–17; Lev ch 18; 19:20, 29; 20:10, 2–21; Num 5:12; Deut 27:20–23	Gen 20:3; 2 Chr 21:11; Prov 6:32; Jer 3:8; Isa 57:3; Jer 3:1, 8–9; 5:7–8; 7:9; 23:14; 29:23; Ezek 16:13–36; 18:6, 11, 15; 22:11; 33:26; Hos 4:2, 13–14
Jesus quotes from Deut 10:12–13 when charging that the Pharisees that they neglected to administer "justice, mercy, and faithfulness." Deuteronomy summarizes all the instructions within Divine Law with these categories as does	Matt 23:23	Deut 10:12–13	Mic 6:8

Appendix A

Topic	New Testament	Divine Law	Prophets
Forbids food offered to idols	Acts 15:20–21, 29; 21:25; 1 Cor 10:14–33; Rev 2:14, 20	Exod 34:15	Ps 16:4; Ezek 23:27, 39
Do not injest animal blood	Acts 15:20, 29; 21:25	Gen 9:4–6; Lev 3:17; 7:27; 17:12–14; 19:26; Deut 12:16, 23; 15:23	1 Sam 14:32–34; Ezek 22:9; 33:25; 39:17–19
Do not east strangled meat, which blood in **not** drained in binding on Gintile believers	Acts 15:20, 29; 21:25	Lev 7:24; Lev 22:8	
Condemns sorcery and witchcraft	Acts 8:9, Gal 5:19–21	Exod 22:18; Deut 18:9–12	1 Sam 15:23; 28:7; 2 Chr 33:6
Obedience of Divine Law Demonstrates We Love God			
We show our love of God through obedience	1 John 5:2–3; Luke 11:28; 2 John 1:6	Deut 6:5–7; 10:12; 11:1, 13, 22; 13:3; 27:10; 30:1–2, 8, 16, 20	2 Kgs 23:25; 2 Chr 31:21; Ps 37:31; 40:8; 119:34; Isa 51:7
"through breaking the law you dishonor God"	Rom 2:23	Num 15:30	
We should uphold Divine Law, adding faith to our obedience (remains in effect after Jesus' death)	Rom 3:31	Most of the Law is "forever: unto all generations: —Exod 3:15; 12:14–17, 24; 15:18; 31:17; Lev 6:18; 16:31; 17:7; 23:14, 23, 31, 41; 25:23; Num 10:8; 15:15; 18:23; **4:40**; 5:29; 18:5; 23:3, 6	2 Sam 22:3, 31; Ps 2:12; 4:5; 5:11; 16:1; 17:7; 18:30; 20:7; 31:1–6, 19; 34:22; 37:3, 5; 40:3–4; 56:4, 11
Those who obey the Law are justified: "For as many as have sinned without law shall also perish without law: and as many as have sinned in the law shall be judged by the law; (For not the hearers of the law are just before God, but **the doers of the law shall be justified**)." (Rom 2:12–13)	Rom 2:12–13	Deut 6:25; 25:1	**1 Kgs 8:32;** 2 Chr 6:23; Prov 17:15; Isa 5:23; 43:9, 26; 45:25; 50:8
The sign of having the holy spirit is that we obey: YHWH places His laws upon our hearts and in our minds, causes us to obey Divine Law.	Heb 8:10; 10:16—quotes from Jeremiah and Ezekiel; 2 Cor 7:1; 1 Pet 1:2; 1 John 3:24	Deut 6:5–7; 10:12; 11:1; 13, 22; 13:3; 27:10; 30:1–2, 8, 16, 20	Ezek 36:26–27; Jer 26:12–13; 31:33–34

Topic	New Testament	Divine Law	Prophets
Those who have God's spirit, serve Him in truth. Truth does not change, it is constant. YHWH is truth and Divine Law defines truth (Ps 119:142, 151; Rom 2:20; 1 John 2:4–7). Truth endures "forever" unto "all generation" (Ps 100:5; 117:2; 146:6). David tells us that he walked in YHWH's truth (Ps 26:3; 86:11). He could not walk in truth if YHWH had not shown that truth through Divine Law. When we have YHWH's spirit, we "obey" the truth YHWH as given to us.	John 3:20–21; **4:23–24**; 17:17; Rom 1:25; 2:8–11; **2:20**; 15:8; **1 Cor 5:8** (quotes Josh 24:14); Eph 5:9; Tit 1:14; 1 Cor 2:12–13; 1 Pet 1:22; **1 John 2:2–4**	Exod 34:6; Deut **32:4**	**Josh 24:14**; **1 Sam 12:24**; 1 Kgs 2:4; 3:6; 2 Kgs 17:37; 20:3; Ps 15:2; **25:10**; 26:3; 31:5; **33:4**; 40:10–11; 51:6; 71:22; 86:11, **15**; 89:49; 100:5; 111:7–8; 117:2; **119:142**, 151; 145:18; Mic 7:20; Prov 22:21; Isa 10:20; 25:1; Ezek 36:26–27; Zec 8:3, 8; Mal 2:6
We Can Obey and Fulfill Divine Law			
YHWH and Jesus thought people could live without sinning	John 5:14; 8:11; 1 Cor 15:34; Eph 4:26; 2 Tim 3:17; 1 John 2:1; 5:18	Exod 20:20; Deut 18:13; 17:19	1 Kgs 8:61; Ps 4:4; **119:11**; Ezek 3:21
We can fulfill Divine "royal" law	James 2:8–9; Rom 8:4	Exod 18:20; 19:5; 23:22; Deut 11:27–28; 13:4; 27:10; 30:2, 8, 11–16, 20; 31:12	Josh 1:7–8; 22:5–6; 24:24; 1 Sam 15:22; 1 Kgs 2:3; 17:37; Jer 26:13; Zec 6:15
Divine Law is not burdensome	1 John 5:2–3	Deut 30:11–16	Ps 119:165
Sin is Transgression of Divine Law			
Sin is breaking Divine Law	1 John 3:4; Rom 3:20; 7:7; James 2:9, 11	Num 15:29; Lev 26:15	Definition of sin is breaking God's Divine Law
People who violate Divine Law by: adultery, fornication, idolatry, sexual immorality, impurity, debauchery, eating food offered to idols, defrauding ones' brother—commit sin.	John 8:34; Rom 6:1, 12; 1 Cor 6:18; 15:34; 2 Tim 3:6; Heb 3:13; 10:26; 12:4; James 1:15; 2:9; 11; 2 Pet 2:14; Rev 2:20–23		
Believers who violate Divine Law cannot enter into God's kingdom	1 Cor 6:9–10; Gal 5:19–21	Lev 26:15; Deut 31:16–18	
People retain their own righteousness	1 John 3:7; 2 Pet 2:8		Ezek 18:20

Topic	New Testament	Divine Law	Prophets
Jesus will judge the Thyatria Church for: fornication, idolatry, adultery, giving "everyone according to their works."	Rev 2:20–23; 22:12		
Jesus encourages the Church of Ephesus to "repent and do the first works," the sins that are listed violate Divine Law	Rev 2:5		

Loved *Does Jesus Exist?*

Share the journey with friends and family!

Scan this QR code to purchase your copy and spark meaningful conversations.

Notes

PREFACE: THE SLEEPING GIANT

1. ALA is an acronym for "Adults that Like Adolescents."

INTRODUCTION: THE CRUX OF THE ISSUE

1. Exod 20:1, 18–19; Deut 4:12, 33, 36; 5:22–28.
2. Richard Elliot Friedman, *The Exodus* (New York: Harper-Collins, 2017), 18–23; James Hoffmeier, *Israel in Egypt* (New York: Oxford Univ. Press, 1996), 3–126; Megan Bishop Moore and Brad Keele, *Biblical History and Israel's Past* (Grand Rapids: Eerdmans, 2011), 112–17, 129–33, 141–42; *YE1* 429–84, 509–600.
3. Eric Cline, *From Eden to Exile: Unveiling the Mysteries of the Bible* (Washington, D.C.: National Geographic Society, 2006), ix; Friedman, *The Exodus*, 19–20.

CHAPTER 1: PROVE ALL THINGS

1. Jordan Pearson, "Salvation through the Church," *Blackfriars* 20/234 (September 1939), 688.
2. See also Deut 7:9; 10:12; 11:1, 13, 22; 13:3; 19:9; 30:6, 16, 20; Josh 22:5; 23:11; Mic 6:8.
3. The Council of Trent edict reads: "Furthermore, in order to restrain petulant spirits, It decrees, that no one, relying on his own skill, shall—in matters of faith, and of morals pertaining to the edification of Christian doctrine—wresting the sacred Scripture to his own senses, presume to interpret the said sacred Scripture contrary to that sense which holy mother Church—whose it is to judge of the true sense and interpretation of the holy Scriptures—hath held and doth hold; or even contrary to the unanimous consent of the Fathers; even though such interpretations were never (intended) to be at any time published. Contraveners shall be made known by their Ordinaries and be punished with the penalties by law established" (*The Council of Trent: The canons and decrees of the sacred and ecumenical Council of Trent*, trans. and ed. J. Waterworth [London: Dolman, 1848], 19–20, https://www.documentacatholicaomnia.eu/03d/1545-1545,_Concilium_Tridentinum,_Canons_And_Decrees,_EN.pdf).
4. Arnold Huijgen, "Alone Together: Sola Scriptura and the Other Solas of the Reformation," in *Sola Scriptura: Biblical and Theological Perspectives on Scripture, Authority, and Hermeneutics*, eds. Hans Burger, et al. (Liden: Brill, 2018), 80–85; Brad S. Gregory, *The Unintended Reformation: How a Religious Revolution Secularized Society* (Cambridge: Harvard Univ. Press, 2012), 89, 93.
5. Art Sippo, Fr. "Did the Catholic Church Forbid Bible Reading?," CatholicBridge.com, eds. Terry Donahue, et al., https://www.catholicbridge.com/catholic/did-the-catholic-church-forbid-bible-reading.php.

    Heinrich Bullinger (a Reformer of the Reformation) clarified *sola Scriptura* by defining the Protestant movement as solely relying on "the holy, Biblical Scripture, because it is the Word of God, has standing and credibility enough in and of itself" (Heinrich Bullinger, *The Opposition of Evangelical and Papal Doctrine*, 1.A.1 [Zurick, 1551], op. cit. in Gregg Allison, *Historical Theology: An Introduction to Christian Doctrine* [Grand Rapids, MI: Zondervan Academic, 2011], 52).

    Gregg Allison (Trinity Evangelical Divinity School) remarks, that *sola Scriptura* (Scripture alone) was "more than a motto, however, this formal principle of Protestantism became a decisive point of division between Protestant churches and the Roman Catholic Church" (Allison, *Historical Theology*, 79). In keeping with the principle of *sola Scriptura*, the *Formula of Concord* articulated the supreme authority of Scripture: 'We believe, confess, and teach that the only rule and norm, according to which all dogmas and all doctors ought to be esteemed and judged, is no other whatever than the prophetic and apostolic writings of both the Old and of the New Testament. . . . But other writings, whether of the fathers or of the moderns, with whatever name they come, are in no way to be equaled to the Holy Scriptures but are all to be esteemed inferior to them" (Allision, 89). See also other reformers who heralded *sola Scriptura* as the issue leading the Reformation. (Allison, 79, 88, 93, 152).
6. Gregg Allison also remarks on the Roman Catholic Church's exclusive claim to Scripture and its interpretation. "Early in his career as a Reformer, Martin Luther was confronted with current church

positions that weighed against common lay people being encouraged to hear and understand the Word of God. One of these positions was that the interpretation of Scripture belonged to the pope, and to the pope alone... At the heart of these positions was the belief that Scripture was 'obscure and ambiguous' and therefore in the need of clarification by the church" (Allison, *Historical Theology*, 128).
7. A sampling of these sects can be found at: "Global Christianity – A Report on the Size and Distribution of the World's Christian Population," PewResearch.org (December 19, 2011), https://www.pewforum.org/2011/12/19/global-christianity-exec/. See also the references listed at Wikipedia: "List of Christian Denominations by Number of Members," https://en.wikipedia.org/wiki/List_of_Christian_denominations_by_number_of_members.
8. Gregory, *Unintended Reformation*, 110.
9. See Lev 26:40–45; Deut 4:27–28; 30:1–10; Prov 1:23; Isa 26:9; 40:2; 44:3; 45:19–25; 52:8; Jer 29:13–14; Ezek 36:26–32; 37:11–17; Hos 5:15–6:3; Joel 2:28.

CHAPTER 2: WRESTLING WITH GOD

1. Edward Young, *The Book of Isaiah:1–18*, vol. 1 (Grand Rapids, Eerdmans, 1965), 75–76.
2. Graham Ogden and Jan Sterk (linguistic scholars with United Bible Societies) observe: "The Hebrew verb rendered 'reason' has the sense of setting things straight, correcting the record, as it were" (Graham S. Ogden and Jan Sterk, *A Handbook on Isaiah*, UBSH, vol. 1 & 2, eds. Paul Clarke, et al. [Reading, UK: United Bible Societies, 2011], 52).
3. Douglas Groothuis (Christian philosopher at Denver Sem.) understands "universal" as: "To be universal means to apply everywhere, to engage everything and to exclude nothing ... God is not circumscribed or restricted by cultural conditions" (Douglas Groothuis, "The Biblical View of Truth Challenges Postmodernist Truth Decay," *Themelios* 26/1 [2000], 22).
4. Deut 4:29–31; 30:1–9; 2 Chr 15:4; Isa 55:6, 7; Jer. 29:13, 14; Neh. 1:9; Duane L. Christensen, *Deuteronomy 1–21:9, Revised*, WBC vol. 6A (Dallas: Thomas Nelson, 2001), 96.
5. My supposition aligned with J. P. Moreland (Talbot School of Theology) who states that "God has revealed understandable, objectively true propositions. The Lord's Word is not only practically useful, it is also theoretically true (John 17:17). God has revealed truth to us and not just himself" (op cit. in Groothius, *Biblical View of Truth*, 21–22). Douglas Groothuis extends this point, stating, "Objective truth is truth that is not dependent on any creature's subjective feelings, desires, or beliefs. Paul makes this point when he discusses the unbelief of some Jews: 'What if some did not have faith? Will their lack of faith nullify God's faithfulness? Not at all! Let God be true, and every person a liar' (Rom. 3:3–4). God's truth is not dependent upon any individual's or group's experiences or interpretations, however strongly felt or culturally entrenched they may be" (Groothius, *Biblical View of Truth*, 22).
6. As I worked through the material, I discovered that without a firm foundation in God's original words in the Old Testament, it would be more difficult to grasp the concepts in Volume 2. Thus, I published my research for Volume 1 in 2015 to lay a conceptual foundation.
7. Nichole McCarthy, et al. "Preponderance of the Evidence," Legal Information Institute, Cornell.edu (March 2022), https://www.law.cornell.edu/wex/preponderance_of_the_evidence; "Burden of Proof-Preponderance," United States District Court: District of Vermont, https://www.vtd.uscourts.gov/sites/vtd/files/BURDEN%20OF%20PROOF%20-%20PREPONDERANCE%20OF%20EVIDENCE.pdf; James Brook, "Inevitable Errors: The Preponderance of the Evidence Standard in Civil Litigation," Digital Commons: New York Law School (1983), https://digitalcommons.nyls.edu/cgi/viewcontent.cgi?article=1524&context=fac_articles_chapters.

CHAPTER 3: WHEN GOD KNOWS YOUR NAME

1. Christensen, *Deuteronomy 1–21:9*, Revised, WBC, 80.
2. James Tabor, *Restoring Abrahamic Faith* (Charlotte, NC: Genesis 2000, 2008), 20.
3. אֶהְיֶה (*ehyeh*), root, הָיָה (*hayah*). SEC 1961; BDB, 226; TWOT (vol. 1), 213; CHALOT, 5; HALOT, 2271, s.v., "היה".
4. See also, John Day, *Yahweh and the Gods and Goddesses of Canaan* (London: Sheffield Academic Press, 2002), 14, 20. For other discussions on the name, see William F. Albright, *Yahweh and the Gods of Canaan* (Winona Lake, IN: Eisenbrauns, 1994), 168–72.

5. יהוה (*Yahweh*). *SEC* 3068–69; *BDB*, 217–18; *TWOT* (vol. 1), 210–12; *HALOT*, 3594, s.v. "יהוה". Robert J. Wyatt, "Names of God," *ISBE* (vol. 2), 507.
6. For those familiar with the Documentary Hypothesis, both the Priestly and Deuteronomist sources recognize YHWH as the Creator's name. See, for instance, Norman Habel, "Yahweh, Maker of Heaven and Earth": A Study in Tradition Criticism," *JBL* 91/3 (September 1972), 321–37.
7. See also Ezek 39:25.
8. Exod 10:7; *20:3*; 23:33; Deut 7:16; 8:19; 11:16; 30:17; Judg 2:3; 8:27; 1 Kgs 9:6; Ps 97:7; 106:36; Jer 13:10; 25:6; Deut 6:4; 32:39; Isa 43:10, 15; 44:24; 46:5. While Israel's God was a singular Deity, He did have messengers or angels who did His bidding—Gen 32:24–30; Exod 23:20–23; Num 22:24–35; Judg 2:1–4; 5:23; 6:11–22; ch. 13; 2 Sam 24:16–17; 2 Kgs 19:35; 22:19–23; 2 Chr 21:12–30.
9. The word "nation" is a modern term. In Hebrew, this idea is termed *goy* or *goyim*. These Hebrew terms, however, have modern connotations alien to the Scriptural text. The most important is that modern Judaism terms any non-Jew a *goy*. The Scriptural text applies the term to any group of people, even Israelites (Gen 12:2; 18:18; 21:18; 35:11; 46:3; Exod 19:6; 32:10; 33:13; Lev 18:26; Deut 4:6, 34; 9:14; 26:5; 32:28; 1 Chr 17:21; Ps 33:12; 83:4; Isa 26:2, 15; 51:4; Jer 31:36; 48:2; Ezek 37:22). To avoid confusion for the reader, I will use the word 'nation' to express the ancient concept of *goy* or *goyim*.
10. Deut 4:7–8; 2 Sam 7:23–24; Ps 73:1; 119:142, 151; 147:19–20; Isa 26:2; Zech 8:3.
11. Albert Green, *The Storm-God in the Ancient Near East*, Biblical and Judaic Studies 8 (Winona Lake: Eisenbrauns, 2003), 67, 278.
12. *UBD*, 413. *SEC* 1168; *BDB*, 127; *TWOT* (vol. 1), 119–21; *CHALOT*, 43–44; *HALOT*, 1325, s.v. "בַּעַל I.B".
13. Green, *Storm-God*, 185, 188, 202, 215, 226–29.
14. Green, *Storm-God*, 255.
15. Green, *Storm-God*, 110.
16. *GDSAM*, 128; and Kurt G. Jung, "Baal," *ISBE* (vol. 1), 377–78.
17. UBD, 413, plural—*Baalim* (הַבְּעָלִים); *SEC* 1168; *BDB*, 127; *TWOT* (vol. 1), 119–21; *CHALOT*, 43–44; *HALOT*, 1325, s.v. "בַּעַל I.B".
18. Exod 23:13; Zech 13:2; *JFB*, 768.
19. Day, *Yahweh and the Gods and Goddesses of Canaan*, 68; emphasis added.
20. Green, *Storm-God*, 278.
21. Ze'ev Meshel, *Kuntillet 'Ajrud (Horvat Teman): An Iron Age II Religious Site on the Judah-Sinai Border*, ed. Liora Freud (Jerusalem: Israel Exploration Society, 2012), 109. See also Hershel Shanks, "The Persisting Uncertainties of Kuntillet 'Ajrud," *BAR* 38/6 (2013), 29–37, 76.
22. Joseph Blenkinsopp, *Ezekiel*, IBC (Louisville, KY: Westminster John Knox Press, 1990), 41, 54.
23. Gerald Keown, Pamela Schalise, and Thomas Smothers, *Jeremiah 26–52*, WBC vol. 27, eds. David Hubbard, et al. (Grand Rapids, MI: Zondervan), 365.
24. William Holladay, *Jeremiah 1*, Hermeneia, ed. Paul D. Hanson (Philadelphia, Fortress Press, 1986), 88–89; John Goldingay, *The Book of Jeremiah*, NICOT, eds. E. J Young, et al. (Grand Rapids: Eerdmans, 2021), 110–12.
25. Goldingay, *Book of Jeremiah*, 110.
26. Andrew R. Fausset, *A Commentary, Critical, Experimental, and Practical, on the Old and New Testaments: Jeremiah-Malachi*, vol. IV (London: William Collins, Sons, 1866), 26.
27. John L. Mackay, *Jeremiah: Chapters 1–20*, vol. 1 (Fearn, Scotland: Christian Focus Publications, 2004), 260–65; Walter C. Kaiser, Jr. and Tiberius Rata, *Walking the Ancient Paths* (Bellingham, WA: Lexham Press, 2019), 97–98; Hetty Lalleman, *Jeremiah and Lamentations*, TOTC vol. 21, eds. David G. Firth, et al. (Downers Grove, IL: InterVarsity Press, 2013), 98–99; Leslie C. Allen, *Jeremiah*, OTL, eds. William P. Brown, et al. (Louisville, KY: Westminster John Knox Press, 2008), 80–81.

Christopher J. H. Wright (Anglican and Old Testament scholar) observes: "YHWH's name-tag on the temple was not a divine insurance policy against the consequences of disobedience and rebellion. The truth (it was the temple of the Lord) had become a lie (if they imagined God could never let it be destroyed and them with it).... Having made the stark point in verse 4, Jeremiah returns to it in verses 8–11, to explain why the words are *deceptive* and *worthless*. The lives of the people have become a daily round of breaking the Ten Commandments. He lists the sixth, seventh, eighth and ninth—which between them include violence and bloodshed, sexual promiscuity, economic oppression and judicial corruption. But every weekend (so to speak) **they would flock to the temple to claim the protection of YHWH on a society that ignored him all week**. Jeremiah mercilessly exposes 'the nonsense—and the effrontery—of tearing up the Ten Commandments and turning up in church, as though saved to sin.' Their worship was deluded and divorced from morality. Their lives made a mockery of the words they spoke in God's presence. Sadly, it was a practice that did not end with Old Testament Israel but remains a temptation among God's people to this day" (Christopher J. H. Wright, *The Message of Jeremiah: Grace in the End*, The Bible Speaks Today, eds. Alec Motyer and Derek Tidball [Nottingham, England: Inter-Varsity Press, 2014], 111–12, emphasis added).

F. B. Huey (Southwestern Baptist Theological Sem.) adduces: "Jeremiah accused the people of repeated violations of the Ten Commandments, specifically mentioning six of them (Eight, Six, Seven, Nine, One, and Two; see Exod 20:1–17; cf. Hos 4:2). They felt no shame about breaking the moral laws of God and then coming to stand in the temple that bore God's name (i.e., belonged to him; Num 6:27; 1 Kgs 9:3). There they would say, 'We are safe.' They believed that observing the temple rituals freed them to return to their 'detestable things' (a word that often bears sexual overtones) without fear of punishment" (F. B. Huey, *Jeremiah, Lamentations*, NAC vol. 16 [Nashville: Broadman & Holman, 1993], 106).

28. Kaiser, *Ancient Paths*, 104–05; Lalleman, *Jeremiah and Lamentations*, 99; MacKay, *Jeremiah*, 260–61.
29. MacKay, *Jeremiah*, 260–61; Kaiser, *Ancient Paths*, 105–06; Lalleman, *Jeremiah and Lamentations*, 99–100; Allen, *Jeremiah*, 81.

CHAPTER 4: KNOWING GOD BY NAME

1. Huey, *Jeremiah, Lamentations*, NAC, 170.
2. Barclay M. Newman Jr. and Philip C. Stine, *A Handbook on Jeremiah*, UBSH (New York: United Bible Societies, 2003), 395.
3. Newman and Stine, *A Handbook on Jeremiah*, UBSH, 396; Fausset, *Jeremiah–Malachi*, CC, 58.
4. "Difference between Baking Soda and Baking Powder," BYJUs.com, https://byjus.com/chemistry/difference-between-baking-soda-and-baking-powder/#:~:text=Baking%20powder%20is%20alkaline%20and,with%20an%20added%20acidic%20ingredient.
5. For a good explanation see, Sally McKenney, "Baking Basics: Baking Powder vs. Baking Soda," Sally's Baking Recipes (May 16, 2023), https://sallysbakingaddiction.com/baking-powder-vs-baking-soda/.
6. Hans Wildberger, *Isaiah 1–12*, CC (Minneapolis, MN: Fortress Press, 1991), 506. Wildberger (Univ. of Zurich, Switzerland) remarks: "One must know the name of a deity if one wants to have contact with the deity. But if one knows his name, then one also has access to him, since the mystery of the deity is included within the knowledge of the name" (Wildberger, 506).
7. Matthew Willis, "Lynching in America," JSTOR Daily (February 12, 2015), https://daily.jstor.org/lynching-america/. You can also search and read online about the murder of James Byrd who was dragged behind a pickup truck in Texas.
8. Kenneth A. Mathews, *Genesis 11:27–50:26*, NAC vol. 1B (Nashville: Broadman & Holman Publishers, 2005), 175; Claus Westermann, *Genesis 12–36, CC* (Minneapolis, MN: Fortress Press, 1995), 228.
9. David Clark and Howard Hatton (both are translators) observe that: "Verse 9 speaks of the conversion of the heathen nations, presumably as a result of the punishment described in the previous verse" (David J. Clark and Howard A. Hatton, *A Translator's Handbook on the Book of Zephaniah*, UBSH [New York: United Bible Societies, 1989], 192).
10. Clark and Hatton also note: "**Lips or speech were made unclean primarily by the worship of false gods (compare Ps 16:4; Isa 6:5),** so when they are made clean or pure again, the result is that the people will call upon the name of the LORD, and serve him with one accord. To call upon the name of the LORD means to pray to and worship him, and so TEV translates '**they will pray to me alone and not to other gods**'" (Clark and Hatton, *Handbook on the Book of Zephaniah*, UBSH, 192, emphasis added). See also, Kenneth L. Barker, *Micah, Nahum, Habakkuk, Zephaniah*, NAC vol. 20 [Nashville: Broadman & Holman Publishers, 1999], 488).
11. David M. Howard Jr., *Joshua*, NAC vol. 5 (Nashville: Broadman & Holman, 1998), 72–73.
12. A case in point is George Harrison's 1970 song, *My Sweet Lord*. The song does not extol Israel's God YHWH or Jesus. The lord he praises and to whom he wants to draw near is the pagan Hindu lord Krishna.
13. Julian of Eclanum in *Commentaries on Job, Hosea, Joel, and Amos*, ACT, trans. Thomas P. Scheck, eds. Thomas P. Scheck, et al. (Downers Grove, IL: IVP Academic, 2021), 129.
14. SEC 376; BDB, 35–36; TWOT (vol. 1), 38–39; CHALOT, 13–14; HALOT, 449, s.v. "אִישׁ‎," I.
15. Duane Garrett (Southern Baptist Theological Sem.) observes: "What is significant, however, is that the hope of future salvation is the basis for current reformation. In the prediction Hosea says that someday, when God restores his people, they will forever banish the name Baal from their religious life. The

very meaning of the term *baʿal*—'lord' or 'husband'—made it easy to interject the word into Israelite worship. One could call Yahweh 'my Baal' and justify it on the grounds that the term means no more than 'my lord.' But since the word was also the name of the Canaanite deity, the devotees of Baal could make use of this semantic overlap to smuggle their cult into Yahweh's worship. We see how completely Baalism would be removed in the promise that God would 'remove the names of the Baals from her lips; no longer will their names be invoked'" (Duane A. Garrett, *Hosea, Joel*, NAC vol. 19A [Nashville: Broadman & Holman Publishers, 1997], 91–92).

One early Italian Church Bishop also understood this text. Julian of Eclanum (386–455 CE) notes that Hosea "is promising that the names of the idols would be removed from the mouth of the chastised nation... she shall no more remember their name... the correction that was complete (Julian of Eclanum in *Commentaries on Job, Hosea, Joel, and Amos*, ACT, 129).

16. See also Exod 23:13; Zech 13:2; Isa 52:5–6.
17. בַּעֲלִי (baali); SEC 376; BDB 35; TWOT (vol. 1), 38–39; CHALOT, 41; HALOT, 1325, s.v. "בְּעָלִים, בַּעַל" I.B. Baalim is the plural form of the word Baal or Baalai.
18. On the Son of man in Psalms 80, James Hamilton (Southern Baptist Theological Sem.) remarks: "Asaph calls on God to visit the son God made strong for himself. Here it becomes apparent that Asaph wants God to restore the nation through his son, and Ps 2:7 has identified that son as the future king from David's line" (James M. Hamilton Jr., *Psalms*, vol. 2, Evangelical Biblical Theology Commentary, eds. T. Desmond Alexander, Thomas R. Schreiner, and Andreas J. Köstenberger [Bellingham, WA: Lexham Academic, 2021], 76).

Daniel Estes (Cedarville Univ.) understands this text similarly: "There may be messianic overtones in this designation, but whatever the specific reference, the people turn to the Lord as the source of strength and success for them and for his appointed son (cf. Ps 89:21[22])." (Daniel J. Estes, *Psalms 73–150*, NAC vol. 13, ed. E. Ray. Clendenen [Nashville: B & H Publishing, 2019], 105. See also, Hans-Joachim Kraus, *A: Psalms 60–150*, CC [Minneapolis, MN: Fortress Press, 1993], 143–44).

CHAPTER 5: BREAKING RELATIVISM'S SPELL

1. Josh Kantrow, "More good stuff from my friend," Facebook: October 12, 9:31 pm. https://www.facebook.com/josh.kantrow/posts/pfbid02p3JvpNAGr5Joxwyra2EDhPSWErCiiDnRPrzTAVeQpEn9q5MXSaLB9iPeffW73TSsl.
2. Norman Snaith, *Isaiah 40–66: A Study of the Teaching of the Second Isaiah and Its Consequences*, VTSup XIV, eds. G. W. Anderson, et al. (Leiden: Brill, 1967), 190.
3. Wyatt Graham, "Does the Mosaic Law Still Apply to Christians?" The Gospel Coalition (February 9, 2021), https://ca.thegospelcoalition.org/columns/detrinitate/does-the-mosaic-law-still-apply-to-christians/; Wayne Jackson, "Is the Law of Moses (Torah) Still Binding?," The Christian Currier, https://christiancourier.com/articles/is-the-law-of-moses-torah-still-binding.
4. Dave Schmidt, "The Christian and the Law of Moses," Southside Church of Christ (March 6, 2011), https://southsidechurchofchrist.com/sermons/the-christian-and-the-law-of-moses.html; "Are Christians Under the Law of Moses?," Verse by Verse Ministry International (March 21, 2015), https://versebyverseministry.org/bible-answers/is-a-christian-under-the-law-of-moses.
5. The term *Shemuah*, translated "report," means tidings or news about something. It derives from the root *shama*, which means "to hear" (שְׁמוּעָה, root שמע. SEC 8052; BDB, 1035; TWOT [vol. 2], 938–39; CHALOT, 377; HALOT, 9720, s.v. "4 ,1 הַשְּׁמֻעָה"; Jan L. Koole, *Isaiah III: Isaiah 49–55*, vol. 2, Historical Commentary of the Old Testament, trans. Anthony Runia, eds. Cornelis Houtman, et al. [Leuven, Belgium: Peeters, 1998], 276). *Shemuah* means tidings, whether those tidings are true or false (2 Kgs 19:7; Prov 15:30; Isa 28:9, 19; 37:7; Jer 10:22; 49:14; Ezek 7:26; 21:7; Oba 1:1).

Jodell's comment: In chapter 28, Isaiah discusses how Ephraim's spiritual drunkenness caused the people to error through strong drink, which departed from the way of YHWH (Isa 28:7). In vv. 9–12 Isaiah tells people how they can emerge from their false ideas to discover truth.
6. Isaiah carefully uses an ancient form for YHWH's commands. This ties Isaiah's words to the instructions in Leviticus and Numbers. Saw (צָו) is the Hebrew word translated "precept." It means a command or instruction (SEC 6673; BDB, 846; TWOT [vol. 2], 758; CHALOT, 304; HALOT, 7895, s.v. "צָו"). It is used in Lev 6:2; 24:2; Num 5:2; 28:2; 34:2; 35:2; Deut 2:4; 2 Kgs 20:1; Isa 28:10, 13; 38:1; Hos 5:11. (See also, John D. W. Watts, *Isaiah 1–33*, Revised Edition, WBC vol. 24 [Nashville: Thomas Nelson, 2005], 431; George Mendenhall, *The Bible and the Ancient Near East: Essays in Honor of William Foxwell Albright*, ed. George

Earnest Wright [Garden City, NY: Anchor Books, 1965], 42). By referencing an ancient and archaic word, Isaiah is tying his criticism in Ch. 28 to the instructions that define YHWH's precepts in Leviticus and Numbers.

Jodell's comment: Isaiah 28 opens by addressing the drunkards of Ephraim and YHWH's judgment of them (vv. 1–4). Verses 5–6 refer to YHWH's future salvation (cf. Isa 11:11; *18:7*; 52:9–15) at the Second Exodus, an idea that Israel could not comprehend since her people had not yet been deported. This may be the "report" to which Isaiah refers to in v. 9. Verses 6–8 refer to "they" as the drunkards of Ephraim. Isaiah 28:9 begins a new section, which returns to the discussion in vv. 5–6 regarding YHWH's future salvation. In verse 9, the singular "he" refers to YHWH and continues the discussion from vv. 5–6. Isaiah asks how these drunken priests can learn knowledge and come to understand Isaiah's report—a report embedded in the Torah's Testimony.

The first time Isaiah mentions commands and lines, it is in the context of YHWH's Divine Law that provided Israel with "rest" (Exod 23:12; 31:15; 33:14; 34:21; 35:2; Lev 16:31; 23:3, 32; 25:4–5; 26:34–35; Deut 3:20; 5:14; 12:9–10; 25:19; 28:65; Josh 1:13–15; 14:26; 21:44). The stammering lips in v. 11 refers to YHWH's then soon-coming judgment against Ephraim's drunken priests, affected by the Assyrians who spoke another language. The rhyme and repetition of v. 10 and v. 13 indicate the priests may have used this phrase as a mnemonic teaching device for children. The Hebrew sounds like: "*tsaw latsaw tsaw latsaw, qaw laqaw qaw laqaw, ze'er sham ze'er sham*" (Graham S. Ogden and Jan Sterk, *A Handbook on Isaiah*, vol. 1 & 2, UBSH, eds. Paul Clarke, et al. [Reading, UK: United Bible Societies, 2011], 728). Israel's priests may have used this phrase as a mnemonic catechism for teaching Torah. However, the mnemonic's rich meaning was lost to rote, meaningless memory learning.

Isaiah's use of (קָו) *qaw*, translated 'line' in v. 10 is similar to Isaiah 18:7 where it is rendered 'powerful.' However, the context of *line* is closer to the original meaning in 28:10. In v. 10, Isaiah contrasts the restful commands YHWH gave to Israel (Isa 28:10) to the drunken commands created by man (Isa 28:13; Hos 5:11). Isaiah terms the latter a "line of confusion" (Isa 34:11) since Israel rejected YHWH's precepts (28:12). Isaiah discusses this *line* again in 28:17, stating that YHWH will lay "judgment to the line" to "sweep away the refuge of lies." Thus v. 10 refers to the instructions in Divine Law that Israel rejected, while v. 13 refers to Israel's manmade laws based upon "lines of confusion" (Isa 34:11; Hos 5:11).

7. David McKenna and Lloyd J. Ogilvie, *Isaiah 1–39*, PCS vol. 17 (Nashville: Thomas Nelson, 1993), 269–70; John F. A. Sawyer, *Isaiah through the Centuries*, WBCS, eds. John F. A. Sawyer, et al. (Hoboken, NJ: Wiley Blackwell, 2018), 165.
8. SEC 6490; *BDB*, 824; *TWOT* (vol. 2), 732; *CHALOT*, 296; *HALOT*, 7688, s.v. "פִּקּוּדִים". *HALOT* defines a precept (פִּקּוּד) as a "responsibility" or "regulation" translating Ps 119:128 as "therefore I find your regulations altogether fair."
9. Stephen Robles, "What is a Precept?," Higher Ground Ministries (2015), Highergroundministries.org, https://highergroundministry.org/precepts?fbclid=IwAR0a5HpU7OllliYgtIkfJZH-LfWSD6e7-C58C-UqnMx0jM4bVM_aRITiZnk.
10. Raymond Westbrook and Bruce Wells, *Everyday Law in Biblical Israel* (Cambridge, UK: Cambridge Univ. Press, 1947), 6.
11. Westbrook and Wells, *Everyday Law*, 1.
12. Westbrook and Wells, *Everyday Law*, 1, parentheses added for clarification.
13. Leslie C. Allen, *Psalms 101–150*, Revised, WBC vol. 21, eds. Bruce Metzger, David Hubbard, Glenn Barker, et al. (Nashville: Thomas Nelson, 2002), 180–92; Nancy deClaissé-Walford, Rolf Jacobson, Beth LaNeel Tanner, *The Book of Psalms*, NICOT (Grand Rapids, MI: Eerdmans, 2014), 882–86.
14. "Innocent Until Proven Guilty: Origin, Law, & Meaning," Study.com (April 6, 2016), https://study.com/academy/lesson/innocent-until-proven-guilty-origin-law-meaning.html; J. T. Yong, "Guilty Until Proven Innocent," The Hill (July 25, 2020), https://thehill.com/opinion/criminal-justice/509018-guilty-until-proven-innocent/; "Cornerstone of Justice," Center for Prosecutor Integrity, http://www.prosecutorintegrity.org/innocence/cornerstone/; Jim Mann, "Even the Bible Points to the Idea of Innocent Until Proven Guilty," DrJimMann.com (October 4, 2018), https://drjimmann.com/2018/10/04/bible-even-points-to-idea-of-innocent-until-proven-guilty/.
15. SEC 4941; *BDB*, 1048–49; *TWOT* (vol. 2), 947–49; *CHALOT*, 221; *HALOT*, s.v. "מִשְׁפָּט".
16. Allen, *Psalms 101–150, WBC*, 180, 184–86; deClaissé-Walford, *Psalms*, NICOT, 882.
17. deClaissé-Walford, *Psalms*, NICOT, 882, 886; Allen, *Psalms 101–150, WBC*, 185.
18. Estes, *Psalms 73–150*, NAC, 414.
19. Martin H. Manser, *Dictionary of Bible Themes: The Accessible and Comprehensive Tool for Topical Studies* (London: Martin Manser, 2009), 1155, Kindle.

20. *SEC* 571; *BDB*, 54; *TWOT* (vol. 1), 51–53; *CHALOT*, 22; *HALOT*, 673, s.v. "אֶמֶת"; Estes, *Psalms 73–150*, NAC, 412, 432, 434. William Holladay (Old Testament scholar at Andover Newton Theological School) defines *emet* as: "permanence, continuance, continually, fidelity, faithfully" (*CHALOT*, 22. Michael Wilcock, *The Message of Psalms: Songs for the People of God*, BST vol. 2, ed. J. A. Motyer [Nottingham, England: Inter–Varsity Press, 2001], 215).

21. **YHWH's voice**—Gen 22:18; Exod 3:18; 4:1, 8; 5:2; 9:23, 28–29; 15:26; 19:5, 19; 23:21; Num 7:89; Deut 4:30. **Charge**—Lev 18:30; 22:9; Num 9:19, 23; Deut *11:1*; 1 Kgs 2:3. **Commandments**—Exod 15:26; 20:6; 24:12; 34:28; Lev 4:13; 22:31; 26:3; Num 15:22–23; 15:40; Deut 4:2, 13; 4:40; 5:10, 29; 6:1–2, 17, 25; 7:9, 11; 8:1–2, 6, 11; 10:4, 13; *11:1*, 8, 13, 22, 27; 13:4, 18; 15:5; 19:9; 26:13, 17–18; 27:10; 28:1, 9; 30:8, 10, 16; Judg 2:17; Ps 78:7; 89:31–32; 103:18–20; 119:35, 66, 151; Isa 48:18. **Statutes/Ordinances**—Exod 12:14, 17; 13:10; Lev 18:4–6, 26, 30 (defined in ch. 18); 19:19, 37; 20:22–23 (defined in ch. 20); 23:14; 23:21, 31, 41; 24:3, 18; 26:15, 43; Num 15:15–16; Deut 6:2; 8:11; 10:13; *11:1*; 28:15, 45; 30:10, 16; 1 Kgs 2:3; 11:11; Ps 89:31; 119:16; Jer 5:24; 10:3; 44:10, 23; Ezek 5:6–7; 11:20; 8:9, 17–21; 20:11–24; *33:15*; 37:24; 44:24.

Jodell's comment: Abraham likely had an early version of Divine Law before it was adapted to a functioning nation. What is unknown are what laws (if any) did YHWH impart to Noah after the flood. Circumstantial evidence indicates both may have had a rudimentary outline of Divine Law. Records from contemporary nations indicate that Passover and Sukkot were known since the days of Abraham (Jan A. Wagenaar, *Origin and Transformation of the Ancient Israelite Festival Calendar* [Otto Harrassowitz Verlag: Wiesbaden German, 2005], 156; *YE1*, 501). It is likely Abraham celebrated both Passover and Sukkot. Later, these ordinances took on new meaning with the Exodus. While administering cultic rites were later transferred to Levi and his family (Abraham's great–grandsons), Genesis chapters 12–22 record Abraham preforming many of these rites for his family. I cover more aspects of the Divine Law that Abraham obeyed in *YE1*, chapters 1–3.

Claus Westermann (Old Testament scholar at Univ. of Heidelberg): "Abraham is here the exemplar of obedience to the law in return for which God bestowed the promises on him" (Westermann, *Genesis 12–36*, CC, 424).

William D. Reyburn and Euan McGreggor Fry (both are translators for UBSH) remark: "**My laws** translates the Hebrew word *torah*, which refers to the first five books of the Hebrew Bible. The word itself means 'teaching,' 'instruction,' or 'guidance.' According to Ps 1:2 obeying the *torah* of the Lord is the source of joy" (William David Reyburn and Euan McGreggor Fry, *A Handbook on Genesis*, UBSH [New York: United Bible Societies, 1998], 592–93).

Kenneth Matthews (Beeson Divinity School): "By employing covenant terminology, the author depicts the complete obedience of Abraham as the ideal for Israel in the land who must observe the provisions of the Sinaitic covenant (e.g., Lev 26:3; Deut 4:40; 30:16)." (Mathews, *Genesis 11:27–50:26*, NAC, 405).

CHAPTER 6: DIVINE BONDAGE?

1. Stephen R. Miller, *Daniel*, NAC vol. 18 (Nashville: Broadman & Holman, 1994), 247; John Goldingay, *Daniel*, WBC vol. 30, Revised Edition, ed. Nancy L. deClaissé-Walford (Grand Rapids, MI: Zondervan Academic, 2019), 464.

John Goldingay (Fuller Sem.) remarks: "Yahweh is אל אמת, the God who is by nature reliable and constant (Ps 31:5 [6])." (*Daniel*, WBC, 464).

American Christian theologian and author J. Dwight Pentecost observes: "Because of her rebellion and disobedience Israel was experiencing **the curses and . . . judgments written by Moses** (cf. v. 13) in Deuteronomy 28:15–68. In spite of the severity of the discipline, including **great national disaster** (Dan. 9:12), the nation was not **turning from her sins** and submitting to the **authority of the Law**, God's truth. **This disaster**, the fall of Jerusalem, was because **God is righteous** (cf. vv. 7, 16) and Israel had **not obeyed Him** (cf. vv. 10–11)." (J. Dwight Pentecost, "Daniel," in *The Bible Knowledge Commentary: An Exposition of the Scriptures*, vol. 1, eds. J. F. Walvoord and R. B. Zuck [Wheaton, IL: Victor Books, 1985], 1360).

2. René Péter-Contesse and John Ellington, *A Handbook on the Book of Daniel*, UBSH (New York: United Bible Societies, 1994), 243.

3. Philip A. Noss and Kenneth J. Thomas, *A Handbook on Ezra and Nehemiah*, UBSH, ed. Paul Clarke et al. (New York: United Bible Societies, 2005), 435.

4. Mervin Breneman, *Ezra, Nehemiah, Esther*, electronic ed., NAC vol. 10 (Nashville: Broadman & Holman, 1993), 237–38.

5. Breneman, *Ezra, Nehemiah, Esther,* 237; Noss and Thomas, *Handbook on Ezra and Nehemiah,* UBSH, 436.
6. Noss and Thomas, *Handbook on Ezra and Nehemiah,* UBSH, 436.
7. Bart Ehrman, *Did Jesus Exist?* (New York: Harper One, 2012), 272.
8. Dennis McCarthy, *Institution and Narrative: Collected Essays* (Rome: Biblical Institute Press, 1985), 30n, 133, 215, 281–82; *YE1,* 67, 222, 241, 277, 253–81; Hayim Tadmore, "Treaty and Oath in the Ancient Near East: A Historian's Approach," in *Humanizing America's Iconic Book,* eds. G. M. Tucker and D. A. Knight (Chico, CA: Scholars Press, 1962), 125–52; Mayer Sulzberger, *Am Ha-Aretz–The Ancient Hebrew Parliament* (Philadelphia: Julias Greenstone, 1909), 6–48; Moshe Weinfeld, "The Covenant of Grant in the Old Testament and in the Ancient Near East," in *Essential Papers on Israel and the Ancient Near East,* ed. Frederick Greenspahn (New York: New York Univ. Press, 1991), 69–102; Meir Soloveichik, et al., eds., *Proclaim Liberty Throughout the Land: The Hebrew Bible in the United States, a Sourcebook* (New Milford, CT: Toby Press, 2019), 7–16; Eric Nelson, *The Hebrew Republic: Jewish Sources and the Transformation of European Political Thought* (Cambridge: Harvard Univ. Press, 2010), 3–4, 16–22; Joshua Berman, *Created Equal: How the Bible Broke with Ancient Political Thought* (New York: Oxford Univ. Press, 2008), 51–108; Milton Konvitz, *Torah and Constitution: Essays in American Jewish Thought,* MJH, ed. Henry L. Feingold (New York: Syracuse Univ. Press, 1988); Daniel J. Elazar, *Covenant and Polity in Biblical Israel, vol. 1,* Biblical Foundations and Jewish Expressions (New Brunswick: Transaction Publishers, 1995); Elazar, "Government in Biblical Israel," *Tradition: A Journal of Orthodox Jewish Thought* 13/14 (Spring–Summer 1973), 105–23; Elazar, "Deuteronomy as Israel's Constitution: Some Preliminary Reflections," Jerusalem Center for Public Affairs: Daniel Elazar Papers Index. http://www.jcpa.org/dje/articles2/deut-const.htm.
9. Dennis Prager through Prager University provides one of the best treatments on why the 10 Commandments were so revolutionary and of such a benefit to society. Dennis Prager, "The Ten Commandments: What You Should Know," Youtube, https://www.youtube.com/watch?v=TK57RiMqTdk. See also R. H. Fuller, *The Foundations of New Testament Christology* (London: Lutterworth Press, 1965), 23.
10. David Wright, *Inventing God's Law: How the Covenant Code of the Bible Used and Revised the Laws of Hammurabi* (Oxford: Oxford Univ. Press, 2013), 3–28, 154–90; George Nedungatt, "The Law of Talion an Ancient Law of Jurisprudence," *Iustitia* 4 (2013), 279–98; Calum Carmichael, "Biblical Laws of Talion," *HAR* 9 (1985), 107–26.
11. Joshua J. Mark, "Code of Ur–Nammu," WorldHistory.org (Oct 26, 2021), https://www.worldhistory.org/Code_of_Ur-Nammu/.
12. Raymond Westbrook, *A History of Ancient Near Eastern Law,* HOSNME 2 (Leiden: Brill, 2003), 361–425.
13. Breneman, *Ezra, Nehemiah, Esther,* 237.
14. Israel's 50–year Jubilee system comprised of Release Years every 7 years. Israel's slavery system functioned as a general welfare system based on indentured service. Those who fell onto hard times and sold themselves into the system to repay debt, served a master up to 7 years. If a person sold himself into slavery in the 3rd year of the Release Year cycle, they would only serve for 4 years since Release Years were based on national cycles (*YE1,* 231–36).
15. Jesus' brother James builds on the precepts within the Law. James builds upon King David's words that "the Law of YHWH is perfect" (Ps 19:7) and Leviticus' instruction to "proclaim liberty throughout the land" (Lev 25:10) when he writes: "But the man who looks intently into the perfect law that gives freedom, and continues to do this, not forgetting what he has heard, but doing it—he will be blessed in what he does" (Jas 1:25, NIV). These ideas are reiterated throughout the Old Testament and are not new to Jesus or the New Testament.
16. Deut 31:17–18; 32:20; Mic 3:4; Isa 8:17; 54:8; 59:2; 64:7; Ezek 39:23; Richard A. Taylor and E. Ray Clendenen, *Haggai, Malachi,* NAC vol. 21A (Nashville: Broadman & Holman, 2004), 454–58.
17. Mt. Horeb is used interchangeably for Mt. Sinai. Over time, names of places change, like Constantinople and Istanbul.
18. Clark and Hatton remark that "the meaning of **Remember** includes not just recollection but also obedience (compare Ps 103:18; 119:55)." (David J. Clark and Howard A. Hatton, *A Handbook on Malachi,* UBSH [New York: United Bible Societies, 2002], 466).
19. Duane L. Christensen, *Deuteronomy 21:10–34:12,* WBC vol. 6B (Dallas: Word, Inc., 2002), 742.
20. The Epic of Gilgamesh dates to as early as 2100 BCE. You can find more information at these sites: "The Search for Everlasting Life," ArtHistoryProject.com, https://www.arthistoryproject.com/timeline/the-ancient-world/mesopotamia/the-epic-of-gilgamesh/gilgamesh-4-the-search-for-everlasting-life/; "Gilgamesh part 3: Crossing the Waters of Death," MythicMojo.com, https://mythicmojo.com/gilgamesh-part-3-crossing-the-waters-of-death/.

21. Christensen, *Deuteronomy 21:10–34:12*, WBC, 743, 747–48. Jeffrey Tigay, *The JPS Torah Commentary on Deuteronomy* דברים, ed. Nahum Sarna (Jerusalem: Jewish Publication Society, 1996), 287; David Brown, A. R. Fausset, and Robert Jamieson, *A Commentary, Critical, Experimental, and Practical, on the Old and New Testaments: Genesis–Deuteronomy*, vol. I (London; Glasgow: William Collins, Sons, 1866), 697.
22. Christensen, *Deuteronomy 21:10–34:12*, WBC, 742.
23. Before his death, Christensen taught at William Carey International Univ. in Pasadena, CA.
24. Christensen, *Deuteronomy 21:10–34:12*, WBC, 743.
25. See also Exod 20:1; 24:3–4, 8; 34:1, 27–28; Deut 4:10–14, 36; 5:22, 28; 6:6; 9:10; 10:2.
26. Eugene H. Merrill, *Deuteronomy*, NAC vol. 4 (Nashville: Broadman & Holman, 1994), 391.
27. Christensen, *Deuteronomy 1–21:9, Revised*, 80.
28. William David Reyburn and Euan McGreggor Fry, *A Handbook on Proverbs*, UBSH (New York: United Bible Societies, 2000), 282; Jay E. Adams, *Proverbs*, The Christian Counselor's Commentary (Cordova, TN: Institute for Nouthetic Studies, 2020), 95.
29. Duane A. Garrett, *Proverbs, Ecclesiastes, Song of Songs*, NAC vol. 14 (Nashville: Broadman & Holman, 1993), 134.

CHAPTER 7: DOES THE NEW TESTAMENT UPHOLD DIVINE LAW?

1. Stephen S. Smalley, *1, 2, 3 John*, WBC vol. 51 (Dallas: Word, Inc., 1984), 162.
2. Sophie Laws (Regent's College) remarks: "James weighs one precept alongside another, arguing for the keeping of the law in its entirety" (Sophie Laws, *The Epistle of James*, BNTC [London: Continuum, 1980], 108).
   Chris Vlachos (Wheaton College) observes that "fulfills" means to "keep" the Law of Moses. (Chris A. Vlachos, *James*, Exegetical Guide to the Greek New Testament, eds. Murray J. Harris and Andreas J. Köstenberger [B & H Academic, 2013], 77). Vlachos understands James to refer to the entire Law. "The phrase means to observe the law *fully*, i.e., in its entirety. This emphasis contrasts with partiality, which, as James will argue, ignores a particular (and essential) aspect of the law" (Vlachos, *James*, 78).
   Douglass Moo (Wheaton College) remarks: "The concept of 'keeping the law' is, of course, very common in the OT, Judaism, and the NT (although the actual verb James uses [*teleō*] occurs with this sense only in Luke 2:39 and Rom. 2:27); and almost always with reference to the law of Moses. . . . 'law' in the NT usually refers to an entire body of commandments rather than to a single commandment" (Douglas J. Moo, *The Letter of James*, PNTC [Grand Rapids, MI: Eerdmans, 2000], 111).
3. David Brown, A. R. Fausset, and Robert Jamieson, *A Commentary, Critical, Experimental, and Practical, on the Old and New Testaments: Acts–Revelation*, vol. VI (London: William Collins, Sons, 1866), 637.
4. For more evidence that Divine Law continues to apply to Christians, see: "Torah Training," 119 Ministries, https://www.119ministries.com/torah-training/; Tom Martincic, "Why All Believers in Messiah Should Observe the Law," EliYah Ministries.com, https://eliyah.com/all-believers-in-messiah-should-observe-the-law/; "Jesus' Teaching on God's Law," Beyond Today (January 27, 2011), United Church of God, https://www.ucg.org/bible-study-tools/bible-study-aids/jesus-christ-the-real-story/jesus-teaching-on-gods-law.
5. Craig Keener (Asbury Theological Sem.) clarifies Jesus' reference to 'jot.' Keener reports that: "Jesus illustrates the eternality of God's law with a popular story line from contemporary Jewish teachers (5:18). Jesus' *smallest letter* (NIV), or 'jot' (KJV), undoubtedly refers to the Hebrew letter *yôḏ*, which Jewish teachers said would not pass from the law. They said that when Sarai's name was changed to Sarah, the *yôḏ* removed from her name cried out from one generation to another, protesting its removal from Scripture, until finally, when Moses changed Oshea's name to Joshua, the *yôḏ* was returned to Scripture. 'So you see,' the teachers would say, 'not even this smallest letter can pass from the Bible.' Jesus makes the same point from this tradition that later rabbis did: even the smallest details of God's law are essential" (Craig S. Keener, *Matthew*, vol. 1, The IVP New Testament Commentary Series [Downers Grove, IL: InterVarsity Press, 1997], Mt 5:17–18).
6. John Stott (All Souls, Anglican Church and leader of the evangelical movement) comments: "Thus the law is as enduring as the universe" (John Stott, ed., *The Message of the Sermon on the Mount: Christian Counter-Culture*, Revised Edition, The Bible Speaks Today [London: IVP, 1978, 2020], 55).
   Chromatius, Biship of Aquileia (388 CE) observes: "Consequently nothing in the divine commandments must be abolished, nothing altered. Everything must be preserved and taught faithfully and

devotedly that the glory of the heavenly kingdom may not be lost" (Chromatius in *Matthew 1–13*, ACCS, ed. Manlio Simonetti [Downers Grove, IL: InterVarsity Press, 2001], 96).

In 1852, Swiss Reformer Henrich Bullinger, remarked: "Let everyone, therefore, be persuaded for certain that the law of God, which is the most excellent and perfect will of God, is forever eternal, and cannot be at any time dissolved, either by humans, or angels, or any other creatures. Let every person think that the law, so far as it is the rule of how to live well and happily, so far as it is the bridle by which we are kept in the fear of the Lord, so far as it is a prick that awakens the dullness of our flesh, and so far as it is given to instruct, correct, and rebuke us, that here, I say, it does remain unabrogated. And, to this day, the law has its belonging in the church of God" (Henrich Bullinger in *Matthew: New Testament*, Reformation Commentary on Scripture, vol. I, eds. Jason K. Lee, William F. Marsh, and Timothy George [Downers Grove, IL: IVP Academic, 2021], 67–68).

Craig Keener understands Jesus to have spoken to his followers by using terms and ideas that they were familiar with: "When Jesus says that he came not to *abolish the Law or the Prophets* but to *fulfill them*, he uses terms that in his culture would have conveyed his faithfulness to the Scriptures" (Keener, *Matthew*, vol. 1, Mt 5:17–18).

John Nolland (Trinity College, Bristol) voices a similar view to those expressed above. "The fulfilment language represents a claim that Jesus' programmatic commitment, far from undercutting the role of the Law and the Prophets, is to enable God's people to live out the Law more effectively" (John Nolland, *The Gospel of Matthew: A Commentary on the Greek Text*, New International Greek Testament Commentary [Grand Rapids, MI: Eerdmans, 2005], 219).

7. Ian Boxall (Catholic Univ. of America) mentions: "In context, the 'least of these commandments' (5:19) probably refers back to the Mosaic commandments of verse 18" (Ian Boxall, *Matthew through the Centuries*, WBCS, eds. John Sawyer, et al. [Hoboken, NJ: Wiley Blackwell, 2019], 122).

Craig Evans (Houston Christian Univ.) places this text in its historical context. The Maccabees were Levitical Jews who faced persecution while liberating the small Judean nation from foreign holocaust and oppression. Their movement began *c.* 165 BCE. The Maccabees founded the Hasmonean Dynasty which ended in *c.* 37 BCE with Herod the Great. This was about 40 years before Jesus' ministry. In 37 BCE, Herod divorced his 1st wife Doris to marry Mariamne, the last Hasmonean princess, in order to unify and pacify the Judean nation. It was this marriage that John the Baptist criticized (Matt 11:2–7; 14:6–12; Mark 1:14; 6:17–29; Luke 3:19–20; 7:18–25; 9:9; *Antiquities of the Jews* 18.5.2).

The Book of Maccabees and the history within the book play a vital role in Jesus' ministry as Jesus quotes from its texts ("Did Jesus or the New Testament Authors Quote from the Apocryphal Books?," Dust off the Bible: Blog Archive (September 17, 2019), https://dustoffthebible.com/Blog-archive/2019/09/17/does-the-new-testament-or-jesus-quote-from-the-apocryphal-books/; Matthew Bryan, "Maccabees in the New Testament," Conciliar Post [September 9, 2019]) Conciliarpost.com, https://conciliarpost.com/theology-spirituality/maccabees-in-the-new-testament/).

This is Craig Evans observation:

"**Do not think** (v. 17) or 'do not suppose' (Greek: *nomizein*): The language here is reminiscent of the determined words of the heroes of the books of the Maccabees, who were concerned with preserving the temple and keeping the Law. A martyr says to the tyrant (i.e., Antiochus IV Epiphanes): 'But do not suppose that you will go unpunished for having tried to fight against God!' (2 Macc. 7:19); or again in a later version: 'Therefore do not suppose that it would be a petty sin if we were to eat defiling food' (4 Macc. 5:19); or yet again: 'Therefore, tyrant, put us to the test; and if you take our lives because of our religion, do not suppose that you can injure us by torturing us' (4 Macc. 9:7). Jesus' opening words, 'Do not suppose . . . ,' followed by a discussion of the value and permanence of the Law, may well have evoked these venerated expressions of fidelity.

"**To abolish the Law** (v. 17): Again, this was the very concern of the Maccabean struggle—to prevent the abolition of the Law. In the preface to his work, the author of 2 Maccabees summarizes the history of Jason that he is about to recount, namely, how Judas Maccabeus and his brothers 'recovered the temple famous throughout the world and freed the city and restored the laws that were about to be **abolish**ed' (2 Macc. 2:22). Again, the words of one of the martyrs parallel the words of Jesus: 'I do not so pity my old age as to **abolish** the ancestral Law by my own act' (4 Macc. 5:33). In the pseudepigraphal *Testaments of the Twelve Patriarchs*, the dying Levi warns his sons that they will have priestly descendants who will 'make void the law, and set at nought the words of the prophets by evil perverseness' (*Testament of Levi* 16:2)."

Evans continues: "Until heaven and earth pass away (v. 18): In Jewish thinking, the heaven and earth would endure until God himself recreated them (as in Isa. 65:17 'I create new heavens and a new earth'; cf. 66:22; *1 Enoch* 91:16; 2 Pet. 3:13; Rev. 21:1). But until that eschatological moment, creation should be thought of as permanent. One thinks of the psalmist, who extols God for creating the heavens, the sun, the moon, and the stars, adding, 'He has established them forever; he has made an ordinance, and it shall not pass away' (LXX Ps. 148:6); or: 'For he knew that his time was but short, but that heaven and earth endure always' (*2 Bar.* 19:2). Thus, Jesus' language is implicitly eschatological: the Law will endure until the End.

"The Law is so important, not the smallest letter or stroke shall pass away from the Law, until all is accomplished (v. 18). God's Law is just as permanent as creation itself (e.g., 4 Ezra 9:37 'the Law, however, does not perish but remains in its glory'; Bar. 4:1 'the Law that endures for ever'; *1 Enoch* 99:2 'the eternal Law'; *2 Bar.* 77:15 'though we depart, yet the Law abides'; Philo, *Life of Moses* 2.3 §14 'But Moses is alone in this, in that his laws, firm, unshaken, immovable, stamped, as it were, with the seals of nature herself, remain secure from the day they were first enacted to now, and we may hope that they will remain for all future ages as though immortal, so long as the sun and the moon and the whole heaven and universe exist'; *Gen. Rab.* 10.1 [on Gen. 2] 'everything has an end, even heaven and earth have an end; only one thing has no end: and what is that? The Law'" (Craig A. Evans, *The Bible Knowledge Background Commentary: Matthew–Luke*, 1st Edition, eds. Craig A. Evans and Craig A. Bubeck [Colorado Springs, CO: David C. Cook, 2003], 112–13).

8. While I presented limited evidence for these additions to Divine Law in *YE1*, chapter 18.II.–III., greater evidence will be presented in my forthcoming book, *The Day of YHWH/The Day of the Lord*, which will follow the *Suffering Servant* trilogy.
9. Evans, *Matthew–Luke*, 346.
10. Craig A. Evans, *Mark 8:27–16:20*, WBC vol. 34B (Dallas: Word, Inc., 2001), 96; Morna D. Hooker, *The Gospel according to Saint Mark*, BNTC (London: Continuum, 1991), 241; Rodney L. Cooper, *Mark*, HNTC vol. 2 (Nashville: Broadman & Holman, 2000), 167.

    Rev. Robert Bratcher observes: "The commandments quoted (from Exod 20:12–16; cf. Deut. 5:16–20) are, with the exception of 'Do not defraud,' numbers VI, VII, VIII, IX, V, in that order, from the Decalogue" (Robert G. Bratcher and Eugene Albert Nida, *A Handbook on the Gospel of Mark*, UBSH [New York: United Bible Societies, 1993], 319).

    Augustine of Hippo (*c.* 400 CE), remarks: "If he wishes to enter into life, he should keep the commandments" (Augustine of Hippo in *Mark*, Revised Edition, ACCS, eds. Thomas C. Oden and Christopher A. Hall [Downers Grove, IL: InterVarsity Press, 1998], 134).
11. Roy E. Ciampa and Brian S. Rosner, *The First Letter to the Corinthians*, PNTC (Grand Rapids, MI: Eerdmans, 2010), 240.

    Mark Taylor (Southwestern Baptist Theological Sem.) remarks: "Each unit within this section addresses a different topic. Garland observes how 5:1–6:20 is bound together by an eschatological focus (5:5; 6:2, 14), a concern for how ethical lapses impact those outside the church (5:1; 6:6, 18–20), sharp commands to desist and flee from sin (5:13; 6:4, 18), and instruction anchored in the Deuteronomic code" (Mark Taylor, *1 Corinthians*, NAC vol. 28, ed. E. Ray Clendenen [Nashville: Broadman & Holman, 2014], 129).

    Richard Pratt (Reformed Theological Sem.) concludes that: "The Corinthians had forgotten a basic Christian doctrine: there is a big difference between believers and unbelievers. **Wicked** people are not destined to **inherit the kingdom of God**—they face a future of divine judgment . . . Paul hoped the Corinthians would remember that people who practice such things would not **inherit the kingdom of God**" (Richard L. Pratt, Jr, *I & II Corinthians*, HNTC vol. 7 [Nashville: Broadman & Holman, 2000], 89).
12. Lee Martin McDonald (Acadia Divinity College) shares the meaning of the Greek in this text. "When Paul asks, 'do you not know?' he suggests that his readers knew what he was saying and that they had been taught on such matters earlier. His list of vices now includes, for the first time, a judgment against homosexuals (Greek, *arsenokoitai,* literally = 'those men who sleep with males'). See later attention given to the issue of homosexuality in 1 Tim. 1:10 (translated 'fornicators' by the NRSV). This is followed by 'and those effeminate' (Greek = *malakoi,* literally, 'the soft ones') and refers to passive partners in homosexual activity. In its broad use in antiquity, the term referred to effeminate males who played the sexual role of females, but the term is broadly translated in antiquity. The practice of homosexuality was condemned in the Greek translation (LXX) of Lev. 18:22 and 20:13 where also the Greek words *arsenos* (Greek for 'male') and *koiten* (Greek for 'bed') are used in the same sentence, and likely were conflated by the Jews, the likely source of Paul's use of *arsenokoitai*" (Lee Martin McDonald, "1 Corinthians," *The Bible Knowledge Background Commentary: Acts–Philemon*, 1st Edition, eds. Craig A. Evans and Craig A. Bubeck [Colorado Springs, CO: David C Cook, 2004], 288).
13. Regarding the modern Church's relationship to the Law, John Stott, observes: "One of the great weaknesses of contemporary evangelical Christianity is our comparative neglect of Christian ethics, in both

our teaching and our practice. In consequence, we have become known rather as people who preach the gospel than as those who live and adorn it. We are not always conspicuous in the community, as we should be, for our respect for the sanctity and the quality of human life, our commitment to social justice, our personal honesty and integrity in business, our simplicity of lifestyle and happy contentment in contrast to the greed of the consumer society, or for the stability of our homes in which unfaithfulness and divorce are practically unknown and children grow up in the secure love of their parents. At least in the statistics of marriage and family life, Jewish performance is higher than that of Christians. One of the main reasons for this is that our churches do not (on the whole) teach ethics. We are so busy preaching the gospel that we seldom teach the law. We are also afraid of being branded 'legalists'. 'We are not under the law', we say piously, as if we were free to ignore and even disobey it. Whereas what Paul meant is that our acceptance before God is not due to our observance of the law. But Christians are still under obligation to keep God's moral law and commandments. Indeed, the purpose of Christ's death was that 'the righteous requirements of the law might be fully met in us', and the purpose of the Holy Spirit's dwelling in our heart is that he might write God's law there" (John R. W. Stott, *The Message of Thessalonians: The Gospel & the End of Time*, The Bible Speaks Today [Downers Grove, IL: InterVarsity Press, 1994], 76).

14. George Milligan, ed., *St. Paul's Epistles to the Thessalonians*, Classic Commentaries on the Greek New Testament (London: Macmillan, 1908), 51.

Paul Ellingworth (Univ. of Aberdeen) and Eugene Albert Nida (American Bible Society), take note of the context of God's calling us to holiness through a life of morality. "In many languages it is necessary to change the location of the negative, for example, 'for God called us, but not for us to live in immorality; rather, he called us to be holy.' *To live in immorality, but in holiness* is literally 'for immorality, but in holiness.' The preposition 'for' suggests 'this was not the purpose God had in mind when he called us,' and 'in' suggests 'to live in a state of holiness'" (Paul Ellingworth and Eugene Albert Nida, *A Handbook on Paul's Letters to the Thessalonians*, UBSH [New York: United Bible Societies, 1976], 84). The only place in the entire Bible that God defines immorality is in His Divine Law. It is to this Law that Jesus, Paul, and the Disciples continually appeal.

Anthony Thiselton (Univ. of Nottingham) clarifies the Greek word for 'holy.' "The Greek word used is *hagiasmos*, which can denote a process or a result (Danker, *Greek–English Lexicon*, 10). The verb from which it derives, *hagiazo-*, to make holy, occurs in the Septuagint or LXX for the Hebrew *q-d-sh*. *Holy* has a primary sense of 'other' or 'separate'" (Anthony C. Thiselton, *1 & 2 Thessalonians through the Centuries*, WBCS, eds. John Sawyer, et al. [West Sussex, UK: Wiley-Blackwell, 2011], 96).

15. C. K. Barret (Univ. of Durham) elaborates on Paul's assertion that Divine Law is holy. "Scripture is holy (1:2) because it comes from God; whatever may be true of other religions and of other codes of morals, those in the Old Testament are the word of God himself. The 'commandment' suggests the special enactments of the Mosaic code (and perhaps Gen. 2:17). These too are holy; they are righteous, in that they command what is right (cf. Gal. 3:21); and they are good, that is, beneficent in their intention. Paul's argument hitherto has evidently been intended to vindicate this holy, righteous, and beneficent character of the law.

"What then is wrong? **Did that which in itself is good** (Prov. 4:2 was sometimes made the basis of an identification of the law with 'the good') **prove in my case to be death?** The question must be asked, because death has in fact resulted (*vv.* 10 f.). But the answer is clear: **No indeed**. The fault does not lie with the law . . . The fault lies entirely with sin" (C. K. Barrett, *The Epistle to the Romans*, Revised, BNTC [London: Continuum, 1991], 136).

Leon Morris (Tyndale House, Cambridge) understands Paul to uphold Divine Law as well. "*So then* introduces the consequence, the conclusion to which this reasoning leads up. The expression is elliptical, and its terseness highlights Paul's point—the law is not sin as was suggested (v. 7). The law may have been used by sin, but that does not make sin and law identical or even put them in the same class. *The law is holy* (JB, 'sacred'), which puts it as far away from sin as possible. The law is God's law, and it takes its character from him. He is holy ('Holy, holy, holy is the Lord Almighty'–Isa. 6:3), and his law accordingly is holy. It is possible that we should see no significant difference between *the law* and *the commandment* (though Godet finds in the law 'the Mosaic system in its entirety' and in the commandment 'each article of the code in particular')." (Leon Morris, *The Epistle to the Romans*, PNTC [Grand Rapids, MI: Eerdmans, 1988], 283).

Joseph Exell (editor for many Bible commentaries) reflects on the "nature of the Law" in the context of Paul's statement. "Its nature is—1. Universal in its extent. It is binding at all times, in all places, and upon all. 2. Perpetual in its obligation: it can allow no change. Other laws, the ceremonial laws, *e.g.*, may be abrogated or altered, but the moral law, being founded upon the Divine nature, knows no change. 'Heaven and earth shall pass away,' etc. 3. Perfect in its character. Being the expression and emanation of the perfect nature and will of God, 'the law of the Lord is perfect, converting the soul'" (Joseph S. Exell, *The Biblical Illustrator: Romans*, vol. 1 [New York: Fleming H. Revell Company, 1900], 582). After citing a thorough review of the Law in Romans 7, Exell concludes that Paul's position is that *"The law (is) vindicated"* (Exell, *The Biblical Illustrator: Romans*, 585, parentheses added).

Robert Mounce (Western Kentucky Univ.) also understands Paul to uphold the Law. He also draws attention to Paul's final verdict that the Law is good. "This verse is the definitive answer to the question raised in v. 7, 'Is the Law itself a sinful thing?' (Weymouth). No, the law is holy. The commandment is 'holy, righteous and good.' Since the law is God's law, it must of necessity reflect the nature of God. The law of a holy God must be consistent with his holy nature (Isa 6:3). A righteous God decrees commandments that are righteous. They are fair and make no unreasonable demands. The law is 'good' because it intends the very best for people. In this entire discussion Paul was not depreciating law as such" (Robert H. Mounce, *Romans*, NAC vol. 27 [Nashville: Broadman & Holman, 1995], 165).

Kenneth Boa (author of over 50 books) also sees Paul upholding the Law. "But here he brings to a conclusion his essential answer to the objector who had asked, 'Is the law sin?' (v. 7). Because the law comes from a holy, righteous, and good God, the law itself must reveal those same characteristics, which it does. Is there an unholy commandment to be found among God's laws? No, because God is holy (Lev. 19:2). Is there an unrighteous commandment to be found among God's laws? No, because God is righteous (Dan. 9:14). Is there an evil commandment to be found among God's laws? No, because God is good (Mark 10:18)." (Kenneth Boa and William Kruidenier, *Romans*, HNTC vol. 6 [Nashville: Broadman & Holman, 2000], 226).

Colin Kruse (Melbourne School of Theology) arrives at the same verdict regarding Paul and the Law. "Paul concludes that the law is not to blame, for in fact the law is good: *So then, the law is holy, and the commandment is holy, righteous and good*. Paul's statement here echoes the words of Deuteronomy 4:8 ('And what other nation is so great as to have such righteous decrees and laws as this body of laws I am setting before you today?') and also of Nehemiah 9:13 ('You came down on Mount Sinai; you spoke to them from heaven. You gave them regulations and laws that are just and right, and decrees and commands that are good'). However, the form of the sentence here in 7:12 (lit. 'So then, on the one hand, the law is holy, and the commandment is holy and righteous and good . . .') indicates the existence of an anacoluthon, the audience expecting the apostle to complete it with something like: 'but on the other hand sin is evil and the real culprit'.

"The significance of the three epithets Paul applies to the law have been described as follows: 'holy'—its origin is God himself whose nature is holy; 'just'—it cannot in any way be said to promote anything that is wrong; 'good'—its provisions are universally positive and desirable" (Colin G. Kruse, *Paul's Letter to the Romans*, PNTC, ed. D. A. Carson [Grand Rapids, MI: Eerdmans, 2012], 303–04).

16. Lev 4:3, 23, 28, 32, 5:15, 18, 6:6; Jacob Milgrom, *Leviticus*, CC (Minneapolis, MN: Fortress, 2004), 24; Mark Rooker, *Leviticus*, NAC vol 3A, ed. E. Ray Clendenen (Nashville: Broadman & Holman, 2000), 275–77; Koole, *Isaiah III*, 269.

17. מִשְׁחַת (*mishchat*); SEC 4893; BDB, 1008; TWOT (vol. 2), 917–18; CHALOT, 214; HALOT, 5792, s.v., "מִשְׁחָת". Leviticus 21:16–24; Rooker, *Leviticus*, NAC, 275–77; Nola J. Opperwall, "Profane," ISBE (vol. 3), 979–80; Jacob Milgrom, *Studies in Levitical Terminology, I: The Encroacher and the Levite the Term 'Aboda* (Eugene, OR: Wipf & Stock, 1970), 38–42.

18. Barclay Moon Newman and Eugene Albert Nida, *A Handbook on Paul's Letter to the Romans*, UBSH (New York: United Bible Societies, 1973), 250; Barrett, *The Epistle to the Romans*, 230; Boa and Kruidenier, *Romans*, 399; Morris, *The Epistle to the Romans*, PNTC, 469.

David Peterson (Oak Hill Theological College) discusses the Greek within this text. "The argument is immediately broadened to include 'any other commandment' of the Mosaic law. These are 'summed up' (ἀνακεφαλαιοῦται) or essentially expressed by the positive command of Lev 19:18 ('Love your neighbor as yourself'). The expression ἐν τῷ λόγῳ τούτῳ ('in this word') identifies this command as a revealed word from God (cf. 9:6, 9, 28), like the 'ten words' of the Decalogue (LXX Exod 34:28; Deut 10:4). Since Jewish writers prior to Paul did not give special prominence to Lev 19:18, it is likely that the apostle was influenced by the tradition in which Jesus combined it with Deut 6:5 and declared that 'all the Law and the Prophets depend on these two commands' (Matt 22:40; cf. Mark 12:31; Luke 10:26–28)." (David G. Peterson, *Romans*, Evangelical Biblical Theology Commentary, eds. T. Desmond Alexander, Thomas R. Schreiner, and Andreas J. Köstenberger [Bellingham, WA: Lexham Press, 2021], 472).

19. תָּמִימָה/*tamim*. SEC 8552; BDB, 1070–71; TWOT (vol. 2), 973–74; CHALOT, 391; HALOT, 10201, s.v., "תָּמִים".
20. שׁוּב/*shub*. SEC 7725; BDB, 996–1000; TWOT (vol. 2), 909–10; CHALOT, 364; HALOT, 9407, s.v., "שׁוּב".

CHAPTER 8: IT'S ALL RELATIVE

1. Jennifer Huizen, "What is Gaslighting?" Medical News Today (November 30, 2023), https://www.medicalnewstoday.com/articles/gaslighting#how-it-works.
2. Reginald Pulliam, "The Eight Stages of Democracy," AL.com (Aug 22, 2016), https://www.al.com/opinion/2016/08/eight_stages_of_democracy.html. China is already seeing America's demise under the Biden administration: "The State of Democracy in the United States: 2022," Ministry of Foreign Affairs of the People's Republic of China (March 20, 2022), https://www.fmprc.gov.cn/eng/wjdt_665385/2649_665393/202303/t20230320_11044481.html; Clifford Ando, "The End of Ancient Democracy?" *Tableau* (Spring 2021), https://tableau.uchicago.edu/ando.
3. America's Founding Documents, "The Declaration of Independence: A Transcript," National Archives, https://www.archives.gov/founding-docs/declaration-transcript.
4. John Quincy Adams (the 6th President of the United States) summed up best the limits that society or government can impose upon a people: "We have no Government armed with power capable of contending with human passions unbridled.... Our Constitution was made only for a moral and religious people. It is wholly inadequate to the government of any other" (John Quincy Adams, "From John Adams to Massachusetts Militia, 11 October 1798," *Founders Online, National Archives*, https://founders.archives.gov/documents/Adams/99-02-02-3102).

CHAPTER 9: PRECEPTS OF TRUTH

1. The Roman Catholic Church, while ignoring Deuteronomy, insists it is the needed intermediary. In 2014 "Pope Francis described as 'dangerous' the temptation to believe that one can have 'a personal, direct, immediate relationship with Jesus Christ without communion with and the **mediation of the church**'" (Cindy Wooden, "The Church is Essential for Faith; There are no 'Free Agents,' Pope Says," *National Catholic Reporter* (Vatican City: June 25, 2014), https://www.ncronline.org/blogs/francis-chronicles/church-essential-faith-there-are-no-free-agents-pope-says.
2. For further discussion, see *YE*1, 1–13.
3. G. W. Bromiley, "Truth," *ISBE* (vol. 4), 926.
4. Patricia Tull Willey, *Remember the Former Things*, SBLDS 161, ed. Michael V. Fox (Atlanta, GA: Scholars Press, 1997), 76.
5. Willey, *Former Things*, 74–76.
6. SEC 571; BDB, 54; TWOT (vol. 1), 52–53; CHALOT, 22; HALOT, 673, s.v., "אָמַת".
7. Manser, *Dictionary of Bible Themes*, 1460, Kindle.
8. "Bertrand Russell—On Truth and Falsehood," BCCampus.com, https://pressbooks.bccampus.ca/classicreadings/chapter/bertrand-russell-on-truth-and-falsehood/. See also, Louis P. Pojman, *Philosophy: The Quest for Truth* (Belmont, CA: Wadsworth Publishing, 1989), 152; A. N. Prior, *The Encyclopedia of Philosophy* (vol. 2), ed. Paul Edwards (New York: Macmillan and The Free Press, 1962), 223–32; Robert Nola and Howard Sankey, *Theories of Scientific Method* (Montreal: McGill-Queen's Univ. Press, 2007).
9. SEC 4171; HALOT, 4928, s.v. "מוּר I."
10. HALOT, 9807, s.v. "שָׁנָה I."
11. Gordon Wenham, *Genesis 16–50*, WBC vol. 2 (Dallas, TX: Word Books, 1994), 29.
12. For the destruction of heavily walled sites in Canaan, see: *YE*1, 515–21. Willaim Dever, "Settlements and Chronologies," in *The Hyksos: New Historical and Archaeological Perspectives*, Univ. Museum Monograph 96/8, ed. Eliezer Oren (Philadelphia: Univ. of Pennsylvania Museum, 1997), 286, 290; Donald Redford, *Egypt, Canaan, and Israel in Ancient Times* (Princeton, NJ: Princeton Univ. Press, 1992), 93, 96; Aharon Kempinski, "The Middle Bronze Age," in *The Archaeology of Ancient Israel*, trans. R. Greenberg, ed. Amnon Ben-Tor (New Haven, CT: Yale Univ. Press, 1992), 166–67.
13. Dating for Shechem destruction: *YE*1, 591–92; Lawrence Stager, "The Shechem Temple Where Abimelech Massacred a Thousand," *BAR* 29/4 (July 2003), 26–35, 66, 68–69; Rivka Gonen, "The Late Bronze

Age," in *The Archaeology of Ancient Israel*, trans. R. Greenberg, ed. Amnon Ben-Tor (New Haven, CT: Yale Univ. Press, 1992), 223.
14. You can read this online at: Jodell Onstott, "YHWH Exists, vol. 1, Chart 9.37: Judah, Israel, Assyria Synchronistic Chronology," Academia.edu, https://www.academia.edu/96075137/YHWH_Exists_vol _1_Chart_9_37_Judah_Israel_Assyria_Synchronistic_Chronology_UPDATED_.
15. *YE1*, 195–97.
16. Steven J. Reynolds, Mary Shepherd, Arun Risbud, et al. "Circumcision Associated With 'Profound' Reduction in HIV-1 Risk," 41st ISDA Conference, Abstracts Volume LB–10 (October 11, 2003), https:// pubmed.ncbi.nlm.nih.gov/15051285/; Rex Russell, *What the Bible Says About Healthy Living* (Ventura, CA: Regal Books, 1996), 22; S. I. McMillen, *None of These Diseases* (New York: Pyramid Books, 1963), 21; For a very general understanding of prothrombin, see: "Prothrombin," Britannica.com http:// www.britannica.com/EBchecked/topic/480073/prothrombin; Peggy Peck, "Circumcision Associated with 'Profound' Reduction in HIV-1 Risk," *Medscape* (October 10, 2003), http://www.medscape.com /viewarticle/462816; Salynn Boyles, "Male Circumcision Cuts Women's Cervical Cancer Risk: Study Shows Circumcision May Help Reduce Spread of HPV," *WebMD Health News*, ed. Laura Martin, (January 2011), http://www.webmd.com/cancer/cervical-cancer/news/20110106/male-circumcision-cuts -womens-cervical-cancer-risk; Christine Rivet, "Circumcision and Cervical Cancer Is There a Link?" *Canadian Family Physician* 49 (September 2003), 1096–97, http://www.ncbi.nlm.nih.gov/pmc/articles /PMC2214289/pdf/14526861.pdf; Xavier Castellsague, F. Xavier Bosch, Nubia Muñoz, et al., "Male Circumcision, Penile Human Papillomavirus Infection, and Cervical Cancer in Female Partners," *NEJM* 346/15 (April 11, 2002), 1105–12, DOI: 10.1056/NEJMoa011688.
17. Sanaz Mollazadeh, Behnaz Sadeghzadeh Oskouei, Mahin Kamalifard, et al., "Association between Sexual Activity during Menstruation and Endometriosis: A Case-Control Study," *Royan Institute International Journal of Fertility and Sterility* 13/3 (October–December 2019), 230–35, https://www.ijfs.ir/article _45552.html; Sanaz Mollazadeh, Khadijeh Najmabadi, Mojgan Mirghafourand, et al., "Sexual Activity during Menstruation as A Risk Factor for Endometriosis: A Systematic Review and Meta-Analysis," *International Journal of Fertility & Sterility* 17/1 (January–March 2023), 1–6, https://www.ncbi.nlm.nih .gov/pmc/articles/PMC9807890/#); F. Samir, S. Badr, A. Al Beidly, A. Alfotouh, et al., "Coital Retrograde Menstruation as a Risk Factor for Pelvic Endometriosis," *Qatar Medical Journal* 20/1 (June 2011), 21–25, https://doi.org/10.5339/qmj.2011.1.9.
18. *YE1*, 700–02. For greater study see *YE1*, 673–895.
19. Bromiley, "Truth," *ISBE* (vol. 4), 926.
20. Wenham, *Genesis 16–50*, WBC, 29.
21. Bromiley notes, "Yet ^{e}met also has a strong implication of righteousness, for God's 'ordinances' are true." (Bromiley, "Truth," *ISBE* [vol. 4], 926).
22. Deut 4:8; Judg 5:11; 1 Sam 12:7; 2 Chr 12:6; Ezra 9:15; Neh 9:8; Ps 7:9, 17; 9:8; 11:7; 19:9; 22:31; 35:24, 28; 36:6, 10; 40:10; 50:6; 51:14; 71:2, 15–16, 19, 24; 72:2; 88:12; 89:16; 97:6; 98:2, 9; 99:4; 103:6; 111:3; 116:5; 119:7, 40, 62, 106, 123, 137–38, 142–44, 160, 164, 172; 129:4; 143:1, 11; 145:7, 17; Isa 5:16; 11:4–5; 41:10; 42:21; 45:19, 23; 46:13; 51:5–6, 8; 56:1; 59:16–17; Jer 12:1; Lam 1:18; Dan 9:7, 14, 16; Mic 6:5; and Zech 8:8.
23. See Ch. 9, endnote 22, above.

CHAPTER 10: "IT'S HARD TO BE A DIAMOND IN A RHINESTONE WORLD"

1. Bromiley, "Truth," *ISBE* (vol. 4), 926.
2. Gary King, Robert Keohane, and Sidney Verba, *Designing Social Inquiry: Scientific Inference in Qualitative Research* (Prineton, NJ: Princeton Univ. Press, 1994); John Stuart Mill, *Philosophy of Scientific Method* (New York: Dover, 2005, reprint); Robert Nola and Howard Sankey, *Theories of Scientific Method* (New York: Routledge Taylor and Francis, 2007).
3. Ehrman, *Did Jesus Exist,* 272. Israel's monotheism did not exclude angels or other entities who took part in the creation process, but they are always subservient to YHWH (Ps 8:5).
4. John Anthony Dunne, "Monotheism," *The Lexham Bible Dictionary,* eds. John D. Barry, et al. (Bellingham, WA: Lexham Press, 2016); John F. A. Sawyer, "Monotheism," *A Concise Dictionary of the Bible and Its Reception* (Louisville, KY: Westminster John Knox Press, 2009), 175; Carey C. Newman, "God,"

Dictionary of the Later New Testament and Its Developments, eds. Ralph P. Martin and Peter H. Davids (Downers Grove, IL: InterVarsity Press, 1997), 412.

5. Throughout Israel's history, her Scripture supports a God who does both good and evil but does so righteously, according to Divine Law—Deut 32:41; Exod 15:26; Isa 43:13; 45:7; Zeph 1:12.
6. See *YE1*, 555–60.
7. Nehemia Gordon, "Hebrew Voices #132—Boiling a Kid in its Mother's Milk," Nehemia's Wall (Aug 18, 2021), https://www.nehemiaswall.com/boiling-a-kid-in-its-mothers-milk (see 29 min. mark).
8. Richard Elliot Friedman, *Commentary on the Torah* (New York: Harper One, 2003), 250; Gordon, "Boiling a Kid in its Mother's Milk" (29 min. mark).
9. Harry Hoffner, "Symbols for Masculinity and Femininity: Their Use in Ancient near Eastern Sympathetic Magic Rituals," *SBL* 85/3 (September 1966), 326–34, 328; Lester Kuyper, "Israel and Her Neighbors," *Reformed Review* 10/3 (1957), https://repository.westernsem.edu/pkp/index.php/rr/article/view/72; Friedman, *Commentary on the Torah*, 250; Jacob Milgrom, "You Shall Not Boil a Kid in Its Mother's Milk," New2Torah.com (Nov 5, 2015), https://new2torah.com/PDF/Milk%20and%20Meat%20-%20Milgrom.pdf.
10. After the flood, Ham and his son Canaan committed a horrific crime against Noah (Gen 9:21–22). For this crime, YHWH removed Canaan's birthright of land and bequeathed it to Shem (Gen 9:26–27), allotting Shem a double inheritance. Noah's judgment became a tradition incorporated into Divine Law (Deut 21:17). When Jacob divided the birthright and blessing among the 12 tribes of Israel, Joseph's sons—Ephraim and Manasseh—inherited the double portion of land in Israel (Gen 48:22). This Biblical practice continued through the patriarchal and ancient Israelite period down to modern Victorian times as *Primogeniture*, with the exception that in biblical Law, women could also inherit land and estates.
11. *YE1*, 186–88.
12. Daniel Estes takes note that this text specifically refers to the revelation of Divine Law to the nation of Israel. "In v. 19 'his word' refers to special revelation, as evidenced in the parallel 'statutes and judgments' in line b. The most likely referent is the Torah, especially the laws given in Exodus through Deuteronomy and mentioned numerous times in Psalm 119. The nation of Israel has the special privilege of receiving the oracles of God (cf. Rom 3:2), along with the special responsibility that entailed (cf. Deut 4:8; Amos 3:2)." (Estes, *Psalms 73–150*, NAC, 618).

    James M. Hamilton, Jr. (Southern Baptist Theological Sem.) concludes: "No other people received Yahweh's rules and statutes and instructions.... The psalmist wants his audience to contrast the way God has revealed himself to them with the way he has not revealed himself to others, and he wants them to do this so that they will feel God's love, so that they will be prompted to obey the command with which he closes the psalm, the command to *hallel* ('praise') Yahweh" (Hamilton, *Psalms*, 514).

    A. R. Fausset (Anglican Bishop of Durham) remarks: "The same reference to God's 'statutes and judgments' occurs in the parallel history, Neh. 9:13, 14; 10:29—the distinguishing glory of Israel. The revelation of God to her at Sinai raised her above all peoples as the only one who knew the will of the one true God (Deut. 33:2–4; 4:32–34; Rom. 3:1, 2)." (A. R. Fausset, *A Commentary, Critical, Experimental, and Practical, on the Old and New Testaments: Job–Isaiah*, vol. III [London: William Collins, Sons, 1866], 409).
13. Barry Webb (Moore Theological College, AU) understands how the past shapes the present. History plays a vital role in Israel's restoration. "They are described in verse 1 as those *who pursue righteousness and who seek the Lord*. They have grasped the heart of true religion: holiness of life flowing from a personal relationship with God... Their expectation of what God will do in the future profoundly shapes how they live in the present. They do not rely on their unaided consciences to tell them how they should live; they *know what is right*, because they have God's *law* in their *hearts* (v. 7). Their whole character and behavior are shaped by the word of God. And yet there are things that trouble them. They are so few in number (v. 1b–2), and so despised (v. 7b). How can the future be theirs? The answer, of course, lay in their history. These struggling believers were true children of Abraham; he was *the rock from which* they had been *cut* (v. 1b). They were not just his physical descendants; they also shared in his faith in God. And look what God did with Abraham! He was only *one* when God called him, but he *blessed him and made him many* (v. 2). Cannot God do the same with them?" (Barry Webb, *The Message of Isaiah: On Eagles' Wings*, The Bible Speaks Today, eds. J. A. Motyer and Derek Tidball [Nottingham, UK: InterVarsity Press, 1996], 201, emphasis is the author's).

    Graham S. Ogden *(United Bible Societies)* and Jan Sterk (Old Testament scholar) also understand the important role history plays in Israel's future restoration. "**Look to Abraham your father and to Sarah who bore you ...** The call to consider the past is repeated in this verse, which identifies the

metaphors of the previous verse as references to Israel's ancestors, **Abraham** and **Sarah**. The purpose of looking back at this history is to remind the people that the God who blessed and multiplied the nation beginning from the days of Abraham will do the same for them. God remains faithful to his promises" (Ogden and Sterk, *Handbook on Isaiah*, UBSH, 1437, emphasis is the authors'). See also, Eusebius of Caesarea (*c*. 300 CE), *Commentary on Isaiah*, ACT, trans. Jonathan J. Armstrong, eds. Joel C. Elowsky, Thomas C. Oden, and Gerald L. Bray (Downers Grove, IL: IVP Academic, 2013), 251; Gary Smith, *Isaiah 40–66*, NAC vol. 15B (Nashville: Broadman & Holman, 2009), 392.
14. Anthony Phillips, *Ancient Israel's Criminal Law* (Oxford: Basil Blackwell, 1970), 11; Raymond Westbrook, *Property, Family in Biblical Law*, LHBOTS 113, eds. David Clines and Philip Davies (Sheffield, JSOT Press, 1991), 38; Elazar, *Covenant and Polity*, 193–95.
15. See Deut 10:13; 26:11; Josh 1:8; 23:14; 1 Sam 12:23; 1 Kgs 8:36; 2 Chr 30:22; Ezra 3:11; Neh 9:13; Ps 25:8; 34:10; 119:39, 68; and Prov 4:2.
16. See *YE1*, 181–90.
17. *CGAE*, 117, 229; Joseph Campbell, *The Mythic Image* (Princeton, NJ: Princeton Univ. Press, 1974); John Currid, *Ancient Egypt and the Old Testament* (Grand Rapids: Baker, 1997), 42; Jan Assmann, *Death and Salvation in Ancient Egypt*, trans. David Lorton (Ithaca, NY: Cornell Univ. Press, 2005), 48–52; K. van der Toorn, *Sin and Sanction in Israel and Mesopotamia* (Maastricht, Netherlands: Van Gorcum, 1985), 23.
18. David Noel Freedman, *The Nine Commandments* (New York: Doubleday, 2000), 34; James Hastings and John Selbie, *Encyclopedia of Religion and Ethics*, vol. 10 (Whitefish, MT: Kessinger, 1908), 483–84; van der Toorn, *Sin and Sanction*, 23; Campbell, *Mythic Image*, 15–44.
19. For more information on this ceremony see: Joshua J. Mark, "The Egyptian Afterlife & the Feather of Truth," World History Encyclopedia Online (March 30, 2018), https://www.worldhistory.org/article/42/the-egyptian-afterlife--the-feather-of-truth/.
20. George Mendenhall, *Ancient Israel's Faith and History* (Louisville, KY: John Knox, 2001), 34. Albertz and Schmitt take a similar view but consider the ritual and symbolism a product of the family rather than state authorities. "The essential interests of families and the actions required to meet these interests largely determined the symbolic systems that were then used to express and manifest family religious beliefs and practices. Rites and rituals of familial religion thus directly expressed family values and were largely shaped by the personal relationships of the family members. . . . and their gods" (Rainer Albertz and Rudiger Schmitt, *Family and Household Religion in Ancient Israel and the Levant* [Winona Lake, IN: Eisenbrauns, 2012], 426).
21. *JM*, 5, 34–37; van der Toorn, *Sin and Sanction*, 24, 94–97; Assmann, *Death and Salvation*, 115, 125; Currid, *Egypt and Old Testament*, 96–102. It should be pointed out that not all ancient religions had a concept of sin. Some cults, such as Egypt's Maat, viewed right and wrong as a set of ethics (Maulana Karenga, *Maat, the Moral Ideal in Ancient Egypt: A Study in Classical African Ethics* [New York: Routledge, 2004], 3–11, 233–35). However, Bleeker has demonstrated ten Egyptian words associated with sin and six other words associated with guilt (C. J. Bleeker, "Guilt and Purification in Egypt," in *Proceedings of the Xth International Congress of the International Association of Religions*, vol. 2 [Leiden: Brill, 1968], 81–87).
22. Assmann, *Death and Salvation*, 115–16. See also Donald Redford, *Oxford Encyclopedia of Ancient Egypt*, vol. 3 (Oxford: Oxford Univ. Press, 2001), 346; Redford, *Oxford Encyclopedia of Ancient Egypt*, vol. 2 (Oxford: Oxford Univ. Press, 2001), 211–14; Bleeker, "Guilt and Purification in Egypt," 81–87.
23. John Pedley, *Sanctuaries and the Sacred in the Ancient Greek World* (New York: Cambridge Univ. Press, 2006), 1, 16, 116; *CGAE*, 135, 117, 136; Campbell, *Mythic Image*; Paul L. Garber and Roland K. Harrison, "Idol," *ISBE* (vol. 2), 794–97; and Othmar Keel and Christopher Uehlinger, *Gods, Goddesses, and Images of God*, trans. Thomas Trapp (Minneapolis, MN: Fortress Press, 1998), 7–9.
24. Celsus, *On the True Doctrine*, trans. R. J. Hoffmann (Oxford: Oxford Univ. Press, 1987), 71; *JM*, 80–81.
25. *JM*, 16, 21–22, 25.
26. *JM*, 35. See also: Hastings, *Encyclopedia of Religion and Ethics*, vol. 10, 282–84; Assmann, *Death and Salvation*, 78; and Bleeker, *Guilt and Purification*, 87.
27. Assmann, *Death and Salvation*, 78–86.

CHAPTER 11: YHWH SUES ISRAEL

1. Fourteen Rebellions occur before Israel enters Canaan: **1. At the Red Sea**—Exod 14:10–12. **2. At the Bitter Waters of Marah**—Exod 15:22–24. **3. Disregarded the Sabbath on Manna**—Exod 16:19–30; Deut 8:3, 16. **4. Rock at Horeb: Massah**— Exod 17:1–7; 33:14; Deut 6:16; 9:22. **5. Golden

Calf—Exod 32:1–35 Deut 9:8–21. **6. Fire at Taberah**—Num 11:1–3; Deut 9:22. **7. Lusting for Flesh at Kibroth-hattaavah**—Num 11:3–10, 18–21, 33; Deut 9:22; Ps 78:30–32. **8. Rebellion of Korah**—Num 16:1–40. **9. Rebellion over Korah's Demise**—Num 16:40–50; Deut 11:6. **10. Rebellion at the Spies Report (*the 10th time*)**—Num 14:1–22; 32:10–14; Deut 9:23. **11. Rebellion at Ai**—Num 14:40–45. **12. Rock at Meribah in Kadesh**—Num 20:1–13, 24; 27:14; Deut 32:51; 33:8. **13. Fiery Serpents near the Red Sea**—Num 21:4–9. **14. Whoredom with Baal-Peor in Moab**—Numbers 25.

2. Gary Smith, *Isaiah 1–39*, NAC vol. 15A, ed. E. Ray Clendenen (Nashville: B & H Publishing, 2007), 93–119; Ogden and Sterk, *A Handbook on Isaiah*, UBSH, 26; John Oswalt, *The Book of Isaiah Chapters 40–66*, NICOT, eds. R. K. Harrison and Robert Hubbard (Grand Rapids, MI: Eerdmans), 40–66, 59, 72, 79, 80, 85, 99, 100, 102, 108, 110, 112, 331, 326; Smith, *Isaiah 40–66*, NAC, 124–27, 198–201, 274, 323–26; Trent Butler, *Isaiah*, HOTC, ed. Max Anders. (Nashville: Broadman and Hollman, 2002), 281, 282; Rikki Watts, "Consolation or Confrontation: Isaiah 40–55 and the Delay of the New Exodus," *Tyn-Bul* 41/1 (1990), 38–44; Michael Thompson, *Isaiah 40–66* (Eugene, OR: WIPF & Stock, 2001), xxvi, 22, 43, 47, 86; Koole, *Isaiah III*, 211.

3. **Israel's charge that YHWH is unrighteous**—Mic 6:3; Ezek 18:25, 29; 33:17–20. **The claim that YHWH is righteous**—Exod 9:27; Deut 4:8; Judg 5:11; 1 Sam 12:7; 2 Chr 12:6; Ezra 9:15; Neh 9:8; Ps 7:9; 7:17; 9:8; 11:7; 19:9; 22:31; 35:24, 28; 36:6, 10; 40:10; 50:6; 51:14; 71:2, 15–16, 19, 24; 72:2; 88:12; 89:16; 97:6; 98:2, 9; 99:4; 103:6; 111:3; 116:5; 119:7, 40, 62, 106, 123, 137–38, 142–44, 160, 164, 172; 129:4; 143:1, 11; 145:7, 17; Isa 5:16; 11:4–5; 41:10; 42:21; 45:19, 23; 46:13; 51:5–6, 8; 56:1; 59:16–17; Jer 12:1; Lam 1:18; Dan 9:7, 14, 16; Mic 6:5; and Zech 8:8.

4. Recent archaeological excavations at Tel Arad have exposed a religious site that competed with the Temple in Jerusalem during King Uzziah's and Ahaz's reign (*c.* 760–715 BCE). The incense altar contained animal dung and cannabis that was used for a drug-induced high (Alex Fox, "Archaeologists Identify Traces of Burnt Cannabis in Ancient Jewish Shrine," *Smithsonian* [June 4, 2020], https://www.smithsonianmag.com/smart-news/cannabis-found-altar-ancient-israeli-shrine-180975016/; Eran Arie, Baruch Rosen, Dvory Namdar, "Cannabis and Frankincense at the Judahite Shrine of Arad," *Tel Aviv* 47/1 (May 28, 2020), 5–28, DOI: 10.1080/03344355.2020.1732046; Christopher Eames "Ancient Israelite Cannabis Altar Points to King Ahaz's Worship," Armstrong Institute of Biblical Archaeology (June 3, 2020), https://tinyurl.com/5466hmyb. Exod 30:34 provides the Biblical formula for incense. The ingredients are specifically described as "sweet." It did not include cannabis, which smells stinky and pungent. YHWH warned, "You shall offer no strange incense thereon" (Exod 30:8). YHWH judged Nadab and Abihu for offering "strange incense" in Lev 10:1–2, demonstrating that mind-altering substances were not to be associated with His theology.

5. Lamar Eugene Cooper (Criswell College) observes: "This paragraph begins and ends with God's response to charges of injustice. Apparently, the charges were based on the claim that Judah was innocent of wrongdoing but was paying for the sins of past generations. They believed they were caught in an unfair process of retribution that meted out punishment indiscriminately. There was nothing, then, the people could do about it" (Lamar Eugene Cooper, *Ezekiel*, NAC vol. 17 [Nashville: Broadman & Holman, 1994], 192).

6. Christopher J. H. Wright, *The Message of Ezekiel: A New Heart and a New Spirit*, The Bible Speaks Today, eds. Alec Motyer and Derek Tidball (Nottingham, England: Inter-Varsity Press, 2001), 202. Fausset, *Jeremiah-Malachi*, 267–70.

7. John Watts (Southern Baptist Theological Sem.) comments that "YHWH's advocate specifically prescribes what proofs are required. The test will turn on the ability of the idols' advocates to predict events and to bring them about as predicted. V. 23 rhetorically addresses the nonexistent gods, challenging them to do something, anything that may 'shock' the assemblage, like the appearance of a ghost. The failure to appear or present proofs is taken as a proof of the nonexistence of their gods. Those who believe in such gods are themselves abhorrent" (John D. W. Watts, *Isaiah 34–66*, WBC vol. 25, Revised Edition [Nashville: Thomas Nelson, Inc., 2005], 659).

Ogden and Sterk provide a thorough understanding of this text. "In this verse God challenges the gods of the nations to prove they control events in the world. **Let them bring them**: The first pronoun **them** refers to the gods, and the second one to the arguments mentioned in the previous verse. Yahweh tells the gods to present their arguments concerning who is the master of history. (French Common Language Version 1997) provides a helpful model here with 'Bring [plural] your arguments....' '**Tell us the former things, what they are:**' The Hebrew noun translated *former things* is an important term in this part of the book. It reappears at 42:9; 43:9, 18; 46:9; and 48:3, but its specific meaning depends on the context in which it is used. Here it clearly refers to past events since it contrasts with **what is to happen**. Yahweh also challenges the gods to prove they knew beforehand the events that have taken place. The

JPS Tanakh footnote on this line points out that it concerns 'former prophecies by your gods which have been fulfilled.' The implication is that there were never any such prophecies. For this line the Good News Bible says 'tell us what they mean,' and Revised English Bible has 'Let them declare the meaning of these past events.' These versions shift the focus from the fulfillment of past prophecies to the meaning of past events.

"*That we may consider them* is literally 'and let us put [them] to our heart,' which means 'let us reflect on them.' The Lord wants to know the evidence the gods have that they successfully predicted past events, so he can think about it. *That we may know their outcome* refers to discovering whether the gods actually predicted past events. *Their outcome* is the occurrence of the past events described as *the former things*. If these events actually happened, then the gods of the nations would be real gods. Some translations link this line to the future events referred to in the last line, so they place it at the end of the verse; for example, for the last two lines Revised English Bible has 'let them predict the future to us that we may know what it holds' (similarly JPS Tanakh, French Common Language Version)." (Ogden and Sterk, *A Handbook on Isaiah*, UBSH, 1116–17).

8. Roger Omanson (Bible translator) and (linguist) John E. Ellington remark: "**So that they did more evil than the nations whom the Lord destroyed before the people of Israel**: The comparison between the people of Judah and the pagan nations who were driven out before the Israelites as they entered the land shows the Judeans to be extremely pagan in themselves" (Roger L. Omanson and John E. Ellington, *A Handbook on 1-2 Chronicles*, UBSH, vol. 1 & 2, eds. Paul Clarke, et al. [Miami, FL: United Bible Societies, 2014], 1327).

9. וַיַאְדִּיר; *weya'dir*; *SEC* 142; *HALOT*, 167, s.v. "אדר" translate as "powerful" or "to glorify;" "to prove to be glorious."

Ogden and Sterk understand Isaiah to be stating the following: "***The Lord was pleased, for his righteousness' sake*** . . . means that because Yahweh is righteous, he was happy to do the things mentioned in the next line. The motivation for God's action is ***his righteousness***, which refers here to his moral purity and justice (see the comments on verse 6). Revised English Bible expresses the sense of this line well with 'it pleased the Lord to further his justice . . . ' Another possible rendering is 'Because the Lord is righteous/just, he was pleased to . . . '

"**To magnify his law and make it glorious**: This is what Yahweh was delighted to do. <u>**To magnify his law** means he caused his teachings to be great</u>. He gave them the most important place in the life of his people. As in verse 4, the Hebrew word rendered **law** is better translated 'teaching' (NRSV, JPS Tanakh) or 'instruction.' <u>**Make it glorious** means Yahweh also gave his teachings a place of honor in the life of his people</u>. The Good News Bible says 'he wanted his people to honor them,' but this rendering shifts the focus from a description of Gods' teachings to his people's response to them (Ogden and Jan Sterk, Handbook on Isaiah UBSH, 1156, underlining added).

On the exalting of Divine Law, Gary Smith remarks: "God's righteousness involves his faithful commitment to do what was right and true. This divine attribute resulted in the establishment of just principles to guide his relationship with his people so that everyone would know the just consequences of righteous and rebellious behavior. God did not hide these facts so that he could unfairly punish people for things they were unaware of, nor did he change the nature of the relationship without telling them. He graciously revealed these righteous guidelines for behavior through a series of written instructions known as his 'instruction, law' (*tôrâ*), as well as God's instructions through prophets like Isaiah. His purpose was not to burden his people with a second-class set of legalistic rules or pedantic restrictive regulations. He viewed these divine instructions as a great and glorious revelation of his character, something that would set the wise Israelites apart from the other nations (Deut 4:6). Other nations would be amazed that they had such wisdom and insight into the will of their God and would marvel that Israel had a God that was so near that he could talk to them when they called on him for help (Deut 4:7). This revelation was a glorious gift of God. Pss 19:7-14 and 119 celebrate the blessedness of having God's revelation as a guide. The person who was walking in a close relationship to God exclaimed that they loved God's instructions (Ps 119:97)." (Smith, *Isaiah 40–66*, NAC, 186).

John Watts remarks: "'YHWH was pleased for his legitimacy's [צדקו] sake that he magnify instruction [תורה] and glorify it' employs some key terms in biblical theology to describe what YHWH is doing through the servant" (Watts, *Isaiah 34–66*, WBC, 672).

10. Regarding the waning of Israel's values, Ralph Smith (SW Baptist Theological Sem.) notes: "One of the problems of Malachi's day was the blurring of moral and theological values. No one seemed to be able to distinguish right from wrong, or the righteous from the wicked" (Ralph L. Smith, *Micah–Malachi*, WBC vol. 32 [Dallas: Word, Inc., 1984], 338).

11. Fourteenth-century French philosopher Jacques Lefèvre d'Étaples understood this text to extol the future restoration of Divine Law, describing a situation similar to our modern era. "'It is time to do, O Lord; they have dissipated your law.' If some precious shrub or shrub of balsam or cinnamon in the world should perish from ignorance, certainly a little sprout is spared in one place. Then knowledge is exceedingly necessary, with which it is cultivated and increased in gardens, lest it should perish at the root. And what is more precious than your law, O Lord of hosts? The law, which is neglected with human ignorance, and disregarded, and lies almost eradicated everywhere, at any rate is preserved in a sacred place and among a few people. Surely knowledge of your law is then especially necessary, so that it may be propagated widely, and so that it may take root, lest it perish completely, and lest all piety and the salvation of all people should perish at the same time with it? 'Surely you will teach and propagate understanding of your precepts? Surely your servants will most justifiably call to you, will cry out, will lament?' 'It is time to do, O Lord; they have dissipated your law.' The time to illuminate, the time to reveal your law, the time to remove and eradicate the ignorance that diminishes, dissipates, and destroys it, and to advance your holy law to the minds of all" (Jacques Lefèvre d'Étaples in *Psalms 73-150: Old Testament*: Explanatory Notes, vol. VIII, Reformation Commentary on Scripture, eds. Herman J. Selderhuis and Timothy George [Downers Grove, IL: IVP Academic, 2018], 278–79).

Andrew Fausset shares a similar understanding: **"It is time for thee, Lord, to work; (for) they have made void thy law.** 'To work;' or, *lit.*, 'to do (it)'—viz., to vindicate thy servant by saving him from his oppressors (*vv.* 121–123). So 'do' is used absolutely, Ps. 22:31; 52:9; Isa. 44:23. Here *the heathen* are charged with breaking God's law—viz., by oppressing Israel, in violation of God's law of righteousness and love written on the conscience in some degree, however in part effaced by degeneracy. The same charge against the inhabitants of the earth is brought in Isa. 24:5. The Book of Job, which concerns one not of Abraham's race, yet regulated by the fear of God and the principles of righteousness, preserved by tradition among some of the Gentiles, shows that the law of God, even in the Old Testament, was not altogether confined to the elect nation. **127. Therefore I love thy commandments above gold, yea, above fine gold**—(Ps. 19:10). 'Therefore'—viz., because of the excellencies of thy law, as detailed already. **128. Therefore I esteem all (thy) precepts (concerning) all (things to be) right; (and) I hate every false way.** We must not choose those precepts which suit our inclinations, whilst we set aside others which oppose our lusts, but 'esteem all God's precepts concerning all things' the obligatory rule of our hearts and lives" (Fausset, *Job–Isaiah*, 371).

12. Mackay, *Jeremiah*, 260–65; Kaiser and Rata, *Walking the Ancient Paths*, 97–98; Lalleman, *Jeremiah and Lamentations*, TOTC, 98–99; Allen, *Jeremiah*, OTL, 80–81.

13. Gary Smith remarks: "The oppression of the poor involved taking homes and fields in 5:12. This was wrong because the land belonged to God (Lev 25:23) and he gave it to various tribes and families. The rich and powerful stole what God gave to others as their eternal inheritance (Exod 19:5; Deut 32:9). Injustice in the courts (5:23) was another way the powerful were able to oppress the poor, enslave them, and take their land. The root *ṣdq*, 'justice,' is used three times in 5:23. These people pay off judges and witnesses so that the guilty people are 'declared just,' but 'justice' for the 'just, innocent' person is denied. This is a sorrowful state of affairs and this behavior is totally opposite the just and holy character of God (5:16)." (Smith, *Isaiah 1–39*, NAC, 178–79).

14. Acts 13:39; Rom 3:19–20; 4:15; 7:1, 6; Gal 2:16, 21; 3:10–11; Heb 7:19; and Jas 2:10.

15. John MacArthur, "What Does 'Sola Scriptura' Mean?," Ligonier.org (Aug 27, 2021), https://www.ligonier.org/learn/articles/what-does-sola-scriptura-mean.

CHAPTER 12: HISTORICITY OF THE NEW TESTAMENT: ARCHAEOLOGY

1. John Creswell, *Research Design: Qualitative, Quantitative, and Mixed Methods Approaches* (Los Angeles: Sage, 2004), 160, 166, 174, 201, 203, 211, 225; Jerome Kirk and Mark Miller, *Reliability and Validity in Qualitative Research, Qualitative Research Methods*, vol. 1, eds. John Van Maanen, et. al. (London: Sage, 1986), 21–33, 41–42; Mark Litwin, *How to Measure Survey Reliability and Validity: The Survey Kit 7* (London: Sage, 1995); Stephen Schensul, et al., *Essential Ethnographic Methods: Observations, Interviews, and Questionnaires: Ethnographer's Toolkit 2* (New York: AltaMira Press, 1999), 271–73; Gerd Theissen, "Historical Skepticism and the Criteria of Jesus Research: My Attempt to Leap over Lessings's Ugly Wide Ditch," in *HSHJ* (vol. 1), 550, 552–555–559, 561, 584. See also Cline, Eden to Exile, ix–xli.

2. Oswalt, *Isaiah Chapters 40–66*, NICOT, 104.

3. See also, Tom Tolmén and Stanley Porter, "How to Study the Historical Jesus," in *HSHJ* (vol. 1), ii–xxi; John Meier, "Basic Methodology in the Quest for the Historical Jesus," in *HSHJ* (vol. 1), 291–331.
4. Ehrman, *Did Jesus Exist,* 42; John Reumann, "Archaeology and Early Christology," in *Jesus and Archaeology*, ed. James Charlesworth (Grand Rapids: Eerdmans, 2006), 664–78; Bruce D. Chilton, "Method in a Critical Study of Jesus," in *HSHJ* (vol.1), 131–32.
5. Matteo Borrini and Luigi Garlaschelli, "A BPA Approach to the Shroud of Turin," *JFS* 64/1 (July 10, 2018), 137–143, https://doi.org/10.1111/1556-4029.13867; P.E. Damon, et al., "Radio Carbon Dating of the Shroud of Turin," *Nature* 337 (February, 1989), 611–15, https://doi.org/10.1038/337611a0.
6. David E. Graves, *The Archaeology of the New Testament* (Moncton, New Brunswick, CAN: Electronic Christian Media, 2019), 101.
7. André Lemaire, "Burial Box of James the Brother of Jesus," *BAR* 28/6 (November/December 2002), 24–33. See also, Hershel Shanks and Ben Witherington, III, *Brother of Jesus: The Dramatic Story and Meaning of the First Archaeological Link to Jesus and His Family* (London: Continuum, 2003); James Tabor, *The Jesus Dynasty: The Hidden History of Jesus, His Royal Family, and the Birth of Christianity* (New York: Simon and Schuster, 2006), 6–36, 305, 321; Neil Asher Silberman and Yuval Goren, "Faking biblical History: How wishful thinking and technology fooled some scholars—and made fools out of others," *Archaeology* 56/5 (September–October 2003), 20–29; Hershel Shanks, "Related Coverage on the James Ossuary and Forgery Trial," Bible History Daily: *BAR* (November 8, 2010), https://bit.ly/352TuiO; Ryan Byrne and Bernadette McNary–Zak, eds., *Resurrecting the Brother of Jesus: The James Ossuary Controversy and the Quest for Religious Relics* (Chapel Hill: University of North Carolina Press, 2009).
8. Archaeometry is the application of techniques and procedures from the hard sciences (physics, chemistry, biology, etc.) and engineering to archaeology-related questions, problems, and studies. Wolfgang E. Krumbein, "Preliminary Report: External Expert Opinion on Three Stone Items," (University of Oldenburg, Germany, September 2005); Amnon Rosenfeld, Howard Feldman, Wolfgang Krumbein, and Carl von Ossietzky, "Archaeometric Analysis of the James Ossuary," Proceedings from 2008 Joint Meeting of The Geological Society of America, Soil Science Society of America, American Society of Agronomy, Crop Science Society of America (Gulf Coast Association of Geological Societies with the Gulf Coast Section of SEPM in GSAAP 40/6), 354.
9. BAR Press Release (June 13, 2012), "Brother of Jesus Proved Ancient and Authentic," Bible History Daily; *BAR* (June 13, 2012), https://bit.ly/30KXmBs; Shanks and Witherington, "Brother of Jesus," xiii, 20, 50, 211; Tabor, *Jesus Dynasty*, 16–20, 129, 305; Byrne and McNary–Zak, *Resurrecting the Brother of Jesus*, 19, 37, 99, 111.
10. Aryeh E. Shimron, et al., "The Geochemistry of Intrusive Sediment Sampled from the 1st Century CE Inscribed Ossuaries of James and the Talpiot Tomb, Jerusalem," *Archaeological Discovery* (2020), 8, 92–115, https://www.scirp.org/pdf/ad_2019120316084496.pdf.
11. James D. Tabor, "The Talpiot 'Jesus' Tomb: A Historical Analysis," in *The Tomb of Jesus and His Family? Exploring Ancient Jewish Tombs Near Jerusalem's Walls: The Fourth Princeton Symposium on Judaism and Christian Origins*, eds. James H. Charlesworth and Arthur C. Boulet (Grand Rapids: Eerdmans, 2013), 247–66.
12. James Tabor and Simcha Jacobovici, *The Jesus Discovery* (New York: Simon and Schuster, 2012).
13. Shimon Gibson and Amos Kloner, "The Talpiot Tomb Reconsidered: The Archaeological Facts," in *Tomb of Jesus and His Family? Exploring Ancient Jewish Tombs Near Jerusalem's Walls: The Fourth Princeton Symposium on Judaism and Christian Origins*, ed. James Charlesworth (Grand Rapids: Eerdmans, 2013), 31–35; Tabor and Jacobovici, *Jesus Discovery*, 17–37.
14. Tabor and Jacobovici, *Jesus Discovery*, 17–18.
15. Gibson and Kloner, "Talpiot Tomb Reconsidered," 29–75.
16. Gibson and Kloner, "Talpiot Tomb Reconsidered," 29, 39.
17. Gibson and Kloner, "Talpiot Tomb Reconsidered," 39.
18. Gibson and Kloner, "Talpiot Tomb Reconsidered," 37–38.
19. Gibson and Kloner, "Talpiot Tomb Reconsidered," 34–35.
20. Gibson and Kloner, "Talpiot Tomb Reconsidered," 39.
21. L. Y. Rahmani, *A Catalogue of Jewish Ossuaries in the Collections of the State of Israel* (Jerusalem: Israel Antiquities Authority, 1994), 222–24, ossuaries nos. 701–09; Amos Kloner, "Tomb with Inscribed Ossuaries," *A Catalogue of Jewish Ossuaries in the Collections of the State of Israel*, 17–21, "Jerusalem," *Atiqot* 19 (1996), ossuaries n. 1–10.
22. Simcha Jacobovici and Charles Pellegrina, *The Jesus Family Tomb: The Discovery That Will Change History Forever* (New York: Harper Element, 2008).

23. Jodi Magness, "Ossuaries and the Burials of Jesus and James," *JBL* 124/1 (Spring 2005), 148.
24. Gibson and Kloner, "Talpiot Tomb Reconsidered," 42; Tabor and Jacobovici, *Jesus Discovery*, 27–37.
25. Gibson and Kloner, "Talpiot Tomb Reconsidered," 43.
26. Gibson and Kloner, "Talpiot Tomb Reconsidered," 50–51.
27. Gibson and Kloner, "Talpiot Tomb Reconsidered," 51 vs. Tabor and Jacobovici, *Jesus Discovery*, 45–47.
28. Tabor and Jacobovici, *Jesus Discovery*, 68–69, 77–89. See also, Matt 12:39–41; 16:4; Luke 11:39–42.
29. Tabor and Jacobovici, *Jesus Discovery*, 70. For further study see: James Tabor, "In-Depth Reading on the Talpiot Tombs: What is the Best Evidence?" TaborBlog.com (August 19, 2021), https://jamestabor.com/in-depth-reading-on-the-talpiot-tombs-what-is-the-best-evidence/. For an alternative translation see Richard Bauckham, "The Four-Line Ossuary Inscription from Talpiyot Tomb B – an Interpretation," ASORblog.org (March 8, 2012). https://asorblog.org/p_1848.html (accessed March 2023); and Christopher Rollston, "The Talpiyot (Jerusalem) Tombs: Some Sober Methodological Reflections on the Epigraphic Materials," Arizona.edu (April 2013), https://bibleinterp.arizona.edu/sites/bibleinterp.arizona.edu/files/images/RollstonTalpiot_0.pdf. A rebuttal to Rollston is also on the Arizona State University Bible and Interpretation Blog. https://bibleinterp.arizona.edu/articles/2013/rol378025. Opposing Chadworth is Bob Cargill, "Why the So-Called 'Jonah Ossuary' Does Not Contain the Name of Jonah," The (Retired) Blog of Robert H. Cargill Ph.D (April 13, 2012), https://bobcargill.wordpress.com/2012/04/13/why-the-so-called-jonah-ossuary-does-not-contain-the-name-of-jonah/.
30. The only type of resurrection the evidence finds possible is a spiritual resurrection. However, this seems to oppose Ezekiel's physical resurrection where dry bones are drawn together (Ezekiel 37).
31. Joel B. Green, "Family, Friends, and Foes," in *HSHJ* (vol. 3), 2436–40.
32. Rahmani, *Catalogue of Jewish Ossuaries*, 222.
33. The other factor that plays into this is the custom of naming a daughter after her mother with a first name, then the distinguishing name second, as a nickname, that was popular from Ptolemaic Egypt until recent modern times. In Egypt, this is witnessed with 7 Cleopatras and 4 Berenices. The popularity of Christianity created a long-lasting tradition where Mary (Maria in Spanish) was given as a first name and the girl's actual name being her second name. The most famous of these in the New Testament is of course, Mary Magdalene.
34. A. Rosenfeld, et al., "The Authenticity of the James Ossuary," *OJG* 4 (2014), 69–78, DOI: 10.4236/ojg.2014.43007.
35. Camil Fuchs, "Demography, Literacy and Names Distribution in Ancient Jerusalem: How many James/Jacob son of Joseph, brother of Jesus were there?" *The Polish Journal of Biblical Research* 4/1 (2005), 3–30.
36. Ehrman, *Did Jesus Exist*, 148.
37. John Chapman, "St. Hegesippus," in *The Catholic Encyclopedia*, vol. 7 (New York: Robert Appleton Company, 1910), http://www.newadvent.org/cathen/07194a.htm.
38. John Meier, *The Marginal Jew: Rethinking the Historical Jesus: The Roots of the Problem and the Person*: AYBRL 1, ed. David Noel Freedman (New York: Doubleday, 1991), 58.
39. Eusebius, *Ecclesiastical History II*, LCL Books I–IV, trans. Kirsopp Lake, ed. G. P. Goold (Cambridge: Harvard University Press, 1949), 171. See also *Ecclesiastical History, II* (23.2), 105.
40. Eusebius: *Ecclesiastical History IV*, 375. Read online for yourself: Kevin Knight, ed., "Eusebius: Church History, IV," NewAdvent.org, http://www.newadvent.org/fathers/250104.htm.
41. Eusebius: *Ecclesiastical History III*, 237.
42. Quoting Hegesippus, Eusebius also notes: "Therefore, they call the church a virgin, for it was not yet corrupted by vain discourses (*Ecclesiastical History IV*, 4.22.4). For Eusebius, vain beliefs began to enter the Church after *c*. 150 CE (Arthur Cushman McGiffert, *From Nicene and Post-Nicene Fathers*, Second Series, vol. 1, eds. Philip Schaff and Henry Wace [Buffalo, NY: Christian Literature Publishing Co., 1890], Revised and edited for New Advent by Kevin Knight, http://www.newadvent.org/fathers/250104.htm).
43. James D. Tabor, "The Talpiot 'Jesus' Tomb," 247–266. James Tabor relates that every known historical reference to the name "Mariamene," variant "Mariamn," refers to Mary Magdalene. Interestingly, the earliest textual reference appears in the third century CE. Thus, Mary Magdalene from the Bible remains the most likely person to whom the inscription refers. For further incidents of names of New Testament people who may appear in other accounts see, the Tabor Blog: https://jamestabor.com/is-there-any-credible-archaeological-evidence-for-the-earliest-followers-of-jesus/.
44. Ehrman, *Did Jesus Exist*, 147.
45. Gen 12:2; 15:4–5, 18; 17:2, 4–6; 22:17; 26:4; 28:14; 32:12; 46:3. See also, *YE1*, 81–121.
46. See also, Tabor, *The Jesus Dynasty*. For an easy-to-read article on the James Ossuary, see: James Tabor, "What's What Regarding the Controversial James Ossuary?" Tabor Blog (February 12, 2016), https://jamestabor.com/whats-what-regarding-the-controversial-james-ossuary/.

47. Graves, *Archaeology of the New Testament*, 101.
48. Bryne and McNary-Zak, *Resurrecting the Brother of Jesus*, 19; Joseph Holden and Norman Geisler, *The Popular Handbook of Archaeology and the Bible: Discoveries that Confirm the Reliability of Scripture* (Eugene, OR: Harvest House, 2013), 304, 314–15, 393, 404. One worthwhile site that explores the pros and cons of the evidence is Paul L. Maier's article, "The James Ossuary," https://www.issuesetcarchive.org/articles/bissar95.htm.

CHAPTER 13: HISTORICITY OF THE NEW TESTAMENT: GREEK & ROMAN SOURCES

1. The word "proof" is too often misused. The only two fields of study capable of proving any issue true or false are mathematics and logic (an extension of math). All other fields of study like astronomy, medicine, political science, etc., rely on the preponderance of evidence.
2. Porter, "The Criteria of Authenticity," in *HSHJ* (vol. 1), 695–714.
3. Meier, *Marginal Jew*, 94–98.
4. Ehrman, *Did Jesus Exist?* 43. See also, Robert Louis Wilken, *The Christians as the Romans Saw Them*, 2nd Edition. (New Haven: Yale University Press, 2003), 1–30; Edgar McKnight, *Jesus Christ in History and Scripture* (Macon, GA: Mercer University Press, 1999), 31–32.
5. Robert Van Voorst, *Jesus Outside the New Testament: An Introduction to the Ancient Evidence*: SHJ (Grand Rapids: Eerdmans, 2000), 25–29; Van Voorst, "Jesus Tradition in Classical and Jewish Wittings," in *HSHJ* (vol. 3), 2151–52; Meier, *Marginal Jew*, 92. To read these letters for yourself, see: "Pliny the Younger, Letters: Book 10:61–151," Attalus.org, trans. J. B. Firth, https://www.attalus.org/old/pliny10b.html. Another great learning resource is: "Epistulae X.96–Pliny the Younger–Ancient Rome–Classical Literature," Ancient –literature.com, http://www.ancient-literature.com/rome_pliny_epistulae_X96.html.
6. S. Angus and A. M. Renwick, "Roman Empire and Christianity," *ISBE* (vol. 4), 207–18.
7. Pliny, the Younger, *Letters, vol. 2, Book X*: LCL, trans. William Melmoth and W. M. L. Hutchinson (London: London Heinemann, 1915), 399–404, parentheses added. Also available online: https://archive.org/stream/letterswithengli02plinuoft/letterswithengli02plinuoft_djvu., pp. 401–05.
8. Van Voorst, "Jesus Tradition in Classical and Jewish Writings," in *HSHJ* (vol. 3), 2157–59.
9. Pliny, the Younger, *Letters, vol. 2, Book X*, 399–404; parentheses added. See also David Horrell, *Becoming Christian: Essays on 1 Peter and the Making of Christian Identity*: LNTS (New York: Bloomsbury T&T Clark, 2013), 183–96.
10. A. N. Sherwin-White, *The Letters of Pliny: A Historical and Social Commentary* (New York: Oxford University Press, 1998), 707–709; Craig de Vos, "Popular Graeco-Roman Responses to Christianity," in *The Early Christian World*, vol. 2, ed. Philip F. Esler (London: Routledge, Taylor and Francis, 2000), 149–66; Geoffrey de Ste. Croix, "Why Were the Early Christians Persecuted?" *SAC*, 210–49; Adrian Sherwin-White, "Why Were the Early Christians Persecuted? An Amendment" in SAC, 250–55; Geoffrey de Ste. Croix, "Why Were the Early Christians Persecuted?—A Rejoinder," Past and Present, 27/27 (1964), 28–33; Everett Ferguson, *Backgrounds of Early Christianity*, 2nd Edition. (Grand Rapids: Eerdmans, 1993), 565–80.
11. Before the council of Nicaea in 325 CE, Christians held various views on Jesus' divinity. Most, especially the Arians worshipped Jesus as a man or as a lesser god to the Old Testament's God the Father. Friendly debates were often enjoyed among Christian leaders. In 380 CE, under the new Augustus, the pro-Nicene sect prevailed, and Jesus suddenly became God's only Son and existed before the Earth itself. See Richard E. Rubenstein, *When Jesus Became God: The Struggle to Define Christianity during the Last Days of Rome* (San Diego: Harcourt, 1999), 221–22; Bart Ehrman, *How Jesus Became God: The Exaltation of a Jewish Preacher from Galilee* (New York: Harper One, 2014), 211–371.
12. Ehrman, *Did Jesus Exist*, 52.
13. Sherwin-White, *Letters of Pliny*, 707–09.
14. Matt 2:2, 8, 11; 8:2; 9:18; 14:33; 15:25; 18:26; 28:9, 17; Mark 5:6; 15:19; Luke 24:52; John 9:38. See also, Van Voorst, "Jesus Tradition in Classical and Jewish Writings," in *HSHJ* (vol. 3), 2151–52.
15. J.W.E. Pearce, "Introduction and Notes," to Cornelius Tacitus, *The Agricola of Tacitus* (London: George Bell, 1901), xi–xiii; Sylvia Fein, *Die Beziehungen der Kaiser Trajan und Hadrian zu den litterati*: Beiträge zur Altertumskunde, 26/26 (Leipzig: Teubner Stuttart, 1994), 210–14.
16. J.W.E. Pearce, "Introduction and Notes," ix–xiii.
17. J.W.E. Pearce, "Introduction and Notes," ix.
18. J.W.E. Pearce, "Introduction and Notes," xii–xiii.

19. Ronald Syme, *Tacitus* (London: Oxford University, 1958), 767.
20. Meier, *Marginal Jew*, 89–91; James Charlesworth, *The Historical Jesus: An Essential Guide* (Nashville: Abingdon Press, 2008), 33.
21. Tacitus, *Annals* 15.44, in *Tacitus V, Annals Books 13–16*, LCL 322, trans. John Jackson (Cambridge, MA: Harvard University Press, 1937), 283. See also, Van Voorst, "Jesus Tradition," in *HSHJ* (vol. 3), 2155–59; Cornelius Tacitus, *Tacitus Annals, Book XV*, ed. Rhiannon Ash (Cambridge Greek and Latin Classics, Cambridge: Cambridge University, 2017), 205–06. See also Cornelius Tacitus, *The Annals*, eds. Alfred John Church and William Jackson Brodribb (New York: Random House, 1942), https://bit.ly/2eJuuSZ.
22. Ehrman, *Did Jesus Exist*, 54–55.
23. You can read this account in Tacitus, *Annals, Book XV*, at: http://penelope.uchicago.edu/Thayer/E/Roman/Texts/Tacitus/Annals/15B*.html.
24. Tacitus, *Annals* (vol. 5), 283–85. See also: Cornelius Tacitus, *The Complete Works of Tacitus*, trans. Alfred John Church and William Brodribb, eds. Moses Hadas, et. al. (New York: The Modern Library, 1942); Matthew Owen and Ingo Gildenhard, *Tacitus, Annals*, 15.20–23, 33–45 (Cambridge: Open Book Publishers, 2013), 237–39; Jona Lendering, "Tacitus on the Christians," Livius.org (2004, modified April 2019), http://www.livius.org/sources/content/tacitus/tacitus-on-the-christians/, or at, https://www.tektonics.org/jesusexist/tacitus.php.
25. See also, Ingo Broer, "The Death of Jesus from a Historical Perspective," in *From Judaism to Christianity: Continuum Approaches to the Historical Jesus*, ed. Tom Holemé (New York: T&T Clark, 2007), 154–58; McKnight, *Jesus Christ: In History and Scripture*, 31–34; Van Voorst, *Jesus Outside*, 39–53; Van Voorst, "Jesus Tradition in Classical and Jewish Writings," in *HSHJ* (vol. 3), 2155–59; Meier, *Marginal Jew*, 89–91.
26. Charlesworth, *Jesus and Archaeology*, 334–36.
27. Van Voorst, "Jesus Tradition in Classical and Jewish Writings," in *HSHJ* (vol. 3), 2152.
28. Suetonius, *Lives of the Caesars*, vol. 2, LCL 38, trans. J. C. Rolf (Cambridge, MA: Harvard University Press, 1914), 53, Online at: http://penelope.uchicago.edu/Thayer/E/Roman/Texts/Suetonius/12Caesars/Claudius*.html.
29. Ehrman, *Did Jesus Exist*, 53; Van Voorst, *Jesus Outside*, 29–38; Van Voorst, "Jesus Tradition in Classical and Jewish Writings," in *HSHJ* (vol. 1), 5152–55; Meier, *Marginal Jew*, 91–92.
30. Van Voorst, *Jesus Outside*, 29–38; Van Voorst, "Jesus Tradition in Classical and Jewish Writings," in *HSHJ* (vol. 3), 2153.
31. Stephen Benko, "The Edict of Claudius of AD 49 and the Instigator Chrestus," *TZ* 25 (1969), 406–18.
32. Ehrman, *Did Jesus Exist*, 53–54.
33. Romans termed religions they deemed illegitimate as "superstitions." Only state-sanction religions were deemed appropriate.
34. Suetonius, *Lives of the Caesars, Book IV*, LCL 38, trans. J. C. Rolfe (Cambridge, MA: Harvard University Press, 1914), 112.
35. McKnight, *Jesus Christ: In History and Scripture*, 33–34.
36. Van Voorst, "Jesus Tradition in Classical and Jewish Writings," in *HSHJ* (vol. 3), 2162–65.
37. Meier, *Marginal Jew*, 92.
38. Lucian, "The Death of Peregrine," 11–13, in *The Works of Lucian of Samosata, vol. 4*, trans. H.W. and F.G. Fowler (Oxford: Clarendon, 1905), 82–83.
39. Lucian, "The Death of Peregrine," (11–13), 82–83.
40. Van Voorst, "Jesus Tradition in Classical and Jewish Writings," in *HSHJ* (vol. 3), 2163.
41. Van Voorst, "Jesus Tradition in Classical and Jewish Writings," in *HSHJ* (vol. 3), 2162.
42. Van Voorst, "Jesus Tradition in Classical and Jewish Writings," in *HSHJ* (vol. 3), 2163.
43. Van Voorst, *Jesus Outside*, 63–64; Van Voorst, "Jesus Tradition in Classical and Jewish Writings," in *HSHJ*, 2163; R. Joseph Hoffmann, trans., *Celsus on the True Doctrine* (New York: Oxford University, 1987), 25–27.
44. Van Voorst, *Jesus Outside*, 57–67; Van Voorst, "Jesus Tradition in Classical and Jewish Writings," in *HSHJ* (vol. 3), 2162–65; Riemer Roukema, "Jesus Tradition in Early Patristic Writings," in *HSHJ* (vol. 3), 2119, 2021–22.
45. Van Voorst, *Jesus Outside*, 65; Van Voorst, "Jesus Tradition in Classical and Jewish Writings," in *HSHJ* (vol. 3), 2165.
46. Celsus, *True Doctrine*, 54. Lincoln Blumell, "A Jew in Celsus' True Doctrine? An examination of Jewish Anti-Christian polemic in the second century C.E.," *SRSR* 36/2 (2007), 302–03.
47. Celsus, *True Doctrine*, 59.
48. Celsus, *True Doctrine*, 63–64.

49. Celsus, *True Doctrine*, 53.
50. Celsus, *True Doctrine*, 15, 28, 61.
51. Celsus, *True Doctrine*, 54 (see also p. 27); Blumell, "A Jew in Celsus," 307, 309.
52. Celsus, *True Doctrine*, 54–55. Fuller not only discusses the divine–man savior myths among pagan cults, but he also cites evidence of a savior–man within Hellenistic Judaism. See also, Fuller, *Christology*, 98.
53. Celsus, *True Doctrine*, 60. The irony is found in Ps 16:4; Isa 42:8; 48:11.
54. Celsus, *True Doctrine*, 61.
55. Celsus, *True Doctrine*, 61.
56. Celsus, *True Doctrine*, 96–97.
57. Celsus, *True Doctrine*, 17, 24. See also, Blumell, "A Jew in Celsus," 297–315.
58. Wendell S. Reilly, "Witness of the Early Church to the Authorship of the Gospels," *CBQ* 1/2 (April 1939), 115–24.
59. Van Voorst, *Jesus Outside*, 67–75; Meier, *Marginal Jew*, 223–24. For a terrific resource for further comprehensive study of the early Christian Scriptures, writings, and Church Fathers, see: "Early Christian Writings," EarlyChristianWritings.com. http:// www.earlychristianwritings.com/.

CHAPTER 14: HISTORICITY OF THE NEW TESTAMENT: JEWISH SOURCES

1. To read this account for yourself, see: Flavius Josephus, *Antiquities of the Jews Book 18*, trans. William Whiston (London: University of Cambridge, 1737), https://penelope.uchicago.edu/josephus/ant-18.html. See also, Van Voorst, *Jesus Outside*, 81–103; Paul Copan and Craig Evans, *Who Was Jesus? A Jewish–Christian Dialogue* (Louisville, KY: John Knox Press, 2001), 55–58; Clare Rothschild, "Echo of a Whisper: The Uncertain Authenticity of Josephus' Witness to John the Baptist," in *Ablution, Initiation, and Baptism in Late Antiquity, Early Judaism, and Early Christianity*, eds. David Hellholm, et al. (New York: De Gruyter, 2010), 255–90.
2. Flavious Josephus, *Jewish Antiquities, Book XVIII–XIX*, LCL 433, trans. Louis Feldman, ed. G.P. Goold (Cambridge: Harvard University Press, 1965), 81–85.
3. Steve Mason, *Josephus and the New Testament* (Grand Rapids: Baker Academic, 2003), 215–17.
4. Mason, *Josephus*, 213–225; Meier, *Marginal Jew*, 66.
5. Mason, *Josephus*, 215.
6. Mason, *Josephus*, 215.
7. Mason, *Josephus*, 215.
8. Mason, *Josephus*, 217–25.
9. Josephus, *Jewish Antiquities*, LCL (Feldman), 83.
10. Cf. Matt 7:19–20.
11. Jesus would later uphold John's theology: Matt 7:16–19; Luke 6:43–44; 13:7; John 15:2.
12. Mason, Josephus, 238.
13. Mason, *Josephus*, 239.
14. Mason, *Josephus*, 239.
15. Mason, *Josephus*, 241–42, 246.
16. Craig Evans, *Jesus and His Contemporaries: Comparative Studies*, Arbeiten Zur Geschichte Des Antiken Judentums Und Des Urchristentums 25 (Leiden: Brill, 2001), 44–45.
17. Mason, *Josephus*, 243.
18. Ehrman, *Did Jesus Exist*, 58–60; Meier, *Marginal Jew*, 56–57; Charlesworth, *Historical Jesus*, 34–35; McKnight, *Jesus Christ: In History and Scripture*, 30–31; Van Voorst, "Jesus Tradition in Classical and Jewish Writings," in *HSHJ* (vol. 3), 2168–71.
19. Mason, *Josephus*, 226.
20. Mason, *Josephus*, 226.
21. Meier, *Marginal Jew*, 79; Mason, *Josephus*, 229.
22. Χριστοῦ—*SEC* 5547; *Thayer's*, 672–73: *LSJ*, 790; Fuller, *Christology*, 63–64, 67–69.
23. הַמָּשִׁיחַ(hammashiah); *SEC* 4899; *BDB*, 603: *TWOT* (vol. 1), 530–32; *CHALOT*, 218–19; *HALOT*, s.v., "מָשִׁיחַ"; Ehrman, *Did Jesus Exist*, 169.
24. Meier, *Marginal Jew*, 60.
25. Heinz Schreckenberg and Kurt Schubert, *Jewish Traditions in Early Christian Literature*, vol. 2, JHIEMC (Leiden: Brill, 1992), 38–41; Andreas J. Kostenberger, L. Scott Kellum, and Charles L. Quarles, *The Cradle*,

the Cross, and the Crown: An Introduction to the New Testament (Nashville: B & H Academic, 2009), 104–08; Henry Wansbrough, *Jesus and the Oral Gospel Tradition* (Sheffield: Sheffield Academic, 1991), 185; Mason, *Josephus*, 9, 185; Evans, *Jesus and His Contemporaries*, 316; James Dunn, *Jesus Remembered: Christianity in the Making*, vol. 1 (Grand Rapids: Eerdmans, 2003), 141; Ken Olson, "Eusebius and the 'Testimonium Flavianum,'" *CBQ* 61/2 (April, 1999), 305; D. S. Wallace-Hadrill, "Eusebius of Caesarea and the Testimonium Flavianum (Josephus, *Antiquities*, XVIII. 63f)," *JEH* 25/4 (March 2011), 353; Fuller, *Christology*, 23.

26. Ehrman, *Did Jesus Exist*, 60–61.
27. Ehrman, *Did Jesus Exist*, 60–61; McKnight, *Jesus Christ: In History and Scripture*, 30–31.
28. Mason, *Josephus*, 8–19, 229, 236.
29. Mason, *Josephus*, 236.
30. Mason, *Josephus*, 229–236; Meier, *Marginal Jew*, 59.
31. Mason, *Josephus*, 230–231.
32. Jerome, "Lives of Illustrious Men 13," in *The Nicene and Post-Nicene Fathers*, Series 2, ed. Phillip Schaff (Peabody, Mass: Hendrickson, 1994), 3:366.
33. Mason, *Josephus*, 230–34; Ken Olson, "A Eusebian Reading of the Testimonium Flavianum," in Eusebius of Caesarea: Tradition and Innovations: CHS, eds. Aaron Johnson and Jeremy Shott (Trustees for Harvard University, Washington, D.C., Cambridge: Harvard University Press, 2013), https://www.academia.edu/4062154/Olson_A_Eusebian_Reading_of_the_Testimonium_ Flavianum_2013.
34. Olson, "Eusebian Reading," 97–113.
35. Olson, "Eusebian Reading," 97–113.
36. Olson, "Eusebian Reading," 97–113. While Mason leaves open the possibility for Eusebius' "helping" of Josephus' text, he credits the early Church historian Hegesippus with the "Christianizing" of the Josephus text (Mason, *Josephus*, 16–19).
37. Olson, "Eusebian Reading," 111.
38. Olson, "Eusebian Reading," 103–05.
39. Steve Mason, "Commentary" in Falavius Josephus: *Judean War* 2, vol. 1b (Leiden: Brill, 2008), 98n743. See also Fernando Bermejo-Rubio, "Was the Hypothetical Vorlage of the Testimonium Flavianum a 'Neutral' Text? Challenging the Common Wisdom on Antiquitates Judaicae 18.63–64," *JSJ* 45 (2014), 326–65. James Charlesworth interprets testimonium flavianum as an overall negative statement that aligns him with the other Judean rebels (*Historical Jesus: An Essential Guide*, 34).
40. Olson, "Eusebian Reading," 104.
41. Olson, "Eusebian Reading," 104.
42. See also, Olsen, "Eusebius and the 'Testimonium Flavianum,'" 305–22.
43. Evans, *Jesus and His Contemporaries*, 43.
44. Ehrman, *Did Jesus Exist*, 62; Mason, *Josephus*, 229, 236.
45. Mason, *Josephus*, 228. The word "Christ" (Greek, *christos*) did not have any special connotation (see Homer's *Illiad* 23.186). It simply means "wetted" or "anointed" (*LSJ*, 790; Mason, *Josephus*, 227–28). The Jewish people of Josephus' day understood the word in terms of an earthly leader. A mashiach or "anointed one" in a Hebrew context was a person anointed as a leader of the people. [הַמָּשִׁיעַ, *SEC* 4886; Mason, *Josephus*, 227–28]. Throughout the Old Testament, the term was used to anoint kings, priests, and even a stone (Gen 28:18, 31:13). Isaiah terms Persia's King Cyrus a "messiah" (Isa 45:1) since God had appointed him for a specific task. Since Josephus' audience was being introduced to the term *christos* and its association with Jesus, Josephus would have explained it. This lack of clarification within the text arouses suspicion.
46. Mason, *Josephus*, 231.
47. Olson, "Eusebian Reading," 103.
48. Olson, "Eusebian Reading," 103.
49. Olson, "Eusebian Reading," 103; Solomon Zeitlin, "The Christ Passage in Josephus," *JQR* 18 (1927–28), 238–39, 253; Mason, *Josephus*, 232.
50. Mason, *Josephus*, 230; Erich Gruen, "Christians as a 'Third Race,'" in *Christianity in the Second Century: Themes and Developments*, eds. James Paget and Judith Lieu (Cambridge: Cambridge University Press, 2018), 21, 235–49.
51. Mason, *Josephus*, 232.
52. Meier, *Marginal Jew*, 66. While Ehrman finds Olson's arguments for Eusebius' authorship compelling and admits some influence, he does not find the original text a complete forgery (*Did Jesus Exist*, 64). Meier successfully demonstrates that the terminology in *testimonium flavianum* is different than that

used in the NT indicating that the Josephus account was not authored or influenced directly by the NT or its authors (*Marginal Jew*, 79–84 n40–43).
53. Shlomo Pines, *An Arabic Version of the Testionium Flavianum and Its Implications* (Jeruslaem: Israel Academy of Sciences and Humanities, 1971), 9–10, http://khazarzar.skeptik.net/books/pines01.pdf; Mason, *Josephus*, 230.
54. Mason, *Josephus*, 233–34; Meier, *Marginal Jew*, 60, 63; Ehrman, *Did Jesus Exist*, 60–61.
55. Mason, *Josephus*, 233.
56. Pines, *Arabic Version*, 9–10.
57. Ehrman, *Did Jesus Exist*, 61. For further reading, see "Early Christian Writings: Josephus and Jesus, The Testimonium Flavianum Question," EarlyChristianWritings.com, http://www.earlychristianwritings.com/testimonium.html.
58. Peter Shäfer, *Jesus in the Talmud* (Princeton: Princeton University Press, 2009), 8, 15–22, 98; Robert Hutchinson, *Searching for Jesus: New Discoveries in the Quest for Jesus of Nazareth—and How They Confirm the Gospel Accounts* (Nashville: Nelson Books, 2015), 287; Van Voorst, "Jesus Tradition in Classical and Jewish Writings," in *HSHJ* (vol. 3), 2171–76.
59. I wrestled with discussing the early versions of the New Testament or the hundreds of books that did not make the NT canon. I found the topic too broad for the subject of this book but recommend the following books for those who would like to study the topic further: Bart Ehrman, *Lost Christianities* (New York: Oxford University Press, 2003), 247–57; Bruce Metzger, *The Early Versions of the New Testament: Their Origin, Transmission and Limitations* (Oxford, UK: Clarendon Press, 1977); Metzger, *The Canon of the New Testament: Its Origin, Development and Significance* (Oxford, UK: Clarendon Press, 1987); and Stanley E. Porter, *How We Got the New Testament: Text, Transmission, Translation*, ASBT (Grand Rapids: Baker Academic, 2013). See online: Luke Stone, "10 Books Not Included in the New Testament," ListVerse.com (ed. Jamie Frater), https://listverse.com/2012/07/06/10-books-not-included-in-the-new-testament/ (accessed July 2023). Listen to Bart Ehrman's online interview at: Fresh Air, "Scholar Bart Ehrman, 'Lost Christianities,'" NPR.org (July 9, 2004), https://www.npr.org/2004/07/09/3250048/scholar-bart-ehrman-lost-christianities.
60. *YE1*, 12.

CHAPTER 15: SOLA SCRIPTURA

1. A sampling of these sects can be found at "Global Christianity—A Report on the Size and Distribution of the World's Christian Population," Pew Research Center (December 19, 2011), https://www.pewforum.org/2011/12/19/global-christianity-exec/. See also the references listed at Wikipedia. "List of Christian Denominations by Number of Members," Wikipedia.org https://en.wikipedia.org/wiki/List_of_Christian_denominations_by_number_of_members.
2. Deut 9:5–6; Ps 36:10; 89:16; 103:17; 119:40; Isa 33:5; 45:8, 24; 51:7; 54:14, *17*; 61:11; *Jer 23:6; 33:16; 51:10*.
3. Exod 34:6; Deut 32:4; Ps 31:5; 57:3; 86:15.
4. These are the New Testament texts that refer to the Old Testament Law and prophets as a sacred writing or scripture: Mark 12:10; 15:28; Luke 4:21; John 2:22; 7:38, 42; 10:35; 13:18; 17:12; 19:24, 28, 36–37; 20:9; Acts 1:16; 8:32, 35; Rom 4:3; 9:17; 10:11; 11:2; Gal 3:8, 22; 4:30; 1 Tim 5:18; 2 Tim 3:16; James 2:8, 23; 4:5; 1 Peter 2:6; 2 Peter 1:20.

   Ambrosiaster (c. 370 CE) writes: "*In the holy Scriptures*: Paul added this on top of his argument, in order to give greater confidence to believers and show his approval of the law" (Ambrosiaster in *Commentaries on Romans and 1-2 Corinthians*, ACT, eds. Thomas C. Oden and Gerald L. Bray, trans. Gerald L. Bray [Downers Grove, IL: IVP Academic, 2009], 3).

   Grant Osborne (Trinity Evangelical Divinity School) remarks: "Throughout Romans, Paul will be anchoring his theological points in Old Testament truth. This statement in verse 2 establishes the promise–fulfillment pattern that will dominate his use of the Old Testament. The verb is made of two parts, *promise* and *before*, with the latter drawing out the main aspect of the promise, that it was given ahead of time through the *prophets*" (Grant R. Osborne, *Romans*, The IVP New Testament Commentary Series [Downers Grove, IL: InterVarsity Press, 2004], 29–30).

   Newman and Nida (both with American Bible Society) understand Paul's reference to Holy Scripture to refer to the Old Testament. "The *Holy Scriptures* is a reference to the Old Testament (see 2 Timothy 3:15 where this same phrase occurs). More often the Old Testament is referred to simply as 'the Scriptures' (Matt 21:42; 22:29; 26:54; John 5:39; etc.)." (Newman and Nida, *Handbook on Paul's Letter to the Romans*, UBSH, 8).

Fausset and Jamieson understand Paul to refer to the Old Testament. "**Which he had promised afore by his prophets in the holy scriptures.** Though the Roman church was Gentile by nation (see *v.* 13), yet, as most of them had been proselytes to the Jewish Faith, they are here reminded that in embracing the Gospel they had not cast off Moses and the prophets, but only yielded themselves the more intelligently and profoundly to the testimony of God in that earlier Revelation (Acts 13:32, 33)." (Brown, Fausset, and Jamieson, *Acts–Revelation*, 191).

Leon Morris: "It would be possible to recall the original meaning of the word and translate here by 'holy writings'. But the reference to the prophets makes it clear that Paul has in mind the Old Testament. We should thus translate with 'holy scriptures'" (Morris, *The Epistle to the Romans*, PNTC, 41).

Colin Kruse: "Paul frequently refers to the writings of the OT as 'the Scripture(s)' (4:3; 9:17; 10:11; 11:2; 15:4; 16:26; 1 Cor. 15:3, 4; Gal. 3:8, 22; 4:30; 1 Tim. 5:18; 2 Tim. 3:16), but only here as 'the *Holy* Scriptures'" (Kruse, *Paul's Letter to the Romans*, PNTC, 41).

Daniel Gurtner (Gateway Sem.): "**He promised beforehand through His prophets in the holy Scriptures:** Though clearly referring to the Old Testament, only here does he call the Scriptures (*graphai*) sacred (*hagiai*), though such was an expression used elsewhere by Jews for their scriptures (Josh., *Ag. Ap.* 2.4 § 45; Philo, *Abr.* 61; *De congr.* 34, 90). Luther said the gospel here provides us an 'entrance into the Old Testament.' Paul clearly sees the content of his gospel as being continuous with what he studied of the Old Testament as a Pharisee" (Daniel M. Gurtner, "Romans," in *The Bible Knowledge Background Commentary: Acts–Philemon*, 1st Edition, eds. Craig A. Evans and Craig A. Bubeck [Colorado Springs, CO: David C. Cook, 2004], 203).

Robert Mounce interprets Paul in the following way: "God made his promise 'through his prophets' in the Old Testament. He entrusted his message to men chosen to speak for him. Beyond that, he allowed his message to be written down. What the prophets wrote became 'Holy Scriptures.' Here we have a brief summary of the method God chose in order to communicate with his people. Scripture originated with God. He used prophets to communicate his will, and they accomplished that purpose by writing down what God was pleased to reveal. The result was Scripture that is holy" (Mounce, *Romans*, NAC, 60).

5. See also, Matt 10:40; Mark 9:37; Luke 4:18; 9:48; 10:16; John 1:33; 4:34; 5:24, 30, 36–7; 6:38–40, 44, 57; 7:16, 28–29, 33; 8:16, 18, 26, 29, 42; 9:4; 11:42; 12:44–45, 49; 13:20; 14:24; 15:21; 16:5; 17:18, 21, 23, 25; 20:21.

6. Throughout his ministry, Jesus appealed to the authority of Israel's written Scriptures: the Law and the prophets. See: Matt 2:23; 5:12, 17–18, 40; 7:12, 15; 11:13; 12:5; 13:17; 16:14; 22:36, 40; 23:23, 29–31, 34, 37; 26:56; Mark 1:2; 6:15; 8:28; Luke 1:70; 2:22–24, 27, 39; 5:17; 10:24, 26; 11:49; 13:28, 34; 16:16–17, 29–31; 18:31; 24:25–27, 44–49; John 1:45; 6:45; 7:2, 19; 8:5; 12:34; Acts 3:18–25; 7:42, 52–53; 13:15, 27; 15:15; 24:14; 26:22; Rom 1:2; 2:20; 3:21.

Chromatius of Aquileia (c. 390 CE) wrote, "While it is sinful to abolish the least of the commandments, all the more so the great and most important ones. Hence the Holy Spirit affirms through Solomon: 'Whoever despises the little things shall gradually die'. Consequently nothing in the divine commandments must be abolished, nothing altered. Everything must be preserved and taught faithfully and devotedly that the glory of the heavenly kingdom may not be lost. Indeed, those things considered least important and small by the unfaithful or by worldly people are not small before God but necessary" (Chromatius of Aquileia in *Matthew 1–13*, ACCS, 96).

Swiss Reformer Heinrich Bullinger (c. 1550 CE) understood this text to support the continued validity of Old Testament Law. "Let everyone, therefore, be persuaded for certain that the law of God, which is the most excellent and perfect will of God, is forever eternal, and cannot be at any time dissolved, either by humans, or angels, or any other creatures. Let every person think that the law, so far as it is the rule of how to live well and happily, so far as it is the bridle by which we are kept in the fear of the Lord, so far as it is a prick that awakens the dullness of our flesh, and so far as it is given to instruct, correct, and rebuke us, that here, I say, it does remain unabrogated. And, to this day, the law has its belonging in the church of God" (Bullinger in *Matthew: New Testament*, Reformation Commentary on Scripture, 67–68).

Brown, Fausset and Jamieson also understood Jesus to confirm the eternal validity of Divine Law. "Not to subvert, abrogate, or annul, but to establish the Law and the Prophets—to unfold them, to embody them in living form, and to enshrine them in the reverence, affection, and character of men, am I come.' **18. For verily I say unto you** [Ἀμὴν = אָמֵן—λέγω ὑμῖν]: Here, for the first time, does that august expression occur in our Lord's recorded teaching, with which we have grown so familiar as hardly to reflect on its full import. It is the expression, manifestly, of *supreme legislative authority*; and as the subject in connection with which it is uttered is the Moral Law, no higher claim to an authority *strictly divine* could be advanced. For when we observe how jealously Jehovah asserts it as His exclusive prerogative to give law to men v. 5 (Lev. 18:1–5; 19:37; 26:1–4, 13–16, etc.), such language as this of our Lord will appear totally unsuitable, and indeed abhorrent, from any creature-lips. . . . The meaning is that 'not so much as the smallest loss of authority or vitality shall ever come over the law.' The expression, 'till all be fulfilled,' is much the same in meaning as 'it *shall* be had in undiminished and enduring honor, from its greatest to its least requirements. . . . in the Christian Church—**he shall be called the least in the kingdom of heaven.** As the thing spoken of is not the practical breaking, or disobeying, of the law, but annulling, or enervating its obligation by a vicious system of interpretation, and teaching others to do the same" (Brown, Fausset, and Jamieson, *A Commentary, Critical, Experimental, and Practical, on the Old and New Testaments: Matthew–John*, vol. V [London: William Collins, Sons, 1866], 30–31).

John Stott understands this text similarly. "His purpose is not to change the law, still less to annul it, but 'to reveal the full depth of meaning that it was intended to hold'" (John R. W. Stott and John R. W. Stott, *The Message of the Sermon on the Mount (Matthew 5–7): Christian Counter-Culture*, The Bible Speaks Today [Downers Grove, IL: InterVarsity Press, 1985], 72).

Donald Hagner (Wheaton College) remarks: "Jesus here emphatically denies (twice, and thus with the greatest emphasis) that he has come καταλῦσαι, 'to destroy,' the law or the prophets. The infinitive here has the sense of 'to abolish,' 'annul,' or 'repeal' (*cf.* its use in 24:2; 26:61; and 27:40 in reference to the destruction of the temple; in reference to the law, cf. 2 Macc 2:22; 4:11; 4 Macc 5:33; and Josephus *Ant.* 16.2.4 §35; 20.4.2 §81). Jesus, therefore, denies that he has come to cancel or to do away with the law or the prophets. . . . The important declaration introduced by this formula is that not a 'jot or tittle' (to use the now traditional language) of the law will pass away (for a rabbinic parallel, cf. *Exod. Shemot Rabbah* 1:6). This, then, is a further and more forceful statement that Jesus has not come to destroy the law (v 17). The repetition of 'one' (ἕν, μία) in the chiastic formulation ἰῶτα ἓν ἢ μία κεραία, 'one iota or one mark,' provides extra emphasis on the absoluteness of the saying (cf. BDF §474[1]). ἰῶτα ('iota') is the smallest letter of the Greek alphabet but translates an underlying reference to the smallest Hebrew letter, the yod (י). The κεραία ('tittle,' lit. 'horn' or 'hook') refers to minute markings of the written text, either those that distinguish similar Hebrew letters (as between ה and ח) or, more probably, the ornamental marks customarily added to certain letters. We have here thus a deliberate hyperbole—an overstatement that is designed to drive home the main point that the law be fully preserved. Jesus' words stress that the law is to be preserved (Donald A. Hagner, *Matthew 1–13*, WBC vol. 33A [Dallas: Word, 1993], 104–06).

7. Pastor and author Stuart K. Weber addresses the concept of 'fulfilled' in v. 17: "There is much debate over what Jesus meant by the word fulfill. The word means 'to fill out, expand.' **It does not mean to bring to an end.** Jesus was not taking away from the law, nor was he adding to it. He was clarifying its original meaning. After all, he was its author. And we must not forget that Jesus, as a Jew, related well to the law—not as it was commonly understood, but as it was originally intended" (Stuart K. Weber, *Matthew*, HNTC vol. 1 [Nashville: Broadman & Holman, 2000], 63, bolding added for emphasis).

Criag Keener also understands v. 17 in terms of Jesus' Jewish heritage: "When Jesus says that he came not to *abolish the Law or the Prophets* but to *fulfill them,* he uses terms that in his culture would have conveyed his faithfulness to the Scriptures" (Keener, *Matthew*, Matt 5:17–18).

8. Scholars and theologians remark on Divine Law's eternal nature with built-in mechanisms to address and resolve Israel's rebellion. Its many provisions offered forgiveness once the sin was acknowledged and terminated. George Athas (Moore College Australia) remarks on the eternal nature of YHWH's Law and covenant, which includes the promise of future restoration: "With the curses and catastrophic nature of exile still ringing loudly, he now raises the prospect of restoration to the land after exile. Even after Israel has failed its covenant obligations, after it has experienced the curses of the covenant and failed to heed their warning, and even after the downfall and destruction of the nation and the exile of its people to other lands, even then there is a glimmer of hope for them. For if at that point the people who survive genuinely repent of the offences that led to the nation's destruction, even then Yahweh will be gracious to them and restore them to the land.

"The remarkable thing about this prospect of restoration is that it is an act of pure grace from Yahweh. If that were not enough, the prospect of future grace includes the promise of inner transformation. Moses asserts that Yahweh would circumcise Israel's heart (30:6)—an unusual image, but one that signifies the radical change of Israel's attitude, which will lead to genuine love of Yahweh and obedience to his ways. This, after all, is the basic mechanism on which the law works (6:4–5). At that point, after curse, collapse and catastrophe, there would be repentance, restoration and reformation" (George Athas,

Deuteronomy: One Nation under God, Reading The Bible Today, ed. Paul Barnett [Sydney, South NSW: Aquila Press, 2016], 307–08).

   Eugene Merrill (Dallas Theological Sem.) takes a deep dive into this verse noting the promise for future obedience and restoration. "Conditions given for Israel's restoration, and both share formulae expressive of repentance. In v. 1 the conditional particle occurs (to be translated 'when' as in the NIV) followed by three necessary responses if forgiveness is to be offered—'take [the blessings and curses] to heart' (v. 1), 'return [šabtâ] to the Lord your God,' and 'obey [šāma'tâ] him' (v. 2). The same conditional particle appears twice in v. 10 ('if' as in NIV, or even 'when' as in v. 1)—'if you obey [tišma']' and 'if you turn [tāšûb]' to him. Two of the three verbs are repeated (šama' and šûb) but in reverse order and in different form. The intensity of the repentance is expressed in exactly the same terminology in vv. 2 and 10, 'with all your heart and with all your soul.' How Israel could be deported from the land and the very earth itself left desiccated and barren, on the one hand, and how the promises of God for Israel's eternal ongoing could continue in effect, on the other hand, now finds resolution. It lies in Israel's repentance and restoration. It was in this sense that 'the things revealed belong to us and to our children forever' (Deut 29:29 [28]). What the nations could not understand on the basis of empirical historical evidence Israel could understand on the basis of God's covenant promises" (Merrill, *Deuteronomy*, 386–87).

   Raymond Brown (a Sulpician priest) writes: " The Lord knew that his people would break the covenant and incur his threatened wrath (29:28), but in his generous love he made advance provision for their restoration. The Lord knows that his idolatrous and apostate people will be driven into exile but a further thing is equally certain—they will be forgiven" (Raymond Brown, *The Message of Deuteronomy: Not by Bread Alone*, The Bible Speaks Today, eds. J. A. Motyer and Derek Tidball [England: Inter-Varsity Press, 1993], 280).

9. The *YHWH Exists*, Volume 2 series will examine the Son of Man prophecies in detail.
10. Criag Evens remarks: "That the **Law of Moses** refers to the Law (or Pentateuch) and that the **Prophets** refer to the Old Testament prophets is undisputed. The debate centers on how to understand the reference to the **Psalms**, which refers to the third division of the Hebrew Bible, now called the Writings. This division includes Psalms, Proverbs, Job, Song of Songs, Ruth, Lamentations, Ecclesiastes, Esther, Daniel, Ezra, Nehemiah, and 1–2 Chronicles. It is thought that **Psalms** refers to the whole list of books that make up this division because it is the first and longest book in the list" (Evans, *Matthew–Luke*, 526).

    Robert Stein (Southern Baptist Theological Sem.) also sees Jesus as appealing to the Law and Old Testament for the fulfilment of prophecy. "**In the Law of Moses:** That is, the first major section of the OT, consisting of the first five books. **The Prophets:** That is, the second major section of the OT consisting of the 'former prophets' (Joshua through 2 Kings) and the 'latter prophets' (the major prophets: Isaiah, Jeremiah, Ezekiel; and the minor prophets: Hosea through Malachi). In Acts 13:15; 24:14; 28:23 the Law and the Prophets appear together and refer to the entire OT. **And the Psalms:** This probably refers to the third major section of the OT called the 'Writings,' which contains the rest of the books in the OT. The first (in the Hebrew arrangement) and largest book in this section is the Psalms. We find the same threefold division of the OT in the prologue of Sirach, where we read twice of the law, the prophets, and the other books (the writings)." (Robert H. Stein, *Luke*, NAC vol. 24 [Nashville: Broadman & Holman, 1992], 620).
11. On Psalms 19, Theodoret of Cyrus (*c.* 420 CE) "calls the Mosaic Law: law, testimony, judgments, commands, decrees. . . . It is called Law in that it regulates and prescribes the best way of life . . . the law of God, being free of every fault, corrects people's souls and makes them faultless" (Theodoret of Cyrus in *Psalms 1–50*, ACCS, vol. VII, eds. Craig A. Blaising and Carmen S. Hardin [Downers Grove, IL: InterVarsity Press, 2008], 154).

    Bracher and Reyburn discuss the perfection found in Divine Law in Psalms 19:7. "The six adjectives used are not all entirely synonymous, but there is overlapping in meaning: *perfect* (see 'blameless' in 18:23); *sure* (see in 12:1 the verb 'to be sure, reliable, faithful'); *right* (with much the same meaning; see 'upright' in 11:2); *pure* (see 18:26; a 'pure commandment' is one that is right, fair, just); *clean* (synonym of *pure*; see 12:6); and *righteous* (fair, just). Translations of these six adjectives vary: New Jewish Version: 'perfect, enduring, just, lucid, pure, true'; In translation the most important thing is to use adjectives that will naturally apply to the subject. In some languages *perfect* is rendered as 'the best,' 'without any fault,' 'could not be better.' TEV: '*trustworthy*' is sometimes rendered 'you can depend on it,' or idiomatically, 'you can put your heart on it'" (Robert G. Bratcher and William David Reyburn, *A Translator's Handbook on the Book of Psalms*, UBSH [New York: United Bible Societies, 1991], 193).

    Hans-Joachim Kraus (Reformed Alliance) provides an excellent treatment of Psalms 19:7. "The תורה is praised as being תמימה in v. 7. תמים is properly a term belonging to the language of sacrifices. The flawless, spotless animal is called תמים. Here the word denotes the sufficiency of 'Holy Scripture' (cf. Deut. 32:4). The effect of this perfect תורה is seen in this, that it 'brings back' the נפש. This means to say that it restores the power of life (cf. Lam. 1:11, 16). A restorative strength emanates from the תורה. It is נאמנה ('dependable') and transmits wisdom to the פתי—the simple, those who are easily led astray (Prov. 1:22; 7:7; 9:6; 19:25; 21:11; Ps. 119:130). Conceptions of the חכמה-theology combine with the postexilic תורה-understanding also in Psalms 1 and 119. Life and wisdom stream forth from the instruction of God. The Torah is instruction for life" (Hans-Joachim Kraus, *Psalms 1–59*, CC [Minneapolis, MN: Fortress Press, 1993], 274).

12. Trent Butler (International Baptist Theological Sem.) in Luke 11:28 observes that: "True blessing comes to those who hear and obey God's Word (see 8:1–21). Dedication to Jesus involves more than saying good things about him. Dedication to Jesus means listening and obeying" (Trent C. Butler, *Luke*, HNTC vol. 3 [Nashville: Broadman & Holman, 2000], 188).

Grant Osborne writes: "In verse 28 Jesus isn't really correcting her but rather using the rabbinic technique of the weightier and the lighter, providing his own beatitude, 'Blessed rather are those who hear the word of God and obey it.' The translation 'but rather' sounds like Jesus is denying her blessing of his mother, but I don't think that is the case. He is saying that even 'more blessed' are those who keep his word. We are at the very heart of discipleship here. The penultimate method of deepening someone's walk with Christ is to immerse them in the word and help them to 'obey' it (see also 8:8, 15, 18, 21). This uses a strong verb for obeying, *phylassō*, to 'watch over, guard,' thus to 'observe' and 'follow' a teaching. So the idea is not just to obey but also to do so in order to guard and keep the teaching from being broken through disobedience" (Grant R. Osborne, *Luke: Verse by Verse*, New Testament Commentaries, eds. Jeffrey Reimer, et al. [Bellingham, WA: Lexham Press, 2018], 309).

John Nolland (Australian Anglican priest) remarks: "The use of μενοῦν (or μὲν οὖν; Tr. above 'yes, but . . . rather') is predominantly Lukan in the NT, so is likely to be Luke's touch here. 'Hearing the word of God and keeping (φυλάσσοντες) [it]' clearly echoes the wording of 8:21 (cf. 6:47): 'hearing the word of God and doing (ποιοῦντες) [it].' (These verbs are paired synonyms in the LXX of Deut 4:6; 28:13, 15; etc.) 8:21 was based on an original that had simply 'do the will of God' (Mark 3:35), but a double form in the source is more likely here to balance the womb and the breasts of v. 27. 'Word of God' is, however, likely to be Lukan (on this phrase see at 5:1)." (John Nolland, *Luke 9:21–18:34*, WBC vol. 35B [Dallas: Word, Inc., 1993], 648–49).

Jannes Reiling (Union of Baptist Church and translator) and Dutch linguist and translator J. L. Swellengrebel take note of the Greek in Luke 11:28. "*hoi akouontes ton logon tou theou kai phulassontes* 'those who hear the word of God and keep it', conjugation is similar to statements in 6:47 and 8:21. *phulassō* is used here in the metaphorical sense of 'keeping/observing' (s.v. 1f), and is virtually equivalent to *poieō* in 6:47 and 8:21. *Translation Blessed rather are*, or, 'yes, but happier are', 'be that as it may, very much blessed are' (Shona 1966), 'that may be true, but those that are-called (i.e., really are) blessed are' (Balinese). *Hear the word of God*, or 'listen to what God says. For the verb conjugation on 1:41; for the noun phrase on 5:1. *Keep it*, or, 'act in accordance with it', 'do what he commands'" (J. Reiling and J. L. Swellengrebel, *A Handbook on the Gospel of Luke*, UBSH [New York: United Bible Societies, 1993], 444).

13. "You shall not hate your brother in your heart . . . do not bear any grudge against the children of your people, but you shall love your neighbor as yourself: I am YHWH" (Lev 19:17, 18). "But the *ger* (immigrant/convert) who lives among you shall be as one born among you. You shall love him as yourself because you were strangers in the land of Egypt: I am YHWH your God" (Lev 19:34; Deut 10:19).

Jay Adams (founder of the modern Biblical counseling movement) comments that John's command to love one another was an old commandment. "Now I urge you, lady (not as though I were writing a new commandment to you, but rather that which we had from the beginning): that we love one another. This is love—that we walk according to His commandments; this is the commandment, even as you heard from the beginning—that you must walk in love" (Jay Adams, *The Gospel of John, The Letters of John and Jesus*, The Christian Counselor's Commentary [Cordova, NB, Nouthetic Studies: Mid-America Baptist Theological Sem., 2020], 2 John 5–6).

Stephen S. Smalley (Anglican Chester Cathedral) also understands John to refer to an old command. "For the thought of this part of v. 5 see the comment on 1 John 2:7, which is echoed here very closely (cf. also 2:3–5, 10; 3:11–18, 23; 4:7, 11, 21). The paradox of 1 John 2:7–8, that the 'old command' of love is also 'new,' is not repeated in the present verse. Here the presbyter contents himself with the statement that the obligation to love, which is laid upon every believer, goes back to 'the very beginning' of Christian experience, the Christian era, or even of creation (for ἀπ' ἀρχῆς see v. 6; also the comments on 1:1; 2:7, 24; 3:11). But, especially in the current Johannine situation, it could bear repetition" (Smalley, *1, 2, 3 John*, WBC, 325).

Gerald Bray (Samford Univ.) provides a similar analysis when quoting Oecumenius: "**Not a New Commandment**. Note that this verse closely resembles what is said in 1 John 2:7 and elsewhere in that letter. John's purpose is to show that what he is saying is something which people already know in principle and have even had some past experience of. It is not something strange and unusual which they will find hard to grasp" (Oecumenius in *James, 1-2 Peter, 1-3 John, Jude*, ACCS, ed. Gerald Bray [Downers Grove, IL: InterVarsity Press, 2000], 234).

Colin Kruse also understands John to reiterate the older commandment. "By making this request he is not seeking to lay on members of the church any new obligation; he is calling on them to obey the command they both received 'at the beginning.'" (Colin G. Kruse, *The Letters of John*, PNTC [Grand Rapids, MI: Eerdmans, 2000], 207–08).

14. **John 5:14:**
Newman and Nida see Jesus' instruction in simple terms: "*Stop sinning* may be rendered 'cease your sinning' or 'no longer sin'" [Barclay Moon Newman and Eugene Albert Nida, *A Handbook on the Gospel of John*, UBSH [New York: United Bible Societies, 1993], 150).

Gary Burge (Calvin Theological Sem.) understands Jesus to link the man's sin to his illness then command the man to no longer sin. "When Jesus sees him he says two things: 'See you *have* become well' is no doubt a recognition that his cure was not short-lived, as many supposed cures were. But then Jesus remarks, 'Stop sinning or something worse may happen to you.' Is Jesus making some link between sin and physical ills? Interpreters have struggled with the meaning of this verse. No doubt Jesus' exhortation must be connected to his warning here. The man's sin and his condition were linked. Scripture indicates that some tragedies may be the result of specific sins (1 Cor. 11:30) and this may be why Jesus chose the man for healing" (Gary M. Burge, "Gospel of John," in *John's Gospel, Hebrews–Revelation*, The Bible Knowledge Background Commentary, eds. Craig A. Evans and Craig A. Bubeck, 1st Edition [Colorado Springs, CO: David C Cook, 2005], 66).

Brooke Foss Westcott (English Bishop, *c.* 1860) and Arthur Westcott (Bishop of Durham) render this text as to: "*sin no more*– The original (μηκέτι ἁμάρτανε, *noli peccare*, Vulgate expresses rather *No longer continue to sin* (cf. 1 Joh. 3:6, 3:9): How his sickness was connected with his sin must remain undefined; but the connection is implied" (Brooke Foss Westcott and Arthur Westcott, eds., *The Gospel according to St. John Introduction and Notes on the Authorized Version*, Classic Commentaries on the Greek New Testament [London: J. Murray, 1908], 83).

John 8:11:
Bruce Milne (First Baptist Church in Vancouver, Canada) provides insight into John 8:11: "Jesus summons the woman to a new obedience to the law—*Go now and leave your life of sin*. It is a mistake to interpret this story as though sin is unimportant. Jesus upheld the law here, even to the point of setting in motion the application of its judgments" (Bruce Milne, *The Message of John: Here Is Your King!: With Study Guide*, The Bible Speaks Today [Downers Grove, IL: InterVarsity Press, 1993], 126).

Newman and Nida understand John 8:11 similarly: "In the Greek text the command *do not sin again* has some built-in redundancy: 'from now on no longer sin.' Most translations, like *TEV*, combine the force of 'from now on' and 'no longer.' *New English Bible* has the same expression as *TEV* has 'don't sin anymore.' *Moffat* maintains the two adverbial expressions, 'and never sin again.' Some translators take the command *do not sin again* as a specific reference to the sin of adultery and so render 'avoid this sin' (*NAB*)." (Newman and Nida, *A Handbook on the Gospel of John*, UBSH, 262–63).

15. Rodney Whitacre (Trinity School for Ministry) does see Jesus requiring something of the healed man that he could not do. "Asking this man to sin no more seems like an impossible request, an intolerable burden, but it is actually part of the good news. In the first place it implies that he has been forgiven (cf. John 8:11; Matt 9:1–8 par. Mark 2:1–12 par. Luke 5:17–26)." (Rodney A. Whitacre, *John*, The IVP New Testament Commentary Series, vol. 4 [Westmont, IL: IVP Academic, 1999], 122). This opinion, however, contradicts Deuteronomy 30:11–16, which states the Law is easy to obey.

16. Deuteronomy expert Jeffrey Tigay (Univ. of Pennsylvania) understands this text to be an oath of affirmation regarding the validity of the teachings and instructions within Divine Law. "The final anathema refers to all other provisions of the Teaching. As Rashi comments, this constitutes an oath to uphold the entire Teaching." (Tigay, *Deuteronomy*, JPS Torah Commentary, 257).

Hebrew and Old Testament scholar Robert Alter (Univ. of California, Berkeley) understands this text similar to Tigay. "This twelfth curse is clearly a summarizing one, which refers not to any specific transgression but a general failure to uphold the words of the Law that Deuteronomy has conveyed" (Robert Alter, *The Hebrew Bible: The Five Books of Moses*, vol. 1 [New York: Norton, 2019], 709).

CHAPTER 16: EQUAL WEIGHTS AND MEASURES

1. Matt 1:22; 2:15, 17, 23; 4:14; 5:18; 8:17; 12:17; 13:14, 35; 21:4; 26:54, 56; 27:9, 35; Mark 14:49; 15:28; Luke 4:21; 24:44; John 12:38; 13:18; 15:25; 17:12; 19:24, 28, 36; Acts 3:18; 13:29; Steve Moyise, "Jesus and the Scriptures of Israel," in *HSHJ* (vol. 2), 1137.
2. New Testament scholar Craig Bloomberg (Denver Sem.) discerns Jesus' teaching stemming straight from Divine Law. Bloomberg notices Jesus "quotes Deut 6:5, replacing 'strength' with 'understanding.' Neither form of the text implies a compartmentalization of the human psyche. Rather, both refer to wholehearted devotion to God with every aspect of one's being, from whatever angle one chooses to consider it—emotionally, volitionally, or cognitively. This kind of 'love' for God will then result in obedience to all he has commanded (cf. Deut 6:1–3, 6–9).

    "Going beyond the original question, Jesus adds a second commandment that is also foundational—Lev 19:18. 'The second is like it' probably means that this commandment is of equal importance. Jewish interpreters had long recognized the preeminent value of each of these laws; Jesus apparently was the first to fuse the two *and* to exalt them above the whole law (though Philo, *Spec. Leg.* 2:15, comes close to doing this). Divine love issues in interpersonal love. 'As yourself' is not a call to self-love but does presuppose it. These two commandments are the greatest because all others flow from them; indeed the whole Old Testament 'hangs' on them. In other words, all other commandments are summed up and/or contained in these" (Blomberg, *Matthew*, NAC, 335).

    Newman and Stine also see Jesus quoting from Divine Law. "The scripture which Jesus quotes is Deuteronomy 6:5. Matthew employs three terms (*heart . . . soul . . . mind*), while four appear in Mark 12:30 ('heart . . . soul . . . mind . . . strength'). The difference may be accounted for on the assumption that Mark combined the readings of two manuscripts of the Septuagint, while Matthew had a preference for the three-membered form of the Hebrew text. In either case no distinction may be drawn between the meanings of the individual terms. In Hebrew thought a person is not divided into various compartments, as is traditionally done in Greek philosophy, and together these terms summarize the totality of what a person really is. As one scholar notes: 'Any one of them would have been sufficient (in terms of Hebrew anthropology) to denote the entirety of a man.' The words of Jesus may be effectively translated 'You must love the Lord your God in all that you think or feel or do'" (Newman and Stine, *A Handbook on the Gospel of Matthew*, UBSH [New York: United Bible Societies, 1992], 695).

    New Testament scholar Craig Keener sees Jesus' teaching in line with commonly held views in Judaism. "Jesus' view does not contrast dramatically with views held by his contemporaries. In the late first century Rabbi Akiba regarded love of neighbor in Leviticus 19:18 as the greatest commandment in the law (*Gen. Rab.* 24:7; Vermes 1993:42); while this is not where Jesus ranks it, it is close. Other Jewish teachers also conjoined love of God with love of neighbor (*Test. Iss.* 5:2; 7:6; *Test. Dan* 5:3; Philo *Decal.* 108–10). Following the Jewish interpretive principle *gĕzerâh šāwâh*, it was natural to link two commandments on the basis of the common opening Hebrew word *wĕ·ahabtā* ('you shall love'; Diezinger 1978; Flusser 1988:479). The first passage Jesus cites in fact portrays the love of God as a summary of the law (Deut 6:1–7); one who loved God would fulfill the whole Torah (Deut 5:29). This passage about loving God was the central and best-known text of Judaism, the *Shema* (*šĕma·*). Likewise, the command to love one's neighbor as oneself (Lev 19:18; compare Lev 19:34; Matt 5:43; Rom 13:9) expresses a general principle, though its original context applied it to a more specific situation. As in 7:12, Matthew reminds us that these commandments epitomize all the commandments in the Bible" (Keener, *Matthew*, Matt 22:34–40).

    Stuart Weber provides insight into Jesus' reliance upon Divine Law. "Jesus drew his answer from the most memorized and recited passage in all the Jewish Scriptures: 'Hear, O Israel! The Lord our God the Lord is one. Love the Lord your God with all your heart and with all your soul and with all your strength' (Deut. 6:4–5). Jesus quoted the Septuagint almost verbatim, but he substituted **mind** (*dianoia*) for the similar sounding 'might' (*dunameos*). We are to take this list as an emphatic way of saying, 'Love God with everything you are in every way possible.' But it was not without significance that our Lord deliberately substituted 'mind' here rather than some other term. Christians need to take a lesson from this. We should learn to *think* critically and biblically. Jesus emphasized his answer by identifying this commandment as **the first and greatest commandment**. This commandment was greatest because of the statement in Deuteronomy 6:4 which preceded it: 'Yahweh is your God, Yahweh alone' (paraphrased). To honor Yahweh as the one true God is to love him exclusively, from among all others who claim to be gods.

"But Jesus went beyond the critics question and added a second command, which is **like** (*homoios*, 'resembling') the first, this time drawing from Leviticus 19:18 (cf. Matt. 19:19): **love your neighbor as yourself.** This commandment and the first complement each other, so Jesus mentioned them together. They are not to be separated. It is impossible to love God without loving people, for his law and heart's desire is to love others. The measure by which we know if we are truly loving people is if we love them as much as we love ourselves (cf. Eph. 5:28–31). V. **22:40**: Finally, Jesus defended his choice of these two commandments by observing that **all the Law and the Prophets hang on these two commandments** (or 'depends' on them)." (Weber, *Matthew*, HNTC, 358. Only underlining is added).

John Nolland arrives at a similar conclusion: "Matt 22:37—There may be another trace of the second source in the use of ὁ δέ for the change of subject, as in Luke 10:26, rather than Mark's fresh use of Jesus' name. Matthew's failure to reproduce Mark's quotation of Deut. 6:4 may be similarly inspired, as also the preference of ἐν ὅλῃ τῇ to Mark's ἐξ ὅλης τῆς in each of the 'with your whole . . .' phrases (the LXX has Mark's ἐξ ὅλης τῆς). For the quotation from Deut. 6:5 Matthew reduces the number of elements from Mark's four to three, in line with the count in the OT text. Again an influence from the second source is most likely, given that Matthew's reduction to three does not conform the set to the OT list, which would have required the dropping of διανοία ('mind/understanding') and not ἰσχύς ('strength'). (The addition of διανοία to the list is likely to be related to its occurrence as a variant to καρδία ['heart'] in the LXX of Dt. 6:5 and other texts.) . . . The call to love God has a strong OT pedigree; it occurs no fewer than ten times in Deuteronomy alone (admittedly a place of special concentration). . . . For the citation from Lev. 19:18 Matthew uses the Markan wording, which is the LXX wording, which in turn is a quite literal translation of the Masoretic Text. This is Matthew's third use of Lev. 19:18 (see 5:43, where the scope of neighbor is extended even to one's enemy; 19:19, where love of neighbor takes the place of the tenth commandment)." (Nolland, *Gospel of Matthew*, 911–12).

Another New Testament scholar understands the text in Matthew to support the same conclusion as the scholars quoted above. Craig Evans provides added perspective: "**And one of them, a lawyer (v. 35)**: One of the Pharisees, a legal expert, steps forward. '**Teacher, which is the great commandment in the Law?' (v. 36)**: Matthew adds Teacher (the equivalent of Rabbi), which lends greater respect to Jesus. Matthew adds in the law, possibly to clarify that it is the written law, not the oral law (or oral tradition) that is at issue. **This is the great and foremost commandment (v. 38)**: Matthew elevates the prestige of the first commandment by adding this summary and the reference to the foremost (lit. 'first') commandment as great. **On these two commandments depend the whole Law and the Prophets (v. 40)**: The Matthean evangelist concludes his account with a rabbinic maxim (cf. *Sipra Lev.* §195 [on Lev. 19:1–4]; §200 [on Lev. 19:15–20]; *m. Hag.* 1:8 'they are the essentials of the Law'; *b. Shabbat* 31a 'that is the whole Law'; *Exod. Rab.* 30.19 [on Exod. 21:1] 'The whole Torah rests on justice')." (Evans, *Matthew–Luke*, 428).

3. T. Rees, "God in the NT," *ISBE* (vol. 2), 500. See also the online version: "God 3," ISBE Online, http://www.internationalstandardbible.com/G/god-3.html.
4. The following websites address this belief: "Revelation: Manifestations of God," The Bahá'í Faith, https://www.bahai.org/beliefs/god-his-creation/revelation/manifestations-god; Nitin Kumar, "Buddha and Christ–Two Gods on the Path to Humanity," Exotic India (Nov 2003), https://www.exoticindiaart.com/article/buddhaandchrist/; "Manifestation of God," Bahaipedia.org, https://bahaipedia.org/Manifestation_of_God.
5. See *YE1*, 6–10.

Old Testament scholar Ralph Smith (Southwestern Baptist Theological Sem.) provides exceptional understanding of the languages that underlie Malachi 3:6. He also notes the underlying dispute Malachi is addressing in vv. 6–7 is Israel's claim that YHWH reneged on His word and had not upheld His contracted promises. "לֹא שָׁנִיתִי 'I do not change,' a qal perfect of שָׁנָה. God is not stating an abstract theological principle concerning the immutability of his nature. He is simply denying the charge of his disputants that he is unreliable, undependable, capricious. The question is about Yahweh's fidelity, not his nature. The unchangeableness of God's nature may be addressed in Ps 90:1; 102:26. Nahum Waldmann says that an **Akkadian equivalent of** שָׁנָה **means, 'to go back on one's word, change, renege.'** He translates this expression, '**For I the Lord have not gone back on my word**' (*JBL* 93 [1974], 544; cf. Prov 24:21).

"This pericope is related to the previous one and to the one that follows in that all three are dispute dialogues between the people and Yahweh. However, this pericope (3:6–12) is not eschatological like the one before and the one after it. The premise is that Yahweh has not changed. Evidently some skeptics became weary of waiting for the promised return of Yahweh as Ezekiel and Haggai had promised. **They were implying that God had changed his mind and was unfaithful to his word.** But Yahweh says that he has not changed and they (the sons of Jacob) have not changed. **The reason he has not returned** (שׁוּב)

in glory to them is they have not returned, 'repented' (שׁוּב) toward Yahweh (v 7). Yahweh accuses them of not keeping his ordinances, of not repenting, and of robbing him.

"Two personal pronouns אֲנִי 'I' and אַתֶּם 'You' are expressed. Yahweh does not change. The sons of Jacob have not changed either. They persist in their sins but they continue to exist. Malachi says that their continuance of rebellion goes back to the time of the fathers (3:7). They have not kept Yahweh's statutes (חֻקּוֹת). The prophet issues a call for Israel to repent, implying that Israel's failure to repent was responsible for the delay in Yahweh's return in glory to his temple. The expression, 'Return to me and I will return to you,' is a repetition of a part of Zech 1:3. The situation is similar to that reflected in Isa 59:1–2" (Smith, *Micah–Malachi*, WBC, 331–32. Bold emphasis added).

Hebrew scholar Richard Taylor (Dallas Theological Sem.) and linguist E. Ray Clendenen (Univ. of Texas, Arlington) understand that the foundational character of God is constant and unchanging. He also sees Israel complaining that YHWH had rescinded His contracted agreements with the nation. Malachi continues to address the Covenant Lawsuit. "The Lord is not a capricious God who may change his plans on a whim. . . . The verse may be translated then, 'Because I, Yahweh, have not changed, you, the sons of Jacob, have not perished.' The point is that if Yahweh were the kind of unfair and unfaithful God they charge him with being, who acted capriciously on the basis of momentary convenience, he would have put an end to them long ago. The verb for 'change,' šānâ, is used of David changing his 'sense,' that is, pretending to be mad out of fear of the Philistines (1 Sam 21:14); it is used of Jeroboam's wife changing or disguising her appearance to gain information from a prophet (1 Kgs 14:2); and it is used of Israel opportunistically changing their allegiance, first to Assyria then to Egypt, depending on what seems most advantageous at the time (Jer 2:36). **The Hebrew word is related to an Akkadian word šanû, which 'is used of altering contracts, agreements, words, and texts.'** Closely related to the message of Malachi, šānâ is used of God in Ps 89:34 [Heb. v. 35]: 'I will not violate my covenant or *alter* what my lips have uttered.' As VanGemeren explains, the point there is that 'the love of God outweighs his judgment. Though he may discipline even acrimoniously, his 'love' (*ḥesed*, Ps 89:33; cf. v. 28) will still extend to the offspring of David. **Though man may show contempt for the covenant, the Lord will never 'violate' . . . his own covenant. What he has promised by oath stands (v. 34)**.'" (Taylor and Clendenen, *Haggai, Malachi*, NAC, 400, 401. Bold emphasis added).

Church Father, Novatian of Rome (*c.* 250 CE) remarks on how YHWH's Divine name preserves His unchanging nature. He writes on Malachi 3:6, saying: "And therefore he says, **'I am who I am.' That which is has this name because it always preserves its same manner of being. Change takes away the name 'that which is'**; for whatever changes at all is shown to be mortal by the very fact that it changes. It ceases to be what it was and consequently begins to be what it was not" (Novatian of Rome *in* "Introduction to the Twelve Prophets," *The Twelve Prophets*, ACCS, ed. Alberto Ferreiro [Downers Grove, IL: InterVarsity Press, 2003], 303).

Renown Anglican scholar A. R. Fausset also understands Malachi to refer to YHWH's unchanging character. **"For I am the Lord**—Jehovah: a name implying his immutable faithfulness in fulfilling His promises: the covenant-name of God to the Jews (Exod. 6:3), called here 'the sons of Jacob,' in reference to God's covenant with that patriarch. I change not. Ye are mistaken in inferring that, because I have not yet executed judgment on the wicked, I am changed from what I once was—viz., a 'God of judgment' (ch. 2:17). **Therefore ye sons of Jacob are not consumed**. Ye yourselves being 'not consumed,' as ye have long deserved, are a signal proof of *my unchangeableness* (Rom. 11:29: cf. the whole chapter, in which God's mercy in store for Israel is made wholly to flow from *God's unchanging faithfulness to His own covenant of love*. So here, as is implied by the phrase, 'sons of *Jacob*' (Gen. 28:13; 35:12). They are spared because I am Jehovah, and they *sons of that Jacob* with whom, and with whose 'seed' of old, I entered into covenant, engaging to him and them the possession of Canaan, and spiritual privileges" (Fausset, *Jeremiah–Malachi*, 722).

Theologian Peter Adam (vicar of St. Jude's Church in Carlton, Melbourne) recognizes the issue in Malachi 6 is YHWH's consistency. Do His words fade like grass or do they remain constant? Adam observes: "The people complain about God's inconsistency, but in fact he remains the same. . . . They complain about the character of God, and take their revenge on him by petty acts of disobedience, but in fact their only hope lies in the character and constancy of God. Without him, they are nothing. *I . . . do not change; therefore you . . . have not perished* (6)." (Peter Adam, *The Message of Malachi: "I Have Loved You," Says the Lord*, The Bible Speaks Today, eds. Alec Motyer and Derek Tidball [England: Inter-Varsity Press, 2013], 102–03).

6. See previous endnote entry (above) regarding Malachi 3:6 and Israel's charge that YHWH had rescinded the promises of His covenant.

7. Fuller, *Christology,* 19, 23-45.

Systematic theologian Eugene Schlesinger (Santa Clara Univ.) understands the harmony between Old and New Testaments thus: "The church fathers commonly viewed the New Testament events—particularly Christ's life, death, and resurrection—as the fulfillment of Old Testament images, practices, and events (de Lubac, *Corpus Mysticum,* 64-65, 194-200)." (Eugene R. Schlesinger, "Sacraments," The Lexham Bible Dictionary, eds. John D. Barry et al. [Bellingham, WA: Lexham Press, 2016], Logos Bible Study Software).

New Testament and Pauline scholar Thomas Schreiner (Southern Baptist Theological Sem.) writes: "It is also fruitful to consider the scriptures from the standpoint of promise and fulfillment: what is promised in the Old Testament is fulfilled in the New Testament. We must beware of erasing the historical particularity of Old Testament revelation, so that we expunge the historical context in which it was birthed. On the other hand, we must acknowledge the progress of revelation from the Old Testament to the New Testament. Such progress of revelation recognizes the preliminary nature of the Old Testament and the definitive word that comes in the New Testament. To say that the Old Testament is preliminary does not cancel out its crucial role, for we can only understand the New Testament when we have also grasped the meaning of the Old Testament, and vice-versa" (Thomas Schreiner, "Preaching and Biblical Theology 101 [PBT-101]," *9Marks Journal* 3/9 [2006], 18).

Evangelist and New Testament theologian Mark Keown (Laidlaw College in Auckland, New Zealand) remarks on John's understanding of fulfillment from the Old Testament. The Old Testament served and guided his intent. "For John, the Christ-event is the key to understanding the Old Testament, and yet reflection on the Old Testament context leads the way to further comprehension of this event and provides the redemptive-historical background against which the apocalyptic visions are better understood: 'the New Testament interprets the Old, and the Old interprets the New'" (Mark J. Keown, *Discovering the New Testament: An Introduction to Its Background, Theology, and Themes,* General Letters & Revelation, vol. III [Bellingham, WA: Lexham Press, 2022], 360).

New Testament scholar James Dunn (Univ. of Durham) observes how Jesus continues to uphold Divine Law. "The exhortation consists of taking up the everyday pragmatism of popular morality of both Greek and Jew, no doubt familiar to his readers as such, and bringing it all to the touchstone and summation of love. First the negative guideline of petit bourgeoisie economics ('Never get into debt') is transposed into the much more positive obligation to active concern for one another (v. 8). Then the basic rules that make possible relationships of trust ('Don't take unfair advantage—no adultery, no killing, no stealing, no envious coveting') are gathered up into the ancient Mosaic command to 'love your neighbor as yourself' (v. 9). And the whole is summed up in a chiastic definition of love in negative terms as avoiding doing wrong to the neighbor and in positive terms as fulfilling the law (v. 10).

"The triple emphasis on love is matched by a triple emphasis on love of neighbor as the fulfillment and summation of the law: 'he who loves the other has fulfilled the law'. No commandment is not covered by the summary, 'Love your neighbor as yourself'. 'Love is the fulfillment of the law'. These are the first references to the law since the somewhat dismissive statements of 10:4-5; and indeed, as his readers would soon realize, these are the last references to the law in the letter as a whole. They therefore fulfill a crucial role: they would reassure that Paul's gospel was not antinomian—on the contrary, he counts fulfillment of the law as something important. Equally important, he reasserts the continuity with the revelation previously given to Israel, not least in the law—the fulfillment is a fulfillment of God's purpose in giving the law to Israel in the first place. For those who had been attracted to Judaism by its strong moral structure, this would be of crucial importance" (James D. G. Dunn, *Romans 9-16,* WBC vol. 38B [Dallas: Word, Inc., 1988], 781-82).

New Testament scholar, T. R. Schreiner draws attention to the tension and conflict in the New Testament's position on Divine Law. "One of the perplexities in reading the NT is that it seems to say contradictory things about the law. In fact, Raisanen makes this his central plank in his book on Paul's view of the law, contending that Paul's theology of the law is inconsistent and contradictory. Raisanen's solution is unsatisfactory, and yet the difficulty is apparent to all careful readers of the NT, since the various statements made about the law are difficult to reconcile. This comes to the forefront in the matter of the abrogation and fulfilment of the law. Some statements imply that the law is still in force and fulfilled in Christ, while others teach that the law has come to an end. The solution to this vexing problem is paradoxical, for NT writers affirm that both are true, *i.e.* the law is abrogated and yet it is also fulfilled" (T. R. Schreiner, "In the New Testament," *New Bible Dictionary,* eds. D. R. W. Wood, et. al. [Downers Grove, IL: InterVarsity Press, 1996], 676).

Nola Opperwall (International Bible Encyclopedia) reflects on Jesus' relationship to Divine Law. "A special question arises in connection with the fulfillment of the OT law. On the one hand the NT

has indications that the fulfilling of the law established its validity as enduring forever: Matt. 5:17, 19, 'I have come not to abolish . . . but to fulfil . . .'. V. 2, 'Whoever then relaxes one of the least of these commandments and teaches men so, shall be called least in the kingdom of heaven; but he who does them and teaches them shall be called great in the kingdom of heaven'; Rom. 8:4, 'in order that the just requirement of the law might be fulfilled in us'; 13:8, 'he who loves his neighbor has fulfilled the law'; Gal. 5:14, 'For the whole law is fulfilled in one word,' 'You shall love your neighbor as yourself'" (Nola J. Opperwall, "Fugitive," *ISBE*, vol. 2, Revised Edition, ed. Geoffrey W. Bromiley [Grand Rapids: Eerdmans, 1979-1988], 368-69).
8. Geza Vermes, *The Authentic Gospel of Jesus* (New York: Pinguin Books, 2003), 373.
9. See also, Charlesworth, "The Historical Jesus: How to Ask Questions and Remain Inquisitive," in *HSHJ* (vol. 1), 91-128.
10. Δοκιμάζειν, *SEC* 1381; Thayer's, 154; *LSJ*, 177; Matthew Henry, *Matthew Henry's Commentary on the Whole Bible, Complete and Unabridged* (Peabody, MA: Hendrickson, 1991), 2226; Christian historian Paula Fredriksen similarly observes the need "to have some sort of criteria to guide our reading" (Paula Fredriksen, *Jesus of Nazareth King of the Jews* [New York: Knopf, 19990], 23).
11. Charlesworth, "How to Ask Questions," in *HSHJ* (vol. 1), 91-128.
12. See also, Gen 22:1; Exod 15:25; 20:20; Deut 8:2, 16; 13:3; 33:38.
13. Gen 32:10; Ps 119:142; Mal 2:6; Rom 2:20.

CHAPTER 17: DOES HARMONY EXIST BETWEEN THE OLD AND NEW TESTAMENTS?

1. Rubenstein, *When Jesus Became God*, xv.
2. See also, 1 Kgs 2:4; Neh 9:13; Ps 19:9; 25:10; 30:9; 43:3; 51:6; 61:7; 69:13; 89:14; 119:142, 151; 146:6; Prov 3:3; 8:7; 14:22; 16:6; Isa 48:1; 59:4, 14-15.
3. There are two opposing views on John 1:17. The first sees the grace and truth established with Jesus parallel to the grace and truth given by YHWH through Moses. The Law remains in effect. The second view understands John to say that YHWH never bestowed grace and truth to ancient Israel through Moses. What I found interesting about both points of view is that they ended up in the same place. While the author of each commentary may uphold the authority of Divine Law when dealing with this particular verse, later on, each commentary's author writes that Divine Law has been fulfilled and replaced by a generic Jesus. The specifics of Divine Law, which Jesus upheld and that make people and nations strong, are replaced by broad categories of "love," which today have evolved into all sorts of deprived immoral behaviors, which violate Divine Law.
1st View: John 1:17 upholds Divine Law:
Canadian attorney and theologian Gerald Borchert (Carson Newman Univ.) sees John upholding Divine Law. "For Christians who have been brought up with a negative view of the law of Moses derived from a misreading of Paul and an unnecessary bifurcating of law and grace, the temptation is to read this verse as a negative slap at the law. But such is hardly the intention of the evangelist. In the Gospel of John, Moses is regarded as a positive servant of God (e.g., 5:45-47; 6:32; 7:19-23). The problem for Jesus in this Gospel was not with Moses and the law; the problem was with the disobedient Jews who *misused* Moses and the law (e.g., 6:31-32; 9:28-29). Moses and the law were together viewed as a gracious gift from God.

"For those, however, who would argue that the law is regarded as a negative factor in the New Testament, they must deal with Paul's strong contrary arguments. Paul was not set against the law (Rom 2:17-3:20) but against the disobedient Jews. He was equally emphatic in his denial (*mē genoito*, 'absolutely not!') of overthrowing the law (Rom 3:31; cf. also 7:7). Paul in Romans was not engaging in double-talk. He regarded the law positively (Rom 9:4). Similarly in this Johannine text the coming of the law through Moses must be understood as a period or stage of grace. Yet it was not the final stage because the full characteristics of God in a personal embodiment of grace (loving-kindness) and truth (genuine steadfastness and fidelity) could not be revealed except through 'Jesus Christ'" (Gerald L. Borchert, *John 1-11*, NAC vol. 25A [Nashville: Broadman & Holman, 1996], 123).
2nd View: John 1:17 opposes and supplants Divine Law:
English theologian Alfred Plummer understands John to supplant Divine Law with Jesus and his teachings. Plummer considers Divine Law to condemn mankind while Jesus' ideas of grace and truth are superior to the revelation at Mt. Sinai. I wondered why Plummer ignored Ezekiel 18 (and ch 33) where repentance and obedience are all that is required for Divine forgiveness (cf. Is 50:2; 59:1-4). To me,

Plummer seemed to cherry-pick his theology. This is what Plummer believes on John 1:17: "The mention of χάρις reminds the Evangelist that this was the characteristic of the new dispensation and marked its superiority to the old: the Law condemned transgressors, χάρις forgives them" (Alfred Plummer, *The Gospel according to S. John*, Cambridge Greek Testament for Schools and Colleges [Cambridge: Cambridge University Press, 1896], 74). As we have seen, Divine Law provides many avenues for repentance and restoration that make individuals, families, and societies whole while preserving the delicate balance between accountability and restoration.

Theodore of Mopsuestia (Bishop of Antioch *c.* 395 CE) tried to reconcile the inherent contradiction in this verse. He understood the "grace" given by the law to differ from the "grace" given by Jesus. For him, true grace had never existed before Jesus since John contrasts Jesus against the Law. The contrast implies that the latter (Jesus) supplants the former (Divine Law). These are Theodore's thoughts: "And he appropriately added, *grace for grace*, indicating the law, as well, with the name 'grace.' **He says, this grace is given instead of that grace [of the law]**. In order that it might not be thought that identical words stood for identical things, he added, *The law indeed was given through Moses; grace and truth came about through Christ.* At one time, he says, the law was given only for our instruction, and certainly was also conferred as grace even though those who received it were unworthy of it. **But now true grace has been given**. Therefore he did not say that through Jesus Christ it was given, but it came about. . . . And so from all this it appears that the Evangelist wanted to describe the dignity of the Messiah in comparison with the law" (Theodore of Mopsuestia in *Commentary on the Gospel of John*, ACT, trans. Marco Conti, eds. Joel C. Elowsky, Thomas C. Oden, and Gerald L. Bray [Downers Grove, IL: IVP Academic, 2010], 18. Bold emphasis is added).

Evangelist Donald Carson tries to present a balanced view. In the end, he also reduces the instructions for morality, immigration policy, justice, health, and government accountability for a just society to "prophecy." Like others before him, Carson views Divine Law solely as prophecy, which Jesus fulfills so Divine Law is no longer needed for the believer's daily life. Carson writes: "*For the law was given through Moses; grace and truth came through Jesus Christ.* On the face of it, then, it appears that the grace and truth that came through Jesus Christ is what replaces the law. . . . others argue that for John the law in some sense continues in force: the Scripture cannot be broken (10:34), and therefore it is unreasonable to think that John in 1:16–17 can view the grace of the gospel, the grace that has come in Jesus Christ, as *replacing* law. But again, close attention to the way the Fourth Gospel treats the Old Testament alleviates the difficulty. In the passages already mentioned, and in a large number of others, the Old Testament Scriptures are understood to point forward to Jesus, to anticipate him, and thus to prophesy of him. In that sense he fulfills them. If even the covenant of law is 'prophetic' in this sense (*cf.* Matt 11:13), **then when that to which it points has arrived, it is in some sense displaced**" (Donald A. Carson, *The Gospel according to John*, PNTC [Grand Rapids, MI: Eerdmans, 1991], 132, 133. Bold emphasis is added).

Cyril of Alexandria (*c.* 415 CE) understood Divine Law to be a law of fear and bondage, which, of course, opposed what YHWH states about His own Law (see pp. 42–43). Cyril reduces the Israelite constitution, which established justice for theft and murder, laws regulating human sexual relations, and constraints on government into "types" and "shadows." His treatment of Divine Law renders it impotent and meaningless. He sees only Jesus as offering circumcision of the heart and spirit yet ignores both Divine Law and the prophets' instruction for humanity to circumcise her own heart—an act God believed humanity was capable of (Deut 10:16; Jer 4:4; Ps 51:10; Ezek 18:31). Cyril's approach to John troubled me because it relegated clear ideas and concepts of right and wrong given directly by YHWH for our benefit into a nebulous idea of a new "grace." This troubled my heart since the OT also understood people having YHWH's holy spirit (1 Chr 28:12; Ps 51:11; Isa 63:10–11). In many ways, I saw this attitude leading to the current moral decline we are living today.

This is what Cyril writes: "Superiority of Grace to Law: And the law too used to give grace to people, calling them to the knowledge of God and drawing away from the worship of idols those who had been led astray. It also pointed out evil and taught good, if not perfectly, yet in the manner of a teacher and usefully. But the truth and grace that are through the Only Begotten do not introduce to us the good that is in types or to limited things that are only profitable as in shadow. Rather, in glorious and most pure ordinances, it leads us by the hand to an ever more perfect knowledge of the faith. **And the law used to give the 'spirit of bondage to fear,'** but Christ gives the spirit of adoption to liberty. The **law likewise brings in the circumcision in the flesh, which is nothing (for 'circumcision is nothing')**. But our Lord Jesus Christ is the giver of circumcision 'in the spirit and heart.' **The law baptizes the defiled with mere water; the Savior baptizes 'with the Holy Spirit and with fire'**. . . . The blessed Paul in few words solved the question, saying of the law and of the Savior's grace, 'For if there was splendor in the dispensation of condemnation, the dispensation of righteousness must far exceed it in splendor." For he says that the commandment by Moses is 'the ministration of condemnation,' but the grace through the Savior he calls 'the ministration of righteousness,' **which he says surpasses in glory**" (Cyril of Alexandria in *John 1–10*, ACCS, ed. Joel C. Elowsky [Downers Grove, IL: InterVarsity Press, 2006], 52. Bold emphasis is added).

St. Augustine also understood a contrast in John 1:17, writing: "The Law Threatened, the Gospel Heals . . . This grace was not in the Old Testament, because the law threatened but did not bring aid; commanded but did not heal; made known but did not take away our feebleness. Instead it prepared the way for that physician who was to come with grace and truth. He is the kind of physician who, when about to come to anyone to cure him, might first send his servant so that he might find the sick person bound. He was not healthy; he did not wish to be made healthy and just in case he should be made healthy, he boasted that he was so. The law was sent; it bound him" (Augustine of Hippo in *John 1–10*, ACCS, ed. Joel C. Elowsky [Downers Grove, IL: InterVarsity Press, 2006], 53).

4. *SEC* 2580; *BDB*, 336, *TWOT* (vol. 1), 303; *CHALOT*, 110; *HALOT*, 3009, s.v. "חן".
5. *SEC* 5485; χάρις; *LSJ*, 778.
6. On Acts 3:19 the Fausset and Jamieson commentary remarks: "**Repent ye therefore, and be converted** [ἐπιστρέψατε]—or, 'turn ye,' **that your sins may be blotted out, when the times of refreshing shall come from the presence of the Lord** [ὅπως ἂν ἔλθωσιν καιροὶ ἀναψύξεως]. It should be 'in order that seasons of refreshing may come from the presence of the Lord;' as nearly every good interpreter admits, and as our translators themselves render this very phrase in Luke 2:35. The rendering 'when' has been borrowed from the Vulgate ('ut cum') and *Beza* ('postquam'); but *Beza's* examples and those of *Scholefield* (who alone now defends it) are not in point; and that rendering is certainly inaccurate. The 'seasons of refreshing' here meant are, as we think, that definite and, to the Jewish mind, familiar period of lengthened repose, prosperity, and joy, which all the prophets hold forth to the distracted Church and a miserable world, as eventually to come, and which is here, as it is in all the prophets, made to turn upon the national conversion of Israel" (Brown, Fausset, and Jamieson, *Acts–Revelation*, 20).

Scholar and editor Joseph Exell observes: "Repent signifies, in its literal meaning, to change one's mind. It has been translated 'after–wit,' or 'after–wisdom'; it is the man's finding out that he is wrong, and rectifying his judgment. But although that be the meaning of the root, the word has come in Scriptural use to mean a discovery of the evil of sin, a mourning that we have committed it, a resolution to forsake it, the love of what once we hated, and the hate of what once we loved" (Joseph S. Exell, *The Biblical Illustrator: Acts* vol. 1 [Grand Rapids, MI: Baker House, 1967], 314).

Greek scholar Scott Kellum (Baptist Theological Sem.) notes: "However, there are striking similarities with the appeal in Acts 2:38. That appeal is undeniably individual (see, e.g., ἕκαστος ὑμῶν, 'each of you'). Furthermore, the first purpose clause, the prepositional phrase εἰς τὸ ἐξαλειφθῆναι (aor. pass. inf. of ἐξαλείφω, 'be erased'), indicates the intent is to have their sins 'wiped out.' It is unlikely that corporate sin alone or the one sin of rejecting the Messiah is meant. Ultimately personal and genuine corporate conversion are intimately connected" (L. Scott Kellum, *Acts: Exegetical Guide to the Greek New Testament*, eds. Andreas J. Köstenberger and Robert W. Yarbrough [Nashville: B & H Academic, 2020], 54).

7. W. Gunther Plaut, *The Torah: A Modern Commentary*, ed. Gunther Plaut (New York: Union of American Hebrew Congregations, 1981), 1343, 1358.
8. Two views exist on John 1:18. The first holds that no one has ever seen God. The second understands anything that Moses or anyone else had seen of YHWH to simply be a type of what is written in the text. It dismisses any literal interpretation.

Canadian scholar Gerald Bochert remarks on the meaning of the Greek in John 1:18. "The Prologue is drawn to a conclusion in this verse with a powerful reminder that no one has ever really seen God. The word order in Greek is extremely emphatic. It begins with 'God,' ends with what is virtually an expression 'not ever,' and gives the force of an utterly indisputable principle" (Gerald L. Borchert, *John 1–11*, NAC, 124).

Murray Harris also remarks how the Greek text understands God the Father is an invisible Deity. He observes that it "emphasizes the 'pastness' of the non-visibility (Burton § 88) and excludes any exceptions: 'no one ever.' God as he is in himself, God in his being (anar. θεός) has never been seen by either the physical or the spiritual eye of humans (cf. 5:37; 6:46; Exod 33:20); he is invisible (see Harris, *Jesus*, 93–94)." (Murray J. Harris, *John, Exegetical Guide to the Greek New Testament* [Nashville: B & H Academic, 2015], 38).

St. Augustine also explains away any literal interpretation. For him, Moses could not possibly see YHWH as the Old Testament states, but He saw a "type" of what the text states. It seemed to me that theologians explained away any contradiction by relegating it to a "type." Augustine also understood

God the Father and Jesus the son to be two separate entities. This is what Augustine believed: "What did Moses see? Moses saw a cloud, an angel, a fire. All that is of the creature bore the type of its Lord, but they did not manifest the presence of the Lord himself. For you have it plainly stated in the law, 'And Moses spoke with the Lord face to face, as a friend with his friend.' . . . An angel then spoke with Moses, my brothers, bearing the type of the Lord; and all those things that were done by the angel promised that future grace and truth. Those who examine the law know this well. . . . If, then, the Son was visible because of his flesh, we grant this, and it is the catholic faith. But if before he took flesh, that is, if before he became incarnate, they say they saw the Son, they are greatly deluded and making a horrible mistake. For those visible and bodily appearances took place through the creature, in which a type might be exhibited. But there is no way that the substance itself was shown and made known. Listen, beloved, to this easy proof. The wisdom of God cannot be beheld by the eyes. Brothers, if Christ is the wisdom of God and the power of God, if Christ is the Word of God, and if the word of man [humankind] is not seen with the eyes, can the Word of God be seen in this way?" (St. Augustine in *John 1–10*, ACCS, 54).

9. Henry, *Matthew Henry's Commentary*, 1919, 1947.
10. Henry, *Matthew Henry's Commentary*, 1919, 1947.
11. On Elijah see Mignon R. Jacobs, *Books of Haggai and Malachi*, NICOT, ed. Robert Hubbard, Jr. (Grand Rapids, MI: Eerdmans, 2017), 328.

    Several reformers who started the Protestant Reformation remarked on Elijah and Enoch's ascents into heaven. Reformer Johannes Bugenhagen remarks: "Here Elijah was visibly taken up out of this world in the same way, I believe, that Enoch was visibly taken up in Genesis. But how they were taken up to heaven or paradise God sees and knows best and we do not need to know" (Johannes Bugenhagen in *1-2 Samuel, 1-2 Kings, 1-2 Chronicles: Old Testament*, Reformation Commentary on Scripture, vol. V, eds. Derek Cooper, Martin J. Lohrmann, et al. [Downers Grove, IL: IVP Academic, 2016], 400).

    Lutheran reformer, Philip Melanchthon observes: "While still living, Enoch and Elijah were taken from this life to God, because God wanted to give visible evidence of the eternal life. For if they were nothing after this life, then they would not be with God; to be with God means to dwell in a new, divine, eternal life" (Philip Melanchthon, *1-2 Samuel, 1-2 Kings, 1-2 Chronicles: Old Testament*, Reformation Commentary on Scripture, vol. V., eds. Derek Cooper, Martin J. Lohrmann, et al. [Downers Grove, IL: IVP Academic, 2016], 401).

    Protestant Reformer Johannes Piscator also writes on Elijah's ascent: "Elisha was encouraged by Elijah to desire from God this blessing of being allowed to see Elijah's assumption to heaven. And when the opportunity was given to him of seeing it, he enjoyed it as long as he could. It appears, from what we can gather, that the assumption of Elijah into heaven was a type of the ascension of Christ into heaven" (Johannes Piscator in *1-2 Samuel, 1-2 Kings, 1-2 Chronicles: Old Testament*, Reformation Commentary on Scripture, vol. V., eds. Derek Cooper, Martin J. Lohrmann, et al. [Downers Grove, IL: IVP Academic, 2016], 401).

    Modern theologian of Old Testament studies Volkmar Fritz (Univ. of Giessen) writes of Elijah being translated into heaven: "Elijah's end is not death and burial but translation to heaven. The chariot of fire has to be interpreted as a divine vehicle, since fire usually signifies the manifestation of divine presence (see Exod 3:2; 13:21; 19:18)." (Volkmar Fritz, *1 & 2 Kings*, CC [Minneapolis, MN: Fortress Press, 2003], 235).
12. Acts 1:9–11; Luke 24:50–51, John 20:17; and Eph 4:8–10. See also Vermes, *Authentic Gospel*, 264.

    Brown, Fausset, and Jamieson: "How paradoxical this sounds: 'No one has gone up but He that came down, even He who is at once both up and down.' Doubtless this was intended to startle and constrain his auditor to think that there must be mysterious elements in His Person" (Brown, Fausset, and Jamieson, *Matthew–John*, 363).

    Gerald Borchert: "For John, with his post resurrection perspective, the Christian gospel was the only way to salvation because Jesus alone descended and 'has ascended' *(anabebēken)* to heaven. He knew the whole incarnational story when he started writing" (Borchert, *John 1–11*, NAC, 181).

    Newman and Nida: "Some scholars maintain that the verb *has gone up* refers to *the Son of Man*, and so implies that he had already ascended to heaven at the time these words were written. That is, they assume that this verse contains John's comments about *the Son of Man* and that it reflects the post-resurrection theology of John, rather than the words of Jesus. It is thus one way of explaining the use of the perfect tense (*has gone up*). However, the statement *no one has ever gone up to heaven* is possibly intended merely to deny that up to that time anyone had gone up to heaven to learn *about the things of heaven*" (Barclay M. Newman and Eugene Albert Nida, *A Handbook on the Gospel of John*, USBH [New York: United Bible Societies, 1993], 84).

13. A few discrepancies in chronology are found in these texts: 2 Chr 16:1; 2 Kgs 1:17; 2 Kgs 15:1. See also *YE1*, 334.
14. New Testament scholar Andreas J. Köstenberger (Midwestern Baptist Theological Sem.) links the idea of "God–breathed" to inspiration, not infallibility. He summarizes that "Scripture, in fact, 'all' Scripture (more likely than 'every')—in the original context, the OT (but see 2 Pet 3:16; 1 Tim 5:18)—is 'inspired by God' (lit., 'God breathed,' θεόπνευστος). The term, an apparent Pauline coinage, is found in subsequent Greek literature (Ps.-Phoc. 129; Sib. Or. 5:308; 5:407 [ca. AD 90–130]), but the concept of the creative, life–giving breath of God and the image of the word of God as breathed by God have deep OT roots (Genesis 1–2; Ps 33:6; Isa 42:5), and the notion of inspiration is not foreign to the OT (Num 24:2; Hos 9:7). The present passage (1 Tim 5:18) is one of the major biblical texts on the divine inspiration of Scripture, focusing on Scripture's origin in God himself" (Andreas J. Köstenberger, *1–2 Timothy & Titus*, Evangelical Biblical Theology Commentary, eds. T. Desmond Alexander, Thomas R. Schreiner, and Andreas J. Köstenberger [Bellingham, WA: Lexham Press, 2021], 267–68).

    Robert Wall similarly understands this text in the context of the Old Testament. "Probably a better context for understanding Paul's meaning of *theopneustos* is Gen. 2:7, where 'God breathed' life into Adam. The impression Paul creates by his allusion to the biblical story of man's creation, then, concerns less the 'production' of the biblical text—since nowhere does Paul mention the inspiration of Scripture's authors—but rather to its ongoing 'performance' when the community's authorized Scriptures are used profitably within the congregation for teaching, reproof, correction, training in righteousness (3:16b). For this reason, when this text is picked up and used by the church's Fathers (cited more than one hundred times through the first four centuries alone!), it is the performance of Scripture—its utility for Christian nurture—more than its production that is mentioned. In this sense, then, God 'breathes newness of life' into those who actually use Scripture to learn God." [Robert W. Wall, "2 Timothy," in *The Bible Knowledge Background Commentary: Acts–Philemon*, 1st Edition, eds. Craig A. Evans and Craig A. Bubeck, [Colorado Springs, CO: David C. Cook, 2004], 673).

    The BFJ Commentary understands this text in a similar light. "Most of the New Testament books were written when Paul wrote this his latest epistle: so he includes in 'All Scripture [every portion of the *hiera grammata*, 'the Holy Scriptures'] is God–inspired,' not only the *Old Testament*, in which alone Timothy was taught when a child (*v.* 15), but the New Testament books, according as they were recognized in churches, having men gifted with 'discerning of spirits,' and so able to distinguish really inspired utterances, persons, and writings (1 Cor. 12:10; 14:37) from spurious. 'All Scripture is God–inspired, *and therefore* useful:' because *we* see no utility in any portion, it does not follow it is not God–inspired. It is *useful* because *God–inspired*; not *God–inspired* because useful. One reason for the Greek article not being before 'Scripture,' may be that, if it had, it *might* have seemed to limit 'Scripture' to the *hiera grammata*, 'Holy Scriptures' (*v.* 15) *of the Old Testament*, whereas the assertion is general: '*all* Scripture' [cf. *pasa prophēteia graphēs*, 2 Pet. 1:20]. Plenary inspiration of every part of the Scriptures, as a living organic whole, is here set forth. The translation, 'all Scripture that is God–inspired is also useful,' would imply that there is some *Scripture* which is not God–inspired. But the exclusive New Testament sense of 'Scripture' forbids this: and who would need to be told that 'all divine Scripture is profitable?' Heb. 4:13 would then have to be rendered, 'All naked things are *also* open to the eyes of Him,' etc.: so also 1 Tim. 4:4 (*Tregelles* 'On Daniel')." (Brown, Fausset, and Jamieson, *Acts–Revelation*, 511).

15. Kenneth Gangel (Dallas Theological Sem.) sees Jesus' words as standing alone. No evidence was needed outside Jesus' claim. "This mention of the Father at the beginning of the testimony list indicates that Jesus believed all his words and actions were already approved and did *not* need any further word" (Kenneth O. Gangel, *John*, HNTC vol. 4 [Nashville: Broadman & Holman, 2000], 104).

    Gerald Borchert understands John 5:31 in relation to Divine Law. "The issue had been stated in 5:30. The defense here began with a restatement of the issue in preparation for the calling of witnesses. There is first an admission of a presupposition that is based on the accepted legal code of the Torah, the foundation book of the Jews who were Jesus' opponents. In cases where there is a need for verifiable testimony, it is necessary that there be two or three witnesses to provide corroboration of the matter (cf. Deut 19:15). That principle was expected to be firmly observed, particularly in capital cases (Num 35:30; Deut 17:6; cf. Heb 10:28), and that principle was accepted as a basic thesis by Jesus (Matt 18:16; John 8:17) and by the early Christians like Paul (2 Cor 13:1). It was assumed that corroboration would assure the courts and others that the ninth word of the Decalogue (Exod 20:16) had been safeguarded because bearing false witness was regarded as an act of personal treason (Prov 25:18)." (Borchert, *John 1–11*, NAC, 243–44).

    Newman and Nida address the various ways in which this verse is translated. "*What I say is not to be accepted as real proof* is literally 'My testimony is not true.' *New English Bible* translates this clause 'that testimony does not hold good'; *Phillips* 'what I say about myself has no value.' *New American Bible* 'you cannot verify my testimony.' *Jerusalem Bible* has 'my testimony would not be valid.' *Moffatt* translates 'If I testify to myself, then my evidence is not valid.' As these translations all indicate, the point is not that Jesus is saying that his testimony concerning himself is untrue but rather that it could not be accepted as legal evidence in a court of law. The same law mentioned here is appealed to in 8:17. According to Jewish law, a man could not be convicted of a crime on the testimony of one witness (Deut 19:15)."

Newman and Nida also argue against a literal translation of this verse since it presents an inherent contradiction. "As noted, it is often important to avoid a literal translation of the second part of verse 31, since it would imply that Jesus' statements were untrue" (Newman and Nida, *Handbook on the Gospel of John*, UBSH, 163–64).

16. The reason Jack had trouble with John 8:17 is that according to Divine Law, at least two witnesses are needed. When only one witness testifies, it can neither convict nor exonerate. The case is dismissed until further evidence is brought to light. John 8:17 seems to imply that Jesus' dual role as both Father and son satisfies the legal requirements for two witnesses. Modernly, this is equivalent to a president of a corporation providing testimony for himself as an individual and having it count a second time as the president of the company, which would not be accepted in a court of law. When I searched for solutions in commentaries, I did not find them very reassuring.

Gerald Borchert sees Jesus opposing the Jews' reliance on Divine Law. Borchert states: "Having thus dealt with the question of judgment, Jesus turned to respond to their charge of his self-witness. In the judgment of Jesus the Pharisees had **placed their ultimate trust in their use of Scripture or the law**, an approach Jesus did not accept. But given their approach—'your law' (8:17)—he dealt with their charge against him on the basis of the legal prescription in Deut 17:6 (the necessity of two witnesses). Employing the *egō eimi* formula ('I am,' which can be detected in the New International Verson rendering), Jesus argued that there were two strong witnesses to his nature: the witness of the unique "I am" and that of the Father on whose mission he had been sent (John 8:18). Some scholars, such as Brown, have argued that Jesus did not in fact meet the criteria of two witnesses" (Borchert, *John 1–11*, NAC, 297. Bold emphasis is added).

Kenneth Gangel understands Jesus to exert that his self-witness of himself is alone sufficient. Gengal concludes: "Throughout this Gospel the author emphasized words of Jesus that referred to his own deity. There was no question in John's theology that Jesus is God. This constant reference to the Father both in relationship and authentication forms a uniquely Johannine trait" (Gangel, *John*, HNTC, 162).

Newman and Nida remark: "The pronoun *your* (*New English Bible* 'your own') is emphatic. **Jesus is pictured as at once hostile to their law and superior to it**. In the Jewish context the *two witnesses* would normally be taken to be two witnesses other than the person actually concerned. However, in the following verse Jesus makes himself one of the witnesses on his own behalf. The Scripture passages referred to are Deuteronomy 17:6 and 19:15. *When two witnesses agree, what they say is true* is literally 'the testimony of two men is true'; *German Common Language* renders 'If two witnesses agree in their testimony, the truth results.' TEV restructuring transforms the noun-orientated structure 'the testimony of two witnesses' to a verb phrase *when two witnesses agree*, which then requires the inclusion of *what they say*" (Newman and Nida, *Handbook on the Gospel of John*, UBSH, 267–68).

CHAPTER 18: PAUL ON THE LAW: PART I

1. The Old Testament supports that humanity is quite capable of observing YHWH's Law (Deut 30:11–14; 32:46–47; Ps 81:13–16; 119:142, 174. See *YE1*, 304–06).
2. British Methodist scholar C. K. Barrett indirectly accuses YHWH of causing people to sin because He gave a moral/social law. Berrett holds that Divine Law "produced" and "increased" transgression. I had to ask, if no law forbids murder, would murder be okay? If no law forbids theft, is theft alright? If YHWH never established Divine Law would He forbear to punish if humanity was constantly murdering each other? This is Barrett's report: **"For the law produces not promise but wrath; and where there is no law, neither is there transgression**. Paul seems here to be anticipating material which he brings out more fully in 5:12 ff.; 7:7–13. The purpose of the law was in part to show how exceedingly sinful sin was **by actually producing and increasing transgression**" (Barrett, *Epistle to the Romans*, 89–90. The final emphasis with bolding and underlining is added).

Ambrosiaster (*c.* 370 CE): *"For the law brings wrath, but where there is no law there is no transgression.* In order to show that no man can be justified before God by the law, nor can the promise be given through the law, Paul says that *the law brings wrath.* It was given in order to make transgressors guilty. But faith is the gift of God's mercy, so that those who have been made guilty by the law may obtain forgiveness. . . . because it is not possible to be saved by the law, but we are saved by God's grace through faith. Therefore the law is not itself wrath, but it brings wrath, in other words, punishment, to the sinner, for wrath is born from sin. **For this reason Paul wants the law to be abandoned** so that the sinner will take refuge in faith, which forgives sins, that he may be saved.

"Paul says that *where there is no law there is no transgression,* because **once the guilty have been removed from the power of the law and given forgiveness, there is no transgression**. For those who were sinners because they had transgressed the law are now justified. For the law of works has ceased, that is, the observance of sabbaths, new moons, circumcision, distinction of foods, and the expiation by a dead animal or the blood of a weasel" (Ambrosiaster, *Commentaries on Romans and 1–2 Corinthians,* ACT, 34). Jodell's Response: I questioned Abrosiater's thesis. Would sinners who abandon the Law by embezzling funds and committing fraud find refuge in faith before YHWH? Jesus' brother James who likely understood Jesus much better than Paul who never met Jesus, indicates that faith alone can save no one: "What does it profit, my brethren, though a man say he has faith, and have not works? can faith save him? . . . Faith without works is dead" (James 2:14, 26).

Joseph Fitzmyer (Catholic priest and scholar) concludes that if YHWH had never given His Divine Law so we did not know that murder, adultery, or homosexuality were wrong that God would (or could) never judge humanity. This begs the question of how YHWH could destroy the people who lived before the flood since there is no indication that they had YHWH's Divine Law. Fitzmeyer's addresses Paul's statement *"but where there is no law, there is no transgression."* Fitzmyer remarks: "A 'transgression' implies a word or deed that violates a law that has been set up. So if there is no law, there can be no violation of it (cf. 5:13). This is a cardinal tenet in Paul's view of the law . . . Without the law, evil may be vaguely apprehended, but it is not regarded as *parabasis,* 'transgression' (see 3:20; 5:13). Because transgression, which calls down divine wrath, arises . . ." (Joseph A. Fitzmyer, *Romans: A New Translation with Introduction and Commentary,* AYBC vol. 33 [New Haven, CT: Yale Univ. Press, 2008], 385).

Jodell's Response: To me, it seemed that without a Divine Law, evil could reign undefined and unabated. People would be oppressed by theft, murder, kidnapping, rape, bribery, and so much more because no law existed. If we never had knowledge of Divine Law, would it then allow these acts to be "transgressionless"? I also saw parallels to modern society that denies any existence of Divine Law. Government violates the rights of man, exploits positions of power, while criminals who commit murder, theft, and rape often are caught and released only to commit those crimes again. The U. S. Constitution does not define rape or theft as crimes, but does that make those actions okay for society? Or, do these actions violate natural law?

Robert Mounce draws a similar conclusion to Fitzmyer. "Where there is no law, there can be no breaking of law. Sin would still exist, but it could not be designated as the specific transgression of a law (cf. Rom 5:13; 7:7–11)." (Mounce, *Romans,* NAC, 127).

Joseph Fitzmyer also addresses Paul's statement on wrath. He claims that God's wrath is manifested by our observing the Law. This implies that YHWH punishes people for obeying His instructions. "In a legal context, Paul implicitly concludes that the world needs a dispensation independent of law. Wrath is manifested not only against unrighteousness, but also against righteousness sought by observing the law, against law–righteousness (Fitzmyer, *Romans,* AYBC, 385).

Jodell's Response: After reading through these and many other commentaries on Paul's treatment of the Law, I had to wonder if any scholar had the faintest idea of a universal standard of truth. It seemed that to them God was arbitrary and capricious. Paul's God seemed fickle. Paul's God could go back on His word. Paul's God could renege on any standard of universal righteousness or truth. Men have been searching outside of Divine Law for over 2,500 years without finding the healing balm that turns the hearts of the fathers towards their children or children towards their parents. Our world remains under Malachi's curse.

Leon Morris also understands Paul to say that our obedience can never merit YHWH's acceptance. It will always be imperfect. He also considers Divine Law as "thrilling and frustrating the evil passions of the heart." He means that the Law causes us to be thrilled with evil–doing. I don't know about you, but reading in Divine Law that bribes are prohibited or that adultery is wrong, has never "excited" me in the least. Divine Law provokes me to detest those actions. This is Morris' understanding: "Paul advances his argument by pointing out that the promise means **that no way of law can be the way to God**" (Jodell's note: contrast Morris with Deut 4:7–8). Morris: "If the way of law is correct, there is no place for promise (Paul has a similar argument in Rom 11:6, that grace and works are mutually exclusive; cf. Gal. 3:18). . . .

(v. 15) Now we come to the true function of law. It *brings wrath*. Hodge sees this as working out in two ways: (a) our imperfect obedience brings the law's curse on us, and (b) law 'excites and exasperates the evil passions of the heart'.... Paul is emphasizing that faith is the only way. Those who come by the way of law are not saved" (Morris, *Epistle to the Romans*, PNTC, 206-08). This view, contradicts Jesus' brother who personally new Jesus and understood his teachings: "O vain man, faith without works is dead" (James 2:20).

3. Henry, *Matthew Henry's Commentary*, 2202-23; *JFB*, 1147.

Jodell's comment: I became frustrated with this study. Previously, I had seen scholars support that Jesus fulfilled the "Law and the Prophets" (see endnotes 2-7 in Ch. 7. "Does the New Testament Uphold the Law"?). In Luke 24:44, Jesus appealed to the "Law of Moses, Prophets, and Psalms" as prophecies he fulfilled. Wouldn't these prophecies naturally also be promises? The Book of Genesis is included in the Hebrew division of Scripture as part of the Law of Moses. The promises YHWH gave to Abraham (which presumably include the promise of Jesus) were also part of the Law: the serpent bruising the woman's heel (Gen 3:15); promises to Abraham; sacrifices as prophecy foreshadowing Jesus' death. These prophecies are part of the Law. The ONLY justification for Jesus (as Jesus himself testifies) is that his mission to save humanity had been foretold in the Law and the prophets. If Jesus does not fulfill the promise of the Law, then he cannot be a savior. In other words, you cannot get rid of Divine Law as a means for defining sin and the blessings that YHWH promises for obedience, then turn around and use that same Law (which you just dismissed) as justification for Jesus' mission on earth.

Paul contradicts all that Jesus taught. Jesus saw himself as the fulfillment of the Law's promises. But Paul states that no promise came through the Law. Yet it is only through the legal fulfillment of the Law that Jesus' mission can succeed. If Jesus did not come through the promise of the Law, then his mission was based upon deception.

One can have faith and obey a rule of Law. Faithfulness to Divine Law does not nullify faith but strengthens it. This is why Jesus stresses the importance of obedience. Divine Law is not only full of promises (Gen 9:12-17; 12:1-3; 15:14, 16; 17:6-8, 16, 19, 21; 22:17-18; 26:3-4; Exod 15:26; Lev 26:40-42, 44-45; Deut 4:29-31; 28:1-14; 30:1-8); it also contains reasonable consequences and policies for theft, perjury, divorce, government accountability, and immigration—to name a few (see *YE1*, pp. 217-22, 241-51). I questioned how anyone could have a reasonable faith without truth. I had already learned that Divine Law establishes truth (see pp. 35-36), so Paul's statements seemed to violate Isaiah 8:20.

I also learned that most scholars see Paul doing away with Divine Law. I had to wonder if they were aware that the beliefs they were supporting contradicted Jesus' words. Both Jesus and Proverbs supported Divine Law as a way of life "wherein there is no death." Israel had access to this path but had rejected it since the days of Moses until Jesus' ministry. I am only quoting a few scholars (below) since they all pretty much present the same point of view: no promise comes through Divine Law.

Ambrosiaster (*c.* 370 CE) considered anyone who wanted to press a legal claim of inheritance under the law to be wicked. For him, all of the contractual covenants that YHWH made with Abraham, which had specific stipulations for inheritance are meaningless: God can renege and resend His word. Amrosiaster writes: "It is clear that if one's inheritance is from the law, the promise which was made to Abraham by faith is nullified, **since the promise was not made through the law**, but the inheritance comes through the righteousness of faith. The apostle shows that **there is something wicked in hoping for an inheritance under the law**" (Ambrosiaster in *Commentaries on Romans and 1-2 Corinthians*, ACT, 34). Jodell's Response: If "the promise was not made through the law" then Paul's argument about YHWH's promises to Abraham's "seed" (Gal 3:16) would also be invalid since it is only in the Law that the inheritance of YHWH's promises to Abraham's seed are defined (Gen 12:7; 13:15-16; 15:5. 13. 18; 16:10; 17:7-10, 12; 21:12-13, 17-18; 24:7, 60; 26:3-4. See also Ch. 3 in *YE1*).

Handley Moule forgets that blessings and promises are conditional for both YHWH and Jesus. Covenants are legal documents that for YHWH are eternally binding. Moule remarks: "If the Law becomes the condition of heirship, *ipso facto* the faith and the promise are void; they *have been cancelled* **by the mere fact of a *legal* condition**" (Handley Moule, *The Epistle of Paul the Apostle to the Romans, with Introduction and Notes*, The Cambridge Bible for Schools and Colleges [Cambridge: Cambridge Univ. Press, 1891], 94. Bolding is added).

Leon Morris attempts to nullify YHWH's promises: "Paul is insisting that the true seed of Abraham are those who come by faith, **not the physical descendants of the patriarch**" (Morris, *Epistle to the Romans*, PNTC, 207. Bold is added).

C. K. Barrett: "It is clear that if the promise had been based upon law **only those** who had the advantage of possessing the law could hope to inherit the promise" (Barrett, *Epistle to the Romans*, 90).

Robert Mounce: "This promise was not given to Abraham in the context of obedience to law. It had its roots in faith. It rested on the 'faith–righteousness' (Montgomery) of the patriarch. Any idea that the inheritance depended on keeping the law would have consequences. For one thing, it would invalidate the principle of faith (v. 14). What role would there be for faith if the promise were contingent on obedience to law?" (Mounce, *Romans*, NAC, 126–27).

Jodell's response to Mounce: Mounce's ideals seemed to contradict reality. A person can both have faith and obedience—a child can both trust his parent's words and obey their instructions. They are not mutually exclusive. The child's obedience to his or her parents demonstrates the child's faith and love. All of YHWH's blessings were dependent upon people walking in His way of life since it was that lifestyle that produced YHWH's blessings. Faith is trusting that YHWH will uphold His own word and deliver on His written promises, which are recorded in His Divine Law (see Leviticus 26 and Deuteronomy 28). Divine Law also allowed for people from other nations to join YHWH's people and to access His blessings (Exod 12:48–49; Lev 19:34; 24:19; Num 9:14; 15:14–16. 29).

4. *YE1*, 105. See also, Joseph H. Hertz, *Torah & Haftorahs Pentateuch & Halftorahs* (London: Soncino, 1997), 95.
5. *YE1*, 105; Exod 15:26; Lev 18:5, 26:3, 15, 46; Deut 4:40; 5:31; 6:1–2, 17; 7:11; 8:11; 10:13; 11:13; 26:17; 27:10; 28:15, 45; 30:10–16; Neh 9:13; Ezek 44:24.
6. *YE1*, 92–95.
7. Plaut, *The Torah,* 109.
8. For a good treatment on this topic, see "The Law of Moses: All or Nothing? (James 2:10)," 119 Ministries (October 28, 2022), http://tinyurl.com/yc2pdvba.
9. See *YE1*, 181–216.
10. Lev 19:15; Deut 1:16–17; 16:18–20; Prov 24:23. See also: *YE1*, 67, 217–306; Lilly Kaufman, "Judge Justly, Four Ways," JTSA.edu (July 28, 2017), http://www.jtsa.edu/judge-justly-four-ways; Sulzberger, *Am Ha-Aretz–The Ancient Hebrew Parliament*, 6–48; Soloveichik, *Proclaim Liberty Throughout the Land*, 7–16; Nelson, *Hebrew Republic*, 3–4, 16–22; Berman, *Created Equal*, 51–108; Konvitz, *Torah and Constitution*; Elazar, *Covenant and Polity* (vol. 1); Elazar, "Government in Biblical Israel," 105–23; Elazar, "Deuteronomy as Israel's Constitution," http://www.jcpa.org/dje/articles2/deut-const.htm.
11. See Dennis Prager's video teachings on these topics, especially the 11-part series on the 10 Commandments: Dennis Prager, "The Ten Commandments, What You Should Know," PragerU on YouTube (December 1, 2014), https://www.youtube.com/watch?v=TK57RiMqTdk&t=2s.
12. The authors of the New Testament often quote or amend teaching from the earliest Jewish Talmudic book, *Pirkei Avos, Ethics of the Fathers* (in English). *Ethics of the Fathers* records teachings by various rabbis and their rebuttal by other rabbis, which is termed *midrash*. Paul may be rebutting the popular Rabbi Elazar ben Azariah, who stated,

"If there is no Torah, there is no worldly occupation; if there is no worldly occupation, there is no Torah . . .where there is no knowledge, there is no understanding; if there is no understanding, there is no knowledge. If there is no flour, there is no Torah; if there is no Torah, there is no flour." (*Pirkei Avos 3:21*)

The context of Rabbi Elazar's teaching is that if the equitable laws are not followed, there will not be any flour to eat. Paul's style reflects the same type of midrash and parallels Elazar's discussion. Paul makes a leap, however, when he states where there is no Torah there is no sin. He ends up contradicting both the Torah and the New Testament (*Pirkei Avos*, ArtScroll Mesorah Series [New York: Noble Book Press, 2016], 33).
13. Chaos is "lawless disorder."
14. Craig Allen, et al., "Venezuela Children Starving," *The New York Times* (December 17, 2017), https://www.nytimes.com/interactive/2017/12/17/world/americas/venezuela-children-starving.html; Andrew Cawthorne, "Mad Max Violence Stalks Venezuela's Roads," Reuters (February 9, 2018), https://www.reuters.com/article/us-venezuela-economy-trucks-wideimage/mad-max-violence-stalks-venezuelas-lawless-roads-idUSKBN1FT1G9; Will Worley, "Venezuela's Hunger Crisis Spills into Colombia," Pacific Standard (May 10, 2018), https://psmag.com/news/venezuela-hunger-crisis-spills-into-colombia.
15. Vanessa Buschschlüter, "Venezuela Crisis: 7.1m Leave Country Since 2015)," BBC News Online Latin America (October 147, 2022), https://www.bbc.com/news/world-latin-america-63279800.
16. *SEC* 4383; *BDB*, 506; *TWOT* (vol. 1), 457–51; CHALLOT, 195; *HALOT*, 5183, s.v. "מִכְשׁוֹל". Offense has the connotation of stumbling (see Lev 19:14; 1 Sam 25:31; Isa 8:14; 57:14; Jer 6:21; Ezek 3:20; 7:19; 14:3–7; 18:30; 21:15; 44:12).
17. Isa 8:16, 20. See also *YE1*, 1, 3–6, 9–12, 23–26. See also in this book: pp. 20, 24, 56, 60, 131.

18. Most scholars agree that the rebellion to which Paul refers is teaching the abandonment of the Law of Moses.

Ellingworth and Nida: "The word is used to describe unfaithfulness to God or the denial of God. This is the meaning of the closely-related English word 'apostasy.' Acts 21:21, the only other place in the New Testament where this term is used, **speaks of those who 'abandon the Law of Moses'** (TEV). The element of rebellion is perhaps implied, and is certainly present in later verses of the present chapter, but the central meaning is that of being unfaithful to, abandoning, or denying something or someone. A previous relationship with the person or belief denied is strongly presupposed" (Ellingworth and Nida, *Handbook on Paul's Letters to the Thessalonians*, UBSH, 163. Emphasis is added).

Frederick Bruce (Sheffield Univ. and Rylands Professor at Manchester Univ.): "The leader of the great rebellion is described by two phrases each containing an adjectival genitive (a Semitic idiom, common in OT and taken over repeatedly into LXX and NT Greek): he is 'the man of lawlessness' (cf. the more idiomatic Greek ὁ ἄνομος of v. 8) and 'the son of perdition,' i.e. he who is destined for perdition (cf. the application of the same phrase to Judas Iscariot in John 17:12). **This person is characterized by his opposition to the divine law and therefore he is doomed to destruction**" (Frederick F. Bruce, *1 and 2 Thessalonians*, WBC vol. 45 [Dallas: Word, Inc., 1982], 167. Emphasis is added).

D. Michael Martin (Gateway Sem.): "Paul listed and elaborated upon proofs in a conditional structure. The negative conditions are stated first, lest 'the rebellion occurs and the man of lawlessness is revealed' (v. 3b). The 'then' clause, however, was left unstated. The New International Version clarifies the sentence by adding 'that day will not come,' which does not occur in the Greek text. Paul's intent was to assert that if the things listed have not occurred, then the day of the Lord could not have arrived. The three things that must take place before the day of the Lord are (1) the rebellion must occur (v. 3), (2) **the man of lawlessness must be** revealed (v. 3), and (3) the restraint/restrainer must be removed (vv. 6–7).... The Jews, for instance, charged Paul with inciting the apostasia of Jews on the grounds that **he encouraged them to desert the teachings of Moses** (Acts 21:21)." (D. Michael Martin, *1, 2 Thessalonians*, NAC vol. 33 [Nashville: Broadman & Holman, 1995], 230, 233. Emphasis is added).

Daniel Gurtner: "It will not come unless the apostasy comes first: Apostasy is used in Josephus to denote a political rebellion, such as that of the Jews against the Romans (*Life* 43 §212–15). **It is also used of religious defection, such as abandoning the Law of Moses** (Acts 21:21) or his ordained leadership (Josh. 22:22; 2 Chron. 29:19; 33:19; Jer. 2:19; *1 Macc.* 2:15). A revolt against the law of God was foretold by some Jews (*Jub.* 23.23–24; *2 Esdr* 5:1–13; *1 Enoch* 91.3–10; 93.8–10; 1QpHab 2:1; cf. *b. Sanh.* 97). **And the man of lawlessness is revealed, the son of destruction**: The leader of this revolt is called **the man of lawlessness**" (Gurtner, "2 Thessalonians," 629–30. Emphasis is added).

Earnest Best (Univ. of Glasgow): "Now Paul implies that there may be people whose identity he does not seem to know but who are misleading the main body of the church. We cannot conclude that they were deliberately falsifying information, but the way in which they understood it would bring misunderstanding" (Ernest Best, *The First and Second Epistles to the Thessalonians*, BNTC [London: Continuum, 1986], 280).

G. K. Beale (New Testament scholar at Reformed Theological Sem., Dallas): "For example, he changes God's laws in Scripture and teaches other laws that contradict divinely revealed truth (Dan 7:25; 8:11–12; 11:30–32). This is one reason he is called *the man of lawlessness*" (G. K. Beale, *1–2 Thessalonians*, The IVP New Testament Commentary Series [Downers Grove, IL: InterVarsity Press, 2003], 210).

19. Throughout the Law of Moses, God associates sin with violations of justice. The Sabbath, for instance, provided a day off for bond slaves, a liberty unprecedented in the ancient world. Torah's Bill of Rights ensured that even bond slaves, the lowest social class, had access to justice and basic human rights. The ceremonial Levitical instructions within Torah for priests and Levites would not have applied to Israel's citizens or to immigrants. If this is the portion of Israel's constitution that Paul was rejecting, he makes no distinction. Instead, he lumps the entire law together, deeming that promises (blessings) cannot flow to people through obedience to YHWH's constitutional Law.

CHAPTER 19: PAUL ON THE LAW: PART II

1. After Martyn's commentary below, I will discuss the games scholars play in trying to make "Second Paul" work. I've offset my thoughts with my name.

J. Louis Martyn (Univ. of New York): "*The promises*. It is curious that Paul should use the plural in a passage in which he is intent on emphasizing the covenantal promise as a punctiliar event (Abraham that refers to a singular and punctiliar seed (Christ). The plural may reflect the fact that God repeated his promise to Abraham several times (note the plural in Gal 3:21). In any case, after the plural in v. 16, Paul returns to the singular in vv. 17–18, showing that he has no intention of referring to the linear history of the promises in the patriarchal generations and thence into the history of Israel (contrast Rom 9:9–13).

"*The text does not say, 'and to the seeds,' as though it were speaking about many people, but rather, speaking about one, it reads, 'and to your seed.'* **Even in focusing his attention on this single verse, Paul ignores two factors: (a) the plain meaning of the word 'seed' in Genesis 17, where it is clearly a collective referring to the people of Israel as the descendants of Abraham, generation after generation;** (b) his own earlier willingness to discuss the issue of the identity of Abraham's plural children (v. 7; cf. v. 29; Rom 4:13–16). Thus, bold move follows bold move, for the Galatians are sure to have learned of the expression 'seed of Abraham' from the Teachers, and the Teachers will have used it in its collective sense, insisting that the Abrahamic blessing, having come long ago to the plural people of Israel, is now flowing to Gentiles who join that people by observance of the Law. Moreover, the collective sense can be proved from Genesis 17, a fact of which the Teachers may very well have taken advantage in offering the Galatians their own interpretation of Paul's letter (Introduction §11).

"Given developments in his Galatian churches, however, the singular is what Paul actually hears in Gen 17:8, and he is sure that that reading honors the true voice of God's scripture (cf. 3:8). Equating promise and covenant, Paul insists that God spoke his covenantal promise to only *two* persons: Abraham and his singular seed. What concerns him, then, is the identity of that seed to whom, in addition to Abraham, the covenantal promise was made" (J. Louis Martyn, *Galatians: A New Translation with Introduction and Commentary*, AYB vol. 33A [New Haven: Yale Univ. Press, 2008], 339–40).

Jodell's on Brown & Jamieson (below): I'd like to share why the typical exegesis of scholars like David Brown completely contradict what is written in the Old Testament. The method usually employed to justify Paul's assertion relies on sweeping generalities that ignore what is actually written in the text. I'll break Brown's commentary into segments to address the issues he raises.

Brown & Jamieson, 1st comment: "*The law* is, by personification, regarded as a second person, distinct from, and subsequent to, *the promise of God. The promise* is everlasting, and more peculiarly belongs to God. *The law* is as something extraneous, subsequent, exceptional, and temporary (*vv.* 17–19, 21–24) **adds**—none adds new conditions, 'making' the covenant 'of none effect' (*v.* 17). So legal Judaism could make no alteration in the fundamental relation between God and man, already established by the promises to Abraham; it could not add as a new condition the observance of the law, in which case the fulfilment of the promise would be attached to a condition impossible for man to perform. The 'covenant' here is one of free grace—a *promise* afterwards carried into effect in the Gospel" (Brown, Fausset, and Jamieson, *Acts–Revelation*, 383. I emended Old English in this quote).

Jodell's Response: In volume 1, we saw that each and every patriarchal covenant incorporated the previous covenant. YHWH rescinded nothing. Additional promises and stipulations were added until all the covenants were codified into a single legal code ending with Deuteronomy. Divine Law (given at Mt. Sinai and on the plains of Moab) was in no way a 'second person.' Divine Law incorporated all previous promises and upheld them. YHWH's covenants began with Noah and shaped moral ideals until Moses' death. Divine Law also accounts for all the promises including YHWH's promise to Eve in Gen 3:15. There is nothing temporary about Divine Law. Over and over again YHWH stresses that Divine Law, which defines truth, is "unto all generations" and "forever" (Exod 3:15; 12:14; 16:32–33; 30:21; 31:16. Exod 12:17, 24; 27:21; 28:43; 31:17; 32:13; 25:23; Deut 4:40). Brown is correct that Divine Law prohibits anyone from adding or deleting from the stipulations, promises, and words contained therein (Deut 4:2; 12:32). What Brown asserts next contradicts everything in the Old Testament.

Brown & Jamieson, 2nd Comment: "God makes a covenant, but one of promise; whereas the law is a covenant of works. **The law brings in a mediator, a third party (vv. 19, 20)**; God makes His covenant of promise with the *one* Seed, Christ (Gen. 17:7), and embraces others only as identified with, and represented by, Christ" (Brown and Jamieson, *Acts–Revelation*, 383).

Jodell's Response: One of the most distinguishing traits in the Old Testament, a trait that separated Israel from all pagan nations, was that Divine Law did not require a mediator. Instead, Divine Law allowed direct access to YHWH (see pp. 78–79, 63, 84–85, 140–41). This was in fact the entire point of Deuteronomy 30:11–16: no one needs to go up into heaven that we can hear, understand, or observe the law. We can easily keep the law for ourselves. Divine Law is not simply a list of arbitrary "do's" and "don'ts". It is a holistic lifestyle that increases longevity, and quality, and joy of living. Eventually, observance of Divine Law can lead to eternal life. Brown asserts that the promises made to Abraham were only for Jesus. This contradicts what is actually written in Genesis. YHWH stresses over and over again that

His promises were for Abraham's collective seed—meaning the offspring that would be as the sand of the seashore. *Zera'*, Hebrew for seed, is never used to indicate one person. It always indicates all progeny. YHWH's covenants and promises with Abraham and his vast number of descendants did not exclude other peoples and nations. The entire point of giving Divine Law to Israel was for it to be shared with all nations (Mic 4:2; Isa 2:3; 56:7; Zech 14:16-21). Anyone who takes hold of YHWH's promises and obeys Divine Law can join YHWH's people (Exod 12:43-50; Isa 56:3-8). Both Paul and Brown ignore what is written in Genesis to make it say the exact opposite of what YHWH promised Abraham. It should also be stressed that the only right any Abrahamic heir has to any of YHWH's promises is through a legal process "under the Law." Every single promise YHWH made to Abraham occurred within the context of covenant. Covenants are legal contracts. The only way to lay claim to these promises is through the stipulations established in YHWH's covenants with Abraham. Given these facts, I had to wonder if the author of 2nd Thessalonians in writing about the "man of lawlessness" was trying to warn us about the Second Paul.

Jodell's on Hansen (below): One method scholars hide behind is disparaging an idea as "Jewish." The written words in Genesis and Divine Law are not specifically, "Jewish." This term did not exist before Sargon and Sennacherib deported the Northern Kingdom of Israel to Assyria. Deportation left only the tribe of Judah and her allied tribes in the region. Judah and her allied tribes soon came to be called "Jews" both by Assyria and by the remaining Judahites in the Promised Land. Hansen (below) attempts to pass off the idea of Israelite nationalism as a "Jewish" idea. This is a red herring. The idea of Israelite nationalism originates within the specific stipulations and promises YHWH made with Abraham. The Jews simply inherited the understanding established by YHWH. As pointed out above, people did not have to be Jews to join YHWH's covenants. To join the covenants, all a person needed to do was make a personal commitment to follow Divine Law and uphold its teachings. Hansen also attempts to distort the idea of a *zera'* being a collective singular seed by relegating the term to "Jewish literature." However, the "Jewish literature" that defines these ideas are YHWH's words to Abraham. These ideas do *not* originate in the later Jewish writings of the Mishnah and Talmud.

G. Walter Hansen (Univ. of Toronto): "Paul carefully examines the terms of the Abrahamic covenant and notes that the promises of this covenant were made to Abraham and to his seed. The term seed, Paul explains, is not plural but singular. Therefore the covenant designated one person, not many people, to be the recipient of the promises. That one person, says Paul, *is Christ*. Except for the lawyers among us who enjoy the minutiae of legal arguments, Paul's discussion may seem to be over our heads. But if we understand Paul's hidden agenda, we will be able to grasp the reason for this technical argument about one term in the Abrahamic covenant. **We have to realize that Paul's definition of *seed* contradicts the Jewish nationalistic interpretation of this term.** Jews were convinced that the term *seed* referred to the physical descendants of Abraham, the Jewish people. Therefore they believed it was absolutely necessary to belong to the Jewish nation in order to receive the blessings promised to Abraham.

"In Jewish literature the generic singular *seed* was usually interpreted as a collective singular, referring to the nation of Israel. But *seed* was also understood by the rabbis to be a specific singular, referring to an individual—for example, Isaac or David or Solomon. Paul's attention to the grammatical form of this term is very much like the rabbinic practice of exegesis. But Paul's interpretation is based on his conviction that Christ is the sole heir and channel of God's promised blessing" (G. Walter Hansen, *Galatians*, The IVP New Testament Commentary Series [Downers Grove, IL: InterVarsity Press, 1994], Gal. 3:16).

Hans Dieter Betz (Univ. of Chicago): "The argument must be seen on two levels: the argument as a whole is designed to show that the 'men of faith,' whom he had demonstrated to be blessed together with Abraham and to be identical with the believers in Christ (3:6-14*), are also the heirs of the covenant and of the promises. This is done merely in preparation to the discussion to follow later. In this passage, Paul takes advantage of the singular 'seed,' in order to exclude the traditional Jewish interpretation and to reserve the role of the heir for Christ" (Hans Dieter Betz, *Galatians: A Commentary on Paul's Letter to the Churches in Galatia*, Hermeneia [Philadelphia: Fortress Press, 1979], 157).

Matthew Harmon (Wheaton College): "Repeatedly throughout Genesis 12-25 God states that a promise is for both Abraham and his seed, but Paul may specifically have Genesis 17:7-10 in mind. While we will discuss Genesis 17 and its context below, here it is important to note that five times in these verses God says to Abraham that **the promises are for 'you and your seed after you'** (Holman Christian Standard Bible). While the noun rendered 'seed' (σπέρμα) can refer to the seed of plants or even semen, in both the LXX and the New Testament it most often refers to descendants or offspring. In Genesis the notion of 'seed' is central. When God announces judgment on the serpent, he says in part, 'I will put hostility between you and the woman, and between your offspring and her offspring. He will strike your head, and you will strike his heel' (Gen 3:15). This conflict between the offspring of the woman and the offspring of the serpent is in fact the central conflict of the Bible, setting the trajectory for the rest of human history. This thread is picked up in Genesis 12:7, where, after promising to make Abram into a great nation (Gen 12:1–3), God says to Abram, 'To your offspring I will give this land.' From this point forward in Genesis, the theme of Abraham and his offspring drives the narrative forward . . .

"God had reassured Abram that his heir would be a son who comes from his own body, not his servant Eliezer (Gen 15:1–21). Impatient with God's timetable, Sarai encourages Abram to impregnate her Egyptian maid Hagar to produce the promise heir (Gen 16:1–16). Thirteen years later God appears to Abram, where he reaffirms his covenant promises to multiply him into the father of nations and even kings (17:1–6). Yahweh continues by swearing: 'I will confirm my covenant that is between me and you and your future offspring throughout their generations. It is a permanent covenant to be your God and the God of your offspring after you. And to you and your future offspring I will give the land where you are residing—all the land of Canaan—as a permanent possession, and I will be their God' (Gen 17:7–8). The context here clearly indicates that multiple descendants are in view. The gift of circumcision as **the sign of this covenant seems to confirm that multiple descendants are in view** (17:9–14)." (Matthew S. Harmon, *Galatians*, Evangelical Biblical Theology Commentary, eds. T. Desmond Alexander, Thomas R. Schreiner, and Andreas J. Köstenberger [Bellingham, WA: Lexham Academic, 2021], 170–72).

Dieter Lührmann (Univ. of Marburg): "In Paul's use of the comparison, **the will/covenant is replaced by the 'promises' as the content of this covenant.** . . . Now, however, Paul points out that according to the wording of the Old Testament texts, the promises were made to the 'offspring' in the singular, not plural. In the Abraham stories the singular means first Isaac (Gen. 12:7; 13:15), but **along with him also the numerous descendants who were likewise promised.** . . . Paul, however, draws a different conclusion: for him 'offspring' is a singular term that he can interpret only as Christ. Here again, *Christ* has the titular sense and thus points to the content of the gospel and of faith. The promise issued to Abraham is first realized in faith in this Christ (cf. Rom. 4:23–25!), and not earlier" (Dieter Lührmann, *Galatians*, CC [Minneapolis, MN: Fortress Press, 1992], 69).

Jodell's reaction to Lührmann: Paul does not point out that according to the wording of the OT texts that YHWH's promises were singular. Instead, Second Paul makes a spurious claim with a broad, sweeping statement that ignores what the text actually states. Paul does draw a different conclusion, but that conclusion defies the written word of YHWH. Paul's statement attempts to nullify YHWH's original words to Abraham. To me, this seems to be a primary reason why there is so much division and disagreement among Christian sects. Some sects gravitate towards First Paul, who upholds Divine Law, while another set of sects gravitate towards the Man of Lawlessness.

2. Gen 15:5; 22:17; 26:4; 32:12; Exod 32:13; Deut 1:10; 10:22; 28:62; 1 Kgs 4:20; 1 Chr 27:23; Neh 9:23.
3. See *YE1*, 81–121.
4. According to Genesis 36 and 1 Chronicles 1, Esau became 12 chieftains long before Jesus' birth. If Jesus was the God who blessed Esau in the Genesis's history, then Jesus would also be the God who issued his own promises. This would mean that God's promises were lies as they were not truly meant for Abraham's seed but were only for the God who blessed himself (an idea that God frowns upon since YHWH cursed those who blessed themselves through deception—Deut 29:19).

   If YHWH's promises to Abraham were only for Jesus, how could Jesus fulfill the promise of becoming 12 Edomite nations when Esau was excluded from inheriting Abraham's covenants?
5. The first two sources below provide context for Scripture's use of God the Father. Jerome, the last source, conflates God the Father with Jesus the son, as though there is no significant difference. While YHWH and Jesus could share the same goals, father and son are two separate entities. Combining them into one unit repeats the fallacy committed by the pagans' worship of baal.

   Andreas J. Köstenberger (Midwestern Baptist Theological Sem.) and Scott R. Swain (Reformed Theological Sem., Orlando): "While the notion of God as Father is not common in the Hebrew Scriptures, in John's Gospel 'Father–Son' is the dominant, controlling metaphor for Jesus' relationship with God. The two persons of God the Father and the Son are thoroughly and inextricably intertwined. Jesus derives his mission from the Father and is fully dependent on him in carrying it out. . . . The emphasis on the Father as the one who sent Jesus and who witnesses to him portrays him as the Authorizer and Authenticator of Jesus. Emphatically, it is Jesus himself who refers to God as 'the' Father and in close to twenty instances even as 'his' Father. 'The Father' is Jesus' natural, almost unselfconscious, way of referring to God" (Andreas J. Köstenberger and Scott R. Swain, *Father, Son and Spirit: The Trinity and John's Gospel*, New Studies in Biblical Theology, vol. 24, ed. D. A. Carson [Downers Grove, IL: InterVarsity Press, 2008], 151).

Sarah Dille: "Deutero-Isaiah portrays God as a father fairly clearly in three texts. In 43:1–7, interacting with the image of the redeeming kinsman, YHWH is portrayed as the father who redeems his sons and daughters from slavery, just as he once redeemed Israel from bondage in Egypt (through the water and the fire). As a father, YHWH *loves* Israel and is the source of Israel's *identity* ('everyone who is called by my name'). The interaction of the father image with exodus imagery appears again in Isa. 50:1–3, where YHWH is again the redeeming father who frees his children from slavery. This unit adds the dimension of YHWH's relationship with the exiles' 'mother,' Zion. Thus, YHWH as a father in Isa. 50:1–3 involves both the redemption of the exiles from slavery and, implicitly, the restoration of Jerusalem.... The begetting father is the creator of Israel's future. A number of the commonplaces of 'father' are highlighted in Deutero-Isaiah's depiction of YHWH as a father. Among these are the father's role in protecting and redeeming his children and preserving the family (43:1–7), the father as one who punishes the children (50:1–3), the father as the source of the child's name (43:7), and the father's role in conception (45:10)." (Sarah J. Dille, *Mixing Metaphors: God as Mother and Father in Deutero-Isaiah* [New York: T & T Clark, 2004], 175–76).

Jerome (*c.* 400 CE): "Now the phrase 'blessed be the God and Father of our Lord Jesus Christ' is to be read in a double sense. It first means that God is blessed as the maker of all things, this being the main clause. To this is then added 'who is also the Father of our Lord Jesus Christ.' **It means that both God and Father are to be referred in common to our Lord. Blessed is the God of the man who has been assumed and the father of him who was the Word of God with God in the beginning!** Not that the assumed one is other than the Word who assumed him, but that he who is one and the same is spoken of now by sublime and now by humble titles, according to what circumstances demand (Epistle to the Ephesians 1.1.3)." (Jerome in *Galatians, Ephesians, Philippians,* ACCS, ed. M. J. Edwards [Downers Grove, IL: InterVarsity Press, 1999], 109).

6. *YE1*, 81–102.
7. CAD 4:415, "ewuru."
8. מִמֵּעֶיךָ, from מֵעָה (*meeh*); *SEC* 4578; *BDB*, 589; *TWOT* (vol. 1), 518–19; CHALLOT, 205; *HALOT*, 5409, s.v., "מֵעָה". The term is understood as a collective plural since many descendants issue forth from one sperm.
9. If this covenant were not mutually binding on both YHWH and Abram, then YHWH could have allowed Eliezer, Lot, or an entirely new entity to inherit his covenants. For Abraham's children to inherit their father's covenants, YHWH had to bind himself to his covenant without being able to act or proscribe measures arbitrary to this treaty with Abram.
10. *YE1*, 73–81.
11. *YE1*, 84–85. See also the use of *me'ah* (מֵעָה), usually translated 'bowels,' in 2 Sam 16:11; 2 Chr 32:21; Ps 71:6; Isa 48:19; 49:1.
12. The early Christians in Judea were Jews: the children of Abraham. Since the New Testament claimed its authority from the *Tanach* (Old Testament), it helped to preserve its text. Remember, the Testimonial Law (Leviticus 26; Deuteronomy 28) foretold that Israel would be scattered among many nations (see *YE1*, 107–15; 718–21; 731–38; 741–44). Many scattered Israelites became early Christians. For further study, see Yair Davidiy's research at: https://hebrewnations.com/publications/books/booklist.html.
13. *YE1*, 1–12; see in this book, pp. 36–37, 79.
14. *YE1*, 153–58, 335, 602–04.
15. Matt 22:30; Mark 12:25; and Luke 20:34–35.
16. Gen 28:10–18; Lev 26:33, 44–45; Deut 4:27–31; 30:2–6; Ps 106:45–48; Amos 9:9–15; Isa 11:12; 43:6–7; 60:1, 4, 9, 12, 14, 16, 18–22; 61:6–7; Jer 23:3–8; Jer 31:7–12; Hos 9:17; Ezek 11:17–19; 34:12–16; 36:22–24, 25–28; 39:27–29. See *YE1*, 106–115 for discussion of these texts.
17. See *YE1*, 98–102.
18. Herod "the Great" had besieged both Jerusalem and Masada while massacring many Judeans to secure his power and subjugate Israel. The Pharisees were aligned with Judea's general populace and opposed Herod's rule. He executed any who opposed him, which greatly curtailed the number of Pharisees and virtually eliminated any opposition. The Sadducees were not hidden from Herod's grasp, either. He executed 45 aristocrats, most of whom were members of the Jewish governing Sanhedrin. He then confiscated their property. The Hasmonean family, who had liberated Judea from foreign domination less than a century before, fell into Herod's crosshairs and most of the family was executed. Herod Antipas succeeded his father, Herod "the Great." He beheaded John the Baptist, who upheld the Torah's morality code for marriage. Antipas' was not just silencing John's criticism but aimed to silence his

movement. Thus, the Judeans during Jesus' lifetime needed deliverance from Herod's oppressive reign. (See H. W. Hoehner, "Herod," *ISBE* vol. 2, 690–98).
19. Instructions for the Effacement Judgment are given in Num 33:50–54. See *YE1*, 553–54, 601–11, 617–72.
20. *YE1*, 98–102, 120–21, 605–08.
21. <u>James Dunn</u>: "Hence probably Paul's reworking of the argument in Rom. 4:13–17—'the promise to Abraham and his descendants that they should inherit the world', 'father of many nations' . . . But it is not critical here, since the argument at this point turns on the two key words: 'promise', which, of course, **is not used in the Genesis passages** (see on 3:18), but which could quite properly summarize the various passages where God says 'I will give', that is, both the land (as above) and a son (15:2–3; 17:16); and 'seed', which was not necessarily dependent on the promise of the land" (James D. G. Dunn, *The Epistle to the Galatians*, BNTC [London: Continuum, 1993], 183. Emphasis added).

<u>Brown and Jamieson</u>: "Therefore, the promise that in Him 'all families of the earth shall be blessed' (Gen. 12:3) joins in this one Seed, Christ, Jew and Gentile, as fellow-heirs on the same terms—viz., by grace through faith; not to some by promise, to others by the law, but to all alike, circumcised and uncircumcised, constituting but one seed in Christ (Rom. 4:13, 16)." (Brown, Fausset, and Jamieson, *Acts-Revelation*, 383).

Theologian and journalist <u>Timothy George</u> (Samford Univ.) remarks: "**In v. 16 Paul said nothing about the content of the Abrahamic covenant,** focusing entirely on the procedural matter of its irrevocability. In v. 17 the substance of the covenant itself comes into view with the word 'promises,' clearly an allusion to the blessings God promised to Abraham in Gen 12 and reiterated in greater detail in Gen 17. Specifically the promises embraced the gift of the land, a multitudinous progeny, and making Abraham a channel of blessing for all the nations.

"As we have seen already in v. 8, Paul had interpreted this last promise to mean that the message of the gospel, that is, justification by faith, would be preached to the Gentiles as well as to Abraham's **natural descendants**. However, here in v. 16 Paul's main point was that all of these promises applied not only to one man, Abraham, but also to his 'seed.' **Now here is the hairsplitting point: the word 'seed,' he observed, is singular, not plural; therefore in its deepest and fullest meaning it refers to one person, not to many**. And that one person, Paul contended, Abraham's true seed, is Christ himself" (Timothy George, *Galatians*, NAC vol. 30 [Nashville: Broadman & Holman, 1994], 247, emphasis added).

<u>Jodell's response to George</u>: Nothing in the Hebrew text indicates that there is a "richer and fullest singular meaning" with the term *seed*. YHWH reiterates many times that the blessings and promises within the Abrahamic covenants are for Abraham's entire family. When I searched each specific promise, the only blessing that could perhaps be applied to Jesus was his being a blessing to all the families of the earth. However, this blessing still did not exclude Abraham's numerous offspring as they and their history are also a blessing to the nations' of the earth and a source for revealing YHWH's righteousness in action through His judgements.

<u>F. Bruce</u>: "If in Gen. 18:18 it is in (or with) Abraham that all the nations of the earth will be blessed, in Gen. 22:18 the promise runs: 'In your offspring (σπέρμα) all the nations of the earth will be blessed' (cf. Gen. 26:4b; 28:14). In Gen 22:18 (and 26:4b) the Hebrew conjugation is the reflexive Hithpael (*hiṯbārᵉḵû*), not Niphal, but even so it is represented by the passive in the LXX. In Sir. 44:21 (ἐνευλογηθῆναι ἔθνη ἐν τῷ σπέρματι αὐτοῦ) the Hebrew text as well as the Greek translation seems to indicate that the nations would be the objects of the blessing. . . . the reference is to a single descendent, Christ, through whom the promised blessing was to come to all the Gentiles. In the second instance the reference is to all who receive this blessing; in v. 29 all who belong to Christ are thereby included in Abraham's offspring. Paul was well aware that the collective noun could indicate plurality of descendants as well as a single descendent" (F. F. Bruce, *The Epistle to the Galatians: A Commentary on the Greek Text*, New International Greek Testament Commentary [Grand Rapids, MI: Eerdmans, 1982], 172).

CHAPTER 20: DIVINE JUSTICE

1. Priest and linguist <u>Rowland Murphy</u> comments: "Whoever fails to observe the Law will be an 'abomination' to the Lord; such a person is a hypocrite and has no basis for uttering a prayer; see Prov 15:8, 29" (Rowland E. Murphy, *Proverbs*, WBC vol. 22 [Dallas: Thomas Nelson, 1998], 215).

<u>Garrett</u>: "Verse 9 adds yet another twist: those who spurn the law will lose the companionship of God, as indicated by his rejection of their prayers. Taken together these verses teach that the law is

a guide to choosing friends and maintaining sound relations with family and God" (Garrett, *Proverbs, Ecclesiastes*, NAC, *Song of Songs*, 223).

Reyburn & Fry: "If one turns away his ear from hearing the law: **Turns away his ear from hearing** is the literal Hebrew expression and means to 'pay no attention,' 'fail to obey,' or 'disregard.' As in verse 4, **the law** here refers to God's law. **Even his prayer is an abomination**: The opening word **even** expresses the sense that what follows is contrary to what people normally think or expect, that is, that God hears and is happy with peoples' prayers. **His prayer** is 'his prayer to God' or 'his praying to God.' For **abomination** see 3:32. We should understand here that the prayer is an **abomination** *to God*, and in some languages the sense may need to be completed in this way. It is expressed in one language as 'God will regard this prayer as something that stinks'" (Reyburn and Fry, *Handbook on Proverbs*, UBSH, 592).

Fausset: "**He that turneth away his ear from hearing the law, even his prayer shall be abomination**—(Zech. 7:11; Acts 7:57, on the first clause; 15:8; Ps. 109:7, on the last). He who will not hear does not deserve to be heard" (Fausset, *Job–Isaiah*, 503).

2. Deut 31:17–18; 32:20; Mic 3:4; Isa 8:17; 54:8; 59:2; 64:7; Ezek 39:23.
3. The precept of YHWH searching hearts and giving each person according to their actions is established in 1 Kgs 8:39; 1 Chr 28:9; Jer 17:10; 32:19.
4. Ian Boxall: "As we move into the *dispositio* of the Thyatiran message (verses 22–25), the threat of the Son of Man coming in judgement is heightened. . . . **Those who have committed adultery with her** would then be her pagan associates (note the parallel with Babylon and 'earth's kings' at 17:2 and 18:3), who are threatened with the **great tribulation** of the last days. Like pagans elsewhere (9:20–21; 16:9, 11), however, they are provided with the opportunity to repent, oddly **of what she has done** (this harder reading is to be preferred to the alternative 'of what they have done'). Those described as **her children**, on the other hand, would be her followers within the Church. They are threatened with being put to **death**" (Ian Boxall, *The Revelation of Saint John*, BNTC [London: Continuum, 2006], 65).

Uriah Smith: "Children are spoken of, which confirms the idea that a sect and its proselytes are meant. . . . And further, the declaration, "I will give unto every one of you according to your works," is proof that the address to this church looks forward prophetically to the final reward or punishment of all accountable beings" (Uriah Smith, *Thoughts, Critical and Practical, on the Book of Revelation*, 2nd Edition, Revised [Battle Creek, MI: Steam Press of the Seventh–day Adventist Publishing Association, 1875], 52).

5. Martin Kaste, "California Cops Frustrated with 'Catch–and–Release' Crime–Fighting," National Public Radio (January 22, 2016), https://www.npr.org/2016/01/22/463210910/california-cops-frustrated-with-catch-and-release-crime-fighting; Chris Lewis, "A Catch–and–Release Justic System Is Not Working for Canadians: Lewis," CP24.com (January 7, 2023), https://www.cp24.com/news/a-view-from-the-top/a-catch-and-release-justice-system-is-not-working-for-canadians-lewis-1.6221736. In November 2024, Californians passed Proposition 36, which upholds penalties for crime, reversing the soft policy where penalties for crime are ignored. See https://www.theguardian.com/us-news/2024/nov/05/california-prop-36-results.
6. Phil Logan: "Bloodguilt—unclean (Num. 35:33–34) and was incurred by killing a person who did not deserve to die (Deut. 19:10; Jer. 26:15; Jon. 1:14). Killing in self–defense and execution of criminals are exempted from bloodguilt (Exod. 22:2; Lev. 20:9). Bloodguilt is incurred (1) by intentional killing (Judg. 9:24; 1 Sam. 25:26, 33; 2 Kings 9:26; Jer. 26:15); (2) by unintentional killing (see Num. 35:22–28 where one who accidentally kills another may be killed by the avenger of blood implying that the accidental murderer had bloodguilt.); (3) by being an indirect cause of death (Gen. 42:22; Deut. 19:10b; 22:8; Josh. 2:19); (4) a person was under bloodguilt if those for whom he was responsible committed murder (1 Kings 2:5, 31–33); and (5) the killing of a sacrifice at an unauthorized altar imputed bloodguilt (Lev. 17:4). The avenger of blood could take action in the first two instances but not in the latter three.

"When the murderer was known in instance (1) above, the community shared the guilt of the murderer until the guilty party had paid the penalty of death. No other penalty or sacrifice could substitute for the death of the guilty party, nor was there any need for sacrifice once the murderer had been killed (Num. 35:33; Deut. 21:8–9). The one who unintentionally killed another [(2) above] might flee to a city of refuge and be safe. If, however, the accidental killer left the boundaries of the city of refuge, the avenger of blood could kill in revenge without incurring bloodguilt (Num. 35:31–32; Deut. 19:13). The community was held to be bloodguilty if it failed to provide asylum for the accidental killer (Deut. 19:10).

"In cases where the blood of an innocent victim was not avenged, the blood of the innocent cried out to God (Gen. 4:10; Isa. 26:21; Ezek. 24:7–9; cp. Job 16:18), and God became the avenger for that person (Gen. 9:5; 2 Sam. 4:11; 2 Kings 9:7; Ps. 9:12; Hos. 1:4). Even the descendants of the bloodguilty person might suffer the consequences of God's judgment (2 Sam. 3:28–29; 21:1; 1 Kings 21:29). Manasseh's bloodguilt and Judah's failure to do anything about it was the cause of Judah's downfall over 50 years after

Manasseh's reign (2 Kings 24:4)." (Phil Logan, "Bloodguilt," *Holman Illustrated Bible Dictionary*, eds. Chad Brand, et al. [Nashville: Holman Bible Publishers, 2003], 227).

7. Evans: "**That upon you may fall the guilt of all the righteous blood shed on earth** (v. 35): The sin of opposing and persecuting God's prophets and righteous ones has been building and compounding for generations. . . . The idea of blood falling **upon** someone is semitic; cf. 2 Sam. 1:16; Jer. 51:35. So is the expression **righteous blood**; cf. Joel 3:19; Jonah 1:14; Prov. 6:17.

"**From the blood of righteous Abel to the blood of Zechariah, the son of Berechiah, whom you murdered between the temple and the altar** (v. 35): Abel, of course, was the son of Adam and the brother of Cain, who murdered him (cf. Gen. 4:1–15, esp. v. 10 "your brother's blood is crying to me from the ground"). The identity of **Zechariah, the son of Berechiah**, who was **murdered between the temple and the altar**. . . . It is sometimes suggested that Jesus refers to Abel and Zachariah in order to encompass the whole of Scripture's witness" (Evans, *Matthew-Luke*, 436–37).

A. Carr: "ἀπὸ τοῦ αἵματος Ἄβελ κ.τ.λ. If the reading υἱοῦ Βαραχίου be retained (it is omitted in the Sinaitic MS.) a difficulty arises; for the Zacharias, whose death 'in the court of the house of the Lord' is recorded 2 Chron. 24:20–22, was the son of Jehoiada. The words, however, do not occur in Luke 11:51, and are possibly interpolated. Zechariah the prophet was a son of Barachias: but of his death no record is preserved. Another explanation has been offered. At the commencement of the Jewish War with Vespasian a Zacharias, son of Baruch, was slain in the Temple by two zealots (Josephus, War iv. 5, 4).

"Accordingly many commentators have thought that Jesus spoke prophetically of that event. The coincidence is remarkable, but the aorist ἐφονεύσατε is decisively against the explanation. The deed had already been accomplished. The space from Abel to Zacharias, son of Jehoiada, covers the whole written history of the Jews; for the Jewish Canon, not being arranged in order of time, began with Genesis and closed with the second book of Chronicles. ἐφονεύσατε. The present generation shares in the guilt of that murder" (A. Carr, *The Gospel according to St Matthew*, Cambridge Greek Testament for Schools and Colleges [Cambridge: Cambridge Univ. Press, 1896], 263).

Stuart Weber: "Their persecutors would be counted among the murderers of all history, the segment of humanity who is guilty of **all the righteous blood that has been shed on earth**. Expanding on this last phrase, Jesus provided the names of the first righteous martyr and one of the latest in Jewish history. Abel was the first recorded murder (possibly the first human death), and his death at his brother Cain's hand was because of Abel's righteousness (Heb. 11:4; 1 John 3:12), which sparked Cain's jealousy (Gen. 4:1–15).

"Jesus finished the seventh and most sobering woe with his pronouncement of judgment. **I tell you the truth** assured the listeners of the validity of his prediction. **All this** included the persecutions and the judgment for them. **This generation** (cf. Matt. 11:16; 13:39, 45; 16:4) should be taken quite literally in this case, since judgment on Israel did come in the form of the A.D. 70 devastation" (Weber, *Matthew*, 380–81).

Jay Adams: "The present **generation** would fill the cup to overflowing. God's wrath, which had been pending for some time, would now be poured forth in great fury upon the generation alive in 70 AD. The punishment of the guilt of the fathers' and Christ's contemporaries would **come upon this generation**" (Jay E. Adams, *The Gospels of Matthew and Mark*, The Christian Counselor's Commentary [Cordova, TN: Institute for Nouthetic Studies, 2020], 182).

8. In Volume 1, I theorized that Cain's last remaining descendant Naamah, married Noah's son Ham, preserving Cain's bloodline (*YE1*, 48–52, 55). Thus, Israel's intermarriage with the Canaanites and Egyptians would have merged bloodlines in many of Israel's families.

CHAPTER 21: VICARIOUS ATONEMENT

1. While I was studying this text, I discovered a strawman argument. According to Divine Law, when a person sinned, they could bring a penalty payment, and the violation was pardoned or forgiven. This is YHWH's instruction: "He shall do with the bullock as he did with the bullock for a **sin offering**, so shall he do with this: and the priest shall make an **atonement for them, and it shall be forgiven them**" (Lev 4:20).

Two Hebrew words are often used for forgiveness: *nasa'* (נָשָׂא) and *salach* (סָלַח). *Nasa'* means to bear, carry, or tolerate. It is used in Exod 34:7 and Num 14:18 when YHWH states He will bear, carry, and tolerate our sins. In Exodus 32:30, Moses sought to make an "atonement" for Israel after the Golden Calf for Israel's "great sin," so YHWH would "forgive their sin" (Exod 32:31–32). *Nasa'* is used here for "forgive." Moses understood atonement to relate to YHWH's carrying, bearing, and tolerating Israel's sin at the Golden Calf.

Salach means a total pardon and is what we normally associate with modern ideas of forgiveness (Lev 4:26, 31, 35; 5:10, 13, 16, 18; 6:7; 19:22; Num 14:20; 15:25–26; 1 Kgs 8:34, 36, 50). This is the term used for when a person brought the required sin offering to atone for their sin. They were pardoned. They were completely forgiven. This was not a matter of simple "ritual purity" or a fiat ceremony. YHWH specifically states that their sin is pardoned once the person fulfills the stipulations for the required penalty. This was not just a requirement under Law, it was also YHWH's promise to the sinner that he would be forgiven.

Paul equates atonement with purification. These are two separate concepts. Being ceremonial clean usually dealt with one's ability to come in contact with Tabernacle or Temple—YHWH's sacred dwelling. Uncleanliness was usually expressed by the term *tame'*. *Some* sins could cause Israel to become ritually impure and these usually dealt with community contagion (leprosy, illness, and bodily discharges). However, uncleanliness/impurity (*tame'*) were not part of the atonement process. They had nothing to do with sin offerings. Purification had nothing to do with a sinner's payment of a penalty, atonement, or forgiveness process that was part of Israel's penalty (sacrificial) system.

This is where it seems scholars are not honest with the text. In Hebrews 9:22, Paul states that things are "cleansed" with blood. The Greek word *Katharizetai* means "to cleanse" and is often limited to the idea of being ceremonially clean (Mark 1:42; 7:19; Luke 5:12–13; Heb 9:14, 23). Paul asserts that "purification" or "cleanliness" is the same thing as "atonement" and "forgiveness." His subtle argument diminishes from the atonement YHWH proscribed by Law as though it does not really offer forgiveness. The implication is that animal sacrifice just fulfills some arbitrary state of purity. If animal sacrifices provided no real atonement or forgiveness for ancient Israel, then did YHWH lie in the stipulations established for Israel? Or, was it all just meant to be symbolic?

Notes: (*nasa'*); SEC 5375; BDB, 669–71; TWOT (vol. 2), 600–01; CHALOT, 246–47; HALOT, 6362 s.v. "נשׂא" 1–2, 14–15. See also: Lev 11:25, 28, 40; 15:10; 16:22; Num 11:12, 14, 17; 13:23; Deut 32:11; Oswalt, Isaiah: 40–66, 386; Koole, Isaiah III, 288–90; Barré, "Textual and Rhetorical–Critical Observations," 4; Oswalt, Isaiah: 40–66, 386; Young, Isaiah Chapters 40–66, 345; Also: Gen 13:6 and Deut 1:9; J. Alec Motyer, *Isaiah*, TOTC vol. 20, ed. Donald Wiseman (Downers Grove, IL: InterVarsity Press, 1999), 377.

סָלַח (*salach*) as לִסְלוֹחַ (*lislowach*); SEC 5545; BDB, 699; TWOT (vol. 2), 626; CHALOT, 256–57; HALOT, 6576, s.v. "סלח"; Exod 34:9; Lev 4:20, 26, 31, 35; 5:10, 13, 16, 18; 6:7; 19:22; Num 14:19–20; 25–26, 28; 30:5, 8, 12; 29:20; 1 Kgs 8:30, 34, 36, 39, 50; 2 Kgs 5:18; 24:4; 2 Chr 6:21, 25, 27, 30, 39; 7:14; Ps 25:11; 103:3; Isa 55:7; Jer 5:1, 7; 31:34; 33:8; 36:3; 50:20; Lam 3:42; Dan 9:19; Amos 7:2.

Below are a few scholars' thoughts on the matter:

Craig Koester (Luther Sem.): "*Indeed, according to the Law almost everything is cleansed with blood.* In addition to sin offerings, blood was used for cleansing from leprosy (Lev 14:6, 14) and for sanctifying priests (Exod 29:20–21). In saying that 'almost' everything was cleansed with blood, Hebrews recognizes that sometimes other agents were used. Water (Lev 15:1–33; 16:26, 28; 22:6) and fire purified (Num 31:21–24; Isa 6:6), while flour was sometimes used for atonement (Lev 5:11), incense (Num 16:46), or gold (Num 31:50). The idea that blood had cleansing power was shared by Greeks and Romans (Euripides, *Iphegeneia at Tauris*, 1223–24; Aeschylus, *Eumenides*, 280–83; cf. Plutarch, *Mor.* 290D). Despite criticisms (§25 COMMENT *a–b*), blood sacrifice was common. . . . To say that 'without blood forgiveness does not occur' summarizes much of the OT practice. Blood was used in the atonement ritual (Lev 16:14–19) and sin offerings (Lev 4:5–7, 16–18, 25, 30, 34), although God could forgive without sacrifices (e.g., Exod 32:32)." (Craig R. Koester, *Hebrews: A New Translation with Introduction and Commentary*, AYBC vol. 36 [New Haven: Yale Univ. Press, 2008], 420, 421. Underlining added).

David Allen (SW Baptist Theological Sem.): "The paragraph concludes with a twofold statement in v. 22. The first statement, 'nearly everything [must] be cleansed with blood,' uses the present tense verb form *katharizetai*, 'to cleanse.' This present tense form is, according to Westfall, 'a marked past-referring present tense form' that functions to summarize 'what the author was highlighting in the repetition of *pas* in the inauguration scenario.' The second statement is 'without the shedding of blood, there is no forgiveness'" (David L. Allen, *Hebrews*, NAC vol. 35 [Nashville: B & H Publishing, 2010], 483).

2. See YE1, 197–204. One study observes: "Blood is considered to be an excellent medium for bacterial growth due to its high nutritive value, temperature, pH and water activity or relative humidity" (K. Nakyinsige, A. B. Fatimah, Z. A. Aghwan, I. Zulkifli, Y. M. Goh, A. Q. Sazili. "Bleeding Efficiency and Meat Oxidative Stability and Microbiological Quality of New Zealand White Rabbits Subjected to Halal Slaughter without Stunning and Gas Stun-killing," *Asian–Australasian Journal of Animal Sciences* 27/3 [2014], 406–13, https://doi.org/10.5713/ajas.2013.13437; "Animal Fat," NutritianFacts.org, https://nutritionfacts.org/topics/animal-fat/).

3. *SEC* 4975; σχεδόν; *LSJ*, "σχεδόν," 686.
4. *SEC* 2511; καθαρίζω means "to cleanse." Specifically, to make "make clean, literally, ceremonially, or spiritually, according to context." Paul's statement aligns with the Law sins many ceremonial sins were not covered or purified by blood atonement (*LSJ*, "καθαρίζω," 338).
5. Haenchen, Funk, and Busse: "Jesus is going away, and soon, and going to the cross and to the Father, and they will seek him in vain, as it has already been explained in 7:33f. But, in that case, it is too late for them; the judgment of God will take place in the destruction of Jerusalem, which is a city standing for the world.... Verse 24 provides the explanation for Jesus' enigmatic saying in verse 21b: **They will die in their sins, if they do not believe that 'I am he.'** This 'I am' (ἐγώ εἰμι) sounds mysterious and is intended to sound mysterious" (Ernst Haenchen, Robert Walter Funk, and John Ulrich Busse, *A Commentary on the Gospel of John: Chapters 7–21*, vol. 2, Hermeneia [Philadelphia: Fortress Press, 1984], 27, 28. Emphasis added).

    Newman & Nida: "'You will die in your sins' is literally 'you will die in your sin.' The Greek text of this verse has the singular 'sin,' but later (verse 24), when Jesus refers to what he has said in this verse, the plural *sins* is used. In the present verse it seems preferable to translate by the singular 'sin,' since here the focus is on the absolute sin of rejecting Jesus.... On the meaning of the phrase *I Am Who I am*, see 4:26. In this passage, as in some others in John's Gospel, the statement 'I Am' is used absolutely, without a predicate. In such instances this expression identifies Jesus with God. The Greek order of this last sentence is the reverse of the order in TEV *(for if you do not believe that 'I Am,' you will die in your sins)*." (Newman and Nida, *Handbook on the Gospel of John*, UBSS, 271, 273).
6. Thomas Schreiner: "Indeed, only Christ suffered 'for the unrighteous' *(hyper adikōn)*. His death was vicarious and substitutionary and the basis upon which people become right with God.... Only Christ through his suffering died *for* the unrighteous, and the suffering of believers could not bring others to God. Indeed, Christ's suffering is the means by which the Petrine Christians were themselves brought to God, showing that they were formerly unrighteous and sinners" (Thomas R. Schreiner, *1, 2 Peter, Jude*, NAC vol. 37 [Nashville: Broadman & Holman, 2003], 182).

    John Elliott: "The substantive *dikaios* ('righteous one' or 'just one'), one who is obedient to God's will, recalls the earlier Christological statement of 2:21–25, which was seen to be reliant on the portrait of the Suffering Servant of Isaiah (Isa 53), identified as the 'righteous one' (*dikaios*, Isa 53:11). This concept of the suffering righteous one, as noted there, belonged to a broader Israelite tradition, eventually assumed messianic import (Wisdom 2:18; *1 Enoch*. 38:2, 3; 53:6 ['the Righteous and Elect One']), and was subsequently applied as a messianic designation to Jesus by his followers" (John H. Elliott, *1 Peter: A New Translation with Introduction and Commentary*, AYBC vol. 37B [New Haven: Yale Univ. Press, 2008], 641).

    Paul Achtemeier (Union Theological Sem.): "The ensuing phrase (δίκαιος ὑπὲρ ἀδίκων, 'righteous [one] for [the] unrighteous [many]') employs language familiar to NT tradition, both as a phrase and, with respect to the word δίκαιος, as a description of Christ. In its latter meaning it indicates why it was possible for Christ's death to be 'for sin' in a unique way,[92] that is, as righteous he did not need to die for his own sin. While it is clear to whom the δίκαιος refers, the ἄδικοι are not so easy to identify. There is ample evidence in the NT, particularly in Paul, that Christ's death was for the benefit of all ἄδικοι ('unrighteous,' hence 'sinners')." (Paul J. Achtemeier, *1 Peter: A Commentary on First Peter*, Hermeneia, ed. Eldon Jay Epp [Minneapolis, MN: Fortress Press, 1996], 247–48).
7. Douglas Stuart (Gordon-Conwell Theological Sem.): So Moses bluntly described the people's sin both in the prior verse in addressing the people, and now to God directly, as a 'great sin' and as idolatry ('they have made for themselves gods of gold'), **a violation of the first two commandments**. The wording 'gods of gold' recalls the language of the second commandment in 20:23, 'Do not make any gods to be alongside me; do not make for yourselves gods of silver or gods of gold....' Moses linked his appeal for forgiveness for Israel's sin to an offer to lose his own eternal life if the people's sin could not be forgiven. God replied that he would not give eternal life to sinners, implying both that Moses was not at fault and that he, God, was fully in charge of judging between the righteous and the wicked and would make the determination of who obtained eternal life. Thus 'Whoever has sinned against me I will blot out of my book' (v. 33) **represents a statement of divine practice, a standard of justice that God maintains**—as well as a strict warning that eternal life is not automatic and that a person who tries to enter it without his sins being forgiven could not succeed" (Douglas K. Stuart, *Exodus*, NAC vol. 2 [Nashville: Broadman & Holman, 2006], 684–85, bolding added for emphasis).

    George Bush (academic and author): "*Whosoever hath sinned against me....* This seems **intended to declare a general rule of proceeding in the divine government, in which an assurance is given that** the innocent shall not be confounded with the guilty, but that punishment should fall where it was justly due, and nowhere else" (George Bush, *Notes, Critical and Practical, on the Book of Exodus*, vol. 2 [Boston: Henry A. Young, 1841], 225, bolding added for emphasis).

Nahum Sarna (Bradeis Univ.): "God responds to Moses' entreaty: **There must be individual accountability**. But the people also bear collective responsibility. Divine promises of national territory to the people of Israel are immutable, but total absolution for the sin of the golden calf cannot be given. Israel receives a suspended sentence; the people is on probation" (Nahum M. Sarna, *Exodus*, The JPS Torah Commentary [Philadelphia: Jewish Publication Society, 1991], 210, bolding added for emphasis).

Willliam Propp (Univ. of California, San Diego): **"Whoever has sinned. Yahweh cannot wipe out Moses, since Moses is innocent. Israel, however, is not innocent"** (William H. C. Propp, *Exodus 19–40: A New Translation with Introduction and Commentary*, AYBC vol. 2A [New Haven: Yale Univ. Press, 2008], 565, bolding added for emphasis).

Brown, Fausset, & Jamieson: The declaration intimates a general rule of the Divine government, that **a clear distinction would be made between the innocent and the guilty, and that punishment would be inflicted only on the strictest principles of justice**. But the declaration primarily referred directly to the peculiar government of Israel, in which Jehovah, as king, would deal with the people who composed that nation, in the distribution of temporal rewards and punishments, according to their respective merits; and the immediate object of making it was to assure Moses that there should not be a national destruction—**that those only should be cut off, whose incorrigible and hopeless sin merited that doom, while all who had remained faithful to the covenant would be spared**" (Brown, Fausset, and Jamieson, *Genesis–Deuteronomy*, 411, bolding added for emphasis).

Marcus Kalisch (Jewish scholar): "*Blot me, I pray Thee, out of Thy book which Thou hast written*; that is, take me from among the living; for in the public registers the names of all citizens are entered, but are erased when the individuals die; and this idea is here transferred to God, who is the ruler of mankind; compare Psalms 69:29; Isaiah, 4:3.—About the *messenger* (מלאכי), see note on 23:21.—*In the day when I visit, I will visit their sin upon them*, that is, I shall not leave them unpunished; and **the plague which ensued must be considered as a chastisement for their sin, which was thereby expiated**. These words cannot mean: whenever they, *or their descendants*, will sin, I shall always punish them in some degree for that transgression also; for this would be in opposition with the promise of God, that He will only punish those who have sinned (v. 33)." (Marcus M. Kalisch, *A Historical and Critical Commentary on the Old Testament: Exodus* [London: Longman, Brown, Green and Longmans, 1855], 580–81, bolding added for emphasis).

John Durham (SE Baptist Sem., Wake Forest): "Moses asks Yahweh to forgive Israel or to erase his own name from the book Yahweh has written, a reference apparently to a register of those loyal to Yahweh and thereby deserving his special blessing (cf. Ps 69:28; Isa 4:3; Ezek 13:9; Durham, 'Psalms,' *BBC* [Nashville: Broadman, 1970], 4:310–12). It is a magnificent petition, but one that dramatizes both the seriousness of Israel's sin and the impossibility of the healing of relationship by anyone save the persons who have compromised it. Yahweh cannot overlook what Israel has done, for their sin has destroyed the basis of his interchange with them. Moses cannot atone by the sacrifice of himself **for a disobedience of which he is not guilty**" (John I. Durham, *Exodus*, WBC vol. 3 [Dallas: Word, Inc., 1987], 432, bolding added for emphasis).

8. *SEC* 6485; פָּקַד/*paqad*; *BDB*, 823; *TWOT* (vol. 2), 731–32 ; *CHALOT*, 296 ; *HALOT*, 7683, s.v. "פקד".
9. Exod 32:4; Lev 18:25; Ps 89:32; Jer 5:9, 29; 9:9; 14:10; 23:2; Amos 3:13.

CHAPTER 22: JUST KEEP SWIMMING

1. Jacob Milgrom (Univ. of California, Berkeley): "There is no doubt that child sacrifice was practiced in the ancient world. Especially impressive are the archaeological excavations in Phoenician colonies, particularly Carthage, that have unearthed special precincts in cemeteries containing hundreds of urns, dating as early as the eighth century BCE, that contain bones of children and animals (but no adults), many of which are buried beneath steles inscribed with dedications to gods. Reliefs from about 500 BCE found at Pozo Moro, Spain, a site bearing Phoenician influence, show an open-mouthed, two-headed monster receiving offerings of children in bowls.

"Neither can there be any question that the practice of 'burning babies' in pagan worship is attested in the Bible. Particularly strong is the evidence of 2 Kgs 23:10: 'He also defiled Topheth, which is in the valley of Ben-hinnom, so that no one might consign his son or daughter to the fire of Molek.' All the identifying words are here: Topheth, Ben-hinnom (the site of the cult), 'consign to fire' (burning), and Molek (the god). This cited verse, 2 Kgs 23:10, is embedded in a chapter that contains bona fide historical information. Moreover, the fact that the cultic practice described in this verse is attributed to Josiah's immediate predecessors, who did, indeed, sacrifice their children (2 Kgs 16:3; 21:6), lends weight to the identification of the other instances of sacrificing children with Molek worship (Deut 12:31; 18:10—a legal passage!).

"Thus the evidence tilts toward the view that Lev 18:21 is expressly prohibiting the practice of sacrificing children to Molek" (Milgrom, *Leviticus*, CC, 206).

2. Patricia Smith, G. Avishai, J.A. Greene, and L.E. Stager, "Aging Cremated Infants: The Problem of Sacrifice at the Tophet of Carthage," *Atinquity* 85 (2011), 859; "Ancient Jewish History: The Cult of Moloch," Jewish Virtual Library, https://www.jewishvirtuallibrary.org/the-cult-of-moloch.

3. Daniel Estes: "In sacrificing their children, they shed innocent blood in murder. Consequently, the land was defiled by their idolatry; and the promised land became a polluted land, just as it had been under the Canaanites, which was why the Lord had ordered the Canaanites obliterated" (Estes, *Psalms 73–150*, NAC, 305).

Leslie Allen: "*Sins in the land punished* (106:34–42). The people's sinning is considered in vv. 34–39, and then the reaction of Yahweh, in vv. 40–42. Entry into the promised land proved a disaster: it exposed the people to fresh temptation to religious syncretism, as the narrative of Judg 1–3 disclosed. For vv. 34–39, Judg 1:21; 2:3, 17; 3:6 may be compared, while v. 37 evokes Deut 32:17. The command to destroy the nations has parallels in Num 33:52; Deut 7:16, 24; and Joshua, while intermarriage is prohibited in Deut 7:1–6 and learning their religious practices in Deut 18:9. The repetition in v. 38 expresses emotional shock. **For the association of child sacrifice with innocent blood, Jer 19:4–5 can be compared**. Here again ancient history held up a mirror to more recent events. The psalmist deliberately paints the Judges period in colors borrowed from the fateful last preexilic centuries (cf. 2 Kgs 17:17; 21:16; Jer 3:1–3). Vv. 40–41 echo Judg 2:14. Yahweh's own people had to be punished. Since nations featured in their sin, God fittingly used nations as agents of punishment, in a reversal of v. 10. As they had become Canaanized, they fell into a canyon of disaster, declares the psalmist (with a wordplay that is more effective on the ancient Hebrew ear than on the modern Western one). This play between כנען, 'Canaan,' in v. 38 and כנע, 'subdue,' in v. 42 ironically makes the punishment fit the crime. Israel suffered national humiliation, which was no stranger to recent generations, including the psalmist's own" (Allen, *Psalms* WBC, *101–50*, 73).

Bratcher & Reyburn: "Because the Israelites had offered their innocent children as sacrifices, both the land (verse 38b) and **they themselves (verse 39a) were made *polluted* and *unclean*, that is, unfit to worship Yahweh**, to have fellowship with him" (Bratcher and Reyburn, *Translator's Handbook on the Book of Psalms*, UBSH, 916. Bold emphasis added).

Anglican bishop John J. Perowne: "Polluted. The strongest word, taken from Num. 35:33; comp. Isa 24:5. The land, the very soil itself, was polluted and accursed, as well as the inhabitants (v. 39)." (J. J. Stewart Perowne, *The Book of Psalms; A New Translation, with Introductions and Notes, Explanatory and Critical*, vol. 2, 5th Edition, Revised [London: George Bell and Sons, 1882], 266).

Andrew Fausset: "**'And shed innocent blood'**—in defiance of Deut. 19:10. **'Even the blood of their sons and of their daughters'**—the very abomination which showed the desperate corruption of the Canaanite, and which caused God to cast them out before Israel (Deut. 12:31; 18:10). **'And the land was polluted with blood'**—forbidden in Num 35:33. Every precaution was taken in God's law to impress the conscience with a horror of bloodshed: so utterly alien is Jehovah's worship to that of Moloch. **39. 'Thus were they defiled with their own works and went a-whoring with their own inventions.'** *Spiritual fornication* alienates the heart from God, and joins it to any idol (Lev. 17:7; Num. 15:39)." (Fausset, *Job–Isaiah*, 336).

4. Jack Lundbom (Garrett-Evangelical Theological Sem.): "The first is a judgment on the city for covenant violations—forsaking Yahweh, going after strange gods, burning incense to them, and shedding innocent blood, which here includes the loathsome practice of child sacrifice at Topheth. The corresponding Temple–Valley Oracle (7:30–31) contains only indictment, focusing on idol worship and child sacrifice. The present oracle ends as the Temple–Valley Oracle ends, with **Yahweh saying that not only did he not command such things, or speak about them, he never even gave them a thought**" (Jack R. Lundbom, *Jeremiah 1–20: A New Translation with Introduction and Commentary*, AYBC vol. 21A [New Haven, London: Yale Univ. Press, 2008], 841, bolding added for emphasis).

Andrew Fausset: "**Blood of innocents**—slain in honor of Moloch (ch. 7:31; Ps. 106:37). **5. They have built also the high places of Baal, to burn their sons with fire for burnt offerings unto Baal,** which I commanded not—nay, more, I commanded the opposite (Lev. 18:21; see ch. 7:31, 32)." (Fausset, *Jeremiah-Malachi*, 67).

F. B. Huey: "They had shed the blood of innocent ones (cf. 2 Kgs 21:16; 24:4), probably a reference to child sacrifice but including people innocent of any crimes. Verses 5–6 are almost identical with 7:31–32 and serve as an additional **reminder that human sacrifice was abhorrent to God**" (Huey, *Jeremiah, Lamentations*, NAC, 187, bolding added for emphasis).

5. For further discussions, see *YE1*, 673–824. Also online at: Jodell Onstott, "The Prophetic Code in Leviticus 26 and Deuteronomy 28," Academia.edu, https://www.academia.edu/100601649/YHWH_EXISTS_vol_1_The_Prophetic_Code_Leviticus_26_and_Deuteronomy.

6. Micah initiates the covenant lawsuit. He mentions YHWH's goodness in delivering Israel from Egypt (6:4), turning Balaam's curses into blessings (6:5), and Israel's belief that sacrifices could substitute for correct behavior (6:7). Each of Micah's statements relate to the accounts recorded within the Law of Moses. When Micah states that YHWH had already shown humanity what was right and good, Micah is specifically referring to YHWH's revelation of righteousness, truth, justice, and how to balance mercy with judgment as defined in Divine Law by quoting from Divine Law itself (Deut 10:12–13).

Dilbert Hillers (Semitic language expert at Johns Hopkins) observes: "In a covenant lawsuit the prophet recites the righteous acts of Yahweh, which leave the people no excuse for infidelity; to their offer of ritual performance comes the charge: do justice, love kindness, and walk wisely with your God.... Finally, as a pinnacle of human delusion, the spokesman [for the people] proposes to offer his son, his firstborn. Such sacrifices were more than mere possibilities, both in other nations of the time and in Israel, at least in certain periods, but the linguistic and archaeological evidence is such that it is difficult to estimate the degree to which such an abomination was practiced.... The reply rejects even the thought of such a sacrifice, and the attitude it reflects.... 'Justice' and 'kindness' are broad terms for what is expected of those to whom one is joined by a social bond such as a covenant; even 'love' fits in the covenant vocabulary" (Delbert R. Hillers, *Micah: A Commentary on the Book of the Prophet Micah*, Hermeneia, eds. Paul D. Hanson and Loren R. Fisher [Philadelphia: Fortress Press, 1984], 75, 78, 79, brackets added for clarity).

E. Henderson: "The questions put in the preceding verses do not involve anything like irony ... but manifestly argue **a deep anxiety about an atonement, and at the same time the grossest ignorance of what was necessary to constitute that atonement. In replying to them, the prophet first of all shows, that the ignorance of the people was culpable. They had been furnished with revelations of the mind of God upon the subject**. הִגִּיד לְךָ, *He* (i.e. Jehovah) *had shown* or *manifested it to you*; or, the verb may be taken impersonally, and rendered in the passive: *It has been shown to you*. No MS. supports אַגִּיד, *I will show*, the reading of the Syriac Vulgate and Arab. Had they searched the Divine records they could not have failed to discover, that, whatever prescriptions relative to sacrifices had been delivered to them, they had never been taught to attach to them any moral efficacy" (E. Henderson, *The Book of the Twelve Minor Prophets: Commentary* [London: Hamilton, Adams & Co., 1845], 257. Old English updated and bolding added for emphasis).

Francis I. Andersen and David Noel Freedman (Referring to the people of Israel): "They are being cross-examined with a barrage of double questions on what they are supposed to know—incidents from their past, what Yahweh has done for them, what he has told them to do for him. The famous prescription that follows is not attested elsewhere in that form; but **the implication is that this has always been the essential requirement. Compare Deut 10:12–13**" (Francis I. Andersen and David Noel Freedman, *Micah: A New Translation with Introduction and Commentary*, AYB 24E [New Haven, CT: 2000], 527, bolding added for emphasis).

Kenneth Barker: "They think ritual alone is a solution when in reality it is part of the problem. No mere ceremony is ever sufficient. 'False worshipers think God's favor, like theirs, can be bought' or earned. They 'offer the Lord everything but what he asks for: their loving and obedient hearts.' '**Offerings ... are no substitute for obedience to God's will. ...**' Finally, the worshipers hypothetically wonder whether sacrificing their firstborn children would atone for their sins (on 'transgression' and 'sin' see comments on 1:5). This, in fact, is what King Ahaz did (2 Kgs 16:3; 2 Chr 28:3). The Ammonites sacrificed their children to their god, Molech (Lev 20:2–5; 1 Kgs 11:5). The detestable practice spread to Phoenicia, Canaan, and even to the Israelites themselves on occasion. **For God's people to engage in child sacrifice would only increase their sins because God expressly prohibited it (Lev 18:21; Deut 18:10)**. Jeremiah condemned such a horrible ritual (Jer 7:31; 19:5; 32:32; for the biblical teaching on redeeming the 'firstborn' see Exod 13:2, 13; 22:29; 34:20). What the Lord really wanted most of all, however, was not the offerings but the hearts, allegiance, and obedience of the offerers (cf. Rom 12:1; Heb 10:4). 'They would offer everything (even what God forbade) excepting only what alone he asked for, their heart, its love and its obedience.' The truth taught in this passage is basically the same as that expressed in 1 Sam 15:22; Ps 40:6–8; 50:8–15, 23; 51:16–19; Isa 1:11–15; Jer 6:19–20; 7:22–23; Hos 6:6; Amos 5:21–24; Zech 7:4–10.

"The Lord through Micah now announces to Israel (Judah) what he does require ('man' here represents corporate Israel). **He does not desire ritual sacrifices divorced from a changed life—a life given over completely to the covenant Lord. Rather, his people must change their ways and actions (Jer 7:3, 5–7)**. Furthermore, he had already revealed what he requires and 'what is good.' Where? In passages like Deut 10:12–13: 'And now, O Israel, what does the Lord your God ask of you but to fear the Lord your God, to walk in all his ways, to love him, to serve the Lord your God with all your heart and with all your soul, **and to observe the Lord's commands and decrees that I am giving you today for your own good.'** Three requirements are specified in v. 8. First, they must 'act justly' (see comments on 3:1). Boice points out, 'To act justly is most important, for it does not mean merely to talk about justice or to get other people to act justly. It means to do the just thing yourself.' Second, they must 'love mercy.' The Hebrew for 'mercy' is *ḥesed*, which essentially and primarily means 'faithful covenant love.' Third, they must 'walk humbly' with their God ('your God' is relational covenant terminology and is the counterpart to 'my people' in v. 3). 'Walk' means to 'live' in a certain way, but the Hebrew for 'humbly' is difficult because it is not the usual word for humility. It almost certainly does not mean 'humbly.' Probably the New International Reader's Version is as accurate as any version. Here is its rendering of the entire verse: 'People of Israel, the Lord has shown you what is good. / He has told you what he requires of you. / You must treat people fairly. / You must love others faithfully. / And you must be very careful to live / the way your God wants you to.' So 'walk humbly' would be better rendered 'walk carefully (with your God),' which ultimately means 'be careful to live the way your God wants you to. . . . **Micah is repelled by sacrifices and worship which are not matched by just dealing and real spirituality. His central concerns are for social justice and true religion**" (Barker, *Micah, Nahum, Habakkuk, Zephaniah*, NAC, 112–14, bolding added for emphasis).

J. P. Lewis: "**Worship and morality cannot be divorced from each other. They are two sides of the same coin**" (J. P. Lewis, *The Minor Prophets* [Grand Rapids: Baker, 1966], 36, bolding added for emphasis).

Daniel Carroll (Dallas Theological Sem.) and Thomas McComiskey (Brandeis Univ.): "The standards of this verse are for those who are **members of the covenantal community and delineate the areas of ethical response that God wants to see in those who share the covenantal obligations. These standards have not been abrogated for Christians, for the New Testament affirms their continuing validity**. We are still called to the exercise of true religion, to kindness, and to humility (1 Cor 13:4; 2 Cor 6:6; Col 3:12; Jas 1:26–27; 1 Pet 1:2; 5:5). Christians are in a covenant relationship with God in which the law (*torah*) has been placed within their hearts (Jer 31:33; cf. Heb 10:14–17), not abrogated" (Daniel Carroll and Thomas McComiskey, *Hosea, Amos, Micah*, Expositor's Bible Commentary, vol. 7 [Grand Rapids: Zondervan, 2017], 436–37, bolding added for emphasis).

7. Leslie Allen: "There was an opportunity for the wicked to put themselves in the shoes of the righteous who were promised life: vv. 5, 9, 19 are echoed here. God would transfer them into that blessed category. Their former disloyalty to the covenant was regrettable, but God would not count it against them (cf. Jer 31:34). Their new right living would be accepted as their passport to the promised land" (Allen, *Ezekiel 1–19*, WBC, 277).

Moshe Greenberg (Hebrew Univ., Jerusalem): "God's constant readiness to accept and save penitents (vss. 21–32). Following the clue of A's structure, **we identify the boundary markers of B as vss. 23 and 32—a statement and a restatement of its essential doctrine**. The former appears as a conclusion from a premise (repentance expunges past sins) and is phrased as a rhetorical question: 'Do I at all desire the death of the wicked man . . . ?' The latter closes the consequential part of the oracle in the form of a declaration and an exhortation: 'For I do not desire the death of anyone . . .'

"The structure of B so far is:

B1	Doctrine	a. **repentance expunges past sins**
		b. God desires repentance
		c. reversion expunges past merits
B2	Cavil and retort	d. not God's ways but yours are perverse
		c'. **reversion expunges merits**
		a'. **repentance expunges past sins**
		d'. not God's ways but yours are perverse

Note how a and c of B1 are woven—inverted!—into B2, with a' (vss. 27f.) twice as long as c' (vs. 26; contrast the equality of a and c), **betraying an emphasis on the doctrine of repentance**. Note also the envelope of d–d', marking off this repartee as a discrete unit while stressing the rigorous consistency of God as opposed to the people's perversity" (Moshe Greenberg, *Ezekiel 1–20: A New Translation with Introduction and Commentary*, AYBC vol. 22 [New Haven: Yale Univ. Press, 2008], 335, 336, bolding added for emphasis).

    Isaac George Matthews (Yale and Crozer Theological Sem.): A Call to Repentance addressed to the house of Israel. A good man will live, but an evil man can escape doom only by turning from his evil and making for himself a new heart (cf. 11:19; 36:26; Jer. 31:34). This, which lays emphasis on the inner life, need not be divorced from the outer acts, but should be the inspiring source of righteous conduct" (I. G. Matthews, *Ezekiel*, American Commentary on the Old Testament [Philadelphia: The American Baptist Publication Society; The Judson Press, 1939], 67).

    Walther Zimmerli (Swiss academic theologian and scholar): "In a parallel formulation vv. 21f consider the case of the wicked man who turns away from his wickedness to keep the commandments, and in v. 24, the case of the righteous man who turns from his righteousness to do what is wrong (cf. further *Babylonian Talmud Berakot* 29a). In regard to both cases **the prophet proclaims the free righteousness of God**, which man encounters in his immediate present and which either deals graciously with him or judges him, granting him life or sentencing him to death, in accordance with his present state.... the question of God's concern for man. **That it is attached to the case of the wicked man who repents shows that Yahweh does not stand coolly indifferent to either possibility but proclaims to the erstwhile wicked man that the gateway of repentance stands open for him in the present**. In his penetrating ... החפץ אחפץ 'Do you really think then that I am pleased with the death of the wicked?' he uncovers his own heart, his hope, and his strong bias for the *life* of man.... Here the fuller details of the description (which follows in second place here) of the repentance of the wicked man makes it clear where the greatest emphasis lies. **The description of the change of heart in vv. 27f recalls the turning away of the son from the wickedness** of his father in v. 14.... In Ezekiel repentance is not, as with Amos and Isaiah (Wolff, Dietrich), described as a return to Yahweh, but as a turning away from wickedness. Here it is a turning away from rebellion. Rebellion is the occasion for falling into guilt. Hence Yahweh commands the casting away (for השליך cf. Matt 5:29f) of the rebellious acts like a dangerous object and the determined acceptance (עשו לכם, cf. the ποιήσατε of Matt 12:33) **of a new heart and a new spirit. The entire casuistic ruling of individual laws (vv. 5ff) is completely and finally subordinated here to an appeal to men to be renewed inwardly and to return to obedience**, such as is to be found again in 11:19 and 36:26" (Walther Zimmerli, *Ezekiel: A Commentary on the Book of the Prophet Ezekiel*, Hermeneia, eds. Frank Moore Cross and Klaus Baltzer [Philadelphia: Fortress Press, 1979], 385, 386, bolding added for emphasis).

8. Ezekiel chs. 18 and 33. Eugene Cooper concludes that "All people are personally responsible to God for their own sin" (Cooper, *Ezekiel*, NAC, 189).
9. 1 Kgs 8:39; 2 Kgs 17:13; 2 Chr 6:30; Job 34:11; Jer 17:10; 32:19; Ezek 7:3–9; 18:30; 20:44; 24:14; Hos 12:2; Zec 1:6; Mal 2:9.
10. Christopher J. H. Wright (Director of Langham Partnership International) provides an exceptional understanding of Ezekiel's position on YHWH's ability to freely forgive the wicked. "The moral integrity of his universe cannot ultimately remain fractured by the presence of deliberate sin unrepented and unpunished. But the exercise of punitive justice gives the Almighty no pleasure at all. What pleases him is that moment of repentance and genuine turning on the part of a sinner which liberates God to exercise his unique and greatest divine capacity in the granting of life. *Life* is God's gift. Life is his creation. Life is his desire. Life is his pleasure.

    "Likewise here, the whole point of this great disputation with the house of Israel has been to bring the wicked to recognize their desperate plight and to turn around. In their wickedness they face the God who decrees with no pleasure that the one who sins will die. In repentance they will face the God who decrees with pleasure that the one who repents will live. Such is Yahweh's radical consistency, in judgment and in compassion.... Ultimately there are only two categories of people before Yahweh—the righteous and the wicked. By argument, illustration and case-study, Ezekiel has insisted (the bad news) that only the righteous can be saved, but also (*the good news*), *that only the wicked need perish*. Only repentance can make the difference, but it truly can and will make all the difference in the world for those who respond.... God offers a free transfer from the camp of the wicked to the community of the righteous. **God offers a free pardon and a new life**. But the offer is open only to those who truly repent. Leaving nothing to misunderstanding, Ezekiel makes it abundantly clear what that required repentance will mean" (Wright, *Ezekiel: A New Heart and a New Spirit*, 202–03, emphasis added).

    Jodell on Fausset: Despite trying to reason around it, A. R. Fausset admits that Ezekiel purposes the same type of repentance that the New Testament would later embrace. Fausset concludes: "(1.) The penitent sinner is dealt with according to his new obedience, not according to his former sins. (2.) The righteous man, who turns from righteousness to sin, shall be punished for the latter, and his former righteousness will be of no avail to him. He shall surely live.... So far from God laying on men the penalty of others' sins, He will not even punish them for their own, if they turn from sin to righteousness; but if they turn from righteousness to sin, they must expect in justice that their former goodness will not atone for subsequent sin (Heb. 10:38, 39; 2 Pet. 2:20–22)... The sinner who penitently turns from his sin to God shall have none of his past transgressions imputed to him, but in his righteousness shall live before God (vv. 21, 22)... What encouragement this assurance gives to the repenting sinner to have an assured hope of pardon, peace, and life! Why should any be lost with such a promise held out to all?" (A. R. Fausset, *Jeremiah–Malachi*, 267, 269).

On Ezekiel 18, Caesarius of Arles (c. 500 CE) writes, "Since no one makes a fool of the Lord, he deceives himself if having led a wicked life for a long time he arises to seek life when he is already half-dead. He should listen to the prophet say, 'If the sinner turns away from his sins'—if he turns away, he says, not if he only talks about it—'he shall live because of the virtue he has practiced.' Surely you have noticed that healing medicine of this kind must be asked with the lips, but it must be brought to completion by deeds" (Caesarius of Arles in *Ezekiel, Daniel*, ACCS, eds. Kenneth Stevenson and Michael Gluerup [Downers Grove, IL: InterVarsity Press, 2008], 80).

Augustine of Hippo (c. 400 CE) writes, "Behold how God advises and arouses you so that you may be converted from your sins and be saved, though late. Behold how he urges one liable to death to live; how gently, how kindly he calls, not refusing his fatherly devotion even to sinners. He continues to call children those who have lost God their Father by their sins. On the Christian Life 2" (Augustine of Hippo in *Ezekiel, Daniel: Ancient Christian Commentary on Scripture*, eds. Kenneth Stevenson and Michael Gluerup [Downers Grove, IL: InterVarsity Press, 2008], 79).

11. See *YE1*, 75, 768–70, 773, 776–77, 780–83, 795, 840, 842.
12. Exod 10:16; 32:33; Lev 4:14; 32:23; Deut 1:41; 9:16; Josh 7:20; 10:10, 15; 1 Sam 7:6; 19:4; 24:11; Ps 41:4; 51:4; Jer 3:25; 8:14.

CHAPTER 23: EXCEPTIONS TO THE LAW?

1. Bart Ehrman, "Bart Ehrman on the Problem of Suffering—UCB," The Bart Ehrman Blog (February 28, 2016), https://ehrmanblog.org/bart-ehrman-on-problem-of-suffering-ucb/.
2. Norman H. Snaith, "Sacrifices in the Old Testament," *Vetus Testamentum* 7/3 (1957), 308–17, https://doi.org/10.2307/1516202.
3. Both Jesus and Divine Law teach that no avenue for expiation exists for intentional sins. Instead, the repentant person relied upon YHWH's mercy.

    Scholar and translator René Péter-Contesse and linguist John Ellington address unintentional sins: "The term used in the text (verse 3) is simply 'sin offering.' The context of this chapter, however, makes it quite clear that unintentional sins are meant.... The priest (offers) sacrifices to God when people sin without meaning to,' or 'Israel seeks pardon for careless sins,' or 'Israel makes offerings to God for unintentional sins,' or 'Offerings to be made when people sin accidentally.'... *Unwittingly*: that is, involuntarily or unintentionally. The word comes from a root which means 'to wander' or 'to get lost.' Both New American Bible and New English Bible translate 'inadvertently,' while Moffatt speaks of 'sinning unawares'" (René Péter-Contesse and John Ellington, *A Handbook on Leviticus*, UBSH [New York: United Bible Societies, 1992], 46, 47).

    Arnold Fruchtenbaum (Ariel Ministries) observes: "That the main idea of the Sin Offering was expiation for sin, but the main idea of the Trespass Offering was satisfaction for restoration of rights that had been violated." In another observation, he notes "that there are four specific lessons of the Trespass Offering. The first lesson is that, in cases of sin that caused harm to others, amends must be made first; restitution had to be made before making the offering. This same principle is taught in Matthew 5:23–24; 6:12. The second lesson is that the sinner must give complete satisfaction. The third lesson is that sin defiles, and this defilement has both spiritual and social dimensions. And the fourth lesson is that the concept of satisfaction and compensation was included here; both satisfaction and compensation were essential" (Arnold G. Fruchtenbaum, *The Messianic Bible Study Collection*, vol. 180 [Tustin, CA: Ariel Ministries, 1983], 18).

    Martin Pakula (Anglican Pastor): "These are offerings for unintentionally breaking the command in verses 17–21, or any other commands God has given (vv. 22–23). If it comes to Israel's attention that somehow they have sinned, they are to bring the sacrifices outlined here, and they will be forgiven (verses 24–26). Verses 24–26 deal with a communal sin, and verses 27–29 deal with one person's unintentional sin. An example of such an unwitting sin would be, say, accidental manslaughter as opposed to premeditated murder" (Martin Pakula, *Numbers: Homeward Bound*, Reading the Bible Today Series, ed. Paul Barnett [Sydney, South NSW: Aquila Press, 2006], 76–77).

Mark Rooker (SE Baptist Theological Sem., NC): "The Lord said to Moses, 'Say to the Israelites: When anyone sins unintentionally and does what is forbidden in any of the Lord's commands—'. . . . Here God informs Moses of what is the required sacrifice *nepeš kî tehĕṭā' bišgāgâ* ('when one sins inadvertently'; New International Version, 'unintentionally'; 4:2). Two roots are introduced for the first time in the Book of Leviticus, the root *ht'* for 'sin' and the root *šgg* for 'inadvertence.' These roots are predominant in the discussion of the last two major offerings, the sin offering and the guilt offering. The root *ht'* occurs fifty-three times, and the root *šgg* occurs seven times in 4:1–6:7; the understanding of these terms is critical to the understanding of these last two offerings. . . . The root *ht'* suggests a violation of the covenant. . . . The word translated 'miss' is from the root *ht'* and indicates that sinning in the religious realm is like 'missing the mark,' that is, not living in accord with God's standards. Violation of God's standard is dealt with by means of the 'sin offering' (*ḥaṭṭa't*, from the same root). The sacrificial animal in effect takes the substance of sin upon itself, removing the guilt from the offender. The root *šgg* has the meaning of 'going astray, commit sin or error' and in relation to the commission of sin carries the connotation of sin by accident or inadvertence" (Rooker, *Leviticus*, NAC, 107, 108).

Intentional Sins:

Dennis Cole (Mcfarland Chair of Archaeology): "But in the case of outright and deliberate rebellion, nothing could compensate for the people's sin, nothing could remove the impurity except the manifestation of the grace and mercy of God" (R. Dennis Cole, *Numbers*, NAC vol. 3B [Nashville: Broadman & Holman, 2000], 252).

Martin Pakula: "But an intentional, or high-handed, sin will not be atoned for by such sacrifices: 'But anyone who sins defiantly, whether native-born or alien, blasphemes the Lord, and that person must be cut off from his people. Because he has despised the Lord's word and broken his commands, that person must surely be cut off; his guilt remains on him' (Num 15:30–31). Such deliberate sin shows contempt for God, and that person will be 'cut off'" (Pakula, *Numbers: Homeward Bound*, 77).

4. Marvin H. Pope, *Job: The Anchor Bible* (Garden City, NY: Doubleday, 1965), lxxxi–ii.

Select Bibliography

ANCIENT AUTHORS BEFORE 800 CE

Ambrosiaster in *Commentaries on Romans and 1–2 Corinthians*. Ancient Christian Texts. trans. Gerald L. Bray. ed. Thomas C. Oden and Gerald L. Bray. Downers Grove, IL: IVP Academic, 2009.

Augustine of Hippo in *Ezekiel, Daniel*. Ancient Christian Commentary on Scripture. eds. Kenneth Stevenson and Michael Gluerup. Downers Grove, IL: InterVarsity Press, 2008.

——— in *John 1–10*. Ancient Christian Commentary on Scripture. ed. Joel C. Elowsky. Downers Grove, IL: InterVarsity Press, 2006.

——— in *Mark*. Ancient Christian Commentary on Scripture. Rev. edition. eds. Thomas C. Oden and Christopher A. Hall. Downers Grove, IL: InterVarsity Press, 1998.

Caesarius of Arles in *Ezekiel, Daniel*. Ancient Christian Commentary on Scripture. eds. Kenneth Stevenson and Michael Gluerup. Downers Grove, IL: InterVarsity Press, 2008.

Celsus, *On the True Doctrine*. trans. R. J. Hoffmann. Oxford: Oxford University Press, 1987.

Chromatius, Bishop of Aquileia in *Matthew 1–13*. Ancient Christian Commentary on Scripture. ed. Manlio Simonetti. Downers Grove, IL: InterVarsity Press, 2001.

The Council of Trent: The Canons and Decrees of the Sacred and Ecumenical Council of Trent. trans. and ed. J. Waterworth. London: Dolman, 1848. https://www.documentacatholicaomnia.eu/03d/1545-1545,_Concilium_Tridentinum,_Canons_And_Decrees,_EN.pdf.

Cyril of Alexandria in *John 1–10*. Ancient Christian Commentary on Scripture. ed. Joel C. Elowsky. Downers Grove, IL: InterVarsity Press, 2006.

Eusebius of Caesarea in *Commentary on Isaiah*. Ancient Christian Texts. trans. Jonathan J. Armstrong. eds. Joel C. Elowsky, Thomas C. Oden, and Gerald L. Bray. Downers Grove, IL: IVP Academic, 2013.

——— *Ecclesiastical History, Books I–IV*. Loeb Classical Library, vol. 153. trans. Kirsopp Lake. ed. G. P. Goold. Cambridge: Harvard University Press, 1949.

——— in "Eusebius: Church History, IV." NewAdvent.org. http://www.newadvent.org/fathers/250104.htm.

Hegesippus in Eusebius: *Ecclesiastical History IV*, 4.22.4 in Arthur Cushman McGiffert. *The Nicene and Post-Nicene Fathers*, Series 2, vol. 1. ed. Philip Schaff and Henry Wace. Buffalo, NY: Christian Literature Publishing Co., 1890. Rev. and ed. Kevin Knight for New Advent. http://www.newadvent.org/fathers/250104.htm.

Jerome. *Epistle to the Ephesians 1.1.3* in *Galatians, Ephesians, Philippians*. Ancient Christian Commentary on Scripture. ed. M. J. Edwards. Downers Grove, IL: InterVarsity Press, 1999.

———. *Lives of Illustrious Men* in *The Nicene and Post-Nicene Fathers*, Series 2, vol. 3. ed. Phillip Schaff. Peabody, MA: Hendrickson, 1994.

Josephus, Flavious. *Antiquities of the Jews Book 18*. trans. William Whiston. London: University of Cambridge, 1737. https://penelope.uchicago.edu/josephus/ant-18.html.

———. *Jewish Antiquities, Books XVIII–XIX*. Loeb Classical Library, vol. 433. trans. Louis Feldman. ed. G.P. Goold. Cambridge: Harvard University Press, 1965.

Julian of Eclanum in *Commentaries on Job, Hosea, Joel, and Amos*. Ancient Christian Texts. trans. Thomas P. Scheck. ed. Thomas P. Scheck, et al. Downers Grove, IL: IVP Academic, 2021.

Lucian. "The Death of Peregrine, 11–13," in *The Works of Lucian of Samosata*, vol. 4. trans. H.W. Fowler and F.G. Fowler. Oxford: Clarendon, 1905.

Novatian of Rome in "Introduction to the Twelve Prophets." *The Twelve Prophets: Ancient Christian Commentary on Scripture.* ed. Alberto Ferreiro. Downers Grove, IL: InterVarsity Press, 2003.

Oecumenius in *James, 1–2 Peter, 1–3 John, Jude.* Ancient Christian Commentary on Scripture. ed. Gerald Bray. Downers Grove, IL: InterVarsity Press, 2000.

Pirkei Avos. ArtScroll Mesorah Series. New York: Noble Book Press, 2016.

Pliny, the Younger. *Letters, vol. II: Book X.* Loeb Classical Library, vol. 59. trans. William Melmoth and W. M. L. Hutchinson. London: London Heinemann, 1915. https://archive.org/stream/letterswithengli02plinuoft/letterswithengli02plinuoft_djvu.

———. "Letters: Book 10:61–151." Attalus.org. trans. J. B. Firth. https://www.attalus.org/old/pliny10b.html.

———. "Epistulae X.96–Pliny the Younger–Ancient Rome–Classical Literature." Ancient–literature.com. http://www.ancient-literature.com/rome_pliny_epistulae_X96.html.

Suetonius. *Lives of the Caesars,* vol. II. Loeb Classical Library, vol. 38. trans. J. C. Rolf. Cambridge, MA: Harvard University Press, 1914. http://penelope.uchicago.edu/Thayer/E/Roman/Texts/Suetonius/12Caesars/Claudius*.html.

Tacitus, Cornelius. *The Annals.* eds. Alfred John Church and William Jackson Brodribb. New York: Random House, 1942. https://bit.ly/2eJuuSZ.

———. *Annals, 15.20–23, 33–45.* eds. Matthew Owen and Ingo Gildenhard. Cambridge: Open Book Publishers, 2013.

———. *Annals 15.44,* in *Tacitus V: Annals Books 13–16.* Loeb Classical Library, vol. 322. trans. John Jackson. Cambridge, MA: Harvard University Press, 1937.

——— in *The Complete Works of Tacitus.* trans. Alfred John Church and William Brodribb. ed. Moses Hadas. New York: The Modern Library, 1942.

——— in *Tacitius.* Ronald Syme. London: Oxford University, 1958.

———. *Tacitus Annals Book XV.* Cambridge Greek and Latin Classics. ed. Rhiannon Ash. Cambridge: Cambridge University, 2017.

———. "Tacitus on the Christians." ed. Jona Lendering. Livius.org (2004, modified April 2019). http://www.livius.org/sources/content/tacitus/tacitus-on-the-christians/.

Theodore of Mopsuestia in *Commentary on the Gospel of John: Ancient Christian Texts.* trans. Gerald L. Bray. eds. Marco Conti, Joel C. Elowsky, Thomas C. Oden. Downers Grove, IL: IVP Academic, 2010.

Theodoret of Cyrus in *Psalms 1–50.* Ancient Christian Commentary on Scripture. eds. Craig A. Blaising and Carmen S. Hardin. Downers Grove, IL: InterVarsity Press, 2008.

GENERAL BIBLIOGRAPHY

A

Achtemeier, Paul J. *1 Peter: A Commentary on First Peter.* Hermeneia. ed. Eldon Jay Epp. Minneapolis, MN: Fortress Press, 1996.

Adam, Peter. *The Message of Malachi: "'I Have Loved You,' Says the Lord."* The Bible Speaks Today. ed. Alec Motyer and Derek Tidball. England: Inter-Varsity Press, 2013.

Adams, Jay E. *The Gospel of John, The Letters of John and Jesus.* The Christian Counselor's Commentary. Cordova, TN: Institute for Nouthetic Studies, 2020.

———. *The Gospels of Matthew and Mark.* The Christian Counselor's Commentary. Cordova, TN: Institute for Nouthetic Studies, 2020.

———. *Proverbs.* The Christian Counselor's Commentary. Cordova, TN: Institute for Nouthetic Studies, 2020.

Select Bibliography

Adams, John Quincy. "From John Adams to Massachusetts Militia, 11 October 1798." Founders Online, National Archives. https://founders.archives.gov/documents/Adams/99-02-02-3102.

Albertz, Rainer and Rudiger Schmitt. *Family and Household Religion in Ancient Israel and the Levant.* Winona Lake, IN: Eisenbrauns, 2012.

Albright, William F. *Yahweh and the Gods of Canaan.* Winona Lake, IN: Eisenbrauns, 1994.

Allen, David L. *Hebrews.* New American Commentary, vol. 35. Nashville: B & H Publishing, 2010.

Allen, Leslie C. *Ezekiel 1–19.* Word Biblical Commentary, vol. 28. Dallas: Word, Inc., 1994.

———. *Jeremiah.* Old Testament Library. ed. William P. Brown. Louisville, KY: Westminster John Knox Press, 2008.

———. *Psalms 101–150.* World Bible Commentary, vol. 21. Rev. edition. eds. Bruce Metzger, David Hubbard, Glenn Barker, et al. Nashville: Thomas Nelson, 2002.

Alter, Robert. *The Hebrew Bible: The Five Books of Moses,* vol. 1. New York: Norton, 2019.

America's Founding Documents. "The Declaration of Independence: A Transcript." National Archives. https://www.archives.gov/founding-docs/declaration-transcript.

"Ancient Jewish History: The Cult of Moloch." Jewish Virtual Library. https://www.jewishvirtuallibrary.org/the-cult-of-moloch.

Andersen, Francis I. and David Noel Freedman. *Micah: A New Translation with Introduction and Commentary.* Anchor Yale Bible, vol. 24E. New Haven: Yale University Press, 2008.

Ando, Clifford. "The End of Ancient Democracy?" *Tableau* (Spring 2021). https://tableau.uchicago.edu/ando.

Angus, S. and A. M. Renwick. "Roman Empire and Christianity." *International Standard Bible Encyclopedia,* vol. 4. Grand Rapids, MI: Eerdmans, 1979–1988, 207–21.

Archer, Jr. Gleason, R. Laird Harris, and Bruce Waltke, eds. *Theological Wordbook of the Old Testament,* 2 vols. Chicago: Moody Bible Institute, 1980.

Arie, Eran, Baruch Rosen, and Dvory Namdar. "Cannabis and Frankincense at the Judahite Shrine of Arad." *Tel Aviv* 1/47 (May 28, 2020), 5–28. DOI: 10.1080/03344355.2020.1732046.

Assmann, Jan. *Death and Salvation in Ancient Egypt.* trans. David Lorton. Ithaca, NY: Cornell University Press, 2005.

Athas, George. *Deuteronomy: One Nation under God.* Reading the Bible Today Series. ed. Paul Barnett. Sydney, South NSW: Aquila Press, 2016.

Avishai, Gal, Patricia Smith, J. A. Greene, and L.E. Stager. "Aging Cremated Infants: The Problem of Sacrifice at the Tophet of Carthage." *Atinquity* 85/329 (2011), 859–74.

B

Barker, Kenneth L. *Micah, Nahum, Habakkuk, Zephaniah.* New American Commentary, vol. 20. Nashville: Broadman & Holman Publishers, 1999.

BAR Press Release (June 13, 2012). "Brother of Jesus Proved Ancient and Authentic." Bible History Daily: *BAR* (June 13, 2012). https://bit.ly/30KXmBs.

Barré, Micael L. "Textual and Rhetorical-critical Observations on the Last Servant Song (Isaiah 52:13–53:12)." *CBQ* 62/1 (January 2000), 1–27.

Barrett, C. K. *The Epistle to the Romans.* Black's New Testament Commentary. Rev. edition. London: Continuum, 1991.

Bauckham, Richard. "The Four–Line Ossuary Inscription from Talpiyot Tomb B – an Interpretation." ASORblog.org (March 8, 2012). https://asorblog.org/p_1848.html (accessed March 2023). Retained at: https://efaidnbmnnnibpcajpcglclefindmkaj/https://larryhurtado.wordpress.com/wp-content/uploads/2012/04/bauckham-talpiyot-tomb-inscription.pdf.

Baumgartner, Walter and Ludwig Koehler. *The Hebrew and Aramaic Lexicon of the Old Testament*, 2 vols. Rev. edition. eds. Johann Stamm, Mervyn E. J. Richardson, et al. Leiden: Brill, 2001.

Beale, G. K. *1-2 Thessalonians*. The IVP New Testament Commentary Series. Downers Grove, IL: InterVarsity Press, 2003.

Benko, Stephen. "The Edict of Claudius of AD 49 and the Instigator Chrestus." *Theologische Zeitschrift* 25 (1969), 406-18.

Berman, Joshua. *Created Equal: How the Bible Broke with Ancient Political Thought*. New York: Oxford University Press, 2008.

Bermejo-Rubio, Fernando. "Was the Hypothetical Vorlage of the Testimonium Flavianum a 'Neutral' Text? Challenging the Common Wisdom on Antiquitates Judaicae 18.63-64." *JSJ* 45 (2014), 326-65.

Best, Ernest. *The First and Second Epistles to the Thessalonians*. Black's New Testament Commentary. London: Continuum, 1986.

Betz, Hans Dieter. *Galatians: A Commentary on Paul's Letter to the Churches in Galatia*. Hermeneia. Philadelphia: Fortress Press, 1979.

Black, Jeremy and Anthony Green. *Gods, Demons and Symbols of Ancient Mesopotamia*. Austin: University of Texas, 1992.

Bleeker, C. J. "Guilt and Purification in Egypt." *Proceedings of the Xth International Congress of the International Association of Religions*, vol. 2. Leiden: Brill, 1968.

Blenkinsopp, Joseph. *Ezekiel*. Interpretation: A Bible Commentary for Teaching and Preaching. Louisville, KY: Westminster John Knox Press, 1990.

Blomberg, Craig. *Matthew*. New American Commentary, vol. 22. Nashville: Broadman & Holman Publishers, 1992.

Blumell, Lincoln. "A Jew in Celsus' True Doctrine? An Examination of Jewish Anti-Christian Polemic in the Second Century C.E." *Studies in Religion/ Sciences Religieuses* 36/2 (2007), 297-315.

Boa, Kenneth and William Kruidenier. *Romans*. Holman New Testament Commentary, vol. 6. Nashville: Broadman & Holman, 2000.

Borchert, Gerald L. *John 1-11*. New American Commentary, vol. 25A. Nashville: Broadman & Holman Publishers, 1996.

Borrini, Matteo and Luigi Garlaschelli. "A BPA Approach to the Shroud of Turin." *JFS* 64/1 (July 10, 2018), 137-43. https://doi.org/10.1111/1556-4029.13867.

Boxall, Ian. *Matthew through the Centuries*. Wiley Blackwell Bible Commentaries. ed. John Sawyer, et al. Hoboken, NJ: Wiley Blackwell, 2019.

———. *The Revelation of Saint John*. Black's New Testament Commentary. London: Continuum, 2006.

Bratcher, Robert G. and Eugene Albert Nida. *A Handbook on the Gospel of Mark*. United Bible Societies Handbooks. New York: United Bible Societies, 1993.

——— and William David Reyburn. *A Translator's Handbook on the Book of Psalms*. United Bible Societies Handbooks. New York: United Bible Societies, 1991.

Breneman, Mervin. *Ezra, Nehemiah, Esther*. electronic edition. New American Commentary, vol. 10. Nashville: Broadman & Holman Publishers, 1993.

Brenton, C. L., trans. *The Septuagint with Apocrypha: Greek and English*. London: Hendrickson Publishers, 1851.

Briggs, Charles A., Francis Brown, and S. R. Driver. *The Brown-Driver-Briggs Hebrew and English Lexicon*. Peabody, MA: Hendrickson Publishers, 2003.

Broer, Ingo. "The Death of Jesus from a Historical Perspective." *From Judaism to Christianity: Continuum Approaches to the Historical Jesus*. ed. Tom Holemé. New York: T & T Clark, 2007.

Brook, James. "Inevitable Errors: The Preponderance of the Evidence Standard in Civil Litigation." Digital Commons: New York Law School 1983. https://digitalcommons.nyls.edu/cgi/viewcontent.cgi?article=1524&context=fac_articles_chapters.

Bromiley, Geoffrey W., et al., eds. *International Standard Bible Encyclopedia*, 4 vols. Grand Rapids, MI: Eerdmans, 1979.

———. "Truth." *The International Standard Bible Encyclopedia*, vol. 4. Rev. edition. ed. Geoffrey W. Bromiley. Grand Rapids, MI: Eerdmans, 1979–1988, 926–28.

Brown, Francis, S. R. Driver, and Charles A. Briggs. *The Brown-Driver-Briggs Hebrew and English Lexicon*. Peabody, MA: Hendrickson Publishers, 2003.

———, A. R. Fausset, and Robert Jamieson. *A Commentary, Critical, Experimental, and Practical, on the Old and New Testaments: Acts–Revelation*, vol. VI. London: William Collins, Sons, 1866.

———, A. R. Fausset, and Robert Jamieson. *A Commentary, Critical, Experimental, and Practical, on the Old and New Testaments: Genesis–Deuteronomy*, vol. I. London: William Collins, Sons, 1866.

———, Andrew Fausset, and Robert Jamieson. *A Commentary, Critical, Experimental, and Practical, on the Old and New Testaments: Matthew–John*, vol. V. London: William Collins, Sons, 1866.

———, Robert Jamieson, and Andrew R. Fausset. *Jamieson, Fausset, and Brown's Commentary*. Grand Rapids, MI: Zondervan, 1961.

Brown, Raymond. *The Message of Deuteronomy: Not by Bread Alone*. The Bible Speaks Today. eds. J. A. Motyer and Derek Tidball. England: Inter-Varsity Press, 1993.

Bruce, Frederick F. *1 and 2 Thessalonians*. Word Biblical Commentary, vol. 45. Dallas: Word, Inc., 1982.

———. *The Epistle to the Galatians: A Commentary on the Greek Text*. New International Greek Testament Commentary. Grand Rapids, MI: Eerdmans, 1982.

Bugenhagen, Johannes in *1–2 Samuel, 1–2 Kings, 1–2 Chronicles: Old Testament, Reformation Commentary on Scripture*, vol. V. eds. Derek Cooper, Martin J. Lohrmann, et al. Downers Grove, IL: IVP Academic, 2016.

Bullinger, Heinrich. *The Opposition of Evangelical and Papal Doctrine*, 1.A.1 Zurick, 1551. *op. cit.* in Gregg Allison, *Historical Theology: An Introduction to Christian Doctrine*. Grand Rapids, MI: Zondervan Academic, 2011.

——— in *Matthew: New Testament*. Reformation Commentary on Scripture, vol. I. eds. Jason K. Lee, William M. Marsh, and Timothy George. Downers Grove, IL: IVP Academic, 2021.

"Burden of Proof–Preponderance." United States District Court: District of Vermont. https://www.vtd.uscourts.gov/sites/vtd/files/BURDEN%20OF%20PROOF%20-%20PREPONDERANCE%20OF%20EVIDENCE.pdf.

Burge, Gary M. "Gospel of John." *John's Gospel, Hebrews–Revelation*. 1st edition. The Bible Knowledge Background Commentary. eds. Craig A. Evans and Craig A. Bubeck. Colorado Springs, CO: David C Cook, 2005.

Bush, George. *Notes, Critical and Practical, on the Book of Exodus*, vol. 2. Boston: Henry A. Young, 1841.

Busse, Ulrich, Ernst Haenchen, and Robert Walter Funk. *John: A Commentary on the Gospel of John*. Hermeneia. Philadelphia: Fortress Press, 1984.

Butler, Trent. *Isaiah*. Holman Old Testament Commentary, vol. 15. ed. Max Anders. Nashville: Broadman and Hollman, 2002.

———. *Luke*. Holman New Testament Commentary, vol. 3. Nashville: Broadman & Holman Publishers, 2000.

Byrne, Ryan and Bernadette McNary-Zak, eds. *Resurrecting the brother of Jesus: The James Ossuary Controversy and the Quest for Religious Relics*. Chapel Hill: University of North Carolina Press, 2009.

C

Campbell, Joseph. *The Mythic Image*. Princeton, NJ: Princeton University Press, 1974.

Cargill, Bob. "Why the So-Called 'Jonah Ossuary' Does Not Contain the Name of Jonah." The (Retired) Blog of Robert H. Cargill, Ph.D (April 13, 2012). https://bobcargill.wordpress.com/2012/04/13/why-the-so-called-jonah-ossuary-does-not-contain-the-name-of-jonah/.

Carmichael, Calum. "Biblical Laws of Talion." *HAR* 9 (1985), 107–26.

Carr, A. *The Gospel according to St Matthew*. Cambridge Greek Testament for Schools and Colleges. Cambridge: Cambridge University Press, 1896.

Carroll, Daniel and Thomas McComiskey. *Micah*. Expositor's Bible Commentary, vol. 7. Grand Rapids: Zondervan, 1985.

Carson, Donald A. *The Gospel according to John*. The Pillar New Testament Commentary. Grand Rapids, MI: Eerdmans, 1991.

Chapman, John. "St. Hegesippus." *The Catholic Encyclopedia*, vol. 7. New York: Robert Appleton Company, 1910. http://www.newadvent.org/cathen/07194a.htm.

Charlesworth, James. *The Historical Jesus: An Essential Guide*. Nashville: Abingdon Press, 2008.

———. "The Historical Jesus: How to Ask Questions and Remain Inquisitive." *Handbook for the Study of the Historical Jesus*, vol. 1. eds. Tom Tolmén, and Stanley Porter. Leiden: Brill, 2011.

Chilton, Bruce D. "Method in a Critical Study of Jesus." *Handbook for the Study of the Historical Jesus*, vol. 1. eds. Tom Holmén and Stanley Porter. Leiden: Brill, 2011.

Christensen, Duane L. *Deuteronomy 1–21:9*. Word Biblical Commentary, vol. 6A. Rev. edition. Dallas: Thomas Nelson, 2001.

———. *Deuteronomy 21:10–34:12*. Word Biblical Commentary, vol. 6B. Dallas: Word, Inc., 2002.

Ciampa, Roy E. and Brian S. Rosner. *The First Letter to the Corinthians*. The Pillar New Testament Commentary. Grand Rapids, MI: Eerdmans, 2010.

deClaissé-Walford, Nancy, Rolf Jacobson, and Beth LaNeel Tanner. *The Book of Psalms*. New International Commentary on the Old Testament. Grand Rapids, MI: Eerdmans, 2014.

Clark, David J. and Howard A. Hatton. *A Handbook on Malachi*. United Bible Societies Handbooks. New York: United Bible Societies, 2002.

——— and Howard A. Hatton. *A Translator's Handbook on the Book of Zephaniah*. United Bible Societies Handbooks. New York: United Bible Societies, 1989.

Clarke, Paul, et al., eds. *United Bible Societies Handbooks*, 2 vols. Reading, UK: United Bible Societies, 2011.

Clendenen, E. Ray and Richard A. Taylor. *Haggai, Malachi*. New American Commentary, vol. 21A. Nashville: Broadman & Holman, 2004.

Cline, Eric. *From Eden to Exile: Unveiling the Mysteries of the Bible*. Washington, D.C.: National Geographic Societies, 2006.

Cole, R. Dennis. *Numbers*. New American Commentary, vol. 3B. Nashville: Broadman & Holman, 2000.

Cooper, Lamar Eugene. *Ezekiel*. New American Commentary, vol. 17. ed. E. Ray Clendenen. Nashville: Broadman & Holman, 1994.

Cooper, Rodney L. *Mark*. Holman New Testament Commentary, vol. 2. Nashville: Broadman & Holman, 2000.

Copan, Paul and Craig Evans. *Who Was Jesus? A Jewish–Christian Dialog*. Louisville, KY: John Knox Press, 2001.

"Cornerstone of Justice." Center for Prosecutor Integrity. http://www.prosecutorintegrity.org/innocence/cornerstone/.

Croix, Geoffrey de Ste. "Why Were the Early Christians Persecuted?" *Studies in Ancient Society*. ed. M. I. Finley. London: Routledge, Taylor & Francis, 1974.

———. "Why Were the Early Christians Persecuted?—A Rejoinder." *Past & Present* 27 (1964), 28–33.

Currid, John. *Ancient Egypt and the Old Testament*. Grand Rapids: Baker, 1997.

D

Damon, P.E. et al. "Radio carbon dating of the Shroud of Turin." *Nature* 337 (February 1989), 611–15. https://doi.org/10.1038/337611a0.

Day, John. *Yahweh and the Gods and Goddesses of Canaan*. London: Sheffield Academic Press, 2002.

Dever, Willaim. "Settlements and Chronologies." *The Hyksos: New Historical and Archaeological Perspectives*. University Museum Monograph 96/8. ed. Eliezer Oren. Philadelphia: University of Pennsylvania Museum, 1997.

"Difference between Baking Soda and Baking Powder." BYJUs.com. https://byjus.com/chemistry/difference-between-baking-soda-and-baking-powder/#:~:text=Baking%20powder%20is%20alkaline%20and,with%20an%20added%20acidic%20ingredient.

Dille, Sarah J. *Mixing Metaphors: God as Mother and Father in Deutero-Isaiah*. New York: T & T Clark, 2004.

Driver, S. R., Francis Brown, and Charles A. Briggs. *The Brown-Driver-Briggs Hebrew and English Lexicon*. Peabody, MA: Hendrickson Publishers, 2003.

Dunn, James D. G. *The Epistle to the Galatians*. Black's New Testament Commentary. London: Continuum, 1993.

———. *Jesus Remembered: Christianity in the Making*. Grand Rapids: Eerdmans, 2003.

———. *Romans 9–16*. Word Biblical Commentary, vol. 38B. Dallas: Word, Inc., 1988.

Dunne, John Anthony. "Monotheism." *The Lexham Bible Dictionary*. ed. John D. Barry, et al. Bellingham, WA: Lexham Press, 2016.

Durham, John I. *Exodus*. Word Biblical Commentary, vol. 3. Dallas: Word, Incorporated, 1987.

E

Ehrman, Bart. "Bart Ehrman on the Problem of Suffering—UCB." The Bart Ehrman Blog (February 28, 2016). https://ehrmanblog.org/bart-ehrman-on-problem-of-suffering-ucb/.

———. *Did Jesus Exist?* New York: Harper One, 2012.

———. *How Jesus Became God: The Exaltation of a Jewish Preacher from Galilee*. New York: Harper One, 2014.

Elazar, Daniel J. *Covenant and Polity in Biblical Israel*. Biblical Foundations and Jewish Expressions, vol. 1. New Brunswick: Transaction Publishers, 1995.

———. "Deuteronomy as Israel's Constitution: Some Preliminary Reflections." Jerusalem Center for Public Affairs: Daniel Elazar Papers Index. http://www.jcpa.org/dje/articles2/deut-const.htm.

———. "Government in Biblical Israel." *Tradition*: A Journal of Orthodox Jewish Thought 13/14 (Spring–Summer) 1973.

Ellington, John and René Péter-Contesse. *A Handbook on the Book of Daniel*. United Bible Societies Handbooks. New York: United Bible Societies, 1994.

——— and Roger L. Omanson. *A Handbook on 1–2 Chronicles*. United Bible Societies Handbooks, vols. 1–2. eds. Paul Clarke, et al. Miami, FL: United Bible Societies, 2014.

——— and René Péter-Contesse. *A Handbook on Leviticus*. United Bible Societies Handbooks. New York: United Bible Societies, 1992.

Ellingworth, Paul and Eugene Albert Nida. *A Handbook on Paul's Letters to the Thessalonians*. United Bible Societies Handbooks. New York: United Bible Societies, 1976.

Elliott, John H. *1 Peter: A New Translation with Introduction and Commentary*. Anchor Yale Bible, vol. 37B. New Haven: Yale University Press, 2008.

Estes, Daniel J. *Psalms 73–150*. New American Commentary, vol. 13. ed. E. Ray. Clendenen. Nashville: B & H Publishing, 2019.

d'Étaples, Jacques Lefèvre. *Psalms 73–150: Old Testament: Explanatory Notes*. Reformation Commentary on Scripture, vol. VIII. eds. Herman J. Selderhuis and Timothy George. Downers Grove, IL: IVP Academic, 2018.

Exell, Joseph S. *The Biblical Illustrator: Acts*. Oak Harbor, WA: Logos Research Systems, 1997.

———. *The Biblical Illustrator: Romans*, vol. 1. New York: Fleming H. Revell Company, 1900.

Evans, Craig A. *The Bible Knowledge Background Commentary: Matthew–Luke*. 1st edition. ed. Craig A. Evans and Craig A. Bubeck. Colorado Springs, CO: David C. Cook, 2003.

———. *Jesus and His Contemporaries: Comparative Studies*. Arbeiten Zur Geschichte Des Antiken Judentums Und Des Urchristentums 25. Leiden: Brill, 2001.

———. *Mark 8:27–16:20*. Word Biblical Commentary, vol. 34B. Dallas: Word Inc., 2001.

——— and Paul Copan. *Who Was Jesus? A Jewish-Christian Dialog*. Louisville, KY: John Knox Press, 2001.

F

Fausset, Andrew R., David Brown, and Robert Jamieson. *A Commentary, Critical, Experimental, and Practical, on the Old and New Testaments: Acts–Revelation*, vol. VI. London: William Collins, Sons, 1866.

———, David Brown, and Robert Jamieson. *A Commentary, Critical, Experimental, and Practical, on the Old and New Testaments: Genesis–Deuteronomy*, vol. I. London: William Collins, Sons, 1866.

———. *A Commentary, Critical, Experimental, and Practical, on the Old and New Testaments: Jeremiah–Malachi*, vol. IV. London: William Collins, Sons, 1866.

———. *A Commentary, Critical, Experimental, and Practical, on the Old and New Testaments: Job–Isaiah*, vol. III. London: William Collins, Sons, 1866.

———, David Brown, and Robert Jamieson. *A Commentary, Critical, Experimental, and Practical, on the Old and New Testaments: Matthew–John*, vol. V. London: William Collins, Sons, 1866.

———, Robert Jamieson, and David Brown. *Jamieson, Fausset, and Brown's Commentary*. Grand Rapids, MI: Zondervan, 1961.

Fein, Sylvia. *Die Beziehungen der Kaiser Trajan und Hadrian zu den litterati*. Leipzig: Teubner Stuttart, 1994.

Feldman, Howard, Amnon Rosenfeld, Wolfgang Krumbein, and Carl von Ossietzky. "Archaeometric Analysis of the James Ossuary." Proceedings from 2008 Joint Meeting of The Geological Society of America, Soil Science Society of America, American Society of Agronomy, Crop Science Society of America. Gulf Coast Association of Geological Societies with the Gulf Coast Section of SEPM in GSAAP 40/6.

———, Ammon Rosenfeld, and Wolfgang E. Krumbein. "The Authenticity of the James Ossuary." *OJG* 4 (March 12, 2014), 69–78. DOI: 10.4236/ojg.2014.43007.

Ferguson, Everett. *Backgrounds of Early Christianity*. 2nd edition. Grand Rapids: Eerdmans, 1993.

Fitzmyer, Joseph A. *Romans: A New Translation with Introduction and Commentary*. Anchor Yale Bible, vol. 33. New Haven: Yale University Press, 2008.

Fox, Alex. "Archaeologists Identify Traces of Burnt Cannabis in Ancient Jewish Shrine." *Smithsonian* (June 4, 2020). https://www.smithsonianmag.com/smart-news/cannabis-found-altar-ancient-israeli-shrine-180975016/.

Fredriksen, Paula. *Jesus of Nazareth King of the Jews*. New York: Knopf, 1999.

Freedman, David Noel. *The Nine Commandments*. New York: Doubleday, 2000.

——— and Francis I. Andersen. *Micah: A New Translation with Introduction and Commentary*. Anchor Yale Bible, vol. 24E. New Haven: Yale University Press, 2008.

Freke, Timothy and Peter Gandy. *The Jesus Mysteries*. New York: Three Rivers Press, 1999.

Friedman, Richard Elliot. *Commentary on the Torah.* New York: Harper One, 2003.

———. *The Exodus.* New York: Harper–Collins, 2017.

Fritz, Volkmar. *1 & 2 Kings.* Continental Commentary. Minneapolis, MN: Fortress Press, 2003.

Fruchtenbaum, Arnold G. *The Messianic Bible Study Collection*, vol. 180. Tustin, CA: Ariel Ministries, 1983.

Fry, Euan McGregor and William David Reyburn. *A Handbook on Genesis.* United Bible Societies Handbooks. New York: United Bible Societies, 1998.

——— and William David Reyburn. *A Handbook on Proverbs.* United Bible Societies Handbooks. New York: United Bible Societies, 2000.

Fuchs, Camil. "Demography, Literacy and Names Distribution in Ancient Jerusalem: How many James/Jacob son of Joseph, brother of Jesus were there?" *The Polish Journal of Biblical Research* 4/1 (2005), 3–30.

Fuller, R. H. *The Foundations of New Testament Christology.* London: Lutterworth Press, 1965.

Funk, Robert Walter, Ernst Haenchen, and Ulrich Busse. *John: A Commentary on the Gospel of John.* Hermeneia. Philadelphia: Fortress Press, 1984.

G

Gandy, Peter and Timothy Freke. *The Jesus Mysteries.* New York: Three Rivers Press, 1999.

Gangel, Kenneth O. *John.* Holman New Testament Commentary, vol. 4. Nashville: Broadman & Holman, 2000.

Garber, Paul L. and Roland K. Harrison. "Idol." *International Standard Bible Encyclopedia*, vol. 2. Grand Rapids, MI: Eerdmans, 1979–1988, 794–97.

Garlaschelli, Luigi and Matteo Borrini. "A BPA Approach to the Shroud of Turin." *JFS* 64/1 (July 10, 2018), 137–43. https://doi.org/10.1111/1556-4029.13867.

Garrett, Duane A. *Hosea, Joel.* New American Commentary, vol. 19A. Nashville: Broadman & Holman, 1997.

———. *Proverbs, Ecclesiastes, Song of Songs.* New American Commentary, vol. 14. Nashville: Broadman & Holman, 1993.

Geisler, Norman and Joseph Holden. *The Popular Handbook of Archaeology and the Bible: Discoveries that Confirm the Reliability of Scripture.* Eugene, OR: Harvest House, 2013.

George, Timothy. *Galatians.* New American Commentary, vol. 30. Nashville: Broadman & Holman, 1994.

Gibson, Shimon and Amos Kloner. "The Talpiot Tomb Reconsidered: The Archaeological Facts." *Tomb of Jesus and His Family? Exploring Ancient Jewish Tombs Near Jerusalem's Walls: The Fourth Princeton Symposium on Judaism and Christian Origins.* ed. James Charlesworth. Grand Rapids: Eerdmans, 2013.

"Gilgamesh part 3: Crossing the Waters of Death." MythicMojo.com. https://mythicmojo.com/gilgamesh-part-3-crossing-the-waters-of-death/.

"Global Christianity – A Report on the Size and Distribution of the World's Christian Population." PewResearch.org (December 19, 2011). https://www.pewforum.org/2011/12/19/global-christianity-exec/.

Goldingay, John. *The Book of Jeremiah.* New International Commentary on the Old Testament. eds. E. J. Young, et al. Grand Rapids: Eerdmans, 2021.

———. *Daniel.* Word Bible Commentary, vol. 30. Rev. edition. ed. Nancy L. deClaissé-Walford. Grand Rapids, MI: Zondervan Academic, 2019.

Gonen, Rivka. "The Late Bronze Age." *The Archaeology of Ancient Israel.* trans. R. Greenberg. ed. Amnon Ben-Tor. New Haven, CT: Yale University Press, 1992.

Gordon, Nehemia. "Hebrew Voices #132—Boiling a Kid in its Mother's Milk." Nehemia's Wall (Aug 18, 2021). https://www.nehemiaswall.com/boiling-a-kid-in-its-mothers-milk, 29 min. mark.

Goren, Yuval and Neil Asher Silberman. "Faking Biblical History: How Wishful Thinking and Technology Fooled Some Scholars—and Made Fools Out of Others." *Archaeology* 56/5 (September–October 2003), 20–29.

Graham, Wyatt. "Does the Mosaic Law Still Apply to Christians?" The Gospel Coalition (February 9, 2021). https://ca.thegospelcoalition.org/columns/detrinitate/does-the-mosaic-law-still-apply-to-christians/.

Graves, David E. *The Archaeology of the New Testament*. Moncton, New Brunswick, CAN: Electronic Christian Media, 2019.

Green, Albert. *The Storm-God in the Ancient Near East, Biblical*. Judaic Studies 8. Winona Lake: Eisenbrauns, 2003.

Green, Anthony and Jeremy Black. *Gods Demons and Symbols of Ancient Mesopotamia*. Austin: University of Texas, 1992.

Green, Joel B. "Family, Friends, and Foes." *Handbook for the Study of the Historical Jesus*, (vol. 3). eds. Tom Tolmén, and Stanley Porter. Leiden: Brill, 2011, 2433–54.

Greenberg, Moshe. *Ezekiel 1–20: A New Translation with Introduction and Commentary*. Anchor Yale Bible, vol. 22. New Haven: Yale University Press, 2008.

Greene, J. A. Patricia Smith, G. Avishai, and L.E. Stager. "Aging Cremated Infants: The Problem of Sacrifice at the Tophet of Carthage." *Atinquity* 85/329 (2011), 859–74.

Gregory, Brad S. *The Unintended Reformation: How a Religious Revolution Secularized Society*. Cambridge: Harvard University Press, 2012.

Groothuis, Douglas. "The Biblical View of Truth Challenges Postmodernist Truth Decay." *Themelios* 26/1 (2000), 11–33.

Gruen, Erich. "Christians as a 'Third Race.'" *Christianity in the Second Century: Themes and Developments*. eds. James and Judith Lieu. Cambridge: Cambridge University Press, 2018.

Gurtner, Daniel M. "Romans." *The Bible Knowledge Background Commentary: Acts–Philemon*. 1st edition. ed. Craig A. Evans and Craig A. Bubeck. Colorado Springs, CO: David C. Cook, 2004.

H

Habel, Norman. "Yahweh, Maker of Heaven and Earth:" A Study in Tradition Criticism." *Journal of Biblical Literature* 91/3 (September 1972), 321–37.

Hagner, Donald A. *Matthew 1–13*. Word Biblical Commentary, vol. 33A. Dallas: Word, Inc., 1993.

Haenchen, Ernst, Robert Walter Funk, and Ulrich Busse. *John: A Commentary on the Gospel of John*. Hermeneia. Philadelphia: Fortress Press, 1984.

Hamilton Jr., James M. *Psalms*, vol. 2. Evangelical Biblical Theology Commentary. eds. T. Desmond Alexander, Thomas R. Schreiner, and Andreas J. Köstenberger. Bellingham, WA: Lexham Academic, 2021.

Hansen, G. Walter. *Galatians*. The IVP New Testament Commentary Series. Downers Grove, IL: InterVarsity Press, 1994.

Harmon, Matthew S. *Galatians*. Evangelical Biblical Theology Commentary. eds. T. Desmond Alexander, Thomas R. Schreiner, and Andreas J. Köstenberger. Bellingham, WA: Lexham Academic, 2021.

Harris, R. Laird, Gleason Archer, Jr. and Bruce Waltke, eds. *Theological Wordbook of the Old Testament*, 2 vols. Chicago: Moody Bible Institute, 1980.

Harris, Murray J. *John, Exegetical Guide to the Greek New Testament*. Nashville: B & H Academic, 2015.

Harrison, Roland K. and Paul L. Garber. "Idol." *International Standard Bible Encyclopedia*, vol. 2. Grand Rapids, MI: Eerdmans, 1979–1988, 794–97.

Hastings, James and John Selbie. *Encyclopedia of Religion and Ethics*, vol. 10. Whitefish, MT: Kessinger, 1908.

Hatton, Howard A. and David J. Clark. *A Handbook on Malachi*. United Bible Societies Handbooks. New York: United Bible Societies, 2002.

——— and David J. Clark. *A Translator's Handbook on the Book of Zephaniah*. United Bible Societies Handbooks. New York: United Bible Societies, 1989.

Henderson, E. *The Book of the Twelve Minor Prophets: Commentary*. London: Hamilton, Adams, 1845.

Hertz, Joseph H. *Pentateuch & Halftorahs*. London: Soncino, 1997.

Hillers, Delbert R. *Micah: A Commentary on the Book of the Prophet Micah*. Hermeneia. eds. Paul D. Hanson and Loren R. Fisher. Philadelphia: Fortress Press, 1984.

Hoehner, H. W. "Herod." *International Standard Bible Encyclopedia*, vol. 2. Grand Rapids, MI: Eerdmans, 1979–1988, 688–98.

Hoffmeier, James. *Israel in Egypt*. New York: Oxford University Press, 1996.

Hoffner, Harry. "Symbols for Masculinity and Femininity: Their Use in Ancient near Eastern Sympathetic Magic Rituals." *SBL* 85/3 (September 1966), 326–34.

Holden, Joseph and Norman Geisler. *The Popular Handbook of Archaeology and the Bible: Discoveries that Confirm the Reliability of Scripture*. Eugene, OR: Harvest House, 2013.

Holladay, William. *A Concise Hebrew and Aramaic Lexicon of the Old Testament*. Grand Rapids, MI: Eerdmans; Leiden: Brill, 1988.

———. *Jeremiah 1*. Hermeneia. ed. Paul D. Hanson. Philadelphia, Fortress Press, 1986.

Holmén, Tom and Stanley Porter, eds. *Handbook for the Study of the Historical Jesus*, 4 vols. Leiden: Brill, 2011.

Hooker, Morna D. *The Gospel according to Saint Mark*. Black's New Testament Commentary. London: Continuum, 1991.

Hornung, Erik. *Conceptions of God in Ancient Egypt*. trans. John Baines. Ithaca, NY: Cornell University Press, 1982.

Horrell, David. *Becoming Christian: Essays on 1 Peter and the Making of Christian Identity*. Library of New Testament Studies. New York: Bloomsbury T&T Clark, 2013.

Howard, David M., Jr. *Joshua*. New American Commentary, vol. 5. Nashville: Broadman & Holman, 1998.

Huey, F. B. *Jeremiah, Lamentations*. New American Commentary, vol. 16. Nashville: Broadman & Holman, 1993.

Huijgen, Arnold. "Alone Together: Sola Scriptura and the Other Solas of the Reformation." *Sola Scriptura: Biblical and Theological Perspectives on Scripture, Authority, and Hermeneutics*. eds. Hans Burger, et al. Liden: Brill, 2018.

Huizen, Jennifer. "What is Gaslighting?" Medical News Today (November 30, 2023). https://www.medicalnewstoday.com/articles/gaslighting#how-it-works.

Hutchinson, Robert. *Searching for Jesus: New Discoveries in the Quest for Jesus of Nazareth–and How They Confirm the Gospel Accounts*. Nashville: Nelson Books, 2015.

J

Jackson, Wayne. "Is the Law of Moses Torah Still Binding?" The Christian Currier. https://christiancourier.com/articles/is-the-law-of-moses-torah-still-binding.

Jacobovici, Simcha and James Tabor. *The Jesus Discovery*. New York: Simon and Schuster, 2012.

——— and Charles Pellegrina. *The Jesus Family Tomb: The Discovery That Will Change History Forever*. New York: Harper Element, 2008.

Jacobs, Mignon R. *Books of Haggai and Malachi*. New International Commentary on the Old Testament. ed. Robert Hubbard, Jr. Grand. Rapids, MI: Eerdmans, 2017.

Jacobson, Rolf, Beth LaNeel Tanner, and Nancy deClaissé-Walford. *The Book of Psalms*. New International Commentary on the Old Testament. Grand Rapids, MI: Eerdmans, 2014.

Jamieson, Robert, David Brown, and A. R. Fausset. *A Commentary, Critical, Experimental, and Practical, on the Old and New Testaments: Acts–Revelation*, vol. VI. London: William Collins, Sons, 1866.

———, David Brown, and A. R. Fausset. *A Commentary, Critical, Experimental, and Practical, on the Old and New Testaments: Genesis–Deuteronomy*, vol. I. London: William Collins, Sons, 1866.

———, David Brown, Andrew Fausset. *A Commentary, Critical, Experimental, and Practical, on the Old and New Testaments: Matthew–John*, vol. V. London: William Collins, Sons, 1866.

———, Andrew R. Fausset, and David Brown. *Jamieson, Fausset, and Brown's Commentary*. Grand Rapids, MI: Zondervan, 1961.

Jung, Kurt G. "Baal." *International Standard Bible Encyclopedia*, vol. 1. Grand Rapids, MI: Eerdmans, 1979–1988, 377–79.

K

Kaiser, Walter C., Jr. and Tiberius Rata. *Walking the Ancient Paths*. Bellingham, WA: Lexham Press, 2019.

Kalisch, M. M. *A Historical and Critical Commentary on the Old Testament: Exodus*. London: Longman, Brown, Green, and Longmans, 1855.

Karenga, Maulana. *Maat, the Moral Ideal in Ancient Egypt: A Study in Classical African Ethics*. New York: Routledge, 2004.

Kaufman, Lilly. "Judge Justly, Four Ways." JTSA.edu (July 28, 2017). http://www.jtsa.edu/judge-justly-four-ways.

Keel, Othmar and Christopher Uehlinger. *Gods, Goddesses, and Images of God*. trans. Thomas Trapp. Minneapolis, MN: Fortress Press, 1998.

Keele, Brad and Megan Bishop Moore. *Biblical History and Israel's Past*. Grand Rapids: Eerdmans, 2011.

Keener, Craig S. *Matthew*. The IVP New Testament Commentary Series, vol. 1. Downers Grove, IL: InterVarsity Press, 1997.

Kellum, L. Scott. *Acts: Exegetical Guide to the Greek New Testament*. eds. Andreas J. Köstenberger and Robert W. Yarbrough. Nashville: B & H Academic, 2020.

———, Andreas J. Kostenberger, and Charles L. Quarles. *The Cradle, the Cross, and the Crown: An Introduction to the New Testament*. Nashville: B & H Academic, 2009.

Kempinski, Aharon. "The Middle Bronze Age." *The Archaeology of Ancient Israel*. trans. R. Greenberg. ed. Amnon Ben-Tor. New Haven, CT: Yale University Press, 1992.

Keown, Gerald, Pamela Schalise, and Thomas Smothers. *Jeremiah 26–52*. Word Biblical Commentary, vol. 27. eds David Hubbard, et al. Grand Rapids, MI: Zondervan, 1995.

Keown, Mark J. *Discovering the New Testament: An Introduction to Its Background, Theology, and Themes*. General Letters & Revelation, vol. III. Bellingham, WA: Lexham Press, 2022.

Kloner, Amos. "Tomb with Inscribed Ossuaries." *A Catalogue of Jewish Ossuaries in the Collections of the State of Israel*, 17–21, Jerusalem." *Atiqot* 29 (1996).

——— and Shimon Gibson. "The Talpiot Tomb Reconsidered: The Archaeological Facts." *Tomb of Jesus and His Family? Exploring Ancient Jewish Tombs Near Jerusalem's Walls: The Fourth Princeton*

Symposium on Judaism and Christian Origin. ed. James Charlesworth. Grand Rapids: Eerdmans, 2013.

Koehler, Ludwig and Walter Baumgartner. *The Hebrew and Aramaic Lexicon of the Old Testament*, 2 vols. Rev. edition. eds. Johann Stamm, Mervyn E. J. Richardson, et al. Leiden: Brill, 2001.

Koester, Craig R. *Hebrews: A New Translation with Introduction and Commentary*. Anchor Yale Bible, vol. 36. New Haven: Yale University Press, 2008.

Konvitz, Milton. *Torah and Constitution: Essays in American Jewish Thought*. Modern Jewish History. ed. Henry L. Feingold. New York: Syracuse University Press, 1988.

Koole, Jan L. *Isaiah III: Isaiah 49–55*, vol. 2. Historical Commentary of the Old Testament. trans. Anthony Runia, eds. Cornelis Houtman, et. al. Leuven, Belgium: Peeters, 1998.

Köstenberger, Andreas J. *1–2 Timothy & Titus*. Evangelical Biblical Theology Commentary. eds. T. Desmond Alexander, Thomas R. Schreiner, and Andreas J. Köstenberger. Bellingham, WA: Lexham Press, 2021.

———, L. Scott Kellum, and Charles L. Quarles. *The Cradle, the Cross, and the Crown: An Introduction to the New Testament*. Nashville: B & H Academic, 2009.

——— and Scott R. Swain. *Father, Son and Spirit: The Trinity and John's Gospel*. New Studies in Biblical Theology, vol. 24. ed. D. A. Carson. Downers Grove, IL: InterVarsity Press, 2008.

Kraus, Hans-Joachim. *Psalms 1–59*. Continental Commentary. Minneapolis, MN: Fortress Press, 1993.

———. *Psalms 60–150*. Continental Commentary. Minneapolis, MN: Fortress Press, 1993.

Kruidenier, William and Kenneth Boa. *Romans*. Holman New Testament Commentary, vol. 6. Nashville: Broadman & Holman, 2000.

Krumbein, Wolfgang E., Howard Feldman, Amnon Rosenfeld, and Carl von Ossietzky. "Archaeometric Analysis of the James Ossuary." Proceedings from 2008 Joint Meeting of The Geological Society of America, Soil Science Society of America, American Society of Agronomy, Crop Science Society of America. Gulf Coast Association of Geological Societies with the Gulf Coast Section of SEPM in GSAAP 40/6.

———, Howard R. Feldman, and Amnon Rosenfeld. "The Authenticity of the James Ossuary." *OJG* 4 (March 12, 2014), 69–78. DOI: 10.4236/ojg.2014.43007.

———. "Preliminary Report: External Expert Opinion on Three Stone Items." University of Oldenburg, Germany (September 2005), 313–21.

Kruse, Colin G. *The Letters of John*. The Pillar New Testament Commentary. ed. D. A. Carson. Grand Rapids, MI: Eerdmans, 2000.

———. *Paul's Letter to the Romans*. The Pillar New Testament Commentary. ed. D. A. Carson. Grand Rapids, MI: Eerdmans, 2012.

Kuyper, Lester. "Israel and Her Neighbors." *Reformed Review* 10/3 (1957), 11–20. https://repository.westernsem.edu/pkp/index.php/rr/article/view/72.

L

Lalleman, Hetty. *Jeremiah and Lamentations*. Tyndale Old Testament Commentaries, vol. 21. eds. David G. Firth, et al. Downers Grove, IL: InterVarsity Press, 2013.

Laws, Sophie. *The Epistle of James*. Black's New Testament Commentary. London: Continuum, 1980.

Lemaire, André. "Burial Box of James the Brother of Jesus." *BAR* 28/6 (November/December 2002), 24–33.

Lewis, Jack P. *The Minor Prophets*. Grand Rapids: Baker, 1966.

Liddell, Henry George and Robert Scott. *Liddell and Scott's Greek–English Lexicon*. ed. Henry Stuart Jones. Oxford: Simon Wallenberg Press, 2007.

Logan, Phil. "Bloodguilt." *Holman Illustrated Bible Dictionary*. eds. Chad Brand, et al. Nashville: Holman Bible Publishers, 2003.

Lührmann, Dieter. *Galatians*. Continental Commentary. Minneapolis, MN: Fortress Press, 1992.

Lundbom, Jack R. *Jeremiah 1–20: A New Translation with Introduction and Commentary*. Anchor Yale Bible, vol. 21A. New Haven: Yale University Press, 2008.

M

MacArthur, John. "What Does 'Sola Scriptura' Mean?" Ligonier.org (Aug 27, 2021). https://www.ligonier.org/learn/articles/what-does-sola-scriptura-mean.

Mackay, John L. *Jeremiah: Chapters 1–20*, vol. 1. Fearn, Scotland: Christian Focus Publications, 2004.

Magness, Jodi. "Ossuaries and the Burials of Jesus and James." *JBL* 124/1 (Spring 2005), 121–54.

Maier, Paul L. "The James Ossuary." *The Lutheran Witness* (January 2003). https://www.issuesetcarchive.org/articles/bissar95.htm.

Mann, Jim. "Even the Bible Points to the Idea of Innocent Until Proven Guilty." DrJimMann.com (October 4, 2018). https://drjimmann.com/2018/10/04/bible-even-points-to-idea-of-innocent-until-proven-guilty/.

Manser, Martin H. *Dictionary of Bible Themes: The Accessible and Comprehensive Tool for Topical Studies*. London: Martin Manser, 2009, Kindle.

Mark, Joshua J. "Code of Ur–Nammu." WorldHistory.org (Oct 26, 2021). https://www.worldhistory.org/Code_of_Ur-Nammu/.

———. "The Egyptian Afterlife & the Feather of Truth." World History Encyclopedia Online (March 30, 2018). https://www.worldhistory.org/article/42/the-egyptian-afterlife--the-feather-of-truth/.

Martin, D. Michael. *1, 2 Thessalonians*. New American Commentary, vol. 33. Nashville: Broadman & Holman, 1995.

Martyn, J. Louis. *Galatians: A New Translation with Introduction and Commentary*. Anchor Yale Bible, vol. 33A. New Haven: Yale University Press.

Mason, Steve. *Josephus and the New Testament*. Grand Rapids: Baker Academic, 2003.

———. "Commentary," in Falavius Josephus, *Judean War* 2, vol. 1b. Leiden: Brill, 2008.

Matthews, Isaac George. *Ezekiel: Commentary*. American Commentary on the Old Testament. Philadelphia: The American Baptist Publication Society, 1939.

Mathews, Kenneth A. *Genesis 11:27–50:26*. New American Commentary, vol. 1B. Nashville: Broadman & Holman, 2005.

McCarthy, Dennis. *Institution and Narrative: Collected Essays*. Rome: Biblical Institute Press, 1985.

McCarthy, Nichole, et al. "Preponderance of the Evidence." Legal Information Institute. Cornell.edu (March 2022). https://www.law.cornell.edu/wex/preponderance_of_the_evidence.

McComiskey, Thomas and Daniel Carroll. *Hosea, Amos, Micah*. Expositor's Bible Commentary, vol. 7. Grand Rapids: Zondervan, 2017.

McDonald, Lee Martin. "1 Corinthians." *The Bible Knowledge Background Commentary: Acts–Philemon*. 1st edition. eds. Craig A. Evans and Craig A. Bubeck. Colorado Springs, CO: David C. Cook, 2004.

McGiffert, Arthur Cushman. *Nicene and Post-Nicene Fathers, Second Series*, vol. 1. eds. Philip Schaff and Henry Wace. Buffalo, NY: Christian Literature Publishing, 1890. Revised and edited for New Advent by Kevin Knight. http://www.newadvent.org/fathers/250104.htm.

McKenna, David and Lloyd J. Ogilvie. *Isaiah 1–39*. The Preacher's Commentary Series, vol. 17. Nashville: Thomas Nelson, 1993.

McKnight, Edgar. *Jesus Christ in History and Scripture*. Macon, GA: Mercer University Press, 1999.

McNary–Zak, Bernadette and Ryan Byrne, eds. *Resurrecting the Brother of Jesus: The James Ossuary Controversy and the Quest for Religious Relics*. Chapel Hill: University of North Carolina Press, 2009.

Meier, John. *The Marginal Jew: Rethinking the Historical Jesus: The Roots of the Problem and the Person*. Anchor Yale Bible Reference Library, vol. 1. ed. David Noel Freedman. New York: Doubleday, 1991.

Melanchthon, Philip. *1–2 Samuel, 1–2 Kings, 1–2 Chronicles: Old Testament*. Reformation Commentary on Scripture, vol. V. eds. Derek Cooper, Martin J. Lohrmann, et al. Downers Grove, IL: IVP Academic, 2016.

Mendenhall, George. *The Bible and the Ancient Near East: Essays in Honor of William Foxwell Albright*. ed. George Earnest Wright. Garden City, NY: Anchor Books, 1965.

———. *Ancient Israel's Faith and History*. Louisville, KY: John Knox, 2001.

Merrill, Eugene H. *Deuteronomy*. New American Commentary, vol. 4. Nashville: Broadman & Holman, 1994.

Meshel, Ze'ev. *Kuntillet 'Ajrud Horvat Teman: An Iron Age II Religious Site on the Judah–Sinai Border*. ed. Liora Freud. Jerusalem: Israel Exploration Society, 2012.

Milligan, George, ed. *St. Paul's Epistles to the Thessalonians. Classic Commentaries on the Greek New Testament*. London: Macmillan, 1908.

Milgrom, Jacob. *Leviticus*. Continental Commentary. Minneapolis, MN: Fortress, 2004.

———. *Studies in Levitical Terminology, I: The Encroacher and the Levite the Term 'Aboda*. Eugene, OR: Wipf & Stock, 1970.

———. "You Shall Not Boil a Kid in Its Mother's Milk." New2Torah.com (Nov 5, 2015). https://new2torah.com/PDF/Milk%20and%20Meat%20-%20Milgrom.pdf.

Miller, Stephen R. *Daniel*. New American Commentary, vol. 18. Nashville: Broadman & Holman, 1994.

Milne, Bruce. *The Message of John: Here Is Your King!: With Study Guide*. The Bible Speaks Today. Downers Grove, IL: InterVarsity Press, 1993.

Moo, Douglas J. *The Letter of James*. The Pillar New Testament Commentary. Grand Rapids, MI: Eerdmans, 2000.

Moore, Megan Bishop and Brad Keele. *Biblical History and Israel's Past*. Grand Rapids: Eerdmans, 2011.

Moreland, J. P. op cit. in Douglas Groothuis. "The Biblical View of Truth Challenges Postmodernist Truth Decay." *Themelios* 26/1 (2000), 11–33.

Morris, Leon. *The Epistle to the Romans*. The Pillar New Testament Commentary. Grand Rapids, MI: Eerdmans, 1988.

Motyer, J. Alec. *Isaiah*. Tyndale Old Testament Commentaries, vol. 20. ed. Donald Wiseman. Downers Grove, IL: InterVarsity Press, 1999.

Moule, Handley C. G. *The Epistle of Paul the Apostle to the Romans, with Introduction and Notes*. The Cambridge Bible for Schools and Colleges. Cambridge: Cambridge University Press, 1891.

Mounce, Robert H. *Romans*. New American Commentary, vol. 27. Nashville: Broadman & Holman, 1995.

Moyise, Steve. "Jesus and the Scriptures of Israel." *Handbook for the Study of the Historical Jesus*, vol. 2. eds. Tom Tolmén, and Stanley Porter. Leiden: Brill, 2011, 1137–67.

Murphy, Rowland E. *Proverbs*. Word Biblical Commentary, vol. 22. Dallas: Thomas Nelson, 1998.

N

Namdar, Dvory, Eran Arie, Baruch Rosen. "Cannabis and Frankincense at the Judahite Shrine of Arad." *Tel Aviv* 1/47 (May 28, 2020), 5–28. DOI: 10.1080/03344355.2020.1732046.

Nedungatt, George. "The Law of Talion an Ancient Law of Jurisprudence." *Iustitia* 4 (2013), 279–98.

Nelson, Eric. *The Hebrew Republic: Jewish Sources and the Transformation of European Political Thought.* Cambridge: Harvard University Press, 2010.

Newman, Barclay M., Jr. and Philip C. Stine. *A Handbook on Jeremiah.* United Bible Societies Handbooks. New York: United Bible Societies, 2003.

——— and Eugene Albert Nida. *A Handbook on the Gospel of John.* United Bible Societies Handbooks. New York: United Bible Societies, 1993.

——— and Philip C. Stine. *A Handbook on the Gospel of Matthew.* United Bible Societies Handbooks. New York: United Bible Societies, 1992.

——— and Eugene Albert Nida. *A Handbook on Paul's Letter to the Romans.* United Bible Societies Handbooks. New York: United Bible Societies, 1973.

Newman, Carey C. "God." *Dictionary of the Later New Testament and Its Developments.* eds. Ralph P. Martin and Peter H. Davids. Downers Grove, IL: InterVarsity Press, 1997.

Nida, Eugene Albert and Barclay M. Newman. *A Handbook on the Gospel of John.* United Bible Societies Handbooks. New York: United Bible Societies, 1993.

——— and Robert G. Bratcher. *A Handbook on the Gospel of Mark.* United Bible Societies Handbooks. New York: United Bible Societies, 1993.

——— and Barclay M. Newman. *A Handbook on Paul's Letter to the Romans.* United Bible Societies Handbooks. New York: United Bible Societies, 1973.

——— and Paul Ellingworth. *A Handbook on Paul's Letters to the Thessalonians.* United Bible Societies Handbooks. New York: United Bible Societies, 1976.

Nola, Robert and Howard Sankey. *Theories of Scientific Method.* Montreal: McGill-Queen's University Press, 2007.

Nolland, John. *The Gospel of Matthew: A Commentary on the Greek Text.* New International Greek Testament Commentary. Grand Rapids, MI: Eerdmans, 2005.

———. *Luke 9:21–18:34.* Word Biblical Commentary, vol. 35B. Dallas: Word, Inc., 1993.

Noss, Philip A. and Kenneth J. Thomas. *A Handbook on Ezra and Nehemiah.* United Bible Societies Handbooks. eds. Paul Clarke, et al. New York: United Bible Societies, 2005.

O

Ogden, Graham S. and Jan Sterk. *A Handbook on Isaiah*, vol. 1–2. United Bible Societies Handbooks. eds. Paul Clarke, et al. Reading, UK: United Bible Societies, 2011.

Ogilvie, Lloyd J. and David McKenna. *Isaiah 1–39.* The Preacher's Commentary Series, vol. 17. Nashville: Thomas Nelson, 1993.

Olson, Ken. "Eusebius and the 'Testimonium Flavianum.'" *CBQ* 61/2 (April 1999), 305–22.

———. "A Eusebian Reading of the Testimonium Flavianum." *Eusebius of Caesarea: Tradition and Innovations.* Center for Hellenistic Studies. eds. Aaron Johnson and Jeremy Shott. Trustees for Harvard University, Washington, D.C. Cambridge: Harvard University Press, 2013. https://www.academia.edu/4062154/Olson_A_Eusebian_Reading_of_the_Testimonium_Flavianum_2013.

Omanson, Roger L. and John E. Ellington. *A Handbook on 1–2 Chronicles*, vol. 1–2. United Bible Societies Handbooks. eds. Paul Clarke, et al. Miami, FL: United Bible Societies, 2014.

Onstott, Jodell. *YHWH Exists*, vol. 1. Baton Rouge, LA: Emmanuel Academic Publishing, 2015.

———. "YHWH Exists, vol. 1, Chart 9.37: Judah, Israel, Assyria Synchronistic Chronology." Academia.edu. https://www.academia.edu/96075137/YHWH_Exists_vol_1_Chart_9_37_Judah_Israel_Assyria_Synchronistic_Chronology_UPDATED_.

———. "The Prophetic Code in Leviticus 26 and Deuteronomy 28." Academia.edu. https://www.academia.edu/100601649/YHWH_EXISTS_vol_1_The_Prophetic_Code_Leviticus_26_and_Deuteronomy.

Opperwall, Nola J. "Fugitive." *The International Standard Bible Encyclopedia*, vol. 2. Rev. edition. ed. Geoffrey W. Bromiley. Grand Rapids: Eerdmans, 1979–1988, 366.

———. "Profane." *The International Standard Bible Encyclopedia*, vol. 3. Revised. ed. Geoffrey W. Bromiley. Grand Rapids: Eerdmans, 1979–1988, 979–80.

Osborne, Grant R. *Luke: Verse by Verse*. New Testament Commentaries. eds. Jeffrey Reimer, et al. Bellingham, WA: Lexham Press, 2018.

———. *Romans*. The IVP New Testament Commentary Series. Downers Grove, IL: InterVarsity Press, 2004.

von Ossietzky, Carl, Wolfgang E. Krumbein, Howard Feldman, and Amnon Rosenfeld. "Archaeometric Analysis of the James Ossuary." Proceedings from 2008 Joint Meeting of The Geological Society of America, Soil Science Society of America, American Society of Agronomy, Crop Science Society of America. Gulf Coast Association of Geological Societies with the Gulf Coast Section of SEPM in GSAAP 40/6.

Oswalt, John. *The Book of Isaiah Chapters 40–66*. New International Commentary on the Old Testament. eds. R. K. Harrison and Robert Hubbard. Grand Rapids, MI: Eerdmans, 1998.

P

Pakula, Martin. *Numbers: Homeward Bound*. Reading the Bible Today Series. ed. Paul Barnett. Sydney, South NSW: Aquila Press, 2006.

Pearce, J.W.E. "Introduction and Notes" to Cornelius Tacitus, *The Agricola of Tacitus*. London: George Bell, 1901.

Pearson, Jordan. "Salvation through the Church." *Blackfriars* 20/234 (September 1939), 686–93.

Pedley, John. *Sanctuaries and the Sacred in the Ancient Greek World*. New York: Cambridge University Press, 2006.

Pellegrina, Charles and Simcha Jacobovici. *The Jesus Family Tomb: The Discovery That Will Change History Forever*. New York: Harper Element, 2008.

Pentecost, J. Dwight. "Daniel." *The Bible Knowledge Commentary: An Exposition of the Scriptures*, vol. 1. eds. J. F. Walvoord and R. B. Zuck. Wheaton, IL: Victor Books, 1985.

Perowne, J. J. Stewart. *The Book of Psalms: A New Translation, with Introductions and Notes, Explanatory and Critical*, vol. 2. Rev. 5th edition. Cambridge: George Bell and Sons, 1882.

Péter-Contesse, René and John Ellington. *A Handbook on the Book of Daniel*. United Bible Societies Handbooks. New York: United Bible Societies, 1994.

——— and John Ellington, *A Handbook on Leviticus*. United Bible Societies Handbooks. New York: United Bible Societies, 1992.

Peterson, David G. *Romans*. Evangelical Biblical Theology Commentary. eds. T. Desmond Alexander, Thomas R. Schreiner, and Andreas J. Köstenberger. Bellingham, WA: Lexham Press, 2021.

Phillips, Anthony. *Ancient Israel's Criminal Law*. Oxford: Basil Blackwell, 1970.

Pines, Shlomo. *An Arabic Version of the Testionium Flavianum and Its Implications*. Jerusalem: Israel Academy of Sciences and Humanities, 1971. http://khazarzar.skeptik.net/books/pines01.pdf.

Piscator, Johannes in *1-2 Samuel, 1-2 Kings, 1-2 Chronicles*. Old Testament: Reformation Commentary on Scripture, vol. V. eds. Derek Cooper, Martin J. Lohrmann, et al. Downers Grove, IL: IVP Academic, 2016.

Plaut, W. Gunther. *The Torah: A Modern Commentary*. ed. Gunther Plaut. New York: Union of American Hebrew Congregations, 1981.

Plummer, Alfred. *The Gospel according to S. John*. Cambridge Greek Testament for Schools and Colleges. Cambridge: Cambridge University Press, 1896.

Pojman, Louis P. *Philosophy: The Quest for Truth*. Belmont, CA: Wadsworth Publishing, 1989.

Pope, Marvin H. *Job*. Anchor Yale Bible, vol. 15. Garden City, NY: Doubleday, 1965.

Porter, Stanley. "The Criteria of Authenticity." *Handbook for the Study of the Historical Jesus*, vol. 1. eds. Tom Holmén and Stanley Porter. Leiden: Brill, 2011.

——— and Tom Holmén, eds. *Handbook for the Study of the Historical Jesus, 4 vols*. Leiden: Brill, 2011.

——— and Tom Tolmén. "How to Study the Historical Jesus." *Handbook for the Study of the Historical Jesus*, vol. 1. eds. Tom Holmén and Stanley Porter. Leiden: Brill, 2011.

Pratt Jr., Richard L. *I & II Corinthians*. Holman New Testament Commentary, vol. 7. Nashville: Broadman & Holman, 2000.

Prior, A. N. *The Encyclopedia of Philosophy*, vol. 2. ed. Paul Edwards. New York: Macmillan and The Free Press, 1962.

Propp, William H. C. *Exodus 19–40: A New Translation with Introduction and Commentary*. Anchor Yale Bible, vol. 2A. New Haven: Yale University Press, 2008.

Pulliam, Reginald. "The Eight Stages of Democracy." AL.com (Aug 22, 2016). https://www.al.com/opinion/2016/08/eight_stages_of_democracy.html.

Q

Quarles, Charles L., Scott Kellum, and Andreas J. Kostenberger. *The Cradle, the Cross, and the Crown: An Introduction to the New Testament*. Nashville: B & H Academic, 2009.

R

Rahmani, Levi Yizhaq. *A Catalogue of Jewish Ossuaries in the Collections of the State of Israel*. Jerusalem: Israel Antiquities Authority, 1994.

Rata, Tiberius and Walter C. Kaiser, Jr. *Walking the Ancient Paths*. Bellingham, WA: Lexham Press, 2019.

Redford, Donald. *Egypt, Canaan, and Israel in Ancient Times*. Princeton, NJ: Princeton University Press, 1992.

———. *Oxford Encyclopedia of Ancient Egypt*, vols. 2–3. Oxford: Oxford University Press, 2001.

Renwick, A. M. and S. Angus. "Roman Empire and Christianity." *International Standard Bible Encyclopedia*, vol. 4. Grand Rapids, MI: Eerdmans, 1979–1988, 207–21.

Rees, T. "God in the NT." *The International Standard Bible Encyclopedia*, vol. 2. Rev. edition. Grand Rapids, MI: Eerdmans, 1979–1988, 500–03.

Reiling, J. and J. L. Swellengrebel. *A Handbook on the Gospel of Luke*. United Bible Societies Handbooks. New York: United Bible Societies, 1993.

Reilly, Wendell S. "Witness of the Early Church to the Authorship of the Gospels." *CBQ* 1/2 (April 1939), 115–24.

Reumann, John. "Archaeology and Early Christology." *Jesus and Archaeology*. ed. James Charlesworth. Grand Rapids: Eerdmans, 2006.

Reyburn, William David and Euan McGregor Fry. *A Handbook on Genesis*. United Bible Societies Handbooks. New York: United Bible Societies, 1998.

——— and Robert G. Bratcher. *A Translator's Handbook on the Book of Psalms*. United Bible Societies Handbooks. New York: United Bible Societies, 1991.

——— and Euan McGregor Fry. *A Handbook on Proverbs*. United Bible Societies Handbooks. New York: United Bible Societies, 2000.

Robles, Stephen. "What is a Precept?" Higher Ground Ministries 2015. Highergroundministries.org. https://highergroundministry.org/precepts?fbclid=IwAR0a5HpU7OllliYgtIkfJZH-LfWSD6e7-C58C-UqnMx0jM4bVM_aRITiZnk.

Rollston, Christopher. "The Talpiyot (Jerusalem) Tombs: Some Sober Methodological Reflections on the Epigraphic Materials." Arizona.edu (April 2013). https://bibleinterp.arizona.edu/sites/bibleinterp.arizona.edu/files/images/RollstonTalpiot_0.pdf

Rooker, Mark. *Leviticus*. New American Commentary, vol 3A. ed. E. Ray Clendenen. Nashville: Broadman & Holman, 2000.

Rosen, Baruch, Eran Arie, Dvory Namdar. "Cannabis and Frankincense at the Judahite Shrine of Arad." *Tel Aviv* 1/47 (May 28, 2020), 5–28. DOI: 10.1080/03344355.2020.1732046.

Rosenfeld, Amnon, Howard Feldman, Wolfgang Krumbein, and Carl von Ossietzky. "Archaeometric Analysis of the James Ossuary." Proceedings from 2008 Joint Meeting of The Geological Society of America, Soil Science Society of America, American Society of Agronomy, Crop Science Society of America. Gulf Coast Association of Geological Societies with the Gulf Coast Section of SEPM in GSAAP 40/6, 354.

———, Howard R. Feldman, Wolfgang E. Krumbein. "The Authenticity of the James Ossuary." *OJG* 4 (March 12, 2014), 69–78. DOI: 10.4236/ojg.2014.43007.

Rosner, Brian S. and Roy E. Ciampa. *The First Letter to the Corinthians*. The Pillar New Testament Commentary. Grand Rapids: Eerdmans, 2010.

Roth, Martha T., et al., eds. *The Assyrian Dictionary of the Oriental Institute of the University of Chicago*, 21 vols. Chicago: The Oriental Institute of the University of Chicago, 1956–2010.

Rothschild, Clare. "Echo of a Whisper: The Uncertain Authenticity of Josephus' Witness to John the Baptist." *Ablution, Initiation, and Baptism in Late Antiquity, Early Judaism, and Early Christianity*. eds. David Hellholm, et al. New York: De Gruyter, 2010, 255–90.

Roukema, Riemer. "Jesus Tradition in Early Patristic Writings." *Handbook for the Study of the Historical Jesus*, vol. 3. eds. Tom Holmén and Stanley Porter. Leiden: Brill, 2011, 2119–47.

Rubenstein, Richard, *When Jesus Became God: The Epic Fight over Christ's Divinity in the Last Days of Rome*. New York: Harcourt Brace, 1999.

"Russell, Bertrand—On Truth and Falsehood." BCCampus.com. https://pressbooks.bccampus.ca/classicreadings/chapter/bertrand-russell-on-truth-and-falsehood/.

S

Sankey, Howard and Robert Nola. *Theories of Scientific Method*. Montreal: McGill-Queen's University Press, 2007.

Sarna, Nahum M. *Exodus*. The JPS Torah Commentary. Philadelphia: Jewish Publication Society, 1991.

Sawyer, John F. A. *Isaiah through the Centuries*. Wiley Blackwell Bible Commentaries. ed. John F. A. Sawyer, et al. Hoboken, NJ: Wiley Blackwell, 2018.

———. "Monotheism." *A Concise Dictionary of the Bible and Its Reception*. Louisville, KY: Westminster John Knox Press, 2009, 175.

Schalise, Pamela, Gerald Keown, and Thomas Smothers. *Jeremiah 26–52*. World Book Commentary, vol. 27. eds David Hubbard, et al. Grand Rapids, MI: Zondervan, 2016.

Schlesinger, Eugene R. "Sacraments." *The Lexham Bible Dictionary*. eds. John D. Barry, et al. Bellingham, WA: Lexham Press, 2016.

Schmidt, Dave. "The Christian and the Law of Moses." Southside Church of Christ (March 6, 2011). https://southsidechurchofchrist.com/sermons/the-christian-and-the-law-of-moses.html.

Schmitt, Rudiger, and Rainer Albertz. *Family and Household Religion in Ancient Israel and the Levant*. Winona Lake, IN: Eisenbrauns, 2012.

Schreckenberg, Heinz and Kurt Schubert. *Jewish Traditions in Early Christian Literature*, vol. 2. Jewish Historiography and Iconography in Early and Medieval Christianity. Leiden: Brill, 1992.

Schreiner, Thomas R. "In the New Testament." *New Bible Dictionary*. eds. D. R. W. Wood, et. al. Downers Grove, IL: InterVarsity Press, 1996.

———. *1, 2 Peter, Jude*. New American Commentary, vol. 37. Nashville: Broadman & Holman, 2003.

———. "Preaching and Biblical Theology 101 PBT-101." *9Marks Journal* 3/9 (2006), 15–22.

Schubert, Kurt and Heinz Schreckenberg. *Jewish Traditions in Early Christian Literature*, vol. 2. Jewish Historiography and Iconography in Early and Medieval Christianity. Leiden: Brill, 1992.

Scott, Robert and Henry George Liddell. *Liddell and Scott's Greek–English Lexicon*. ed. Henry Stuart Jones. Oxford: Oxford University Press, 1843. Reprint, Oxford: Simon Wallenberg Press, 2007.

"The Search for Everlasting Life." ArtHistoryProject.com. https://www.arthistoryproject.com/timeline/the-ancient-world/mesopotamia/the-epic-of-gilgamesh/gilgamesh-4-the-search-for-everlasting-life/.

Selbie, John and James Hastings. *Encyclopedia of Religion and Ethics*, vol. 10. Whitefish, MT: Kessinger, 1908.

Shanks, Hershel and Ben Witherington, III. *Brother of Jesus: The Dramatic Story and Meaning of the First Archaeological Link to Jesus and His Family*. London: Continuum, 2003.

———. "The Persisting Uncertainties of Kuntillet 'Ajrud." *BAR* 38/6 (2012), 29–37, 76.

———. "Related Coverage on the James Ossuary and Forgery Trial." Bible History Daily: *BAR* (November 8, 2010), https://bit.ly/352TuiO.

Sherwin-White, Adrian. *The Letters of Pliny: A Historical and Social Commentary*. New York: Oxford University Press, 1998.

———. "Why Were the Early Christians Persecuted? An Amendment." *Studies in Ancient Society*. ed. M. I. Finley. Oxford, UK: Routledge, 1974.

Shimron, Aryeh E., et al. "The Geochemistry of Intrusive Sediment Sampled from the 1st Century CE Inscribed Ossuaries of James and the Talpiot Tomb, Jerusalem." *Archaeological Discovery* (2020), 8, 92–115. https://www.scirp.org/pdf/ad_2019120316084496.pdf.

Silberman, Neil Asher and Yuval Goren. "Faking Biblical History: How Wishful Thinking and Technology Fooled Some Scholars—and Made Fools Out of Others." *Archaeology* 56/5 (September–October 2003), 20–29.

Sippo, Fr. Art. "Did the Catholic Church Forbid Bible Reading?" CatholicBridge.com.eds. Terry Donahue, et al. https://www.catholicbridge.com/catholic/did-the-catholic-church-forbid-bible-reading.php.

Smalley, Stephen S. *1, 2, 3 John*. Word Biblical Commentary, vol. 51. Dallas: Word, Inc., 1984.

Smith, Gary V. *Isaiah 1–39*. New American Commentary, vol. 15A. ed. E. Ray Clendenen. Nashville: B & H Publishing, 2007.

———. *Isaiah 40–66*. New American Commentary, vol. 15B. ed. E. Ray Clendenen. Nashville: B & H Publishing, 2009.

Smith, Patricia, Gal. Avishai, J.A. Greene, and L.E. Stager. "Aging Cremated Infants: The Problem of Sacrifice at the Tophet of Carthage." *Atinquity* 85/329 (2011), 859–74.

Smith, Ralph L. *Micah–Malachi*. Word Biblical Commentary, vol. 32. Dallas: Word, Inc., 1984.

Smith, Uriah. *Thoughts, Critical and Practical, on the Book of Revelation*. Rev. 2nd edition. Battle Creek, MI: Steam Press of the Seventh-day Adventist Publishing Association, 1875.

Smothers, Thomas, Gerald Keown, and Pamela Schalise. *Jeremiah 26–52*. Word Biblical Commentary, vol. 27. eds. David Hubbard, et al. Grand Rapids, MI: Zondervan, 2016.

Snaith, Norman. *Isaiah 40–66: A Study of the Teaching of the Second Isaiah and Its Consequences*. VTSup XIV. eds. G. W. Anderson, et al. Leiden: Brill, 1967.

———. "Sacrifices in the Old Testament." *Vetus Testamentum* 3/7 (1957) 308–17. https://doi.org/10.2307/1516202.

Soloveichik, Meir, et al., eds. *Proclaim Liberty Throughout the Land: The Hebrew Bible in the United States, a Sourcebook*. New Milford, CT: Toby Press, 2019.

Stager, Lawrence E., Patricia Smith, G. Avishai, and J.A. Greene. "Aging Cremated Infants: The Problem of Sacrifice at the Tophet of Carthage." *Atinquity* 85/329 (2011), 859–74.

———. "The Shechem Temple Where Abimelech Massacred a Thousand." *BAR* 29/4 (July 2003), 26–29, 31, 33–35, 66, 68.

Stein, Robert H. *Luke*. New American Commentary, vol. 24. Nashville: Broadman & Holman Publishers, 1992.

Sterk, Jan and Graham S. Ogden. *A Handbook on Isaiah*, vol. 1–2. United Bible Societies Handbooks. ed. Paul Clarke, et al. Reading, UK: United Bible Societies, 2011.

Stine, Philip C. and Barclay M. Newman, Jr. *A Handbook on Jeremiah*. United Bible Societies Handbooks. New York: United Bible Societies, 2003.

——— and Barclay M. Newman, Jr. *A Handbook on the Gospel of Matthew*. United Bible Societies Handbooks. New York: United Bible Societies, 1992.

Stott, John R. W. *The Message of the Sermon on the Mount: Christian Counter-Culture*. Revised. The Bible Speaks Today. London: IVP, 2020.

———. *The Message of the Sermon on the Mount Matthew 5–7: Christian Counter-Culture*. The Bible Speaks Today. Downers Grove, IL: InterVarsity Press, 1985.

———. *The Message of Thessalonians: The Gospel & the End of Time*. The Bible Speaks Today. Downers Grove, IL: InterVarsity Press, 1994.

Strong, James. *Strong's Exhaustive Concordance*. Grand Rapids, MI: Baker Books, 1997. (Denotes Strong's number only)

Stuart, Douglas K. *Exodus*. New American Commentary, vol. 2. Nashville: Broadman & Holman, 2006.

Sulzberger, Mayer. *Am Ha-Aretz–The Ancient Hebrew Parliament*. Philadelphia: Julias Greenstone, 1909.

Swain, Scott R. and Andreas J. Köstenberger. *Father, Son and Spirit: The Trinity and John's Gospel*. New Studies in Biblical Theology, vol. 24. ed. D. A. Carson. Downers Grove, IL: InterVarsity Press, 2008.

Swellengrebel, J. L. and J. Reiling. *A Handbook on the Gospel of Luke*. United Bible Societies Handbooks. New York: United Bible Societies, 1993.

Syme, Ronald. *Tacitus*. London: Oxford University, 1958.

T

Tabor, James. "Is There Any Credible Archaeological Evidence for the Earliest Followers of Jesus?" Tabor Blog (March 21, 2022). https://jamestabor.com/is-there-any-credible-archaeological-evidence-for-the-earliest-followers-of-jesus/.

——— and Simcha Jacobovici. *The Jesus Discovery*. New York: Simon and Schuster, 2012.

———. *The Jesus Dynasty: The Hidden History of Jesus, His Royal Family, and the Birth of Christianity*. New York: Simon and Schuster, 2006.

———. *Restoring Abrahamic Faith*. Charlotte, NC: Genesis 2000, 2008.

———. "The Talpiot 'Jesus' Tomb: A Historical Analysis." *The Tomb of Jesus and His Family? Exploring Ancient Jewish Tombs Near Jerusalem's Walls: The Fourth Princeton Symposium on Judaism and Christian Origins*. eds. James H. Charlesworth and Arthur C. Boulet. Grand Rapids: Eerdmans, 2013.

———. "What's What Regarding the Controversial James Ossuary?" TaborBlog (February 12, 2016). https://jamestabor.com/whats-what-regarding-the-controversial-james-ossuary/.

Tadmore, Hayim. "Treaty and Oath in the Ancient Near East: A Historian's Approach." *Humanizing America's Iconic Book*. eds. G. M. Tucker and D. A. Knight. Chico, CA: Scholars Press, 1962.

Tanner, Beth LaNeel, Nancy deClaissé-Walford, and Rolf Jacobson. *The Book of Psalms*. New International Commentary of the Old Testament. Grand Rapids, MI: Eerdmans, 2014.

Taylor, Mark. *1 Corinthians*. New American Commentary, vol. 28. ed. E. Ray Clendenen. Nashville: B & H Publishing, 2014.

Taylor, Richard A. and E. Ray Clendenen. *Haggai, Malachi*. New American Commentary, vol. 21A. Nashville: Broadman & Holman, 2004.

Thayer, Joseph H. *Thayer's Greek–English Lexicon of the New Testament*. Edinburgh: T & T Clark, 1896. Reprint, Peabody, MA: Hendrickson Publishers, 2005.

Thiselton, Anthony C. *1 & 2 Thessalonians through the Centuries*. Wiley Blackwell Bible Commentaries. eds. John Sawyer, et al. West Sussex, UK: Wiley-Blackwell, 2011.

Thomas, Kenneth J. and Philip A. Noss. *A Handbook on Ezra and Nehemiah*. United Bible Societies Handbooks. eds. Paul Clarke, et al. New York: United Bible Societies, 2005.

Thompson, Michael. *Isaiah 40–66*. Eugene, OR: WIPF & Stock, 2001.

Tigay, Jeffrey. *The JPS Torah Commentary on Deuteronomy* דברים. ed. Nahum Sarna. Jerusalem: Jewish Publication Society, 1996.

Tolmén, Tom and Stanley Porter. "How to Study the Historical Jesus." *Handbook for the Study of the Historical Jesus*, vol. 1. eds. Tom Holmén and Stanley Porter. Leiden: Brill, 2011.

van der Toorn, K. *Sin and Sanction in Israel and Mesopotamia*. Maastricht, Netherlands: Van Gorcum, 1985.

U

Uehlinger, Christopher and Othmar Keel. *Gods, Goddesses, and Images of God*. trans. Thomas Trapp. Minneapolis, MN: Fortress Press, 1998.

Unger, Merrill F. *Unger's Bible Dictionary*. Chicago: Moody, 1957.

V

Vermes, Geza. *The Authentic Gospel of Jesus*. New York: Penguin Books, 2003.

Vlachos, Chris A. *James. Exegetical Guide to the Greek New Testament*. eds. Murray J. Harris and Andreas J. Köstenberger. Nashville: B & H Academic, 2013.

van Voorst, Robert. *Jesus Outside the New Testament: An Introduction to the Ancient Evidence*. Studying the Historical Jesus. Grand Rapids: Eerdmans, 2000.

———. "Jesus Tradition in Classical and Jewish Wittings." *Handbook for the Study of the Historical Jesus*, vol. 3. eds. Tom Holmén and Stanley Porter. Leiden: Brill, 2011, 2149–81.

de Vos, Craig. "Popular Graeco-Roman Responses to Christianity." *The Early Christian World*, vol. 2. ed. Philip F. Esler. London: Routledge, Taylor and Francis, 2000.

W

Wagenaar, Jan A. *Origin and Transformation of the Ancient Israelite Festival Calendar*. Otto Harrassowitz Verlag: Wiesbaden German, 2005.

Wall, Robert W. "2 Timothy." *The Bible Knowledge Background Commentary: Acts–Philemon*. 1st edition. eds. Craig A. Evans and Craig A. Bubeck. Colorado Springs, CO: David C. Cook, 2004.

Wallace-Hadrill, D. S. "Eusebius of Caesarea and the Testimonium Flavianum (Josephus, *Antiquities, XVIII*. 63f.)." *The Journal of Ecclesiastical History* 25/4 (March 2011), 353–62.

Waltke, Bruce, R. Laird Harris, Gleason Archer, Jr., eds. *Theological Wordbook of the Old Testament*, 2 vols. Chicago: Moody Bible Institute, 1980.

Wansbrough, Henry. *Jesus and the Oral Gospel Tradition*. Sheffield: Sheffield Academic Press, 1991.

Watts, John D.W. *Isaiah 1-33*. Word Biblical Commentary, vol. 24. Rev. edition. Nashville: Thomas Nelson, 2005.

———. *Isaiah 34-66*. Word Biblical Commentary, vol. 24. Rev. edition. Nashville: Thomas Nelson, 2005.

Watts, Rikki. "Consolation or Confrontation: Isaiah 40–55 and the Delay of the New Exodus." *TynBul* 41/1 (1990), 31–59.

Webb, Barry. *The Message of Isaiah: On Eagles' Wings*. The Bible Speaks Today. eds. J. A. Motyer and Derek Tidball. England: Inter-Varsity Press, 1996.

Weber, Stuart K. *Matthew*. Holman New Testament Commentary, vol. 1. Nashville: Broadman & Holman, 2000.

Weinfeld, Moshe. "The Covenant of Grant in the Old Testament and in the Ancient Near East." *Essential Papers on Israel and the Ancient Near East*. ed. Frederick Greenspahn. New York: New York University Press, 1991.

Wells, Bruce and Raymond Westbrook. *Everyday Law in Biblical Israel*. Cambridge, UK: Cambridge University Press, 1947.

Wenham, Gordon. *Genesis 16-50*. Word Biblical Commentary, vol. 2. Dallas, TX: Word Books, 1994.

Westbrook, Raymond and Bruce Wells. *Everyday Law in Biblical Israel*. Cambridge, UK: Cambridge University Press, 1947.

———. *A History of Ancient Near Eastern Law*. Handbook of Oriental Studies: The Near and Middle East, vol. 2. Leiden: Brill, 2003.

———. *Property, Family in Biblical Law*. The Library of Hebrew Bible/Old Testament Studies, 113. eds. David Clines and Philip Davies. Sheffield: JSOT Press, 1991.

Westcott, Arthur and Brooke Foss Westcott, eds. *The Gospel according to St. John Introduction and Notes on the Authorized Version*. Classic Commentaries on the Greek New Testament. London: J. Murray, 1908.

Westcott, Brooke Foss and Arthur Westcott, eds. *The Gospel according to St. John Introduction and Notes on the Authorized Version*. Classic Commentaries on the Greek New Testament. London: J. Murray, 1908.

Westermann, Claus. *Genesis 12-36*. Continental Commentary. Minneapolis, MN: Fortress Press, 1995.

Whitacre, Rodney A. *John*. The IVP New Testament Commentary Series, vol. 4. Westmont, IL: IVP Academic, 2010.

Wildberger, Hans. *Isaiah 1-12*. Continental Commentary. Minneapolis, MN: Fortress Press, 1991.

Wilcock, Michael. *The Message of Psalms: Songs for the People of God*. The Bible Speaks Today, vol. 2. ed. J. A. Motyer Nottingham. England: Inter-Varsity Press, 2001.

Wilken, Robert Louis. *The Christians as the Romans Saw Them*. 2nd edition. New Haven: Yale University Press, 2003.

Willey, Patricia Tull. *Remember the Former Things*. Society of Biblical Literature Dissertation Series 161. ed. Michael V. Fox. Atlanta, GA: Scholars Press, 1997.

Witherington, Ben, III and Hershel Shanks. *Brother of Jesus: The Dramatic Story and Meaning of the First Archaeological Link to Jesus and His Family*. London: Continuum, 2003.

Wooden, Cindy. "The Church is Essential for Faith; There are no 'Free Agents,' Pope Says." *National Catholic Reporter*. Vatican City (June 25, 2014). https://www.ncronline.org/blogs/francis-chronicles/church-essential-faith-there-are-no-free-agents-pope-says.

Wright, Christopher J. H. *The Message of Ezekiel: A New Heart and a New Spirit*. The Bible Speaks Today. eds. Alec Motyer and Derek Tidball. Nottingham, England: Inter-Varsity Press, 2001.

———. *The Message of Jeremiah: Grace in the End*. The Bible Speaks Today. eds. Alec Motyer and Derek Tidball. Nottingham, England: Inter-Varsity Press, 2014.

Wright, David. *Inventing God's Law: How the Covenant Code of the Bible Used and Revised the Laws of Hammurabi*. Oxford: Oxford University Press, 2013.

Wyatt, Robert J. "Names of God." *International Standard Bible Encyclopedia*, vol. 2. Grand Rapids, MI: Eerdmans, 1979–1988, 504–09.

Y

Yong, J. T. "Guilty Until Proven Innocent." *The Hill* (July 25, 2020). https://thehill.com/opinion/criminal-justice/509018-guilty-until-proven-innocent/.

Young, Edward. *The Book of Isaiah:1–18*, vol. 1. Grand Rapids, Eerdmans, 1965.

Z

Zimmerli, Walther. *Ezekiel: A Commentary on the Book of the Prophet Ezekiel*, 2 vols. Hermeneia. eds. Frank Moore Cross and Klaus Baltzer. Philadelphia: Fortress Press, 1979.

Zwingli, Huldrych in *New Testament: John 1–12*. Reformation Commentary on Scripture, vol. IV. eds. Craig S. Farmer, Timothy George, et al. Downers Grove, IL: IVP Academic, 2014.

CURRENT EVENTS

Allen, Craig, et al. "Venezuela Children Starving." *The New York Times* (December 17, 2017). https://www.nytimes.com/interactive/2017/12/17/world/americas/venezuela-children-starving.html.

Buschschlüter, Vanessa. "Venezuela Crisis: 7.1m Leave Country Since 2015." BBC News Online Latin America (October 14, 2022). https://www.bbc.com/news/world-latin-america-63279800.

Cawthorne, Andrew. "Mad Max Violence Stalks Venezuela's Roads." Reuters (February 9, 2018). https://www.reuters.com/article/us-venezuela-economy-trucks-widerimage/mad-max-violence-stalks-venezuelas-lawless-roads-idUSKBN1FT1G9.

Kantrow, Josh. "More Good Stuff from My Friend." Facebook: October 12, 9:31pm. https://www.facebook.com/josh.kantrow/posts/pfbid02p3JvpNAGr5Joxwyra2EDhPSWErCiiDnRPrzTAVeQpEn9q5MXSaLB9iPeffW73TSsl.

Kaste, Martin. "California Cops Frustrated with 'Catch–and–Release' Crime–Fighting." National Public Radio (January 22, 2016). https://www.npr.org/2016/01/22/463210910/california-cops-frustrated-with-catch-and-release-crime-fighting.
Lewis, Chris. "A Catch–and–Release Justic System Is Not Working for Canadians: Lewis." CP24.com (January 7, 2023). https://tinyurl.com/22tt6cws.
Worley, Will. "Venezuela's Hunger Crisis Spills into Colombia." Pacific Standard (May 10, 2018). https://psmag.com/news/venezuela-hunger-crisis-spills-into-colombia.
"The State of Democracy in the United States: 2022." Ministry of Foreign Affairs of the People's Republic of China (March 20, 2022). https://www.fmprc.gov.cn/eng/wjdt_665385/2649_665393/202303/t20230320_11044481.html.
Willis, Matthew. "Lynching in America." JSTOR Daily (February 12, 2015). https://daily.jstor.org/lynching-america/.

SELECT MEDICAL & APPLIED SCIENCE SOURCES:

"Animal Fat." NutritianFacts.org. https://nutritionfacts.org/topics/animal-fat/.
Boyles, Salynn. "Male Circumcision Cuts Women's Cervical Cancer Risk: Study Shows Circumcision May Help Reduce Spread of HPV." WebMD Health News. ed. Laura Martin (January 2011). http://www.webmd.com/cancer/cervical-cancer/news/20110106/male-circumcision-cuts-womens-cervical-cancer-risk.
Castellsague, Xavier, F. Xavier Bosch, Nubia Muñoz, Chris Meijer, Keerti Shah, Silvia de Sanjose, José Eluf-Neto, Corazon Ngelangel, Saibua Chichareon, Jennifer Smith, Rolando Herrero, Victor Moreno, Silvia Franceschi. "Male Circumcision, Penile Human Papillomavirus Infection, and Cervical Cancer in Female Partners." *NEJM* 346/15 (April 11, 2002), 1105–12. DOI: 10.1056/NEJMoa011688.
Huizen, Jennifer. "What is Gaslighting?" Medical News Today (November 30, 2023). https://www.medicalnewstoday.com/articles/gaslighting#how-it-works.
McMillen, S. I. *None of These Diseases.* 3rd edition. Grand Rapids, MI: 2000.
Mollazadeh, Sanaz, Behnaz Sadeghzadeh Oskouei, Mahin Kamalifard, Mojgan Mirghafourvand, Nayyereh Aminisani, Mehri Jafari Shobeiri. "Association between Sexual Activity during Menstruation and Endometriosis: A Case–Control Study." *Royan Institute International Journal of Fertility and Sterility* 13/3 (October–December 2019), 230–35. https://www.ijfs.ir/article_45552.html.
Mollazadeh, Sanaz, Khadijeh Najmabadi, Mojgan Mirghafourand, et al. "Sexual Activity during Menstruation as A Risk Factor for Endometriosis: A Systematic Review and Meta–Analysis." *International Journal of Fertility & Sterility* 17/1 (January–March 2023), 1–6. https://www.ncbi.nlm.nih.gov/pmc/articles/PMC9807890/#.
Nakyinsige, K., Fatimah, A. B., Aghwan, Z. A., Zulkifli, I., Goh, Y. M., & Sazili, A. Q. "Bleeding Efficiency and Meat Oxidative Stability and Microbiological Quality of New Zealand White Rabbits Subjected to Halal Slaughter without Stunning and Gas Stun-killing." *Asian–Australasian Journal of Animal Sciences*, 273 (2014), 406–13. https://doi.org/10.5713/ajas.2013.13747.
Peck, Peggy. "Circumcision Associated with 'Profound' Reduction in HIV–1 Risk." Medscape (October 10, 2003). http://www.medscape.com/viewarticle/462816.
"Prothrombin." Britannica.com. http://www.britannica.com/EBchecked/topic/480073/prothrombin.
Rivet, Christine. "Circumcision and Cervical Cancer Is there a link?" *Canadian Family Physician* 49 (September 2003), 1096–97. http://www.ncbi.nlm.nih.gov/pmc/articles/PMC2214289/pdf/14526861.pdf.
Russell, Rex. *What the Bible Says About Healthy Living.* Ventura, CA: Regal Books, 1996.

Samir, F., S. Badr, A. Al Obeidly, A. A. Alfotough, A. Farid, N. Alsamny, B.E. Ahmed. "Coital Retrograde Menstruation as a Risk Factor for Pelvic Endometriosis." *Qatar Medical Journal* 20/1 (June 2011), 21–25. https://doi.org/10.5339/qmj.2011.1.9.

Steven J. Reynolds, Mary Shepherd, Arun Risbud, Raman Gangakhedkar, Ronald Brookmeyer, Anand Diveker, Sanjay Menendale, Robert Bollinger. "Circumcision Associated With 'Profound' Reduction in HIV–1 Risk." 41st ISDA Conference Abstracts Volume LB–10 (October 11, 2003). https://pubmed.ncbi.nlm.nih.gov/15051285/.

SELECT METHOD & STATISTICS

Creswell, John. *Research Design: Qualitative, Quantitative, and Mixed Methods Approaches.* Los Angeles: Sage, 2004.

"Global Christianity–A Report on the Size and Distribution of the World's Christian Population." Pew Research Center (December 19, 2011). https://www.pewforum.org/2011/12/19/global-christianity-exec/.

King, Gary, Robert Keohane, and Sidney Verba. *Designing Social Inquiry: Scientific Inference in Qualitative Research.* Princeton, NJ: Princeton University Press, 1994.

Kirk, Jerome and Mark Miller. *Reliability and Validity in Qualitative Research, Qualitative Research Methods,* vol. 1. eds. John Van Maanen, et. al. London: Sage, 1986.

"List of Christian Denominations by Number of Members." Wikipedia.org. https://en.wikipedia.org/wiki/List_of_Christian_denominations_by_number_of_members.

Litwin, Mark. *How to Measure Survey Reliability and Validity.* The Survey Kit 7. London: Sage, 1995.

Meier, John. "Basic Methodology in the Quest for the Historical Jesus." *Handbook for the Study of the Historical Jesus,* vol 1. eds. Tom Holmén and Stanley Porter. Leiden: Brill, 2011.

Mill, John Stuart. *Philosophy of Scientific Method.* Free Press, 1950 Reprint, ed. Earnest Nagel. New York: Dover, 2005.

Nola, Robert and Howard Sankey. *Theories of Scientific Method.* New York: Routledge Taylor & Francis, 2007.

Schensul, Stephen, et al. *Essential Ethnographic Methods: Observations, Interviews, and Questionnaires.* Ethnographer's Toolkit 2. New York: AltaMira Press, 1999.

Theissen, Gerd. "Historical Skepticism and the Criteria of Jesus Research: My Attempt to Leap over Lessings's Ugly Wide Ditch." *Handbook for the Study of the Historical Jesus,* vol. 1. eds. Tom Holmén and Stanley Porter. Leiden: Brill, 2011.

FOR FURTHER RESEARCH

"Are Christians Under the Law of Moses?" Verse by Verse Ministry International (March 21, 2015). https://versebyverseministry.org/bible-answers/is-a-christian-under-the-law-of-moses.

Bryan, Matthew. "Maccabees in the New Testament." *Conciliar Post* (September 9, 2019).

Davidiy, Yair. "List of Books." HebrewNations.com. https://hebrewnations.com/publications/books/booklist.html.

"Did Jesus or the New Testament Authors Quote from the Apocryphal Books?" Dust off the Bible: Blog Archive (September 17, 2019). https://dustoffthebible.com/Blog-archive/2019/09/17/does-the-new-testament-or-jesus-quote-from-the-apocryphal-books/.

"Difference between Baking Soda and Baking Powder." BYJUs.com. https://byjus.com/chemistry/difference-between-baking-soda-and-baking-powder/#:~:text=Baking%20powder%20is%20alkaline%20and,with%20an%20added%20acidic%20ingredient.

"Early Christian Writings." EarlyChristianWritings.com. http://www.earlychristianwritings.com/.

"Early Christian Writings: Josephus and Jesus, The Testimonium Flavianum Question." EarlyChristian Writings.com. http://www.earlychristianwritings.com/testimonium.html.

Ehrman, Bart. Fresh Air: "Scholar Bart Ehrman, 'Lost Christianities.'" NPR.org (July 9, 2004). https://www.npr.org/2004/07/09/3250048/scholar-bart- ehrman-lost-christianities.

———. *Lost Christianities*. New York: Oxford University Press, 2003.

"Gilgamesh Part 3: Crossing the Waters of Death." MythicMojo.com. https://mythicmojo.com/gilgamesh-part-3-crossing-the-waters-of-death/.

"Innocent Until Proven Guilty: Origin, Law, & Meaning." Study.com (April 6, 2016). https://study.com/academy/lesson/innocent-until-proven-guilty-origin-law-meaning.html.

"Jesus' Teaching on God's Law." Beyond Today (January 27, 2011). United Church of God. https://www.ucg.org/bible-study-tools/bible-study-aids/jesus-christ-the-real-story/jesus-teaching-on-gods-law.

Kumar, Nitin. "Buddha and Christ–Two Gods on the Path to Humanity." Exotic India (November 2003). https://www.exoticindiaart.com/article/buddhaandchrist/.

"The Law of Moses: All or Nothing? James 2:10." 119 Ministries (October 28, 2022). http://tinyurl.com/yc2pdvba.

"List of Christian Denominations by Number of Members." https://en.wikipedia.org/wiki/List_of_Christian_denominations_by_number_of_members.

McKenney, Sally. "Baking Basics: Baking Powder vs. Baking Soda." Sally's Baking Recipes (May 16, 2023). https://sallysbakingaddiction.com/baking-powder-vs-baking-soda/.

"Manifestation of God." Bahaipedia.org. https://bahaipedia.org/Manifestation_of_God.

Martincic, Tom. "Why All Believers in Messiah Should Observe the Law." EliYah Ministries.com. https://eliyah.com/all-believers-in-messiah-should-observe-the-law/.

Metzger, Bruce. *The Early Versions of the New Testament: Their Origin, Transmission and Limitations*. Oxford, UK: Clarendon Press, 1977.

———. *The Canon of the New Testament: Its Origin, Development and Significance*. Oxford, UK: Clarendon Press, 1987.

Porter, Stanley E. *How We Got the New Testament: Text, Transmission, Translation*. Acadia Studies in Bible and Theology. Grand Rapids: Baker Academic, 2013.

Prager, Dennis. "The Ten Commandments: What You Should Know." YouTube. https://www.youtube.com/watch?v=TK57RiMqTdk.

"Revelation: Manifestations of God." The Bahá'í Faith. https://www.bahai.org/beliefs/god-his-creation/revelation/manifestations-god.

Stone, Luke. "10 Books Not Included in the New Testament." ListVerse.com. ed. Jamie Frater. https://listverse.com/2012/07/06/10-books-not-included-in-the-new-testament/.

Tabor, James. "In–Depth Reading on the Talpiot Tombs: What is the Best Evidence?" TaborBlog.com (August 19, 2021). https://jamestabor.com/in-depth-reading-on-the-talpiot-tombs-what-is-the-best-evidence/.

Tacitus, *Annals, Book XV*. https://penelope.uchicago.edu/Thayer/E/Roman/Texts/Tacitus/home.html.

"Torah Training." 119 Ministries. https://www.119ministries.com/torah-training/.

Scripture Index*

GENESIS

1:2…13
5:7–32…165
5:24…140
9:4–5…167
9:4–6…187
10:1, 21–25…78
11:10–29…78
12…154
12:1–3…13
12:3…154
15:4–6…150
15:6…147
15:16…23, 75, 78
17:1…54
17:4–9…153
17:7…150
17:20…149
18:18…154
18:19…36, 47, 78, 112, 161
18:20, 23–25…160
18:25…70, 73, 89
20:3…186
21:12…152
21:13…149
22…180
22:17…149
22:17–18…153
22:18…154
24:60…153
26:3…64
26:3–5…149
26:4…149, 153, 154
26:5…37, 40, 112, 146
28:14…149, 154
31:10…185
32:10…36

EXODUS

3…20
3:4…12
3:11, 11–15…24
3:13–15…13, 27, 47
3:15…27, 47, 187
6:2–3…24
12:14–17, 24…187
15:18…187
15:26…45, 46, 56, 172
16:4…133
18:20…12, 188
19:8…172
20:1–5…172
20:1–17…185
20:2…62
20:5…1, 22, 178
20:6…31
20:7…13, 22, 27, 47
20:8…132
20:14…186
20:18, 22…138, 139
20:20…188
20:22…138
20:23…172
21:1…33
21:1 – 24:3…40
21:28–36…168
22:16–17…186
22:18…187
22:27…22
22:31…53, 186
23:7…33, 160, 161 177
23:19…77
23:24…1
23:33…193
25:1…177
29:12, 13…181
29:14…168
31:17…187
32:13…152
32:30–35…171
33:11…11
33:12–13, 16…136
33:17…11, 136
33:23…138
34:6…7, 22, 188
34:6–7…160, 164
34:7…171, 172
34:14…22
34:15…187
34:26…77
35:1…44
35:11, 14…45
36:16…136

LEVITICUS

1:8, 12…181
1:9…181
2:2…181
3:10–11, 14–17…181
4–5…181
4:3, 13–21…181
4:4, 7, 13–15, 18, 19, 21, 25–30, 31, 34, 35…181
4:28, 32…181
5…169
5:6, 9…181
5:11–13…169
6:12, 15, 21…181
6:18…187
7:4–5, 11–18…181
7:15–18…181
7:24, 27…187
8:15…181
8:17…168
9:9…181
9:11…168
11:46–47…53
16:11, 15–26…181
16:27…168
16:31…187
17…167, 168
17:3–4…168
17:4…167, 168
17:7…187
17:10, 11, 13–14…167
17:12–14…187
17:13, 16…168
18…186
18:21…23, 162, 173
18:22…52
18:26–30…77
19:5…188
19:6–7…181
19:13…51, 53, 185
19:18…32, 47, 49, 51, 126, 129, 132, 185, 186
19:20…186
19:26…77, 187
19:28…77
19:29…186
20:2–4…23
20:2–5…162
20:4, 5…173
20:2–21…186
20:10…186
20:10–27…52
20:13…52
20:23…77
22:8…187
22:25…54
23:14…187
23:22…188
23:23, 31, 41…187
25:10…42, 43
25:23…187
26:1–44…67, 68, 72, 76
26:1…1, 67
26:1–13…53

* This index does excludes Scripture citations within the footnotes.

26:4-39...21
26:13...35, 42
26:14-39...21

26:15...188
26:16...xxvi, 175
26:19...175

26:42...152
26:44-45...4
26:46...40

27:10...72, 89
27:33....89

NUMBERS

4:40...187
5:12...186
5:29...187
10:8...187
14:18...160, 164, 171, 172, 178

15:15...187
15:29...188
15:30...187
18:5, 23...187
20:1-6...64, 72, 89

20:8, 11-12...64
23:3, 6...187
23:19-20...63, 72, 89
30:2...67, 72, 89
33...154

35:31-33...177
35:33...173

DEUTERONOMY

1:8, 10...152
1:16-18...xxx
1:17...49
3:22...7
4:2...20, 51, 68, 131
4:5-8...18, 41, 45, 46, 47, 185
4:7...22, 78, 84, 140
4:12...138
4:24...22
4:28-9...4, 7, 122
4:33, 36...138
4:39...76
4:40...185
5:1-21...185
5:6...62
5:9...1, 160, 163, 164, 171, 172, 178
5:22-25...138
5:32...67, 72, 89
6:4-5...76
6:5...1, 55, 129
6:5-7...187
6:6...55
6:12...62
6:13...20
6:15...22
6:18...41, 46, 185

6:25...121, 187
7:9...31, 68, 72, 89
8:2...175
8:3...88, 185
10:12...187
10:12-13...175, 186
11:1...187
11:13...129, 187
11:22...187
11:27-28...188
12:5-8...181
12:16, 23...187
12:27...181
12:28...45, 80, 185
12:30-31...78, 80
12:32...21, 51, 68, 131
13:3...4, 187
13:4...188
14:2, 21...77
14:22-23...181
15:19-23...181
15:23...187
16:4...133
16:18...45, 46, 47
17:6...142
17:14-20...83
17:19...188
18:9-12...187

18:9-14...78, 81, 90
18:10...173
18:13...54, 188
19:5...188
19:9-10...163
19:10....33
19:10-13...164
19:13...33, 164, 186
19:15...142
21:8-9...33, 164
21:20-21...161
24:16...170, 171, 176
25:1...33, 70, 73, 89, 161, 177
27:10...187, 188
27:20-23...186
27:26...127
28...76
28:1-14...54
28:1 - 30:9...67, 68, 72, 76
28:15-68...21
28:18, 22, 23-24...175
28:58-62...172
28:58-68...154
30:1-2...187
30:2...188
30:1-3...124

30:1-9...4
30:1-10...4
30:6...129
30:8...187, 188
30:10-16...44, 47, 159
30:11...45
30:11-16...8, 126, 185, 188
30:12...63
30:14...45
30:15-16...64, 185
30:16...187
30:16-20...31
30:19...53
30:20...187, 188
30:19-20...185
30:20...187
31:12...188
31:16-18...188
31:17-18...140
31:20...17
32:4...70, 73, 89, 132, 188
32:20...140
32:24...7
32:47...185
34:6...7, 185

JOSHUA

1:7-8...41, 45, 46, 47, 185, 188

1:8...41
3:10...12

22:5-6...188

24:14...22, 133, 135, 188

JUDGES

2:13...81, 90

5:11...70, 73, 89

9:28...67

1 SAMUEL

1:10–18…78
8:5…83
8:20…16
12:7…70, 73, 89
12:24…188
14:2–34…187
15:22…188
15:23…187
15:28–29…64, 72, 89
19:5….164
26:23…70, 72, 73, 89
28:7…187

2 SAMUEL

7:12…151
11:14–17…177
12:10–11, 13…178
12:14–19…179
16:22…178
22:3…187
22:21, 25…70, 73, 89
22:31…70, 187

1 KINGS

2:3, 4…188
2:31…164
3:6…188
8:32…70, 73, 89, 161, 162, 187
8:61…188
10:2…17
11:7…173
13:9…64
14:1, 17…175
15:5…177
16:32…81, 90
17…175
18…14
18:25…81, 90
23:4–5…81, 90

2 KINGS

2:11…140
11:7…173
17:13…148
17:37…188
20:1–3…175
20:7…78
21:7…15
23:14–16…65, 70, 89
23:25…187
24:3–4…164
24:4…164

1 CHRONICLES

27:23…152

2 CHRONICLES

6:23…161, 162, 172, 187
7:14…8, 175
9:9…17
12:6…70, 73, 89
15:4…192
17:37…188
18:26…27, 47
20:3…188
21:11…186
24:20–24…164
31:21…187
33:6…187
33:9…17, 85
33:18–19…79
59:1…79

NEHEMIAH

9:8…70, 73, 89
9:13…40, 47, 185

JOB

33:26…70, 73, 89
36:3…70, 73, 89
40:8…70, 73, 89

PSALMS

1:6…70, 73
2:12…187
4:4…188
4:5…187
5:8, 10…185
5:11…18
5:12…70, 73, 8
7:17…70, 73, 89
10:17…35
11:7…73, 89
15:2…137, 188
15:4…65, 66, 69, 72, 89, 89
16…16
16:1…187
16:4…16, 187
17:7, 15…187
18:30…187
19:7…47, 56, 57, 65, 125, 132
20:7…187
22:31…70, 73, 89
25:5…137
25:10…7, 137, 188
26:3…188
27:11…184
30:11–16…8
31:1–6…18

31:5...7, 188
31:19...187
33:4....7, 27, 47, 188
34:18...133
34:22...187
36:5...72, 89
36:6...73
37:3, 5...187
37:31...187
37:37...146
40:3-4, 8...187
40:10-11...7
40:10...72, 89, 188
40:11...137, 188
44:1, 20-21...21
45:7...73, 89
48:10...73, 89
50:6...89
51:6...7, 73, 188
51:7...45
51:14, 16...177, 178
51:17...133

53...9
56:4, 11...187
57:3...7
40:8...27
40:10-11...7
44:1, 20-21, 22...21
67:4...115
71:16...73, 89
71:19...70, 73, 89
71:22...188
72:1...73, 89
80:4-6...26
80:6...25
80:17-18...26, 182
82:5...135
82:6...123
84:11-12...137
86:11...27, 47, 188
86:15...7, 188
89:1-8...72, 73, 8
89:34...66, 72
89:49...188

90:1-17...69
90:5-8...xxxi, 3
92:2...89
97:5...15
98:2...73
100:5...7, 35, 188
102:27...65, 72, 89
103:15-18...3
106:36...19
106:38...164, 173
117:2...35
111:7...65
111:7-8...188
111:8-10...185
117:2...188
119...33
119:9....34
119:11...188
119:15, 27...34, 47
119:34...187
119:45...34
119:55-56...35, 185

119:63...34
119:75, 86...72, 89
119:89-92...69, 72
119:90-91...89
119:100...34, 47
119:104...34
119:105...56
119:126...87, 159
119:138...72, 89
119:142...36, 70, 89, 141, 185, 188
119:150-51...35
119:151...188
119:142...36, 45, 73
119:165...41, 45, 46, 47, 146, 188
135:13...25
145:18...135, 188
145:18-19...22
146:6...185, 188
147:19...14
147:19-20...79

PROVERBS

3:5...133
6:17...165
6:32...186
8:17...4

12:28...46, 47, 64, 185
6:23...64
10:17...64
15:19...184

17:15...187
21:18...170
22:21...188

28:4...xxvii, xxviii, xxix, xxx, xxxii, 57
28:9...148, 157

ECCLESIASTES

1:2...xxxii

ISAIAH

1:5...29
1:17-18...5, 182
1:18...5, 133, 182
2:3...122
2:4...xxvi
2:4-5...4
5:16...73, 89
5:20...xxxi, 30
5:20-23...87
5:23...187
8:17...140
8:20...72, 152, 181
10:20...135, 188
11:9...4, 32
12:4...23
25:1...65, 72, 89, 188

25:7...122, 135, 183
26:3...151
28:9-10, 12...31
29:18...135
40:4...184
40:7...65
40:7-8...3, 65, 70, 72, 89, 185
40:8...47, 65, 185
41:10...73, 89
41:21...84, 86
41:22...85
42:4...122
42:8...14, 27
42:16...135
42:17-18...42

42:21...73, 89, 122, 159
43:9...187
43:10-12...77
43:26...18
44:9 – 46:13...81, 90
45:19...73, 89
45:25...187
48:3-5, 12-13, 16...184
48:17-18...42, 45, 46, 47, 146, 185
49:6...78
49:7...72, 89
50:8...187
51:1-2...79
51:2...4, 184
51:1, 1-7...4

51:7...187
52:8...121
52:14...54
52:15...xxvi
53...9, 124, 134, 180, 183
53:5...xxvi, 180
53:6-7...180
53:9...124
53:10...155
54:8...140
54:17...121
55:12...15
56:1...73, 89
56:2-8...132
56:7...182
57:3...186

57:15…133
58:10…135

59:1…79
59:17…62

60:1-2…136
64:7…140

65:24…26
66:2…133

JEREMIAH

2:8…16, 81, 90
3:1…186
3:1-2…173
3:8-9…186
3:15…32
5:7-8…186
5:28, 30-31…17, 87
7:6…164
7:8-10…16, 17, 53, 87, 186
8:8…114
9:24…73, 89

9:25…149
10:1-16…81, 90
10:10…12
10:15-16…78
10:25…23
11:13, 17…81, 90
12:16…81, 90
14:22…78
16:19-2…19, 78
16:21…20
19:4…174
19:5…81, 90, 174

21:8…64
22:3…164
23:14…186
23:16…78
23:26-27…17, 81, 90
23:27…81
24:7…122, 148
26:12-13…187
26:13…188
26:15…164, 165
29:11-14…4
29:13…122

29:23…186
31:33…122, 148
31:33-34…187
31:34…4, 122, 148
32:29…81, 90
32:35…162
33:5…140
33:18…182
34:8-9…42
34:8-22…85
50:2…16
51:17-19…78

LAMENTATIONS

3:22-23…69, 72, 89

EZEKIEL

3:21…188
13:19…xxx
16:13-36…186
18…49, 84, 88, 175, 176
18:6, 11, 15…186
18:19-23…176
18:20…50, 176, 188
18:20-21…46, 50
18:22…176
18:25…73, 84, 89, 176
18:27-28…46, 85

18:29…84, 176
18:29-30…84
18:31-32…4
22:9…187
22:11…18
23:27…187
23:39…173, 187
26:22-30…4
33:15…31, 46, 47, 64, 88, 147, 155, 185
33…49, 84, 88

33:15…31, 46, 47, 64, 147, 155
33:16, 17…176
33:18…88
33:20…176
33:25…187
33:26…186
33:26-27…187
36:22-30…4
36:27…122
37:14…185

38:16…122, 148
39:17-19…187
39:23-24…140
40…182
44:24…40

DANIEL

9:7…73, 89

9:13…39, 135

HOSEA

2:16-17…25
3:4-5…182

4:1…85

4:2, 13-14…186

5:15-6:3…4

AMOS

3:1-2…79

5:4…4

9:9…124

MICAH

4:3…xxvi, 4
5:2…124

6…88
6:2-3…84

6:5…73, 89
6:7, 8…175

6:8…175, 186
7:20…188

NAHUM

1:2...22
1:5...15

ZEPHANIAH

1:4...81, 90
3:9...24

ZECHARIAH

1:4...139
6:15...188
8:3...188
8:8...73, 89, 188
8:16, 19...135
13:9...26
14:21...182

MALACHI

2:6...185, 188
3:6...66
3:6-7...131
4:4...158
4:4-6...43, 86, 185

NEW TESTAMENT

MATTHEW

2:23...141
3:1-12...111
3:2...137
3:7-10...52, 111-12
3:10...172
4:4-7...185
4:17...137
5...123
5:17-19...50, 123, 127, 129, 133, 185
5:18...122, 133
5:19-20...186
5:44...154
7:17-19...172
10:40...21
11:28...31
11:30...126
12:33...172
14:3-11...111
15:24...21
16:27...16
19...50-51
19:17...31, 51, 185
19:18...51
19:18-19...51, 50-51, 183, 185, 186
22:30...152
22:37-40...129
23:23...186
23:29, 30, 35-36...164
23:38...165
27:56...95

MARK

3:1-12...111
6:3...94, 95
6:16-29...111
6:29...111
7:20-23...186
9:37...21
10:19...51, 185, 186
15:28...124
15:47...95

LUKE

3:1...101
3:7-9...52, 111-12
4:43...21
6:27, 35...154
7:19-20...111
9:48...21
10:16...21
11:28...125, 126, 185, 187
11:50-51...164
13:3...137
13:4...172
13:5...137
16:17...133, 185
18:20...185, 186
18:31...125
23:35...114
24:4...125
24:27...124
24:44...125, 133

JOHN

1:17...136, 137, 158
1:18...137, 138, 158
1:29, 36...181
1:45...133
2:12...95
3:13...140
3:20-21...188
4:23-24...188
5:14...126, 137, 185, 188
5:23...21
5:30...123
5:31, 32, 33...142
5:37...137, 158
5:37-38...21
7:17...185, 188
7:26...114
7:38, 42...124
8:11...126, 137, 185, 188
8:17-18...142
8:21...170
8:32...36, 183
8:34...188
8:42...123
10:34-35...123
14:6...139
14:15...31
14:31...131-32

15:2...172

17:17...54

ACTS

1:9...140
2:45...105
3:18...124
3:19...137
4:34 – 5:1-8...105

4:36...95
8:9...187
8:32...180, 181
9:22...114
13:8...151

13:44...168
15:20...186
15:20-21...187
15:29...186, 187
18:1-2...103

19:26...168
21:25...186, 187

ROMANS

1:2...123
1:25...187
2:4, 6...162
2:8-11...188
2:12-13...187
2:20...188
2:23...187

3:2...151
3:20...188
3:27...105
3:31...187
4:13...149
4:14-16...145, 148
5:19...131

6:1, 12...188
7:1, 6...88
7:7...188
7:12-13...53
7:12, 13, 16. 22-23...53
8:4...55, 185, 188
12:2...133

13...55
13:8-10...185
13:9-10...55
13:11...56
14:3...149
15:8...188

1 CORINTHIANS

2:12-13...188
3:8...162
3:16-17...53
5:1, 19-21...186

5:8...188
6:8-10...52, 185, 186
6:9-10, 18...188
6:9-13, 18...186

7:2...186
10:8...186
10:14-33...187
15:22...170

15:34...188

2 CORINTHIANS

7:1...187

12:21...186

GALATIANS

1:4...165
1:19...95

3:16, 17-19...149

5:19-21...186, 187, 188

6:2...105

EPHESIANS

4:26...188
5:2...182

5:3, 5-6...186
5:9...188

6:1...126, 185, 186

6:13-14...62

PHILIPPIANS

4:18...182

COLOSSIANS

3:5...186

1 THESSALONIANS

4:3...52
4:3-4...186

4:5...52

4:6-7...52, 186

5:21...1, 132

2 THESSALONIANS
2:3...148

TITUS
1:14...188

PHILEMON
4:18...182

1 TIMOTHY
1:10...186
1:20...161
6:12...143
6:16...139

2 TIMOTHY
2:22...186
3:6...188
3:15...123
3:16...40, 141
3:17...188
4:14...162

HEBREWS
3:13...188
4:15...131
8:10...187
9:22...167, 168
9:26...161, 177
10:1...54
10:5...182
10:16...187
10:26...182, 188
12:1....143
12:4...188
13:4–5...186

JAMES
1:15...188
2:8–9...49, 185, 186, 188
2:9, 11...188
2:49...49, 185
2:12...105
2:21–25...147

1 PETER
1:2...187
1:20...161, 177
1:22...188
1:23–25...185
3:18...170

2 PETER
2:8...49, 188
2:14...188

1 JOHN
2:1...188
2:2...165
2:2–4...188
2:4–7...188
3:4, 7...49, 188
3:24...187
4:1...133
5...126
5:2–3...125, 132, 159, 187, 188
5:18...188

2 JOHN
1:5, 6...126, 185
1:6...187

JUDE

1:1...95, 96
1:7...186

REVELATION

2:5...189
2:14...186, 187
2:20...187
2:20–23...182, 186, 188, 189
2:21–22...182
2:21–23...182
2:23...162
3:15–17...3
5:6–8, 12–13...181
6:1, 16...181
7:9–10...181
9:21...186
12:11...181
13:8...161, 177
17:1–2...186
19:2...186
20:12–13...162
21:8...186
22:12...162, 189
22:15...186
22:18...21

www.ingramcontent.com/pod-product-compliance
Lightning Source LLC
Chambersburg PA
CBHW071856290426
44110CB00013B/1171